HISTORY OF
United States Naval Operations
IN WORLD WAR II

★

V O L U M E   E L E V E N

The Invasion of France and Germany
1944–1945

Rear Admiral Alan G. Kirk USN

Commander Western Naval Task Force
On deck of U.S.S. *Augusta* at Plymouth

HISTORY OF UNITED STATES NAVAL
OPERATIONS IN WORLD WAR II
VOLUME 11

The Invasion of France and Germany

1944–1945

SAMUEL ELIOT MORISON

UNIVERSITY OF ILLINOIS PRESS
Urbana and Chicago

First Illinois paperback, 2002
© 1957 by Samuel Eliot Morison; © renewed 1985
by Augustus P. Loring and W. Sidney Felton
Reprinted by arrangement with Little, Brown and Company, Inc.
All rights reserved
Manufactured in the United States of America
P 5 4 3 2 1

∞This book is printed on acid-free paper.

Library of Congress Cataloging-in-Publication Data
Morison, Samuel Eliot, 1887–1976.
History of United States naval operations in World War II / Samuel Eliot Morison
p.   cm.
Originally published: Boston : Little, Brown, 1947–62.
Includes bibliographical references and index.
Contents: v. 1. The Battle of the Atlantic, September 1939–May 1943—v. 2. Opera-
tions in North African Waters, October 1942–June 1943—v. 3. The Rising Sun in
the Pacific, 1931–April 1942—v. 4. Coral Sea, Midway and Submarine Actions, May
1942–August 1942—v. 5. The Struggle for Guadalcanal, August 1942–February
1943—v. 6. Breaking the Bismarcks Barrier, 22 July 1942–1 May 1944—v. 7. Aleu-
tians, Gilberts and Marshalls, June 1942–April 1944—v. 8. New Guinea and the
Marianas, March 1944–August 1944—v. 9. Sicily—Salerno—Anzio, January 1943–
June 1944—v. 10. The Atlantic Battle Won, May 1943–May 1945—
v. 11. The Invasion of France and Germany, 1944–1945
ISBN 0-252-06963-3 (v. 1); ISBN 0-252-06972-2 (v. 2); ISBN 0-252-06973-0 (v. 3);
ISBN 0-252-06995-1 (v. 4); ISBN 0-252-06996-x (v. 5); ISBN 0-252-06997-8 (v. 6);
ISBN 0-252-07037-2 (v. 7); ISBN 0-252-07038-0 (v. 8); ISBN 0-252-07039-9 (v. 9);
ISBN 0-252-07061-5 (v. 10); ISBN 0-252-07062-3 (v. 11)
1. World War, 1939–1945—Naval operations, American. I. Title.
D773.M6   2002
940.54'5973—dc21   00-064840

University of Illinois Press
1325 South Oak Street   Champaign, IL 61820-6903
www.press.uillinois.edu

THIS EMBATTLED SHORE
PORTAL OF FREEDOM
IS FOREVER HALLOWED BY
THE IDEALS, THE VALOR AND THE SACRIFICES
OF OUR FELLOW COUNTRYMEN

— Inscription on the Colonnade of the
American Military Cemetery at Omaha Beach

Preface

THIS volume has been a long time in the making. During Operation NEPTUNE Lieutenant George M. Elsey USNR was detached from the staff of the Naval Aide at the White House and temporarily attached to that of Rear Admiral Kirk, commander of the American forces for the invasion; and during the "Omaha" assault, on board U.S.S. *Ancon*, wrote a vivid and careful account of his observations for this History, and collected copies of documents that would otherwise have disappeared. Lieutenant Commander Leonard Ware USNR, then a member of Admiral Stark's staff in London, performed a similar function as special historical observer on board Admiral Moon's flagship, U.S.S. *Bayfield*, in the "Utah" assault. These two officers were the historian's "eyes" for the invasion of Normandy. For Southern France, Lieutenant Henry D. Reck USNR of my staff was temporarily attached to that of Admiral Hewitt and viewed Operation DRAGOON from the deck of his flagship, U.S.S. *Catoctin*, subsequently transferring to *Augusta*. He, too, brought to this History valuable personal observations and documents, and after his return to Washington did intensive research on all Mediterranean operations. After participating in the Marianas operation I sailed to the Mediterranean in U.S.C.G.C. *Campbell*, and, in company with Lieutenant Commander F. Murray Forbes USNR, studied the landing beachheads of Provence not long after they had been secured; in January 1945 at Naples I profited by long discussions with Captain Robert English and other officers of Admiral Hewitt's staff.

Work on this volume was suspended in 1948 while others were being prepared. In the meantime many books on the Normandy operations had appeared. Rear Admiral Bern Anderson USN (Ret.) of my staff began intensive research on Parts I and II in 1954, when he was still helping me with Volumes IX and X, bringing to bear on problems of OVERLORD his firsthand knowledge of amphibious operations in the Southwest Pacific. At the same time I began working over the materials collected by Lieutenant Reck and myself in 1944–1945, as well as those in the archives of the United States Navy at Washington. Mr. Roger Pineau was of constant assistance to me in this work, and did an outstanding job in elucidating the problems of Operation DRAGOON.

During the summer of 1955, after I had written the first draft of this volume, Admiral Anderson and Mr. Pineau accompanied me in making a fresh examination of the landing beaches in France, both from the sea and from the land. The French Navy, through the kind offices of Capitaine de Vaisseau Rostand, chief of the Service Historique de la Marine, placed at my disposal the coastal escort vessel *Le Vigilant* for examining the southern coast. Commandant Rostand accompanied us himself, to our great pleasure and profit. *Lansquenet*, a French warship of similar type, was assigned to me for the examination of the landing beaches in Normandy. Médecin en Chef Hervé Cras, well known to readers of French naval history by his pen name, Jacques Mordal, accompanied us on this second expedition, as well as on a motor tour through Calvados and the Cotentin Peninsula, and to Granville and Saint-Malo. In England we visited the principal centers of United States naval activities in 1943–1944. My beloved wife, Priscilla Barton Morison, who in the seven years of our marriage has been my constant companion and best critic, accompanied me on all those journeys by land and by sea.

The Service Historique de la Marine, the Historical Section, Admiralty, and the staff of Professor J. R. M. Butler, editor of the official British war history, placed their records and files at my disposal, and answered many questions. I wish particularly to thank Rear Admiral Roger Bellairs RN, the Librarian of the Admiralty (Commander Peter K. Kemp), Captain Stephen W. Roskill RN, Major L. F. Ellis, Commandant Rostand and Médecin en Chef Cras, for their many suggestions and other assistance. Admiral of the Fleet Lord Mountbatten of Burma, Admiral Walter F. Boone USN,

Admiral Sir Charles Little RN, Admiral Sir George Creasy RN, The Right Reverend Robert C. Mortimer, Bishop of Exeter; Lieutenant General Sir Frederick Morgan and Colonel George Thompson have helped me in many and various ways. Konteradmiral Ruge and Dr. Jürgen Rohwer have furnished valuable information on German naval forces. In this country four leading flag officers, Admiral Hewitt, Admiral Kirk, Admiral Deyo and Admiral Hall, have patiently answered many queries, as have General of the Army George C. Marshall and General W. Bedell Smith. Over a hundred naval officers and many enlisted men who participated in these events have given me information to amplify or explain the records. The historians of other United States Armed Forces, Colonel Kent Roberts Greenfield, Chief Historian Department of the Army, and Dr. Albert F. Simpson, Chief of the Air Force Historical Division, have always been coöperative and helpful.

In addition to the outstanding assistance afforded by Rear Admiral Anderson and Mr. Pineau (now Lieutenant Commander USNR), Mr. Donald R. Martin, former Chief Yeoman USNR, who has been with me now for almost fourteen years, compiled the task organizations and did important bits of research. He also typed most of the final draft, in which he was assisted by Yeoman 3rd Class Edward Ledford, and by my civilian secretaries Miss Antha E. Card and Mrs. Christopher Laing. And I am deeply grateful to two old friends and former shipmates, Rear Admiral John B. Heffernan and Rear Admiral Ernest M. Eller, successive Directors of Naval History, as well as to Captain F. Kent Loomis, their exec., and to Miss Loretta MacCrindle, head of the Historical Records Branch of the Division of Naval History.

Two successive Presidents of the United States Naval War College at Newport, R.I., the late Vice Admiral Lynde D. McCormick and Rear Admiral Thomas H. Robbins, have given this work their countenance and support. The charts were prepared in the drafting room of the War College under the direction of Mr. John Lawton and drafted by Mr. Joseph A. Domingoes Jr. and Mr. Frederick J. Wagner. Captain E. S. L. Goodwin read the ms. intensively.

The problem of elimination and condensation has been difficult and perplexing. In other volumes of this series which cover amphibious operations, I attempted to describe the movements of ground forces in some detail as long as they were within range of naval gunfire support; and in the Pacific this has meant that my account is a reasonably complete history of each operation. In Operations OVERLORD and DRAGOON, however, where the Navy transported and covered the invasion of a continent, it would have been presumptuous as well as impracticable for me to attempt to tell the story of ground and air operations in any detail. I have had to confine myself to the planning and the assault, leaving others to carry on the story from the point where troops were established ashore. And, as this is a history of United States Naval Operations, I have been unable to give the very formidable British part in Operation NEPTUNE–OVERLORD the space commensurate to its importance. That is why seven chapters are devoted to the American sectors (Utah and Omaha) and to Cherbourg, as against only one to the British sector of the landings.

In order to avoid excessive number and length of footnotes, I shall here give the full titles of the principal sources which have been drawn upon for this volume, indicating first the key words by which they are cited.

1. *Printed Books of Official Series*

Of volumes already published in the official *U.S. Army in World War II* series, with the imprint "Office of the Chief of Military History, Department of the Army, Washington, D.C.," the following have been most helpful: —

HARRISON. Gordon A. Harrison, *Cross-Channel Attack* (1951).

MATLOFF & SNELL. Maurice Matloff and Edwin M. Snell, *Strategic Planning for Coalition Warfare 1941–1942* (1953). The volume covering the period 1943–1944, by Dr. Matloff alone, I have used in ms.

Pogue. Forrest C. Pogue, *The Supreme Command* (1954).

Ruppenthal. Roland G. Ruppenthal, *Logistical Support of the Armies*, I, May 1941–Sept. 1944 (1953). Vol. II, which covers the rest of the war in Europe, I have used in ms.

In the earlier *American Forces in Action* series, the following volumes give additional details of the landings: —

Omaha Beachhead (1946), written by Lt. Col. Charles H. Taylor aus.

Utah Beach to Cherbourg (1947), written by Dr. Ruppenthal.

Craven & Cate III. *The Army Air Forces in World War II*, prepared under the editorship of Wesley Frank Craven and James Lee Cate. Vol. III, *Europe: Argument to V–E Day* (Jan. 1944 to May 1945), University of Chicago Press 1951.

Of the British *History of the Second World War, United Kingdom Military Series*, edited by Professor J. R. M. Butler, the following volume is the most thorough and detailed on this period: —

Ehrman V. John Ehrman, *Grand Strategy*, Vol. V: *Aug. 1943–Sept. 1944*. London, H.M. Stationery Office, 1956.

2. *Overall Action Reports ("Despatches" if British)*

Hewitt. Commander U.S. Eighth Fleet (Vice Admiral H. Kent Hewitt) to Cominch, 29 Nov. 1944, "Invasion of Southern France. Report of Naval Commander Western Task Force." A very full and comprehensive Report on Operation dragoon.

Leigh-Mallory. *Air Operations by the Allied Expeditionary Air Force in N.W. Europe from Nov. 15, 1943 to Sept. 30, 1944. Despatch by the late Air Chief Marshal Sir Trafford Leigh-Mallory.* Dated Nov. 1944. Printed as *Fourth Supplement to the London Gazette of 31 Dec. 1946.* London, H.M. Stationery Office, 1947.

RAMSAY. *The Assault Phase of the Normandy Landings. Despatch submitted by Admiral Sir Bertram H. Ramsay, Allied Naval Commander-in-Chief Expeditionary Force.* Printed as Supplement to the *London Gazette* of 7 Oct. 1947.[1] London, H.M. Stationery Office, 1947. This is the introductory part and summary of Admiral Ramsay's "Report by the Allied Naval C. in C. Expeditionary Force on Operation Neptune," dated Nov. 1944.

SACMED REPORT. *Report of the Supreme Allied Commander Mediterranean* [Field Marshal Sir Henry Maitland Wilson] *to the Combined Chiefs of Staff on the Operation in Southern France, August 1944.* Washington, Government Printing Office, 1946. The "Revised Draft of SAC Despatch," undated, given to the writer at Caserta in 1945, contains details not in the printed version.

SEVENTH ARMY REPORT. *Report of Operations. The Seventh United States Army in France and Germany 1944–1945.* Three vols. Heidelberg, 1946. Pending the publication of an account of DRAGOON in the U.S. Army series, this is the best overall printed book on that operation.

COMNAVEU ADMINISTRATIVE HISTORY. Commander U.S. Naval Forces in Europe (Admiral Harold R. Stark), typed volumes in the Naval Administrative Series, at Office of Naval History, Washington. Volume IV: "Supply and Logistical Activities" (including U.S. Naval Bases in England), Volume V: "The Invasion of Normandy"; Volume VII: "U.S. Naval Task Forces and Groups in Europe."

3. Memoirs and Accounts by Participants

BRADLEY. Omar N. Bradley, *A Soldier's Story.* New York 1951. The best single account of the Normandy operation.

Closing the Ring. Winston S. Churchill, *The Second World War,* Vol. V: *Closing the Ring* (Boston 1951). Vol. VI: *Triumph and Tragedy* (Boston 1953) also covers this period.

[1] Date corrected in copy furnished to me from 7 to 28 Oct. 1947.

Preface   XV

Crusade in Europe. Dwight D. Eisenhower, *Crusade in Europe.* New York 1955. Also available in Permabooks, paper-covered.

KING & WHITEHILL. Ernest J. King and Walter Muir Whitehill, *Fleet Admiral King, A Naval Record.* New York 1952.

MORGAN. Lt.-Gen. Sir Frederick Morgan ("Cossac"), *Overture to Overlord.* London 1950. (The American edition is paged differently.) The indispensable account of planning OVERLORD.

STIMSON & BUNDY. Henry L. Stimson and McGeorge Bundy, *On Active Service in Peace and War.* Two Vols. New York 1948.

This volume is dedicated to the memory of Rear Admiral Don P. Moon. A native of Indiana, he graduated from the Naval Academy fourth in the large class of 1916, which has given the United States Navy at least a score of distinguished flag officers.[2] When serving on board *Arizona* in World War I, he invented various new devices for plotting, fire control and range tables, and, after that war was over, qualified as an expert in naval ordnance. The principles of his Master of Science dissertation, "Errors Inherent in Direction Fire" (1921) at the University of Chicago, were subsequently tested and found to be correct. Between wars he served on board several ships as gunnery or fire control officer, in the design section of the Bureau of Ordnance, and on the staff of the Naval War College. At the outbreak of World War II he was in command of Destroyer Squadron 8 of the Atlantic Fleet. As such, he played a notable part on the North Russia run (as I have described in Volume I), as well as in Operation TORCH. After the conclusion of that invasion of North Africa, Admiral King, who had a very high opinion of Captain Moon, made him a member of his staff in Washington. Subsequently, owing to his strong desire for sea duty, he was appointed by Admiral King to command an amphibious group in the Mediterranean. In January 1944, when it was decided to broaden the landings in NEPTUNE, he was promoted Rear Admiral

[2] Including Admirals Radford, Fechteler, Joy and Carney, and Rear Admirals Davidson, Rodgers, Wilkes and Durgin who figure largely in this volume.

to command Force "U" which effected the landings on Utah Beach.

Admiral Moon was a completely dedicated and conscientious officer who had to see personally that everything under his command was taut and shipshape; and his probably excessive efforts in that direction led to his tragic death on 5 August 1944 when he was about to command one of the assault groups in Operation DRAGOON.

It is a pleasure to conclude this volume on board one of the finest new ships of the United States Navy, the 2700-ton frigate *Mitscher*, in which I am sailing south as a guest of the captain, Commander Sheldon H. Kinney USN.

SAMUEL E. MORISON

OFF SAN SALVADOR
   Lat. 23°59′20″ N
   Long. 74°09′30″ W

6 January 1957

Contents

Contents

List of Illustrations

(*All photographs not otherwise described are Official United States Navy. Frontispiece, American Embassy Brussels Press Section photo*)

List of Maps and Charts

Abbreviations

Officers' ranks and bluejackets' ratings are those contemporaneous with the event. Officers and men named will be presumed to be of the United States Navy unless it is otherwise stated; officers of the Naval Reserve are designated USNR. Other service abbreviations are USA, United States Army; USCG, United States Coast Guard; USCGR, Reserve of same; USMC, United States Marine Corps; RAF, Royal Air Force; RCN, Royal Canadian Navy; RN, Royal Navy; RNR, Royal Navy Reserve; RNVR, Royal Navy Volunteer Reserve.

Abbreviations of Landing Craft and Ship Types will be found facing Appendix I.

A.A.F. – United States Army Air Force
A/S – Antisubmarine
B.C.S. – British Chiefs of Staff
Bu – Bureau; Buord – Bureau of Ordnance; Bupers – Bureau of Naval Personnel
C.C.S. – Combined Chiefs of Staff
C. in C. – Commander in Chief
Cincmed – Allied Commander in Chief, Mediterranean
Com – Commander; Comdesron – Commander Destroyer Squadron
Cominch – Commander in Chief, United States Fleet (Admiral King)
Comlancrabeu – Commander U.S. Landing Craft and Bases, Europe
Comnaveu – Commander U.S. Naval Forces, Europe (Admiral Stark)
C.N.O. – Chief of Naval Operations
C.O. – Commanding Officer
Cossac – Chief of Staff, Supreme Allied Command (General Morgan)
CTF – Commander Task Force; CTG – Commander Task Group
CVE – Escort Aircraft Carrier
DD – Destroyer; DD tank – dual drive amphibious tank
DE – Destroyer Escort
E-boat – German motor torpedo boat or other small type
F.F.I. – Forces françaises de l'Intérieur
H.M.C.S. – His Majesty's Canadian Ship; H.H.M.S. – His Hellenic Majesty's Ship; H.M.S. – His Majesty's Ship; H.N.M.S. – Her Netherlands Majesty's Ship

HQ – Headquarters
J.C.S. – Joint Chiefs of Staff
MAS – Italian motor torpedo boat
MTB – British motor torpedo boat
NCDT – Naval Combat Demolition Team; same as UDT
N.O.B. – Naval Operating Base
N.O.I.C. – Naval Officer in Charge
O.N.I. – Office of Naval Intelligence
O.T.C. – Officer in Tactical Command
PT – American motor torpedo boat
R.A.F. – Royal Air Force
R.C.T. – Regimental Combat Team
Sacmed – Supreme Allied Commander, Mediterranean
Secnav – Secretary of the Navy
Shaef – Supreme Headquarters, Allied Expeditionary Force
S.f.c.p. – Shore fire control party
TF – Task Force; TG – Task Group; TU – Task Unit
UDT – Underwater Demolition Team
U.S.C.G.C. – United States Coast Guard Cutter

AIRCRAFT DESIGNATIONS

Numeral in parentheses indicates number of engines

B–24 – Liberator bomber (4); by Navy called PB4Y
C–47 – Skytrain transport (2)
Do–217 – Dornier heavy bomber (2)
F4F–4 – Wildcat (Grumman) fighter (1); F6F – Hellcat (Grumman) fighter (1)
FW–190 – Focke-Wulf fighter (1)
FW–200 – Focke-Wulf heavy bomber (4)
He–111 – Heinkel medium bomber (2)
Ju–88 – Junkers medium bomber (2)
Me–109 – Messerschmitt fighter (1)
OS2U – Kingfisher, Navy (1) scout-observation float plane
P–38 – Lightning fighter (2); P–47 – Thunderbolt (1)
SOC – Seagull (Curtiss-Wright) reconnaissance (1)
Spitfire – Vickers-Armstrong fighter (1)

PART I

Normandy:
Operation NEPTUNE–OVERLORD

CHAPTER I

Grand Strategy and High Politics[1]

1941–1943

1. Strategic Concepts

THE FINAL DEFEAT of Germany by military action was the object of nearly four years of planning and discussion by the British and American high commands. To understand why it took the shape that it did, we must go back to 1940 and try to explain the tortuous road of strategic discussion and planning before the final agreement set forth in the Combined Chiefs of Staff directive of 12 February 1944 to General Eisenhower:

"You will enter the Continent of Europe, and, in conjunction with the other United Nations, undertake operations aimed at the heart of Germany and the destruction of her armed forces."

One major lesson of World War I, the lack of plans for American participation when the United States reluctantly decided to get into it, had been well learned by President Roosevelt, Admiral Stark, General Marshall, and almost everyone who had a responsible position in the American armed forces.

The European situation after the fall of France, in June 1940, aroused everyone who was seriously concerned with defending the Western Hemisphere. "Neutrality Patrol" and other purely defensive measures were first adopted; but Admiral Stark, then Chief of

[1] The Ruppenthal, the Matloff & Snell, the Harrison and the Pogue volumes in the *U.S. Army in World War II* series. *Crusade in Europe;* Winston Churchill's volumes; Robert E. Sherwood *Roosevelt and Hopkins* (1948); King & Whitehill; William D. Leahy *I Was There* (1950); Tracy B. Kittredge ms. "History of U.S.-British Naval Relations 1939–42"; "Digest of Operation ROUNDUP, including notes on Operation SLEDGEHAMMER, etc.," June 1944, a historical monograph written under Comnaveu (Admiral Stark).

Naval Operations, expressed his opinion that in the event of a two-ocean war Germany would be a more dangerous enemy than Japan, and to defeat Germany an American Expeditionary Force in Europe would be required.[2] Shortly after this remarkably prophetic report was written, the senior American military planners invited their British opposite numbers to confer with them in Washington. At that conference the basic strategic decision for the participation of the United States in World War II was agreed upon, nine months before the Japanese attack on Pearl Harbor brought America actively into the war. Between January and March 1941, these officers worked out an overall plan, known as the ABC–1 Staff Agreement of 27 March 1941, for collaboration *if and when* the United States was drawn into the war.[3] It was agreed that Germany, as the strongest Axis power, with the greatest economic and military potential, must be defeated first. At that time, it was hoped that Japan could be persuaded to remain neutral; yet, if she should decide otherwise, the future Allies would still endeavor to defeat Germany first — as eventually they did.

These early meetings and understandings helped the United States to withstand the shock of the Japanese attack on Pearl Harbor, and to cement the most successful Grand Alliance in modern history. The atmosphere of this alliance was not always sweet, and the way was never easy; but it withstood serious setbacks and defeats, gave rise to a glorious victory, and for more than ten years after the end of the war remained the principal bulwark of the free world against its erstwhile ally, Soviet Russia.

There is no doubt that the British in general, and Mr. Churchill in particular, intended to invade Europe when they considered the time to be ripe. At the ARCADIA Conference in Washington in December 1941, two weeks after Pearl Harbor, when the basic strategic decision was confirmed, Mr. Churchill presented to the American Joint Chiefs of Staff his strategic concept for the defeat

[2] See Volume I of this History pp. 42–43. A more extended digest of this report, dated 12 Nov. 1940, is in Matloff & Snell pp. 25–28.

[3] See Volume I 38–49 for a discussion of these early staff meetings with the British, and for details on the evolution of this agreement.

of Germany. In brief, this consisted of (1) a tight naval blockade of the Axis countries; (2) an intensive aërial bombardment of Germany; (3) propaganda to break down German morale and arouse rebellion among the conquered peoples; (4) a series of peripheral landings by small armored forces at points on the coast from Norway all the way around to the Ægean; and (5) a "final assault on the German citadel." [4]

In this concept Churchill was responding to English history. His countrymen preferred what Captain Liddell Hart calls "the indirect approach." "We are particularly liable to yield to the temptation to dispersal," wrote Major General Sir Frederick Maurice in 1929.[5] They remembered that they had got at Napoleon by the back door of the Iberian Peninsula, and that direct-attack strategy in World War I had cost them a million men killed and two million wounded. To avoid the static trench warfare of that earlier Great War, with its useless and terrible bloodletting, they sought other means to defeat Germany — blockade; bombing; peripheral probing for a weak spot, and, when they found it, a final drive for victory. The very title of one of Churchill's volumes, *Closing the Ring*, indicates his belief in this strategy of squeeze, probe and push — which also has an American precedent, General Winfield Scott's "Anaconda Plan" for defeating the Southern Confederacy by blockading its coast and seizing the Mississippi.

There was another good reason for this British concept. The United Kingdom was fully mobilized for war early in 1942. She had no unused pool of resources, and lacked the capacity for a head-on attack on the German Army; but she had the men, the troop lift and the naval power to probe around the periphery of *Festung Europa* in search of a weak spot. Thus British leaders had to be opportunist in their strategic thinking. As Colonel Greenfield has well stated, "The British idea was to use the forces of the Allies as they accumulated in jabs all around 'the ring' with forces capable of hitting hard, but so used as to be able to disengage and hit again

---

[4] Churchill *The Grand Alliance* pp. 645–59.
[5] *British Strategy* p. 85.

somewhere else. Meanwhile the Allies would back the Soviets to the limit with supplies and equipment, achieve complete domination of the seas, tighten the blockade of the Axis, bomb its vitals and the morale of its people from the air, give aid to guerillas and other elements of internal resistance in all occupied areas, and continually encourage these by propaganda. Having thus worn the enemy down until he was weak, they would finally move in for the kill with an offensive directed at some vital point in his territory." [6]

The American strategic planners took a very dim view of this British concept.[7] They had little to work with early in 1942, but with the resources of the New World to draw upon they could look forward to large-scale military operations and long-range plans. They admitted the value of blockade, bombing, propaganda, and (to a limited extent) of hit-and-run raids; but they did not believe Germany could be defeated or even greatly weakened by such methods. From the first, they insisted that the Allies must plan, build up and concentrate for one big powerful drive at the earliest possible date, to meet the German Army head-on and strike at the heart of the Axis. And that was the way it was finally done, after long strategic wrangling and a series of Mediterranean operations which the British insisted upon before they would consent to back up a major power push. The American strategic concept also explains why all top American planners, from early 1942, were pressing the British to agree on a firm date for the major operation. Without it they could not decide what sort of army was needed or have time to train it properly, or what kind of landing and beaching craft would be required, and how many, or what to procure from American factories — all with a war against Japan going on. Very few British strategists except General Morgan — certainly not Mr.

---

[6] Kent R. Greenfield *The Historian and The Army* (1954) p. 44, a neat presentation of the opposing views.

[7] They had heard an outline of them at Argentia in August 1941, and presented a critique of them on 20 September which remarked significantly that the British views "do not envisage the offensive use of such forces on a sufficient scale . . . to accomplish the complete defeat of Germany." In other words, the British at that time, naturally enough, could not anticipate either American entrance into the war or the immense military potential of the United States. But their opposition to the big power push continued long after these conditions had changed.

Churchill — ever understood this. The British strategists' thinking tended to regard all high-level plans and decisions as tentative, subject to discussion and alteration, especially if circumstances changed; they were always asking us to be more flexible.[8] But the Americans, who were counted on to build or supply the bulk of the landing craft, aircraft, matériel and at least half the man power, had to be fairly rigid, had to have target dates; they could not retool factories, shift flotillas of beaching craft from one ocean to another, dispatch divisions thousands of miles for a full-scale operation, as though it were a raid from England on the Channel Islands.

There was also a tendency among the British to regard the wars against Japan and the European Axis as two distinct and separate wars, in which the basic strategic decision required both the British Commonwealth and the United States to throw everything they had against Germany before any vigorous offensive was started against Japan. The Americans, on the contrary, regarded the global war as one war, in which it would be useless to defeat Germany if Japan were allowed to work her will in the Pacific Ocean and the Far East.

Given the widely differing resources and circumstances of the two countries, American exasperation over the difficulty of pinning down the British to a decision, and the British feeling that Americans were opinionated and inflexible, it is a tribute to the leaders of both countries that they were able to agree on a major operation like OVERLORD.

2. SLEDGEHAMMER *and* ROUNDUP

The first positive American plan for the defeat of Germany came from the very man who executed the eventual combined plan — the operations we are describing in this volume. On 26 February 1942 Major General Dwight D. Eisenhower, chief of the war plans

[8] For an extreme example of the British desire to switch an operation to a new target at the eleventh hour, and American resistance to such a change, see Chapter XIII.

division of the War Department, completed a set of conclusions and recommendations on world strategy. In it he declared, "We should at once develop, in conjunction with the British, a definite plan for operations against Northwest Europe." [9] This, together with other recommendations, was sent to the Joint Strategic Committee of the Joint Chiefs of Staff, which included some of the best brains in the armed forces: Rear Admiral Richmond Kelly Turner (chairman), Captain Forrest Sherman and Lieutenant Colonel Albert C. Wedemeyer USA. Starting with the agreed decision that Germany was to be beaten before Japan, they studied each and every littoral of *Festung Europa* from northern Norway to the Black Sea. They appreciated the importance for the future of having Anglo-American rather than Russian troops overrunning Europe. They were fully aware of the "soft underbelly" strategy so persistently inculcated by Mr. Churchill and his Chiefs of Staff; but where were the soft spots in the underbelly? Every landing place they studied on the Mediterranean shore of Axis-held Europe led to a mountain defile, and none was within reach of a possible Allied naval base eighty miles away — the then limit of effective fighter-plane cover, as well as of the smaller landing craft. Consequently they could see no other possible jumping-off place for the big assault than the British Isles, and no better gateway than Northern France for the entrance of our forces into the Continent.

The committee, after going thoroughly into capabilities, with experts, on troop training, supply, construction of landing craft, and procurement of weapons, tanks and aircraft, decided that an Anglo-American amphibious invasion of Northern France across the English Channel would be practicable in the spring or summer of 1943. [10]

Their report was favorably received by the War Department; especially by Secretary Stimson and General George C. Marshall, the Chief of Staff. The Navy, in view of the difficulty of sending ground forces to Britain before the U-boats were defeated, and of

[9] Matloff & Snell p. 159. Their chaps. vii and viii have the best account of this period of planning.

[10] Conversations with General Wedemeyer in 1956 and with Admiral Forrest Sherman on 1 May 1946.

constructing enough landing craft and training enough sailors to man them for a 1943 invasion, received the report with little enthusiasm. Nevertheless the Navy responded by inaugurating an ambitious program of building landing craft and training crews,[11] coördinating it with the Army's "Victory Program" for building up ground and air forces.

On 27 March 1942 the Army planners, on the basis of the Joint Strategic Committee's report, presented to President Roosevelt an outline plan for an invasion of Europe in the spring of 1943, with 48 divisions and 5800 aircraft, the United States alone to furnish 3250 planes and about one million troops. The Marshall Memorandum, as this draft is called, contemplated three phases: —

1. Preparation, involving (*a*) Build-up of ground forces and matériel in Great Britain; this, essentially a logistic movement, and called Operation BOLERO, had already begun. (*b*) Aërial bombardment of and coastal raids on German-occupied Europe. (*c*) An emergency cross-Channel operation (SLEDGEHAMMER)[12] to establish a beachhead on the Cotentin (Cherbourg) Peninsula in 1942, in the event either of an imminent collapse of Russia or unexpected weakness in the German hold on France.

2. The main cross-Channel operation to seize broad beachheads somewhere between Boulogne and Le Havre. First called Operation ROUNDUP,[13] this, with a shift of target, eventually became the NEPTUNE–OVERLORD of 1944.

3. Consolidation of the beachhead and advance into the heart of Germany.

The President approved this Memorandum on 1 April 1942 and immediately sent General Marshall, Colonel Wedemeyer and Harry Hopkins to London to present it to the British, in the hope of obtaining an early decision. They felt the urgent necessity of fixing a

[11] See Volume II 28–29.

[12] This code name had already been used for an emergency operation by the British Joint Planners.

[13] This code name, too, had already been used by the British planners for a small-scale landing plan in Dec. 1941. (Ruppenthal I 52.)

target date before grappling with the immense logistical problem of establishing an American army of a million men, with modern equipment and troop lift, in England. Furthermore, it was hoped to commit the British to this direct strategy before their forces had been dissipated in peripheral operations, like the brilliant but unnecessary capture of Madagascar.

General Marshall presented his plan to the British War Cabinet, and to the Chiefs of Staff and their planning committee. It reached them at the right moment, because the British planners had already outlined a very similar scheme, from which the two code names were taken. Their skepticism as to the American ability to implement so grand a scheme within a year seems to have been to a large extent removed, because all three bodies formally accepted the Marshall Memorandum as a basis for planning on 14 April 1942.[14]

Our Allies, however, were silenced rather than convinced. They could not — at any rate did not — present convincing arguments against the 1943 ROUNDUP, because their objections were fundamentally historical and emotional. Britain had suffered terribly from the static warfare of World War I, and her more mature planners feared that a premature invasion of France would result either in another Dunkirk or interminable trench warfare. "You must remember," said Professor Lindemann, Mr. Churchill's friend and counsellor, to General Marshall, "you are fighting our losses on the Somme." [15]

The British had already thrice been thrown out of Europe in World War II — from Norway, Dunkirk and Greece; they could not afford to have it happen a fourth time. And the American advocates of SLEDGEHAMMER, the proposed landing near Cherbourg in 1942, were embarrassed because the United States would be able to contribute only token forces; the operation would have to be

---

[14] Matloff & Snell p. 188.

[15] Told to the writer by General Marshall in 1956. Professor Lindemann (now Viscount Cherwell) was an eminent physicist from Oxford on whom Churchill relied for advice on scientific matters, and on many other matters as well. "The Professor," as he was called in British military circles, was more respected than liked; but "By God, he was right that time — " has been the reaction of more than one high-ranking Briton to whom I have repeated this incident.

mainly British as to ground forces, air cover and troop lift. It was kept "on the books" as a possible diversion to encourage Russia and please her friends in Great Britain and America (the "Open Second Front Now" propaganda was in full blast); but the Americans were in no position to insist on it even when (as in July 1942) it became in General Marshall's opinion an indispensable preliminary to ROUNDUP in 1943. By that time the United States would be able to pull her weight; yet we could not resist the British objections since Sir Alan Brooke and other members of the British Chiefs of Staff had felt the bite of the German Army, which no member of the American Joint Chiefs of Staff had experienced.

General Marshall believed that everything was settled, in principle at least, when he flew back to the United States in April 1942. But the more the British thought about SLEDGEHAMMER–ROUNDUP and discussed it among themselves, the less they liked it. The Prime Minister sent Admiral Lord Louis Mountbatten to present his misgivings to President Roosevelt and, as a counterproposal for 1942, an amphibious landing in North Africa. Mr. Roosevelt, with his historic memories of Decatur and Somers and the Barbary Corsairs, and a love of peripheral operations almost equal to Mr. Churchill's, liked the North Africa idea. But the Secretary of War, Henry L. Stimson, and his other military advisers did their best to keep him firm to the SLEDGEHAMMER-ROUNDUP plan. The prior visit to Washington of the Russian Foreign Minister Molotov, to present the urgent need of a "second front" in 1942, to some extent counteracted the arguments of the popular "Dickie" Mountbatten.[16] But on 19 June Churchill himself arrived at Hyde Park, with the primary purpose of arguing Roosevelt out of the agreed-upon plan and into the North African operation which became TORCH. During the six days that he was in the United States he made his mark on the President's mind.

The forensic situation, as we may call it when describing only plans and arguments, was about as follows in the last week of June 1942: —

[16] Stimson & Bundy pp. 418–24; Sherwood *Roosevelt and Hopkins* pp. 556–79.

1. The British were unwilling to put on SLEDGEHAMMER in 1942 and, since they would have to provide most of the forces involved, their wishes could not be ignored. And they were becoming increasingly skeptical of victory in a cross-Channel operation in 1943.

2. The Joint Chiefs of Staff might be willing to cut out SLEDGE-HAMMER, but were eager to concentrate on the BOLERO build-up in the European theater for a decisive cross-Channel thrust in 1943 and averse to diverting forces elsewhere in Europe or to Africa.

3. The political chiefs — Churchill and Roosevelt — could not face their people without doing *something* in the European theater in 1942; they could not stand the onus of fighting another "phony war."

4. Since *something* must be done in 1942, the invasion of North Africa, where the British had been forced to yield Tobruk on 21 June, was the only practicable operation which offered any strategic advantage. Yet, as both General Marshall and Admiral King predicted, as soon as forces started funneling into North Africa, arguments for postponing the cross-Channel operation to 1944 would become irresistible.

Shortly after his return to England Mr. Churchill declared to the British Chiefs of Staff that SLEDGEHAMMER "had been dead for some time" and should be given a decent burial. The British Chiefs, generally responsive to Churchillian prodding,[17] so reported to the War Cabinet, which sent notice to Washington on 8 July that they had definitely decided *not* to mount SLEDGEHAMMER. And, in a separate message to the President, the Prime Minister urged the North African invasion as the best thing for 1942, with a landing in Norway as an alternative.[18]

[17] General Marshall observed to the writer that Churchill often saw the British Chiefs of Staff twice daily and made it difficult for them to refuse anything he urged strongly; Roosevelt saw the Joint Chiefs of Staff but seldom, and generally took their advice. The British Chiefs, in fact, sometimes appealed to the J.C.S., through Sir John Dill, head of the British Joint Staff Mission in the United States, to "get them out of" things Churchill had ordered them to do! (Compare *Crusade in Europe* p. 61.)

[18] *Hinge of Fate* p. 433.

SLEDGEHAMMER was not to die without a struggle. At the meeting of the Joint Chiefs of Staff on 10 July General Marshall, after frankly discussing the whole matter with Sir John Dill, declared that he still regarded the North African invasion as bad strategy; he believed that, if we must "do something" in 1942, it should lead to a more important result than could be attained in or through North Africa. But he admitted that no cross-Channel operation could be carried out if Britain went along only as a reluctant dragon. He then made the radical proposal that, if America were forced to accept the British strategy of no SLEDGEHAMMER and no firm commitment even for ROUNDUP, the American build-up in Britain be halted, and the mass of United States ground forces be deployed for decisive action in the Pacific. Admiral King joined Generals Marshall and Arnold and Admiral Leahy in sending a memorandum to that effect to the President. F.D.R. (then at Hyde Park) required an outline plan for this radical shift of forces to be delivered to him by air that very afternoon. On 14 July, after he had digested it, he telegraphed to General Marshall that he disapproved the Pacific proposal and was sending him to London with King and Hopkins to make a last fight for SLEDGEHAMMER–ROUNDUP.[19]

Was the J.C.S. proposal a bluff, intended to prod the British into firming up ROUNDUP even if SLEDGEHAMMER had to be sacrificed? Henry L. Stimson, the Secretary of War, so thought at the time. Sir John Dill, who had Marshall's full confidence, evidently did not think so, for he cabled his Government not to press too hard for North Africa, lest Britain lose American aid in Europe.[20] On the part of the two naval members of the J.C.S. it was certainly no bluff. Admirals King and Leahy firmly believed in the basic strategy of defeating Germany first; but so long as it was doubtful when — if ever — the British would consent to a cross-Channel operation,

[19] Matloff & Snell p. 270; Harrison p. 28.
[20] *Hinge of Fate* pp. 439–40; Stimson & Bundy p. 425. In 1956 I asked General Marshall the direct question, "Was it a bluff?" His answer is interesting: "It was partly bluff and partly really meant. I cannot pretend now to interpret my feelings in 1942. But I am certain of this: President Roosevelt did not want any bluffing in these high strategy matters." The implication is that the J.C.S. were prepared to make the Pacific shift if F.D.R. had given the word.

they disliked sending to the United Kingdom American men and matériel which were desperately needed in the war with Japan.

On 15 July the President held a long and tense session with the J.C.S. On the following day he directed Marshall, King and Hopkins to agree with the appropriate British authorities upon "definite plans" for the rest of 1942 and "tentative plans" for 1943. "You should strongly urge immediate all-out preparations" for SLEDGE-HAMMER, regardless of the Russian situation, and only if "completely convinced" that it is "impossible of execution," to "determine upon another place for U.S. troops to fight in 1942." Plans for ROUNDUP for 1943 should be immediately considered and preparations made for it.[21]

3. TORCH *Substituted*

Marshall, King and Hopkins, reaching London 19 July, promptly conferred with the top American commanders then in England — Admiral Stark and Generals Eisenhower, Mark Clark and Spaatz — who had already drafted an outline plan for a landing near Cherbourg in late September or early October. Armed with this, they pled with Mr. Churchill and the British Chiefs of Staff for SLEDGE-HAMMER as necessary preliminary to a 1943 ROUNDUP. They met unanimous opposition, and a firm argument for North Africa. Mr. Roosevelt was informed of the deadlock. He replied that they must settle for something that would get an American army into action against Germany in 1942, and mentioned five possible targets ranging from Norway to the Persian Gulf. Accordingly, on 25 July, Marshall, King and Hopkins agreed to the North African operation, which now received the hopeful code name TORCH.

"Thank God!" cabled F.D.R. to Churchill.[22]

[21] Sherwood *Roosevelt and Hopkins* pp. 603–05.

[22] Same pp. 610–12; Matloff & Snell p. 278. One strong argument of the British which struck a responsive chord in Admirals Stark and King was that the Channel weather in late September was too foul for an amphibious operation. The argument was used in reverse when Mr. Churchill was trying to have OVERLORD postponed from June to September 1944 in order to get in a few licks in the Ægean. He then pointed out that William the Conqueror landed at Hastings on 28 Sept. 1066!

General Marshall recalls that, as he got out of bed in his London hotel a day or two later, Admiral King entered to look over the memorandum on this decision to be presented to the British Chiefs of Staff. King observed that everyone should understand that TORCH would inevitably draw so many forces into the Mediterranean that no cross-Channel operation would be possible before 1944. He wished everyone to admit this frankly, instead of nourishing the notion that we could have our strategic cake and eat it too. He insisted on adding to the American memorandum: —

"That it be understood that a commitment to this operation [TORCH] renders ROUNDUP in all probability impractical of successful execution in 1943 and therefore that we have definitely accepted a defensive, encircling line of action for the Continental European Theater, except as to air operations." [23]

The British War Cabinet declined to receive the proposal in that bald form, probably because they wished to keep their hands clean of responsibility for postponing the invasion of Europe in case they were accused of delaying the war. King's statement had to be emasculated to the extent that it meant nothing: — "That there be no avoidable reduction in the preparation for ROUNDUP as long as there remains any possibility of its successful execution before July 1943. . . ." [24]

Owing to the willingness of the British Chiefs of Staff to continue planning for ROUNDUP, Marshall and King returned to Washington feeling that the final choice between that operation and TORCH had not been made. The President promptly informed them that *he* had decided for North Africa, preparations for which had top priority. This was one military decision that Roosevelt made on his own responsibility and against the advice of his principal military advisers. [25]

In August the Allies suffered two blows: the American and Australian defeat by the Japanese Navy in the Battle of Savo Island, and the Anglo-Canadian repulse at Dieppe. The former served no-

[23] Matloff & Snell p. 280.
[24] King & Whitehill p. 404.
[25] *Roosevelt and Hopkins* p. 615.

tice that Japan had quickly recovered from her setback at Midway, and the latter served to confirm the British in their feeling that any invasion of France short of overwhelming strength might be disastrous.

For some time Mr. Churchill insisted that he could have TORCH in 1942 and ROUNDUP in 1943. In November 1942, after the successful landings in North Africa had been made, the resulting slow-down of the BOLERO build-up in Britain shook his confidence, and General Eisenhower told him that no major operation against the Continent would now be practicable before 1944. He then sought Mr. Roosevelt's assurance (25 November) that planning for ROUNDUP was still going on. The President gave him the desired assurance, but at the same time warned him that the drain of American resources into the Mediterranean made it all but impossible to count on a cross-Channel invasion before 1944.

That, as we all know, is what happened. And that is what General Sir Alan Brooke, chairman of the B.C.S. and Chief of the Imperial General Staff, wanted. He shared the American belief that the ultimate key to victory was a successful landing in France. But, after weighing ponderables and imponderables, he concluded that no such operation could succeed until the German Army had been worn down by the Russians, the Luftwaffe bled white by Allied air power, the U-boats thwarted, and American war production expanded. Brooke had no respect for the Churchillian strategy of jabbing all around the ring from the North Cape to Rhodes; on the contrary, he wanted all diversions to be arranged in the Mediterranean like a ladder, with TORCH as the bottom rung. The successful ascent of this ladder, planted on what he called the "imperial base" in the Middle East, would open the Suez Canal, save an estimated million tons of shipping, take German forces off Russia's back, and, in general, give us a weaker Germany to deal with in 1944.[26] The Americans, once having been persuaded to place their feet on the bottom rung of this Mediterranean ladder, were unable

[26] Sir Arthur Bryant *The Turn of the Tide* (1957).

to resist the logic of the Sicilian and Salerno landings later that year, and the long, arduous push up the boot of Italy. They were in for it.

The Americans had pressed hard for a strategic decision, but for a long time all they could get from their British colleagues was a strategic drift into the Mediterranean. Probably it was well for the cause that they did. SLEDGEHAMMER was too much of a gamble; if we had obtained a lodgment near Cherbourg in 1942, the Germans should have had little difficulty in bottling us up there. The politicians were right; something *had* to be done in 1942, and the Mediterranean ladder did bring substantial strategic benefits, even though it postponed the cross-Channel operation to 1944, and led up the hard spine of the Apennines instead of to a "soft underbelly" of Germany.

CHAPTER II

Plans and Preparations[1]

March 1943–May 1944

1. *The "Cossac" Planning Group*

ALTHOUGH Operation TORCH had given the kiss of death to ROUNDUP, General Marshall continued to feel her fluttering pulse and endeavor to rally her declining strength. After fighting for her all through the Casablanca Conference in January 1943,[2] the only concession he could extort from the British was an agreement to set up a special Anglo-American planning staff, responsible for planning (1) minor amphibious operations, (2) a possible landing on the Continent to seize strategic centers in the event of enemy collapse, and (3) the seizure of a Continental bridgehead in 1943, leading to rapid exploitation by a large-scale invasion in 1944. The Combined Chiefs of Staff also recommended that a supreme commander for the invasion of Europe be named "at once" — it was not done for almost a year — and that, pending his appointment, the Anglo-American planning staff be set up.

Lieutenant General Frederick E. Morgan received the news on 13 March 1943 that he had been appointed "Chief of Staff to the Supreme Allied Commander (designate)," and that he was to organize the Anglo-American planning staff at once. At that time he commanded a British Army Corps which had been readied to enter Spanish Morocco in case Franco threw in his lot with Hitler. General Morgan brought to this new task a vast energy, an outstanding ability to organize, and a sense of humor which enabled

[1] Same sources as for Chapter I, plus Morgan *Overture to Overlord* and Ehrman V.
[2] See Volume IX 6-11.

him to make British and American officers, with their differing attitudes, traditions and procedures, work together in a spirit of harmony and dedication to a common objective. First evidence of his wit was the code name for his staff, an abbreviation of his title: "Cossac." Deputy Cossac was Brigadier General Ray W. Barker USA, assigned from the headquarters of "Etousa" (European Theater of Operations U.S. Army). General Barker, having had experience with the Combined Planners, was "able to gallop straight on without missing a beat." The United States Navy was represented by Captains Lyman A. Thackrey and Gordon Hutchins; the Royal Navy by Rear Admiral George E. Creasy and Commodore John Hughes-Hallett. There were representatives, too, of the air forces, the Canadian Army, the Engineers, and every branch of the armed services which might conceivably be concerned in the operation – and who would not? By the close of 1943, Cossac comprised 489 officers – 215 of them American – and 614 ratings, 204 of them American. Their headquarters at Norfolk House, St. James's Square, London, fortunately had plenty of room.

Cossac's first directive, of 23 April 1943, required that it draft a scheme of elaborate diversionary operations to keep the Germans moving and guessing, a plan for immediate entrance into the Continent (Operation RANKIN) in the event of a sudden German collapse, and a plan for the major assault on France in 1944.

Work on these plans had barely started when the TRIDENT Conference of the Combined Chiefs of Staff with the President and Prime Minister convened at Washington, in May 1943. Here for the first time a tentative date was set, 1 May 1944, for the major invasion of Northern France that eventually became known as NEPTUNE-OVERLORD.

General Morgan's staff, after surveying all possible targets between Norway and Portugal, narrowed down their choice to two stretches of Northern France – (1) the Pas-de-Calais and the coast of Picardy between Gravelines and the Somme; and (2) Calvados and the Bay of the Seine, that part of Normandy between Caen and the base of the Cotentin Peninsula. The first (the old ROUNDUP plan) was closer to Britain, but very heavily defended; and it would require broadening to include either Antwerp or Le Havre as a major port of entry, in order to keep up the momentum of the assault. For all experience had shown that, if momentum is not maintained, an amphibious operation bogs down; and momentum was more important here than anywhere. The Calvados alternative, less heavily defended, also lacked a major port; but on 26 June 1943 Cossac decided to concentrate on planning for this latter target.

During the greater part of its existence, Cossac was embarrassed by two main factors: (1) the want of a supreme commander, for which President Roosevelt was responsible; and (2) the aversion of many important Englishmen, from Mr. Churchill down, to *any* cross-Channel operation until Germany was so beaten down that it would be a walkover. Were these British diehards right, that any cross-Channel operation was an undue risk; or were the Americans right in insisting that it could and must be done? Admiral Lord Mountbatten broke the deadlock, by inviting Cossac staff to thrash it out with his people at Combined Headquarters in Largs, Scotland, at the end of June. There, under the combined influence of Mountbatten hospitality, an unusually perfect stretch of Scots weather, and the bagpipes of the local Home Guard, the "unbelievers" were converted and all agreed that a three-division cross-Channel operation was feasible, with the Bay of the Seine as target.

By early July General Morgan had an outline plan for an initial assault of three divisions, to be followed by eight more; Cherbourg to be seized within two weeks and Southern France to be invaded at the same time. This was the basis for the plan actually followed in 1944. It was reviewed and discussed in the QUADRANT Conference of the C.C.S. with the President and Prime Minister at Quebec in August, 1943. By that time the situation was far more favorable to the Allies than it had been in the early months of the year. The back of the U-boat offensive had been broken. Sicily was in the bag. The Central Solomons had been secured and the Gilbert and Marshall Islands were about to be invaded. In the discussion Mr. Churchill made the pregnant suggestion that the forces allocated to OVERLORD be increased 25 per cent and that a landing should also be made on the Cotentin Peninsula. Although he was still promoting prior Mediterranean operations, it was agreed at Quebec that OVERLORD be the main Allied effort in 1944 and the first charge on available resources; that the target date of 1 May be confirmed; and that the Cossac plan, with such augmentations as the planners thought necessary, be approved.

Thus, after more than a year of discussion, a firm decision was made to proceed with the major invasion of the Continent, and to give it top priority for 1944. Nevertheless Mr. Churchill and several important British generals still had mental reservations as to its desirability or probable success, until or unless conditions were exactly right; and among many strategists there still remained the lively hope for an easier substitute. Even before the QUADRANT Conference was over, the Prime Minister caused to be inserted a minute in the proceedings to the effect that, as a possible alternative to the invasion of Normandy, Cossac must work on an invasion of Norway.[3] In mid-November 1943, when Rear Admiral Kirk arrived in London to prepare for his command of the Western Naval Task Force in OVERLORD, he found that Admiral Stark, as well as almost every top British commander, expected Germany to collapse before the end of the year; that Operation RANKIN would replace OVERLORD. This feeling that "something might turn up" to make the cross-Channel invasion unnecessary was one of the heavy handicaps to serious planning by Cossac's staff; but the delay of President Roosevelt in appointing a supreme commander was also frustrating.

[3] Morgan p. 173. Mr. Churchill was always loyal to the concept of an *eventual* power to push against Germany, but he wanted to try all sorts of other operations first. He wrote to General Marshall 12 March 1944, "I am hardening very much on this operation as the time approaches," and on 20 April he told Asst. Sec. War J. J. McCloy and General McNarney that, if *he* had planned OVERLORD, he would have waited until Norway had been "cleared up," Turkey was in the war, "and the Danube under threat," before it was launched. Matloff II chap. xv pp. 58–9 of mimeographed draft.

2. *Choice of a Supreme Commander*

The choice of a supreme commander was long postponed after planning had reached the stage where one was desperately needed to make decisions and to insist on sufficient forces being allocated. At the QUADRANT meeting it was decided that he was to be an American; but which American, Marshall or Eisenhower? Marshall outranked Eisenhower, and Churchill, who had seen enough of the Chief of Staff to recognize his sterling qualities, wanted him, as did Roosevelt. But Admirals King and Leahy and General Arnold begged the President to keep him in Washington, as the indispensable key figure on the Joint Chiefs of Staff. By September 1943 the question had got into the American press. Newspapers hostile to Roosevelt charged that Marshall was being "kicked upstairs" as a result of a left-wing plot to get him out of Washington. The implication is that the Democrats wished to build up Marshall as a war hero to succeed Roosevelt, a rôle which the Republicans were reserving for General MacArthur. Throughout this unfortunate controversy General Marshall kept silent and refused to express his own preference.[4]

The fears of the Joint Chiefs that the British would again try to postpone OVERLORD were realized at the SEXTANT Conference at Cairo in late November 1943. Naples was now secured and Italy had joined the Allies, but Mr. Churchill proposed to set up the following timetable: capture Rome in January 1944, Rhodes in February; get Turkey into the war; open up the Ægean as a supply route to Russia; and then get around to OVERLORD — maybe in the fall. The Joint Chiefs agreed to postpone a decision until the Com-

[4] General Marshall informed the writer in 1956 that he did not regard the opposition to himself as political, but that he had felt that he would be more useful to the cause in Washington; besides, he realized that, if he were appointed supreme commander in Europe after such a press campaign, he would be an embarrassment to President Roosevelt, no matter how hard his endeavors to the contrary, as Leonard Wood had been to President Wilson, McClellan to President Lincoln; and as MacArthur already was to F.D.R.

bined Chiefs met at Teheran, since Russia's views must be ascertained.

At Teheran, Stalin, much to the delight of Mr. Roosevelt, put a stopper on the flow of Churchillian oratory; and the Marshal equally pleased the Prime Minister by giving the President a dig in the ribs on his failure to make up his mind about a supreme commander. After Churchill had outlined his proposed safaris into the Eastern Mediterranean, and admitted that they would delay OVERLORD for six to eight weeks (ignoring Morgan's warning that weather conditions in the Channel would require it to be launched not later than July), Stalin bluntly inquired as to who would be the supreme commander? Roosevelt and Churchill admitted that this was not yet settled. "Then nothing will come out of these operations," said Stalin. He then called the attention of all present to the necessity of *not* starting diversions from the most important operation. OVERLORD, he said, should not be postponed; and it should be reinforced by a landing in the South of France.[5]

Churchill yielded. On 30 November 1943 General Sir Alan Brooke announced that the C.C.S. had agreed to launch OVERLORD in May 1944 and to mount a supporting operation against the South of France. At Cairo, on 3 December, the President announced his decision to appoint Eisenhower Supreme Commander. The public announcement was made on Christmas Eve; and the Supreme Commander, after a brief visit home, arrived in London 14 January 1944 to take up his new and tremendous responsibility. Cossac was now absorbed in Eisenhower's staff — Supreme Headquarters Allied Expeditionary Force, better known as "Shaef." General Bedell Smith remained "Ike's" chief of staff; and General Morgan, although offered the command of an army corps, generously de-

---

[5] President Roosevelt, after his return to the U.S., told the writer that he believed Churchill was trying to get OVERLORD postponed to 1945, and that he and Stalin had prevented it. On the other hand, it was F.D.R. who proposed "several things we could do" while waiting for OVERLORD and without delaying it beyond June 1944, such as (*a*) to increase the forces in Italy (*b*) operate from the northern Adriatic (i.e. Trieste-Ljubljana Gap) and (*c*) capture Ægean Islands. Was he merely "fishing" for Stalin's reaction?

clined it in favor of becoming Eisenhower's deputy chief of staff in order to "keep the wheels rolling."

The appointments of Allied naval, ground force and air commanders had already been made. These were Admiral Sir Bertram H. Ramsay, General Sir Bernard Montgomery, and Air Chief Marshal Sir Trafford Leigh-Mallory.

Admiral Ramsay, the Allied Naval Commander Expeditionary Force, from whom components of the United States Navy in Operation NEPTUNE–OVERLORD took orders, was a remarkable character. Retired as a rear admiral in 1938, after notable service in Dover Patrol in World War I, Ramsay had been recalled to active duty the following year at the age of fifty-six for the important home command of Flag Officer, Dover. As such he had been the main instrument in the evacuation of the British Army from Dunkirk in May and June 1940. After serving as Admiral Sir Andrew Cunningham's chief naval planner for Operation TORCH, he had played a distinguished part in Mediterranean amphibious operations, in which he had been closely associated with General Eisenhower.[6] Rear Admiral Hall, who served under Admiral Ramsay, described him as "quiet, brilliant, intelligent, determined and easy to get on with." All who knew him praise his tact, his attractive personality and his grasp of military as well as naval problems.

3. *"Mulberry," "Pluto" and "Buco"* [7]

A major problem of the planners was to provide the assault force with ammunition, supplies and reinforcements over the beaches during the critical period before Cherbourg could be brought into use. Weather statistics indicated that a storm in the Channel should be expected in every month of the year, and that fair weather seldom lasted more than a few days; yet no prolonged landing opera-

[6] See Volume IX 148–49, and portrait at p. 162.
[7] Cdr. Alfred Stanford USNR, deputy commander Mulberry A under Capt. A. Dayton Clark, gives an excellent account of these inventions in his *Force Mulberry* (1951); see also Ruppenthal I 269–82.

tion could succeed without fair weather. The only way, then, to guarantee momentum, the uninterrupted flow of men and matériel, was to provide sheltered water off the beaches. The novel, not to say colossal, solution is a tribute to British brains and energy.

The Admiralty and Mountbatten's outfit had been working intermittently on this problem since early in the war. Commodore Hughes-Hallett RN thought up a "quite improbable four-footed pierhead that could climb up and down its own legs and could be connected to the shore by an articulated pontoon pier that would carry traffic," the whole protected by a barrier of big caissons.[8] When a rough plan for these was called to Mr. Churchill's attention in May 1942, he scribbled on the foot: "They must float up and down with the tide. . . . Let me have the best solution worked out. Don't argue the matter. The difficulties will argue for themselves." They did.

For over a year nothing was done about this scheme except to experiment in a mild way, under the direction of Brigadier Sir Bruce White, a civil engineer. General Morgan has told how it was brought into the purview of Cossac more or less by accident, when the initial plan was being discussed on a hot July day in 1943. After the Army members had insisted that OVERLORD could not be launched unless they were assured of a major port within a few days, and pointed out that Cherbourg was too strongly defended to be taken at once, Commodore Hughes-Hallett remarked, " Well, all I can say is, if we can't capture a port we must take one with us." Next morning, he brought the artificial harbor project into Cossac. It was later given the name "mulberry." Intensive production began in Great Britain, under conditions of the most excruciating secrecy.

In their final form two artificial harbors were produced, both built by British labor: "Mulberry A" for the American beaches, and "Mulberry B" for the British sector. Any ship approaching a mulberry would first encounter a floating breakwater composed of "bombardons," floating steel structures, to break up wave action.

[8] Morgan p. 262.

Next came the 2200-yards long breakwater of thirty-one concrete caissons called "phœnixes," each as tall as a five-story house, to be towed across the Channel and sunk. The phœnixes formed a sea wall on two sides of an artificial harbor about two square miles in area, equal to that of the harbor of Gibraltar, and big enough for seven Liberty ships and twelve smaller vessels to moor. Within each harbor were three "whale" pontoon-section runways anchored on their seaward ends to the "Lobnitz" pierheads — named after the engineer who designed them to rise and fall with the tide. This combination would enable LSTs to unload at any stage of the tide, and provide their wheeled cargoes with a one-way road for rolling ashore.

In addition to the mulberries were the "gooseberries," to provide sheltered water for landing and other craft at the beachhead. Each consisted of a line of ancient ships (called "corncobs") which were to be sunk parallel to the shore in about three fathoms of water. Each of the two American landing beaches and all three of the British were provided with a gooseberry.

This was a tremendous project, greedy of steel and man power, costing in the neighborhood of twenty-five million pounds. Over 70 ships, including 25 American merchantmen, were sacrificed to make the gooseberries. About 132 tugboats, of which 51 were contributed by the United States Army and 19 by the Navy, were required to tow the entire works, except the corncobs, across the Channel. Captain E. J. Moran USNR was appointed to control the entire tugboat fleet and Captain A. Dayton Clark was placed in charge of the American "Mulberry A."

"Pluto," another British project, was an abbreviation of "Pipeline under the Ocean." [9] This was an original means of supplying the invading armies promptly with the vast quantities of petroleum products that they required; for tankers were in short supply at the time, and it was feared that U-boats would concentrate on them after the landings. British petroleum engineers found the solution in

[9] Ruppenthal I 323–24; Ens. Rufus J. Moon "Operation PLUTO" in U.S. Naval Inst. *Proceedings* LXXX (June 1954) 647–53.

a small flexible pipe which could be laid from a ship steaming at five to ten knots.

In connection with these devices we may mention an organization which, like them, came into play after the initial assault: the build-up control known as "Buco." This was the means of coping with the immense follow-up required to overwhelm the Germans before they could move reinforcements into the beachhead. Allied troops had to be moved from billeting areas to embarkation points in accordance with priorities fixed by Army commanders, and all available ships and beaching craft had to be organized in a tight shuttle service to ferry troops and equipment promptly across the Channel. To handle this complex movement the Build-up Control Organization (Buco) was set up, consisting of Army, Navy and Air Force officers from the British and American services. Admiral Ramsay, anticipating unpredictable delays and changes, did not attempt to prescribe convoy schedules beyond D-day plus 3, when he expected that a cross-Channel rhythm could be established.

4. *Cossac Plan Becomes* NEPTUNE–OVERLORD [10]

Before General Eisenhower left the Mediterranean, he worked with Generals Montgomery and Bedell Smith over the Cossac plan, which had been approved at the Quebec Conference. He decided that the narrow front and three-division assault called for by the plan were insufficient, and ordered both officers, who would reach London ahead of him, to press for a broader front and a five-division assault.[11] That they did, when briefed by Cossac on 3 January 1944. General Morgan had always favored a broader assault, but a three-division front was the best that he could do with the forces allocated. His planners now proposed to extend the landing front from 20 to 50 miles in length, from a point on the east coast

[10] Admiral Ramsay "Despatch" and "Operation Neptune-Naval Plan"; Admirals Kirk and Hall, Action Reports; Comnaveu Administrative History Vol. V; sources mentioned in Chapter I, note 1.
[11] W. Bedell Smith *Eisenhower's Six Great Decisions* (1956) p. 30.

of the Cotentin Peninsula to the River Orne; and to include one airborne and five infantry divisions in the initial assault. This scheme received Eisenhower's approval when he assumed command in mid-January, and he recommended it to the C.C.S. on the 23rd.

This new plan, adding what became the "Utah" area to the original "Omaha" and the British assault beaches, raised the question of where to find additional assault shipping. It was estimated that six more attack transports, 47 LST (Landing Ship, Tank), 71 LCI (Landing Craft, Infantry) and 144 LCT (Landing Craft, Tank) would be required for the added troop lift. These vessels could be obtained only if the target date were postponed from 1 May to 1 June, in order to get another month's American production; and that, too, only if the South of France assault were reduced, postponed, or scrapped. The B.C.S. and J.C.S. now reversed rôles; the British insisting on concentrating on OVERLORD even if ANVIL (as the Southern France operation was then called) had to be given up, and the Americans clinging to the southern invasion.

General Eisenhower was in a grave dilemma. Before leaving the Mediterranean, his staff had drawn up a plan for ANVIL, which he believed to be essential to the success of OVERLORD. And, in addition to the six divisions, he wanted a second airborne division to drop behind the Cotentin beaches. But where could the additional beaching craft and air lift be found? "Ike" viewed OVERLORD and ANVIL as a double envelopment, but was willing to postpone both operations for a month in order to obtain more shipping. The vicissitudes of ANVIL will be discussed in Chapter XIII; suffice it here to say that that much kicked-around operation was postponed to 15 August 1944 in order that some of the troop-lift and gunfire support could double in OVERLORD. At one point in the discussion, Mr. Churchill growled that "The destinies of two great empires . . . seem to be tied up in some God-damned things called LSTs." [12]

While this debate was at its height, the C.C.S. approved the widened beachhead and the strengthened assault. On 1 February 1944

[12] Harrison p. 64. General Marshall told the writer in 1956 that the only really bitter fight he had witnessed in the C.C.S. was over 27 LSTs.

Admiral Ramsay, General Montgomery (whose Twenty-First Army Group had initial command over all ground forces), and Air Chief Marshal Leigh-Mallory issued the NEPTUNE Initial Joint Plan. NEPTUNE, a code name adopted to provide additional security, applied to all documents which mentioned the target date and place of the assault, as well as to the officers authorized to know such details; but it came to be used generally for the assault or amphibious phase of Operation OVERLORD.

This Initial Joint Plan, supplemented by Admiral Ramsay's 28 February Naval Outline Plan, provided that the British Second Army (Lieutenant General Sir Miles C. Dempsey) would be landed by the British Eastern Naval Task Force (Rear Admiral Sir Philip Vian RN) on the beaches later named "Gold," "Juno" and "Sword," between Arromanches and the mouth of the Orne. The United States First Army (Lieutenant General Omar N. Bradley) was to be landed by the Western Naval Task Force (Rear Admiral Alan G. Kirk) on both sides of the Carentan estuary on two sets of beaches, at first called "X" and "Y." Admiral Kirk suggested that X, which adjoined the British, be called "Omaha," and Y, "Oregon," since both names were familiar to Americans and could not easily be confused in voice transmission. He observed somewhat ruefully that Oregon got into the hands of the Army and emerged as "Utah," which ends on the same sound as Omaha; but there is no evidence that the similarity created any confusion. The expanded frontage required a second United States naval assault force to land VII Corps U.S. Army (Major General J. Lawton Collins). The command of this Force "U" was given to Rear Admiral Don P. Moon, who reported on 6 March 1944. Rear Admiral Hall, Commander XI Amphibious Force, also commanded Force "O" for Omaha, to land V Corps (Major General Leonard T. Gerow). Follow-up Force "B," under Commodore C. D. Edgar, was designated to land XIX Corps (Major General Charles H. Corbett) on the Omaha beaches on the afternoon of D-day.

Rear Admiral Alan G. Kirk as Commander Western Naval Task Force became the key American Naval figure in NEPTUNE–

OVERLORD, from the time he reported in mid-November 1943. At the age of fifty-six he was rounding out his thirty-ninth year of service in the United States Navy. As naval attaché to the London Embassy at the outbreak of the war in Europe, and as chief of staff to Admiral Stark in 1942, he had become thoroughly conversant with English ways, problems and personalities. As Commander Amphibious Forces Atlantic Fleet he had made himself master of that branch of naval warfare, and in the Sicilian operation he led the difficult assault on the eastern flank.[13] Kirk set up headquarters at 19 Grosvenor Square, adjoining those of Admiral Stark. A somewhat delicate relationship with his former chief developed because he had the right to report directly to Cominch on all matters pertaining to the operation.

Admiral Harold R. Stark, Commander United States Naval Forces Europe ("Comnaveu"), known as London's "oldest American resident," had been an active participant in all planning since early 1942. Although he now had the additional title of Commander Twelfth Fleet, he was outside the chain of command for OVERLORD. As such he does not appear in the assault picture; but this benign, white-haired admiral had a personal influence that far outweighed his responsibilities.

General Eisenhower established his first headquarters at 20 Grosvenor Square; but, wishing to be outside London, shifted Shaef in March 1944 to Bushy Park near Hampton Court. Admiral Ramsay and Air Chief Marshal Leigh-Mallory were at Norfolk House, where the planners continued to operate after Cossac was absorbed in Shaef. General Montgomery was at St. Paul's School on Hammersmith Road. General Bradley established two headquarters: that of First Army for the assault at Clifton College near Bristol, and that of First United States Army Group in Bryanston Square, London.

Once these commands were organized, planning for the operation was carried on concurrently at every level. Admiral Kirk and

[13] For brief biography and account of the Scoglitti landings, see Volume IX 126–47. His principal staff officers were Capt. Arthur D. Struble, chief of staff; Capt. Edward A. Mitchell; and Capt. Timothy A. Wellings.

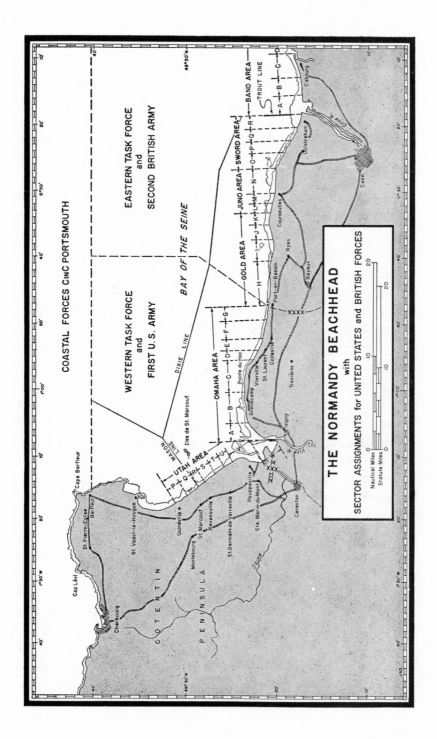

COASTAL FORCES CinC PORTSMOUTH

EASTERN TASK FORCE
and
SECOND BRITISH ARMY

WESTERN TASK FORCE
and
FIRST U. S. ARMY

BAY OF THE SEINE

BAND AREA

TROUT LINE

SWORD AREA

JUNO AREA

GOLD AREA

DIXIE LINE

OMAHA AREA

UTAH AREA

MASON LINE

THE NORMANDY BEACHHEAD
with
SECTOR ASSIGNMENTS for UNITED STATES and BRITISH FORCES

Nautical Miles
Statute Miles

Cherbourg

Cap Lévi

Cape Barfleur

St. Pierre-Eglise

Barfleur

St.Vaast-la-Hougue

Quineville

Montebourg

St.Marcouf

Ravenoville

St.Germain-de-Varreville

Poupperville

Ste.Marie-du-Mont

Carentan

Iles de St. Marcouf

Pointe du Hoc

Grandcamp

Vierville

St. Laurent

Colleville

Treviéres

Isigny

Port-en-Bessin

Ryes

Bayeux

Courseulles

Caen

Ouistreham

Orne R.

Cabourg

COTENTIN PENINSULA

Douve R.

Vire R.

Aure R.

staff conferred with and advised Admiral Ramsay and staff on United States naval methods and techniques, and translated the terms and forms of British naval orders into standard American naval nomenclature. It was astonishing how the two salty languages had diverged since the sailing navies were superseded by armor and steam. The planning methods of the two navies also were very different. The British were accustomed to making detailed plans at top level; the Americans to issuing broad directives to lower echelons, who were encouraged to work out their own details. Admiral Ramsay's operation orders, issued 10 April, consumed, with their twenty-two Annexes, no fewer than 1100 printed pages, and contained much that, with us, would have been left to subordinates. Admiral Ramsay frankly stated: "This is probably the largest and most complicated operation ever undertaken and involves the movement of over 4000 ships and craft of all types in the first three days. The Operation Orders are therefore necessarily voluminous."

One of the knottiest problems that affected all levels of planning was timing the assault — the selection of D-day and H-hour. Airborne troops could be dropped by night, provided there were enough moonlight to enable them to identify targets. It was essential that initial assault forces cross the English Channel during darkness, and the problem was to get enough darkness, since in that latitude in June it begins to grow light at 0300 and by 0430 day has broken. There was no question, after abundant experience, but that a daylight landing was desirable. An unusual factor was the tide. On that Norman coast the average range is 18 feet, and the maximum 25 feet. The beach gradients are very gradual, only about one foot in a hundred. Under such conditions the Army wished to make the initial landings at an hour close to high water in order to lessen the time required for troops to cross the exposed beaches, and it wanted a second high tide during D-day to land the follow-up forces. The

Navy, on the contrary, argued for a low-water landing so that craft could ground outside the beach obstacles and land demolitioners to clear them before the tide rose.

On 1 May 1944, after reconnaissance planes had reported a great increase in the number of obstacles, a meeting was held at Shaef headquarters to make a final decision about H-hour, the landing time for the first boat waves. After several days' discussion, and as a compromise, it was decided that H-hour should be one to three hours after extreme low water,[14] and between 12 minutes before and 90 minutes after sunrise, which on 6–8 June 1944 would be at 0558 by the double daylight saving time (Zone Baker, or minus 2) which we agreed to use. Five different H-hours, with a total spread of 85 minutes between the earliest (0630) and latest (0755), were eventually set for the five groups, to meet different conditions on their respective beaches. In addition to satisfying the tidal and sunlight requisites, the planners, like Bottom and Quince, had to "look in the almanack; find out moonshine, find out moonshine" of sufficient intensity to please the aviators; and they managed to provide them with a full moon.

In June there were only two groups of three days each which fulfilled all desired conditions: the 5th through the 7th, and the 18th through the 20th. D-day would have to be the first in which the weather was suitable for landing troops on exposed beaches. But, if we waited for the rare day in June when everything was perfect, the operation might never come off. The final choice, like the plan itself, had to be a compromise; and it had to be made well in advance, on the weathermen's guess, because assault elements must begin moving toward their objectives six days ahead. Provision also had to be made for postponement if the weather suddenly turned foul, and elaborate schedules were drawn up for the ships' reversing course and putting into emergency ports.

[14] Admiral Hall wanted H-hour at Omaha to be two hours before low water — in order to give the demolition teams ample time to remove the beach obstacles there — and said that his force "O" could handle a night landing; but General Montgomery put his foot down on a "staggered" assault.

5. *Preliminary Operations* [15]

As with all major amphibious assaults, NEPTUNE was preceded by a number of preliminary operations designed to obtain intelligence, harass the enemy, and seal off the target.

Air reconnaissance by the R.A.F. to obtain photographs of the landing beaches, of enemy gun emplacements and troop concentrations, had been going on almost continuously for a year. For NEPTUNE this work was the most important source of military intelligence, because little if anything could be obtained from the Forces Françaises de l'Intérieure (the F.F.I.) in the target sectors. There was very little *résistance* in Normandy; partly because there were no mountains to serve as hideouts, partly because the Germans had effectively sealed off the future bridgehead, and partly because of the somewhat bovine disposition of the Norman peasantry.

Besides the air photographic flights, there was a certain amount of reconnaissance by British submarines (of which this writer has no information), and frequent night visits of British motor torpedo boats and American PTs to the Far Shore to pick up what information they could. One of the American participants relates how his PT crew were "tee'd off" when they were told to bring in a few buckets of sand from each of the Omaha beaches. That was a risky job and it seemed to make no sense. General Morgan, however, reveals that it made plenty of sense. Long after the beaches had been selected, a scientist who claimed local knowledge came up with the alarming statement that these beaches consisted largely of peat, with only a thin covering of sand; and if that were true, our thousands of vehicles would bog down before reaching dry land. Fortunately the reconnaissance parties found that it was completely false.[16]

Offensive minelaying off the German-held coast, which had been going on since 1941, was intensified after 17 April 1944. Two Brit-

[15] Craven & Cate III; Pogue, Harrison, and Ehrman V.
[16] Morgan p. 182; information from Lt. Cdr. Terry Griffin and Cdr. Philip Bucklew in 1956.

ish minelayers, four flotillas of British ML (112-foot Fairmile motor launches), and six flotillas of British MTB (motor torpedo boats), aided by aircraft of Bomber Command, laid 6850 mines between that date and D-day. Nearly two thirds of them were dropped off Channel ports between Ijmuiden, the E-boat base in Holland, and Brest. Of the minecraft, only one, a motor torpedo boat, was lost — victim of a German mine; but their escorts did not get off so easily. Early in the morning of 29 April, off the Isle de Bas, Brittany, H.M.C.S. *Athabaskan* and *Haida*, covering the operations of a minelaying flotilla, engaged two German torpedo boats. After a short and spirited gunfire action, *T-27* was driven ashore afire and became a total loss; but *Athabaskan* suffered a lethal hit aft which caused her to explode and sink.

Most extensive and controversial of all preliminary movements were the air operations, designed to isolate the Normandy battlefields before the landings. These were superimposed upon Operation POINTBLANK — the big bombing, already under way, directed toward weakening German military and civilian economy and destroying the Luftwaffe. POINTBLANK was conducted jointly by the R.A.F. Bomber Command (Air Chief Marshal Sir Arthur Harris) and the U.S. Strategic Air Force (Lieutenant General Carl A. Spaatz). "Tooey" Spaatz arrived in England in January 1944, at about the same time that Air Chief Marshal Leigh-Mallory was completing the air plans for OVERLORD.

In December 1943, Intelligence uncovered the existence of a large number of German missile-launching sites in the Pas-de-Calais, aimed at London, together with a smaller number in the vicinity of Cherbourg, aimed at Bristol. The threat to England was so serious that sustained air attacks on these sites by heavy bombers were begun, and continued until the last of them were captured by Allied troops.[17] This effort naturally weakened Operation POINTBLANK

[17] Harrison p. 215 and Craven & Cate III chap. iv conclude that these bombings delayed the V-bomb attacks, which did not start until 12 June, and reduced their strength. The late start was due to Hitler's refusal to give the word until he had a sufficient stockpile for a sustained offensive; and Gen. Dornberger, who had charge of the guided missiles, states in his book *V-2* (N.Y. 1954), pp. 172–75, that the bombing did not seriously interrupt his program.

and diminished the bomb tonnage that could be dropped on German military and industrial targets.

Air Chief Marshal Leigh-Mallory and his staff developed their general air plan for operations preliminary to OVERLORD in January 1944. The most controversial feature was the "transportation plan" for bombing rail centers and marshaling yards in France, Belgium and Germany. The object was to cripple the enemy's transportation system and check the movement of German reinforcements into Normandy. To be successful, the attacks would have to extend over at least three months and employ a substantial portion of the big bomber fleet. General Spaatz and other strategic airmen objected. They had not yet thoroughly whipped the Luftwaffe; and they argued that, without obtaining prior and complete control of the air, we might be defeated at the beachhead. Air Chief Marshal "Bomber" Harris, however, favored the transportation plan; and a bitter dispute developed — the more so because Leigh-Mallory was a "Tactical" airman whom the "bomber barons" of "Strategic" hated to follow — much as an old-time admiral would have resented a general's being placed in command over his fleet.

An even touchier command problem had to be settled first. In the Combined Chiefs' directive of 12 February 1944 to the Supreme Commander, no mention was made of his controlling strategic air forces. General Eisenhower, who in the Mediterranean had experienced the difficulty of getting Strategic to coöperate, insisted that if he were not given command over it, he would "simply have to go home." [18] The C.C.S. then agreed to accept any plan agreed upon by the Supreme Commander and Marshal of the Royal Air Force Sir Charles Portal. Tedder, as Eisenhower's deputy, and Portal for the R.A.F., worked out a compromise which finally appeared in this C.C.S. directive of 7 April 1944 to the Supreme Commander: "The U.S. Army Strategic Air Force and British Bomber Command will operate under the direction of the Supreme Commander in conformity with agreements between him and the Chief of the Air Staff as approved by the Combined Chiefs of

[18] Harrison p. 220.

Staff." [19] If "direction" and "command" are synonymous, Eisenhower had won his point. But, as late as 12 May, Admiral Ramsay's war diary notes that the top air officers insisted "that fighter protection in the assault area must be organized on the principle of unity of the entire operation; individual protection could not be permitted in any part of the area." General Morgan well observed that "considerable time" would elapse "before anybody at all will be able to set down in the form of an organisational diagram the channels through which General Eisenhower's orders reached all of his aircraft."

Thus, General Eisenhower's command was not really unified as were General MacArthur's in the Southwest Pacific and Admiral Nimitz's in the Central Pacific. It did not meet the test of one officer, and one only, being in command of all elements in an assault. By exception, Admiral Kirk and General Bradley agreed that the former would command both Army and Navy in the Western Naval Task Force between embarkation and the General's establishing his command ashore.[20] But this did not include the air cover to that task force. The R.A.F. and A.A.F. were far more coöperative in OVERLORD than they had been in the Mediterranean, but they still retained a large measure of independence. During the assault phase, for instance, a tactical commander like Admiral Hall with an air support control group in his flagship could not order fighter planes vectored out to protect his fleet; he could only request air support from Leigh-Mallory's headquarters in England, a process that required considerable time. If the Luftwaffe had been more active on D-day, this command set-up might have been disastrous. Under the circumstances, the principle of mutual coöperation worked well in OVERLORD; but that is not to say it would work well in any future war against a more formidable air power.[21]

While argument waxed hot about the air command, another was in progress over Leigh-Mallory's "transportation plan" to seal off

[19] Pogue, p. 125; compare Harrison pp. 219–23, and Craven & Cate III 79–83.
[20] CTF 122 (Vice Adm. Kirk) Op Plan 2–44, Apr. 21 1944.
[21] Data given the writer by Rear Adm. Edward A. Mitchell (Ret.), who was on Admiral Kirk's staff during the invasion.

the beachhead by bombing German-controlled roads and railways in France. Eisenhower and Tedder accepted it as the best possible employment for the bombers prior to the amphibious assault, and "Tooey" Spaatz was converted; but the British Ministry of Home Security estimated that it might inflict up to 160,000 casualties on French civilians and lose the support of the F.F.I. Churchill pressed Eisenhower and Tedder to yield, but they yielded not. F.D.R., asked to intercede, replied that he was unwilling to impose restrictions on responsible commanders in the field that might, in their opinion, impair the success of the invasion. Churchill accepted this verdict reluctantly, and on 17 April the plan went into effect.

The widespread misgivings about the transportation plan were completely unwarranted, and it brought immediate and spectacular results. Before long some 1600 trains, 600 of them carrying German Army supplies, were "back-tracked" in France; and by 26 May all rail traffic over the Seine between Paris and the sea was stalled. The Germans tried to relieve the battered railways by pooling motor transport for critical military needs, but there was also a shortage of trucks. In addition, the transportation bombing hampered the building of coast defenses by creating shortages of cement and steel; 28,000 workers of the Todt organization were withdrawn from fortification work and put into the effort to keep the French railways running.

The transportation plan, like the D-day air drop, was essential to the success of NEPTUNE–OVERLORD. And the French people, according to General Eisenhower, "far from being alienated, accepted the hardships and suffering with a realism worthy of a farsighted nation." [22]

[22] Pogue p. 134.

CHAPTER III

German Plans to Meet the Invasion [1]

1942–1944

ALTHOUGH Hitler's concern over the possibility of Allied landings in the West goes back to December 1941, when he decreed the creation of an "Atlantic Wall" of mutually supporting strongpoints from Norway to Spain, we may well begin the story of his defense plans in March 1942 when he appointed Generalfeldmarschall Gerd von Rundstedt C. in C., West. Von Rundstedt, trained in the traditions of the old Imperial and Prussian armies, was keen, vigorous and able, despite his sixty-seven years. He made no effort to conceal his scorn for the "Bohemian lance corporal" and the Nazi régime, but his integrity and devotion gained him the Fuehrer's respect.

Hitler's principal reaction to British commando raids of 1942, especially that of 19 August on Dieppe, was to order construction of the Atlantic Wall to be pushed "fanatically," so that concrete structures immune to bombing and naval gunfire would protect a

[1] War Diary of the Chief of Staff of the German Army, Volumes IV and V. Essays prepared after the war by German commanders for U.S. Army Historical Section: Generaloberst Franz Halder "Private War Journal" 1939-42; "O.B. West, A Study in Command," five essays by Generals Zimmerman, Von Buttlar, Speidel, Von Rundstedt and Blumentritt; Gen. Pemsel "Chief of Staff Seventh Army Report"; "Rommel and the Atlantic Wall," five essays by Vice Adm. Ruge and Lt. Gen. Dihm; "Report of the Commander, Panzer Group West," three essays by Generals Geyr von Schweppenburg and Von dem Knesebeck. Similar essays prepared for O.N.I.: Vice Adm. Ruge "Treatise on Normandy Invasion"; Vice Adm. Weichold "German Naval Defense against Allied Invasion of Normandy"; Luftwaffe Oberst W. Gaul "The German Air Force and the Invasion of Normandy"; "Fuehrer Conferences, 1939-45," between the Commander in Chief, Navy, and Hitler; "Fuehrer Directives, 1939-45"; Siegfried Westphal *The German Army in the West* (London, 1951); Hans Speidel *Invasion 1944* (Chicago, 1950); Capt. Liddell Hart *German Generals Talk* (1948), and his ed. of *The Rommel Papers* (1953); Gen. Heinz Guderian *Panzer Leader* (1952).

continuous belt of weapons commanding the principal ports and beaches. Some 15,000 concrete strongpoints manned by 300,000 men were to be completed by 1 May 1943.[2] It was a hopeless order to fill in the time allotted. After the war Von Rundstedt remarked that it would have required ten years to build the Atlantic Wall to the strength that Hitler had required, or as propaganda had represented it to be. After making a minute inspection of the coast, Von Rundstedt submitted a report in October 1943, to the effect that coastal fortifications were inadequate and that the troops were spread too thin. He concluded that his command was only "conditionally ready for action." [3]

Hitler really attended to this report. On 3 November 1943 he issued a basic order for the defense of the West. All indications, he announced, pointed to the enemy's planning an invasion of France by the spring of 1944 at the latest. The most likely point was in the Pas-de-Calais, the Strait of Dover. Defenses there must be strengthened to the maximum extent. No more troops were to be withdrawn from the West without his personal permission. In the event that the enemy succeeded in making a landing, he must be thrown into the sea by a powerful counterattack. This implied the formation of a strategic mobile reserve, which was the heart of Von Rundstedt's scheme of defense, and what he had always wanted. Finally, Hitler exhorted, "All persons in authority will guard against wasting time and energy in useless quibbling about jurisdictional matters and will direct all efforts toward strengthening our defensive and offensive power." [4]

Following this forthright declaration, Hitler typically threw a wrench into the already confused machinery of the command structure, giving the tactical command, in the event of an invasion, to Field Marshal Rommel. On 6 November 1943 he was designated "Commander Army Group for Special Employment" and given the task of studying the defenses of the western coast and drafting op-

[2] Harrison pp. 136–37; Adm. Ruge's "Treatise on Normandy" also indicates that the Germans learned a great deal from the Dieppe raid.
[3] "O.B. West" pp. 24, 29–30.
[4] "Fuehrer Directives 1942–45" pp. 99–102; Harrison pp. 464–67.

erational plans for fighting an enemy invasion. On 15 January 1944, he was also appointed Commander Army Group B, and placed under Von Rundstedt's command — with certain reservations. He was given command of the Seventh and Fifteenth Armies, in the event of an invasion; but his bailiwick covered a combat zone which extended inland for only 15 or 20 miles from the French coast. Most of the armored divisions were not under his command but were formed into a Panzer Group under General Geyr von Schweppenburg. The German Navy and the Luftwaffe were practically independent of both, and Himmler retained enough control over his storm troopers to decide where they were to be employed. There was also a training command in France whose principal task seems to have been to provide replacements for the Russian front. Writing of this confused command structure, Geyr von Schweppenburg said, "It was impossible to obtain clear-cut decisions on the broader controversial issues. The ship was not steered; it drifted." [5] But it was he, more than anyone else, who prevented helmsman Rommel from taking a firm grasp of the wheel.

Rommel's and Von Rundstedt's concepts of defense have been oversimplified into "defense on the beach only" *vs.* "defense in depth." Rommel wanted almost as much depth as Von Rundstedt, but the starting point of his scheme was underwater mines. Next came beach obstacles, then the Atlantic Wall of casemated and mobile guns, and finally, infantry and armored divisions within four or five miles of the beach, in position to join the fight on D-day. He regarded the high-water mark to be the main fighting line, supported by strongpoints extending three to four miles inland, the spaces between them to be either inundated (as at Utah) or so studded with land mines — millions of them — that no soldier or vehicle could get through. Von Rundstedt cared naught for mines and beach obstacles, and very little for the Atlantic Wall; he would rely on a big mobile infantry and armored reserve, posted far enough to the rear all along the coast so it might be moved to counterattack the invaders before they could organize a beachhead.

[5] "Report of the Commander, Panzer Group West" p. 17.

Rommel regarded this scheme as completely impractical for want
of means to deal with Allied air power. His ideas had evolved from
his experience in Africa, where the British had made an extensive
use of minefields, and where the R.A.F. had "nailed to the ground"
his tanks and vehicles for two or three days at a time. Knowing how
weak the Luftwaffe had become, he predicted that the R.A.F. and
A.A.F. could prevent reserves posted far in the rear from reaching the beachhead in time to be decisive. That is precisely what they
did. The actual plan adopted was predominantly Rommel's, but
lacked one crucial feature, a tactical reserve of armored divisions
stationed not more than five miles from the coast. It was the Panzer
commander, Geyr von Schweppenburg, who defeated this use of
his armor, pointing out that experience at Gela in Sicily and at Salerno had proved tanks to be no match for naval artillery.[6] He persuaded Generaloberst Jodl, chief of the operational staff of the high
command, not only to keep his armored divisions outside Rommel's
command, but to post them in the hinterland. In reviewing the actual operation, we shall see that the really critical time for the Allies was the morning of D-day. If Rommel had been able, at that
time, to throw two or three armored divisions at the Omaha beach
or the British sector, the situation for the invaders would indeed
have been serious.

In all their discussions of ways and means to stop an amphibious
assault, the Germans never referred to the experiences of their Japanese ally, who could at least have told them some things not to
do. But it seems that the German military mission at Tokyo never
managed to extract information from Imperial Headquarters.
Similarly, British and American military missions in Russia ran
against a steel wall in their efforts to observe fighting on the Eastern Front, or to obtain useful hints on meeting German tactics.
Both Japan and Russia were eager to receive material aid from
their Western allies, but were so suspicious of them as to refuse any
return.

[6] "Report of the Commander, Panzer Group West." See Volume IX of this
History, Chapters VI–VII, XII–XIII.

German top commanders never did agree as to when the Allied invasion of the Continent would come, or where. Grossadmiral Doenitz, Commander in Chief of the Navy after January 1943, wavered in his guesses, as did Hitler; but other admirals inferred the right target from the pattern of British mining in the English Channel — minecraft had neglected the Bay of the Seine. Fortunately for the Allies, the counsels of these German sailors were not heeded by the rest of the high command, which, like Hitler, was *landsinnig*. Von Rundstedt believed that the landing would occur in the narrowest part of the English Channel, somewhere between Le Havre and Dunkirk. Although German coastal defenses were stronger here than elsewhere, Von Rundstedt believed that the Allies would accept that hazard in order to deploy in the plains of Picardy and dash for the Ruhr. Rommel in the spring of 1944 thought it would come farther west; but most of the German generals did not imagine that the Allies would be so "foolish" as to get tied up in the *bocage* country of Normandy. And there was an additional reason for the Germans to defend and the Allies to attack the Pas-de-Calais; for here were the launching platforms for the new "vengeance" weapons — the V-1 robot bombs and V-2 rockets — that Hitler was preparing to loose on England.

Hitler made a close guess as to the target in the course of an impassioned speech to his principal commanders on 20–21 March. He pointed out that, in view of the Allies' control of the seas, they could choose time and place of invasion. He considered the Cherbourg and Brest peninsulas to be their most likely targets. In any event, said Hitler, the enemy assault must be liquidated within a few hours, in order to "prevent the reëlection of Roosevelt," who "with luck, would finish up somewhere in jail!" [7] Churchill, too, would be "finished" and the Allies would never be able to launch another invasion.

---

[7] *The Rommel Papers*, p. 465. Hitler made one sound prediction at this meeting, that the first Allied objective would be to obtain a large port. To prevent that, he had already issued an order designating all major ports as "fortresses"; and on 23 March he issued a new order that any port which could not be held must be completely destroyed and blocked.

Rommel by this time realized that time was short. He studied the coast carefully, improvised weapons for special situations, installed more land mines and underwater obstacles. Land mines were his favorite defensive weapon. He demanded the delivery of ten million a month, a goal which could not even remotely be met. About four million mines were laid in the Atlantic Wall before D-day, but Rommel wanted one hundred million, which would have meant a density of some 160,000 mines per square mile in the potential invasion area. If he had attained this impossible objective, the Allies would have been forced to lay on a prolonged naval bombardment before landing. Rommel also made extensive use of flooding the lowlands behind the coast: the lower valleys of all rivers west of Dieppe, including the Carentan region near Isigny, and the area behind the Utah beaches.[8]

Hitler himself established priorities for the construction of defense positions. No. 1 was the Pas-de-Calais; No. 2 the Channel Islands;[9] No. 3 "Fortress Cherbourg"; No. 4 the east coast of the Cotentin Peninsula, including the future Utah beaches; No. 5 the future Omaha and the British sector. Somehow or other, No. 5 got the most attention, after Nos. 1 and 2. Although the heaviest concentrations of German coastal artillery were emplaced to protect Le Havre, Cherbourg and the Channel Islands, the future American and British landing beaches were very well covered. The artillery, in conjunction with beach obstacles and mines, should have defeated a landing if the guns had been well served, if the Allies had had no gunfire support ships, and if the Germans had counterattacked promptly — three big "ifs"!

The German generals in their "alibi" essays, prepared after the war, complained of the low quality of their troops — most of whom, if we took their statements literally, were misfits, invalids, overaged, or young boys. Most of the infantry in Rommel's com-

---

[8] Ruge "Treatise on Normandy" p. 18. Also, the Dunkirk area was thoroughly flooded.

[9] Hitler's amazing concern for the Channel Islands (his entourage called it *Inselwahn*, island madness) was due to his wish to annex them to Germany after victory, and to an obsession that the British would make a big effort to retake them, which must be bloodily repulsed.

mand were organized in "static" divisions, with no motor transportation, as they were expected to man fixed positions; these were the ones that had the "misfits," the proportion of whom was greatly exaggerated. A German mobile infantry division was superior to an American infantry division in fire power, especially in automatic weapons, and was manned by troops in top physical condition and fully equipped. Best of the German infantry divisions were the paratroops, of which two divisions were in the area behind the landings in June 1944. In addition to the large number of captured French and Russian tanks still used by the armored divisions there were 1608 German tanks in the West at the end of April 1944, 514 of them the powerful Mark V Panthers.

A really formidable defense force had been built up in the West by June 1944. Since November 1943 the number of combat divisions under Von Rundstedt's command had increased from 46 to 58. Of the 58 divisions available on D-day, 33 were either static or reserve divisions; but all save one of the remaining 25 were composed of high quality troops, adequately trained, many of whom had seen service in Russia.[10]

On 6 June (D-day) there were six armored and 19 other divisions in the German Fifteenth Army, which was deployed north of the Seine and (because of Patton's deception, pinning it down) took no part in the fighting for weeks. The German Seventh Army (Generaloberst Dollman), upon which the landings fell, comprised one armored (the 21st Panzer) and 13 other divisions, the majority of which were in Brittany. The Allies would outnumber the defenders at the point of attack; but their great problem was to build up by sea faster than the Germans could reinforce by land. Taking all France in view, the Germans would outnumber the Allies for at least two weeks; and as standard amphibious doctrine required a 3-to-1 superiority of attack over the defense, it will be appreciated that the success of Operation NEPTUNE–OVERLORD was no foregone conclusion.

[10] Harrison pp. 235, 239–41, and Map VI for location of German divisions. In 1942, when Operation SLEDGEHAMMER was in the cards, there were only 30 divisions in the area.

The German Navy's rôle in the event of an invasion of France was largely defensive. Total enemy surface forces in Western France on 6 June were three destroyers in the Bay of Biscay, five torpedo boats of about 1000 tons, and about 30 E-boats in the Channel ports and at Brest. Admiral Krancke, Commander Naval Group West, had under him three major naval commands: Western Defense Forces (Konteradmiral Brüning at Cherbourg), the E-boat command, and that of the submarines in Bay of Biscay ports. These amounted to 36 U-boats, eight equipped with snorkel, which were designated to attack invading forces. The E-boats made reconnaissance patrols along the south coast of England, but only on dark, cloudy or not-too-stormy nights, and Brüning ran nightly patrols of small craft along the French coast from the mouth of the Somme to the Channel Islands. But Admiral Krancke regarded the period 4–6 June as unsuitable for a landing: the tide was "not right," and the waters too rough for an invasion force. So on the crucial nights the E-boats and patrol craft stayed snug in port.

A German barrage of contact and antenna mines was laid along the central axis of the English Channel in the early spring of 1944. These, fortunately for us, were fitted with "flooders" to sink them by June, when the invasion menace was presumed to be over; but a number of stragglers exploded and damaged Allied craft.

Far more of a menace was the highly secret pressure or oyster mine, planted on the bottom and exploded by any change in water pressure exerted by the hull of an approaching ship. The Luftwaffe was eager to make optimum use of these, a few hundred of which, dropped by aircraft in each embarkation harbor, might completely have broken up the invasion. Providentially for the Allies, this program was badly bungled. Although the pressure mine had been invented early in the war, it was long denied production by the German Naval Staff, for fear of the secret's leaking out and being used against Germany in the Baltic. Hitler, however, intervened and ordered 4000 units to be manufactured for use against possible Allied invasion of the Continent. Half this lot was sent to the airdrome at Le Mans and stored in underground hangars, and at the same time two squadrons of minelaying aircraft were readied in a part of Germany safe from Allied bombers, to be used for planting the mines when the invasion alert was sounded. But Reichsmarschall Goering fouled up the plan. In May, fearing that the invasion would come through Brittany and overrun Le Mans, he ordered the mines removed to Magdeburg, and the transfer was completed on 4 June (D-day minus 2).

On the morning of 7 June the high command issued orders to lay these mines immediately; but, owing to the weakness of the Luftwaffe and the strength of the Allied Air Forces, four days were required to fleet them up from Magdeburg to airfields within reach of Normandy beaches. Over 4000 of them had been laid by aircraft in the Bay of the Seine and on the Breton coast by the end of July; but as early as 20 June the British collected a specimen at Luc-sur-Mer, flew it to the Thorney Island airdrome, had a complete description of it in Admiralty hands within a few hours, and countermeasures were immediately applied. A fortunate break indeed for the Allies!

Beach obstacles were installed by the Army. Obsolete tank obstacles, such as the "Czech hedgehog" or "horned scully," consisting of three iron bars intersecting at right angles like a giant jackstone, and the so-called "Belgian barn doors" — gatelike obstacles about seven feet high — were rounded up and placed on the beaches. Steel piles and wooden stakes also were driven into the sand and fitted with mines. It was planned to install four belts of beach obstacles extending between one fathom under the high-water mark and two fathoms under the low-water mark on all possible landing beaches. Up to 13 May over half a million of these obstacles had been emplaced along the Channel, and the installations off Omaha were nearly completed by 6 June, D-day.[11]

Even more feeble than the Navy as a defense force was the Luftwaffe Third Air Fleet with headquarters in Paris, and its operating arm in the West. By 1944 it had almost been driven from the skies over northern France. Its total fighting strength on 5 June 1944

[11] *The Rommel Papers* p. 459.

was 481 aircraft, including 64 reconnaissance and 100 fighter planes.

On the night of 27–28 May about 15 bombers attacked shipping in Portland Harbor, with slight success; *Thomas Jefferson* and two LCTs had superficial damage from near misses. An even feebler bombing attack was made on Brixham shortly before D-day. The Germans concluded from all this that a large landing operation was being prepared, but they still had no indication of where or when the Allies would strike. The High Command, even after the Luftwaffe had reported the heavy shipping concentration in the west of England, still believed that the region between Dieppe and Dunkirk was the most probable target.

Thus, D-day saw the Germans in France only partially ready to meet an invasion. The Luftwaffe and the Navy were hopelessly outclassed. Most of the German troops in Calvados and the Cotentin were deployed along the Atlantic Wall, within a few miles of the coast, with no strategic reserve. Yet it would convey a wrong impression to underestimate the defensive strength of the Atlantic Wall. Incomplete as it was — inadequate as it proved to be for stopping the magnificent élan of the American, Canadian and British troops, supported by overwhelming naval gunfire and airpower — this crust of steel and concrete, girdled with mined obstacles, was the most formidable barrier encountered by any amphibious assault in history. It might even have been a fatal barrier, but for the Allies' priceless asset of surprise.

Surprise was maintained by the Allies almost up to H-hour of D-day. Admiral Krancke, by plotting the Allied bombing pattern, narrowed down the target to somewhere between Boulogne and Cherbourg. Rommel did even better, reaching the conviction that the Bay of the Seine and the east coast of the Cotentin Peninsula were threatened. He moved a mobile division into the Cotentin region and wanted to send an armored division too. But Hitler refused. The Fuehrer, whose March guess had been so nearly correct, had now received a fresh inspiration from his crystal ball. Any landing in Normandy, he insisted, would be but a diversion; the big assault would come north of the Somme. Von Rundstedt, who agreed, therefore defeated the efforts of Rommel to remove to Normandy troops from the Fifteenth Army in the Pas-de-Calais.

The foul weather that set in on 4 June threw all German commanders off their guard, since, lacking observation stations west of the Continent, they were unable to predict the favorable break in the weather forecast by Allied meteorologists.[12] Admiral Krancke's Paris headquarters announced on the 4th that "at the present moment a major invasion cannot be assumed imminent." Rommel was certain that there would be none between 5 and 8 June because the tides then, to his way of thinking, were "not right." He was actually at home in Germany on the morning of D-day when news of the landings caught up with him.[13] General Dollman, Seventh Army Commander, felt equally secure. His regimental and divisional commanders were expected to attend a war game at Rennes, scheduled for 6 June; and many had already arrived when the invasion began. Not until the small hours of D-day, after the Allied paratroops had dropped, was any serious alert issued.

Thus, the efforts of Shaef, the Navies and the British Government to keep secret the time and place of the landings were completely successful.

[12] The *Schatzgräber* weather station in Greenland had been evacuated at the beginning of June and no weather-reporting U-boats were in a position to detect the comparatively small area of high pressure, which, moving eastward, caused the foul weather to pass.

[13] *The Rommel Papers* p. 470; Weichold p. 10.

CHAPTER IV

Coiling the Spring[1]

January 1942–May 1944

1. *The Americans in Britain*

IN ONE RESPECT the invasion of Normandy differed from every other amphibious operation in World War II. In the Pacific islands and the Mediterranean the assault forces, together with relatively small reserves, constituted the principal overwater movement to the objective. Garrisons, supply and maintenance arrived later, but most of the troops were committed in the assault. In Normandy, however, the beachhead was also a bridgehead. On the heels of the assault, other combat troops followed at a planned rate for building up Allied forces in France faster than the Germans could bring up reserves. One and one-half million American troops alone, including twenty combat divisions, were assembled in Great Britain for the assault and the immediate follow-up. Preparing these units to be able to move into France with their supplies and equipment was in itself a major operation, which received the code name BOLERO.

The first American troops arrived in Northern Ireland 26 January 1942. When General Marshall visited London in April, he expected that an American army of one million men would be assembled for the proposed cross-Channel operation in 1943. Lieutenant General John C. H. Lee USA arrived in England on 24 May to establish Service of Supply for the European Theater of Operations,

[1] Same sources as Chapter I note 1, together with Ramsay, Ruppenthal, Bradley, Morgan, Comnaveu Administrative History Vols. I, II and V; Lt. Col. Randolph Leigh *48 Million Tons to Eisenhower* (1945), Cdr. Kenneth Edwards RN *Operation* NEPTUNE (London 1946); Rear Admirals Kirk, Hall and Moon Action Reports, Lt. Cdr. Leonard Ware USNR "Report to Comnaveu on U.S.N. Bases in U.K." 1944.

and to supervise the reception of this huge force, under a subcommittee of the Joint Staff Planners. The problem was complicated by the fact that the resources of the United Kingdom, including industry, were already fully mobilized for war and that civilians were strictly rationed. No surplus food for the expected visitors existed.

Since the Americans had disembarked in western ports of the United Kingdom, they were sent into cantonments in the west and southwest of England, while the British and Canadian troops assembled in the eastern and southeastern counties. That is why the United States Army was assigned the western flank of the assault.

Operation BOLERO was an added burden to the short supply of ships, already few enough for the transfer of matériel to England and Russia. The North African and Mediterranean operations also diverted men and shipping from BOLERO, and for a time this troop movement fell off to a mere trickle; but it did continue. A few statistics will make clear the story of its progress in the two years before D-day: — [2]

DATE	TOTAL U.S. TROOPS IN UNITED KINGDOM (CUMULATIVE)	TOTAL SUPPLIES AND EQUIPMENT IN LONG TONS (CUMULATIVE)
31 January 1942	4,058	108
31 July 1942	81,273	181,979
31 January 1943	122,097	881,554
31 July 1943	238,028	1,492,757
31 January 1944	937,308	3,497,761
30 May 1944	1,526,965	5,297,306

The United States Navy's contribution to this movement was to share in escort of convoy and antisubmarine warfare, activities which we have already described in Volume X of this History.

In July 1942, long before a firm date for the invasion of the Continent had been agreed upon, the Navy established Advanced

[2] Ruppenthal I 100–03, 129, 135, 232–33, 237. Matloff *Strategic Planning* II chap. xv states that the number of U.S. Army combat divisions in the U.K. rose from 11 on 1 Jan. 1944 to 20 on 1 June, and the number of U.S.A.A.F. air groups from 51 to 102.

Group Amphibious Force, Atlantic Fleet, under Rear Admiral Andrew C. Bennett. His headquarters had just been set up at Rosneath, Firth of Clyde, when, owing to the adoption of Operation TORCH, landing craft and crews were diverted to North Africa, whither Admiral Bennett proceeded; and on 2 November Admiral King ordered that the Rosneath base be turned back to the British with the proviso that it be returned to United States control on sixty days' notice.

The next significant step was taken on 15 July 1943 when Admiral King established the Landing Craft and Bases Europe command at Falmouth, Cornwall. Rear Admiral John Wilkes became "Comlancrabeu" on 1 September, and also temporary commander of the newly activated XI Amphibious Force, which at that time consisted of 5 LCT and 95 landing craft. Appointments of the principal naval commanders of the assault forces shortly followed, as we have seen: Admiral Sir Bertram Ramsay RN in overall command, Rear Admiral Alan G. Kirk over the Western Naval Task Force; Rear Admiral Sir Philip Vian RN over the Eastern Naval Task Force; Rear Admiral John L. Hall to command XI Amphibious Force and Force "O" for Omaha; and Rear Admiral Don P. Moon to command Force "U" for Utah. By 1 December 1943 all except Moon were in England, engaged in active planning; and in January 1944 Admiral Hall, as Com XI 'Phib, took charge of training United States sailors and soldiers in amphibious warfare; but Admiral Wilkes as "Comlancrabeu" was responsible for the training and readiness of all landing and beaching craft, without which the operation could not have gone on.

2. *The Battle of the Beaching Craft* [3]

A frequent complaint of the British against their American ally during these preparations, and also of Shaef planners against the

[3] By "beaching craft" I mean LST, LCT and LCI (Landing Ship, Tank, Landing Craft, Tank, and Landing Craft, Infantry). These, in British usage, and by many Americans, are grouped with LCM, LCVP and other davit-carried boats as

General Dwight D. Eisenhower, Rear Admiral Alan G. Kirk,
and Rear Admiral Morton L. Deyo
On board U.S.S. *Tuscaloosa* at Belfast Lough, May 1944

"Ike," "Alan," and "Mort"

Rear Admiral Don P. Moon USN

Navy, was its alleged failure to supply enough landing and beaching craft; or, as it was sometimes put, starving NEPTUNE to fatten the Pacific Fleet. In a milder form the criticism was directed at the Navy's keeping planners guessing as to what they could count on. The root of the trouble was the long delay in fixing a date for OVERLORD. In April 1942, when the SLEDGEHAMMER–ROUNDUP plan appeared to be on, the Navy gave "triple-A priority" to building beaching and landing craft, greatly to the detriment of the destroyer escort and escort carrier programs.[4] When the 1942–1943 Channel crossing was abandoned, and for a year the British refused to firm it up for 1944, the Navy saw no reason to pile up amphibious craft in England for an operation that might never take place. In June 1942 the main stream of new construction was diverted to the Pacific, where these craft were desperately needed.

On 3 September 1943, as a result of the decisions reached at the Quebec Conference, Admiral King issued a revised delivery schedule for beaching and landing craft. He promised to provide for OVERLORD 110 LST, 58 LCI, 146 LCT, 250 LCM and 470 LCVP. Included in this schedule were expected transfers from VIII 'Phib in the Mediterranean to the amount of 48 LST, 24 LCI, 41 LCT, 48 LCM and 81 LCVP. Obviously this was not enough, especially after the base of the attack was widened by including the Utah beaches.

There was also a discrepancy between British and American estimates of the number of troops and vehicles that could be handled per boat. These estimates added up to a British calculation that only 152,000 men and 19,000 vehicles could be carried cross-Channel in craft which the Americans insisted could take 176,000 men and 20,000 vehicles.[5] And it was sharpened by the fact that hundreds of these craft belonging to the Royal Navy, including many built in the United States, were lying about on English beaches and in

---

"landing craft." The reader may here be reminded that the LST is a fairly formidable ship, 327 feet long, costing at that time around $1,500,000, capable of lifting 2000 deadweight tons.

[4] See Volume II 28 and X 35.

[5] Matloff II chap. xv pp. 37–8 of mimeographed draft.

English harbors in the spring of 1944, more or less damaged in training exercises — yet not repaired because the Admiralty did not wish to spend more money on overtime work in the busy British shipyards.[6] Admiral King naturally did not feel compelled to mop up for the Admiralty's labor policy.

In order to resolve this controversy, General Marshall sent Major General John E. Hull of his operations division, and Admiral King sent Rear Admiral Charles M. ("Savvy") Cooke, his top planning officer, to London, where on 13 February 1944 they began the "Landing Craft Conference" at Norfolk House with Shaef staff and Admirals Kirk and Hall. Although the question of how many and how much was complicated by the larger one as to whether there should be a Southern France invasion at the same time as NEPTUNE, or later, or not at all, it was finally agreed that 20 British LST and 21 British LCI be shifted from the Mediterranean to England; that 7 more LST be sent over from the United States; and that the gap in troop- and vehicle-lift remaining between what the British considered necessary and what this increase would provide should be filled by (1) increased loadings of LST and LCT, according to the American pattern, and (2) increased serviceability.

This decision, reached on 24 February, was promptly accepted by the President and the Prime Minister.[7] And it turned out that NEPTUNE had everything that was needed.

This compromise settled the question of American and British contributions, but was succeeded by a secondary and exasperating problem as to how many United States beaching craft could safely be transferred from other theaters. General Somervell, as well as several high-ranking British officers, insisted that many additional LST could be spared from the Pacific Fleet. The Navy re-

[6] Morgan pp. 212, 268–69. Another reason was the comparatively slow repair schedules in British dockyards.

[7] Matloff II chap. xv pp. 37–44 of mimeographed draft. Admiral Hall informed me in 1956 that he and his staff instructed General Montgomery and staff in methods of increasing the loads.

plied in mid-March that it had sent no LST to the Pacific for several months and that these vessels were being pulled out of training establishments for dispatch to England so rapidly that nobody would soon be left to train new crews.[8]

This situation was somewhat eased by Eisenhower's consent on 21 March to postpone ANVIL. That removed one of the unknown quantities in the loading equation which, as General Bedell Smith remarked, were "enough to drive a man insane." And it released more LST from the Mediterranean.

Actually Cominch did better by NEPTUNE than he had promised. By D-day Admiral Ramsay had at his disposal 168 LST of the United States Navy besides 61 American-built LST of his own Navy; 245 LCI, half American and half British; over 900 LCT, of which 664 were British.[9] As a last-minute contribution, Admiral King, only a few weeks before D-day, had 60 of the Coast Guard's 83-foot cutters rounded up and shipped to England, where at one of the United States Naval bases they were converted to rescue ships. Divided equally between the Eastern and the Western Naval Task Forces, they performed valiantly off the British and the American beaches in Normandy, rescuing wounded and drowning men from sunk or damaged landing craft and other vessels, and aircraft, and transferring them to LSTs for treatment and transfer to hospitals in England.[10]

A legitimate complaint on the part of Shaef was Admiral King's tardiness in allocating battleships, cruisers and destroyers for gunfire support. And this was crucial; since nothing in NEPTUNE was more certain than that very heavy naval gunfire would be necessary to break down the Atlantic Wall; air bombs couldn't get at it. Admiral King appears to have believed that the Royal Navy could have handled the job for both naval task forces; but it could not, partly because the Admiralty felt that it must keep strong elements of the Home Fleet in northern waters in case the German Navy

[8] Same pp. 45–47.
[9] See table in Note at end of this section.
[10] *The Coast Guard at War, Landings in France* XI pp. 115–37.

attempted a token Jutland.[11] At Christmastide Admiral Kirk sent to Washington a list of gunfire support ships that he required, but nothing happened until the time of the Landing Craft Conference in London. At a dinner that he gave at the Connaught Hotel to Admirals Cooke, Moon, Wilkes and Hall, the last-named sounded off in no uncertain terms about the want of gunfire support for landings at Omaha; and, although Cooke admonished Hall for his strong language, he saw to it that the Western Naval Task Force got the ships. Three battleships, *Nevada, Texas* and *Arkansas*, and an additional destroyer squadron for gunfire support, arrived in April, but a division of the new 2200-ton destroyers did not reach British waters until a few days before the invasion.[12]

The Royal Navy supplied the lion's share of gunfire support ships; and it also furnished a large majority of minecraft, many specialized types of small craft, and all the Fairmile motor launches and dan-buoy layers. In the end, the United States and Royal Navies shared the burden for NEPTUNE–OVERLORD, each to the best of its ability; and each won its just share of the honors and the glory.

NOTE ON ALLOCATION OF BEACHING AND LANDING CRAFT

For a careful statement of the British point of view, with tables of the number of each leading type supplied by the U.S.N. and R.N., see Chester Wilmot *The Struggle for Europe* pp. 176–80. His figures of numbers "on strength" 1 May are correct, except for two mistakes in addition; but misleading. "On strength" is an English translation of the U.S.N. term "on hand," which means roughly completed, but not

[11] On D-day the Home Fleet comprised 3 battleships, 3 carriers, 3 heavy cruisers, 4 light cruisers and 10 destroyers; several escort carriers with their screen were also available. At that time there were only three German ships larger than destroyers — *Prinz Eugen, Nürnberg,* and *Emden* — capable of going to sea.

[12] See Appendix I for task organization. At Utah-Omaha there were available 22 U.S.N. warships, 8 R.N., 2 French, and 1 Dutch, for gunfire support. The numbers assigned for both British and American sectors were as follows:

	R.N. and R.C.N.	U.S.N.	French and Dutch
Battleships	3	3	0
Monitors	2	0	0
Cruisers	17	3	3
Destroyers	37	31	5
Gunboats	0	0	2

necessarily ready for active duty (see Volume I of this History p. 236 for explanation). He also is mistaken in saying that the U.S.N. used 87 LST to invade the "small island of Saipan"; actually only 79 were used for both Saipan and Guam.

Fortunately I can quote authentic figures from Combined Staff Planners Memo. for Information No. 24, dated 19 June 1944, giving numbers of United States and British landing ships and craft *"serviceable and operational"* in different theaters on 1 June 1944. Those for the most significant types follow: —

	LST	LCI(L)	LCT	LCM	LCVP	LCA
U.S. in 12th Fleet (U. Kingdom)	168	124	247	216	1089	0
British in United Kingdom	61	121	664	265	0	646
U.S. in Mediterranean	23	59	44	185	395	0
British in Mediterranean	2	32	64	95	0	138
U.S. on East Coast, U.S.A.	95	89	58	57	341	0
U.S. on West Coast, U.S.A.	0	41	1	60	181	0
U.S. in all Pacific Areas	102	128	140	1198	2298	0
British on E. Indies Station	0	4	2	67	0	46

The first and second lines are the most important for our purpose, since everything there mentioned went into NEPTUNE; but those in all other combat areas are entered for purposes of comparison. It will be observed that the Pacific Ocean was not exactly swarming with landing ships, tank. Referring to Line 5: of the 95 LST on the United States East Coast, all but 2 were in Chesapeake Bay and Gulf of Mexico and just completed. Of the LCT in the first line, 10 were "reverse lend-lease" British-built. All 61 British LST in Line 2 were American-built. Total number LST and all other types built in the United States for the Royal Navy during the entire war will be found in Appendix III.

3. United States Naval Bases in Britain [13]

By 1 December 1943 training had started at the reactivated Rosneath base in Scotland, and in North Devon, where the confluent Taw and Torridge Rivers empty into Barnstaple or Bideford Bay. Here are plenty of sandy beaches, with gradients and high-ranging tides similar to those of the Norman coast. Rear Admiral Wilkes on 1 September 1943 began organizing other bases in the West Coun-

[13] Cdr. Amphib. Bases "A History of the U.S. Naval Bases in the U.K." mimeographed Nov. 1944 and incorporated in Comnaveu "Administrative History"; Budocks *Building the Navy's Bases in World War II* (1947).

try and in South Wales and on 13 October he set up headquarters at Falmouth. Three Seabee regiments were sent to England, one to take part in the invasion, the others for base construction and maintenance; more came later. By 3 February 1944 there were American Naval bases at the following places in the United Kingdom:

I. Amphibious Training Centers

Rosneath, reactivated 20 August 1943 as Amphibious Training Center. Also as a receiving station, the location of fire-fighting and gunfire support schools and of four "Drews," or parties for operating captured enemy ports. On 14 February 1944, 6329 officers and men were there.

Plymouth, Devon, established 3 November, 1943. Headquarters afloat for Rear Admiral Hall, and for Comlancrabeu (Rear Admiral Wilkes) from 3 January 1944. Maintenance and repair crews for naval ships and craft and a major port of embarkation. Ninety officers and 1495 men.

Falmouth, Cornwall, established September 1943. LST–30, first of her class to arrive from the United States, reported here 28 October and launched an LCT from her deck before an admiring crowd.

Dartmouth, Devon, established November 1943. An advanced amphibious base, moved 27 December into Royal Naval College, which was also the seat of the XI Amphibious Force training center. Main functions of the base unit were to repair and service landing and beaching craft. Number of men swelled to over 2000 and at one time 4000 sailors were being quartered at Dartmouth in tent cities.

Salcombe, Devon, established October 1943. Amphibious training center, especially for Landing Craft, Infantry; and a maintenance and repair base for Landing Craft, Tank.[14]

[14] Lt. Frank Dearing USNR and Lt. (jg) Fred M. Kirby USNR *Salcombe 1943–1945,* an illustrated pamphlet printed at Kingsbridge, Devon.

U.S. NAVAL BASES AND FACILITIES
(With Headquarters of principal
U.S. Army units)
BRITISH ISLES
June 1944

- Ⓝ Advanced Naval Base
- Ⓐ Advanced Amphibious Base
- Ⓣ Amphibious Training Base
- Ⓗ Naval Hospital
- Ⓓ Naval Ammunition Depot
- Ⓕ Naval Facility
- Ⓢ Supply Depot

Appledore and Instow, North Devon, established 29 July 1943 to provide training for landing craft crews, and assist the Army in accustoming soldiers to boat work. S.S. *President Warfield*, an old Chesapeake Bay steamer, provided most of the living quarters. By November 1943 comprised 60 officers and 700 men.

Milford Haven and Penarth, South Wales, established November 1943. Amphibious training centers and maintenance bases. Trained crews of various types of ships and did emergency repairs.

Teignmouth, Devon, established November 1943 for training and repair of LCM (landing craft, mechanized). Moved to Weymouth in April 1944.

II. Advanced Amphibious Training Sub-bases

St. Mawes, Cornwall, established 7 September 1943 to assemble, maintain and operate a flotilla of landing craft and give advanced training to their crews. By February 1944, 70 officers and 596 men were attached.

Fowey, Cornwall, established 25 October 1943 primarily for training of crews of small craft. In March 1944 a Hospital Training Corps School was set up, primarily for the medical crews in LST; [15] 150 medical officers and 2850 hospital corpsmen attended it before D-day. Drew Six, 130 officers and 1005 men, also trained here.

Calstock and Saltash, Cornwall. Repair sub-bases for servicing small craft and minesweepers.

III. Supply Depots and Repair Bases

Exeter, Devon, established October 1943. The great U.S. Naval Amphibious Supply Base which grew to 200 officers and 2600 men by D-day. See further below.

[15] Many American LST in NEPTUNE doubled as hospital ships, carrying vehicles, tanks etc. to the Far Shore, and returning with casualties. They were provided with the proper equipment for first aid, medical care and even surgery. Each

Launceston, Cornwall, established 6 September 1943. Supply depot for spare parts. Stocked all engine parts for LST, YMS, AM, SC, and PC; and compass material for all amphibious craft.

Tiverton, Devon, established September 1943. Naval stores and spare parts subdepot.

Bugle, Cornwall, established February 1944, in abandoned quarries. Naval ammunition depot.

Hedge End, Ludgershall, Wilts, established October 1943 as diesel engine overhaul base, maintained jointly with U.S. Army.

IV. Miscellaneous Bases

Netley, Hants, established 1 April 1944. U.S. Naval Base Hospital No. 12, in the Royal Victoria Hospital, overlooking Southampton Water. In June, July and August 1944 over 500 patients, 54 per cent of them wounded in action, and including British, Canadians and French as well as United States Army, Navy, Coast Guard and Merchant Marine, were admitted here.[16]

Deptford, on the Thames below London, established February 1944. Advanced amphibious maintenance base, especially for LST and other beaching craft from the Mediterranean for assignment to the British follow-up force for NEPTUNE; 25 officers and 425 men by 1 May. Owing to the location, this base was exposed to frequent enemy bombings, but on 1 June was able to report that the 38 American LST attached to Force "L" were 100 per cent operational. It became a main target for German V–1 bombs on and after 13 June. *LST–312* and *LST–384,* when moored abreast, received a direct hit on 8 July, were heavily damaged and lost 14 men killed and 11 badly wounded.

The biggest — except possibly Dartmouth — and one of the most interesting of these "Little Americas" in Britain was the Naval Sup-

---

had two Navy Medical Corps jgs, one Army surgeon, 2 Army noncom operating room technicians and 40 Navy hospital corpsmen attached.

[16] Capt. Henry W. Hudson (MC) USNR *The Story of Snag 56* (1946).

ply Base at Exeter, the shire town of Devon. Under the direction of Captain Ralph B. Hunt, Admiral Wilkes's logistics officer, nine holes of the Exeter golf course were taken over by the Seabees in September 1943 and a railway spur was built to the site. By 3 February 1944, when Commander V. F. Blakeslee became its C.O., the Exeter base had 176 buildings, housing 2352 officers and men, and had built or taken over 109 industrial buildings; it covered 95 acres, with an additional 75 acres of open-storage areas outside the city. Sections of Exeter had already been badly bombed in 1942; fortunately the establishment of the supply depot did not attract further attention from the Luftwaffe. Here spare parts of every sort, unloaded at the seaports by U.S. Army Transportation Corps, were deposited, and thence they were issued. Hot food containers were prepared here and supplied to all United States landing craft, and to British landing craft carrying American troops, in the great invasion.[17]

This influx of American sailors, and of the far more numerous American soldiers, was accomplished with a minimum of friction. Many of the "Yanks" had been long enough in England to meet the people and appreciate their point of view; later arrivals were indoctrinated as to English manners and customs, and cautioned what to expect and what not to demand. At Plymouth one American Naval unit collected a sum of two hundred pounds to give a party for the town children. "I well remember," writes the then commander of the local garrison, "the kindness of your fellows during and after an air raid. . . . The destruction made a great impression on your younger men and this kindness and sympathy at that time made a great impression on the people. They helped by digging out people and removing furniture from bombed houses."

[17] Lt. Cdr. Leonard Ware "History of U.S. Naval Bases in the U.K." pp. 200–13. As an example of the service that the Exeter base performed, after the invasion was well under way an Army request arrived there at midnight for ten tons of welding rod to enable a tank outfit in France to put dozer blades on tanks for cutting through the hedgerows. Next morning trucks carrying the stuff from Exeter were arriving at Portland, and by nightfall the entire order had been delivered in France.

At Exeter, according to the Chief Constable of that city, relations between the American sailors and the civilian population "were very good; they had practically no trouble. There was a large proportion of colored sailors, but even so no trouble. . . . By and large the American sailors were extremely popular; the majority of houses had one as a regular visitor. They were extremely generous in sharing out food parcels." Relations were particularly pleasant in Cornwall, where every sailor in the St. Mawes base was "adopted" by some Cornish family. Significant, too, are the friendships that continued after the war between American veterans and their former hosts, in contrast to the mutual recriminations that followed World War I; and, one may add, in spite of the efforts of Communists and their supporters to make bad blood.

Rear Admiral John Wilkes [18] was responsible for the readiness and training of all beaching and landing craft and for mounting troops to take part in the numerous training exercises organized by Admiral Hall. He shifted his headquarters to Hamoaze House, Devonport, in order to be nearer the center of amphibious activity, and to keep in close touch with C. in C. Plymouth, Admiral Sir Ralph Leatham RN. Captain V. E. Korns headed his exceptionally able staff. Admiral Wilkes, a bundle of nervous energy, had plenty of objects upon which to expend it. For instance, in April 1944 extensive alterations were called for on beaching craft — the installation of a new radio, modification of the bow doors, fitting bulwark doors for side loading, and the like; and every LST received a great increment of antiaircraft artillery.

On 4 January 1944 Admiral Hall broke his flag in amphibious command ship *Ancon*, then in Plymouth Harbor. The active train-

---

[18] John Wilkes, b. Charlotte, N.C., 1895, a great-grandson of the famous Commodore Charles Wilkes of the Pacific Exploring Expedition and the Mason and Slidell episode of 1861. Naval Academy '16, served in *Frederick* during World War I, and in submarines, several of which he commanded, 1919–33. Navigating officer *Indianapolis* 1935–37, Comsubrons 5 and 20 of Asiatic Fleet 1939–42 (see Volume III, Index). C.O. *Birmingham* in Sicilian Operation. "Comlancrabeu" Aug. 1943–25 June 1944, when appointed Com U.S. Ports and Bases, France. Headed administrative command of Amphibious Forces Pacific Fleet May–Dec. 1945, when designated Com Submarines Atlantic Fleet. Com Naval Forces, Germany, 1948–51, when he retired.

ing program was already under way. He had the most varied duties of any attack force commander. He not only commanded XI 'Phib, but until 1 March, when the attack organization went into effect, supervised the training of ships in Force "U" as well as his own assault force "O." All U.S. fire support ships reported to him and conducted shore bombardment exercises under his command. This was as it should be, for Admiral Hall had a longer experience of amphibious assault than any other American flag officer in the European theater.[19] His chief of staff, Captain E. H. von Heimberg, and his plans officer, Captain Marion L. Little, did the detailed planning for the assault, the loading and the follow-up. This staff remained on board U.S.S. *Ancon* but the "school" for amphibious training and gunfire support was set up at the Royal Naval College, Dartmouth. Admiral Hall was not only exceedingly able; his calm, assured, self-controlled temperament spread confidence. Two nights before D-day, when the foul weather and the postponement were giving almost everyone the jitters, the Admiral said to a friend of the writer, "I do not expect to be repulsed on *any* beach."

4. *Final Training and Rehearsal*

Training exercises for the United States V Army Corps began on 15 December 1943 at Slapton Sands in Start Bay, and in the nearby Torbay. Slapton was an unspoiled beach of coarse red gravel, fronting a shallow lagoon, backed by grassy bluffs very similar to those on the Far Shore. When the people of nearby villages were evacuated it was an almost perfect place to simulate the landings at Omaha. Training was long and thorough, but complicated by the progressive arrival in England of gunfire support ships and small craft with green crews.[20]

[19] Excepting Admiral Hewitt, who could not be spared from the Mediterranean. For brief biography of Admiral Hall, see Volume IV, 92*n* and portrait in frontispiece.

[20] All craft down to and including the 173-foot Patrol Craft steamed across the

One of the many remarkable achievements of this operation was the readiness of the thousands of ships and craft taking part. Admiral Ramsay assumed that 90 per cent of the LST and 85 per cent of the LCT and LCI would be operational on D-day. But Admiral Kirk was able to report on 1 June that, owing to "the splendid efforts of Rear Admiral John Wilkes and his staff," 99.3 per cent of all types of United States beaching and landing craft were ready to go. The corresponding British figure was 97.6 per cent. This amazingly high order of readiness won Admiral Ramsay's accolade. In his opinion, "The very highest credit is due to all concerned in the maintenance and repair organizations of both countries for this achievement, which is the more outstanding when it is remembered that the majority of the assault ships and craft had to be used continuously during months of training before the operation."

On 26 April 1944 Admiral Ramsay and staff moved into battle headquarters at Southwick House, an ancient country mansion with an extensive park, seven miles north of Portsmouth dockyard. Here he was frequently visited by Admiral Kirk, and by "Ike," who maintained a sort of trailer-village in a hazel copse about a mile away, protected from German reconnaissance planes by bushy trees and from intruders by a squad of trigger-happy sentries. "Monty" had another caravan (as the British call a motor trailer) in the park. During the next six weeks, Southwick House was the nerve center of NEPTUNE–OVERLORD, and it was here that the great decisions about D-day were made.

The culmination of the joint training program was a pair of full-scale rehearsals in late April and early May. Admiral Moon's Force "U," was the first to rehearse. Troops and equipment embarked in the same ships and for the most part in the same ports whence they would leave for the Far Shore. During the night of 26–27 April they proceeded through Lyme Bay with the minecraft sweeping ahead of them as if crossing the Channel. As German E-boats some-

---

Atlantic on their own bottoms; Landing Craft, Tank, were carried in three sections on freighters or, when already assembled, on the decks of Landing Ships, Tank; and the 110-foot subchasers (SC) were carried on the decks of Liberty ships.

times prowled the Channel on favorable nights, C. in C. Plymouth, who was responsible for protecting the rehearsal, threw patrols across the mouth of Lyme Bay, consisting of two destroyers, three MTB and two MGB motor gunboats. Another MTB patrol was laid on to watch Cherbourg. Following a "bombardment" on Slapton Sands, the "landings" were made during the morning of 27 April, and unloading continued throughout that day and the next, when a follow-up convoy of eight LST was expected.

When that convoy was maneuvering in Lyme Bay around midnight 27–28 April with one escort vessel, H.M.S. *Azalea*,[21] flares were observed, which were supposed to be a part of the exercise; but at about 0130 April 28, when gunfire broke out astern, all vessels went to general quarters. They were being attacked by nine German E-boats out of Cherbourg, which had dashed in past the patrols without being recognized. At 0204, *LST–507* was struck by a torpedo. All electric power failed, the craft burst into flames, the fire got out of control and survivors abandoned ship. A few minutes later *LST–531* was hit by two torpedoes, burst into flames, and within six minutes rolled over and sank. At 0228, *LST–289* opened fire on an E-boat which retaliated with a torpedo hit. A dozen men were killed, but the LST managed to make port under her own power. For about half an hour, the five landing ships remaining afloat exchanged fire with the E-boats, which were also engaged by two British destroyers of the covering force, but escaped by the use of smoke and high speed. The loss of life in this brief action — 197 sailors and 441 soldiers — was greater than the invasion forces suffered on D-day at Utah beach.[22]

The final rehearsals, under the code name FABIUS, were held between 3 and 8 May, together with a marshaling exercise for the troops. Admiral Ramsay assumed complete operational control of

[21] The second escort vessel had engine trouble, returned to Plymouth and was not relieved.

[22] Figures from CTU 125.11.4 (Com LST Group 32, Cdr. B. J. Skahill) Action Report, enclosing those of all surviving LSTs and senior survivors' reports of the two sunk. Aside from the loss of life, this action reduced the reserve of LSTs for NEPTUNE to zero, but Admiral King ordered three more to be transferred from the Mediterranean.

FABIUS, which simulated NEPTUNE as closely as possible without actually crossing the Channel and landing in Normandy.

Admiral Hall's Force "O" rehearsed at Slapton Sands; the three British attack forces used beaches east of Portsmouth. The general effect of these exercises, coming at the peak of a prolonged training, was to create in all hands a feeling of confidence, and the four weeks' interval between them and D-day was profitably employed to unravel snarls and destroy snags.

Rehearsals completed, the troops returned to their embarkation ports and marshaling camps, where they were held until it was time to reëmbark for the assault.

5. The "Fast-anchored Isle"

English ports have never been so congested with ships and sailors, or the English land so full of troops, as on the eve of NEPTUNE. Although the large number of Americans (roughly 1,100,000 soldiers, 124,000 sailors, and 427,000 aviators) [23] was an inconvenience to the English, it assured them that this massive invasion of the Continent, for which they had been waiting four years, would go over.

The British assault forces concentrated at Portsmouth, Southampton, Poole, the Solent between the Isle of Wight and the mainland, and at Spithead, which is not a promontory but the channel between the same island and Portsmouth. American forces were assigned to a number of embarkation ports and harbors on the South Coast, between Portland and Falmouth, with the center of

---

[23] Detailed breakdown in Ruppenthal I 232 for 30 May 1944, and Admiral King *U.S. Navy at War* p. 137.

Ground forces	620,504	ARMY AIR FORCES	426,819
Service of Supply and HQ	459,511	NAVAL FORCES	124,000
E.T.O., miscellaneous	20,131		

Of the naval forces, 15,000 were attached to combatant ships, 87,000 to landing and beaching craft and 22,000 to the naval bases; thus housing of some sort had to be found for about 100,000 U.S. sailors and Coastguardmen ashore. There were not far from 1,627,000 "Yanks" bedded down on British soil before the invasion began, and 25,000 more on board ships in the harbors. The Admiralty estimate for sailors afloat on 6 June is 52,889 Americans, 112,824 British.

gravity at the famous old seaport and naval base of Plymouth, where Sir Francis Drake had embarked to fight the Spanish Armada, and whence the *Mayflower* had made her final start for the New World. But these West Country ports were too small to hold all American forces afloat. The naval gunfire support ships and many of the destroyers for the Western Naval Task Force were based on Belfast Lough in Northern Ireland, where they had plenty of room for maneuver and training.

After the middle of March the congestion of troops and the flow of military traffic into southern England created a critical situation. In the interest both of movement and of security, General Eisenhower asked the British government to impose several new restrictions on the long-suffering population. All nonmilitary traffic between southern England and the rest of the United Kingdom was stopped. In April the British government forbade civilians to visit any part of the coast between Norfolk and Cornwall.[24] Commanders at all levels were deeply concerned with security of the operation plans. The usual "Top Secret" classification was considered inadequate for the more critical details, which were placed under a super-secret classification known as "Bigot." Officers authorized to have access to such plans had special clearances which entitled them to be "bigoted."

On 22 May something happened that threw all "bigoted" officers into a near panic. A crossword puzzle in the London *Daily Telegraph*, when solved, was found to contain several of the leading code words then being used, such as NEPTUNE, OVERLORD, OMAHA, UTAH, WHALE and MULBERRY. Had the whole secret leaked out? A discreet but thorough investigation by British Intelligence reported that the puzzle in question had been devised by two retired schoolmistresses of unimpeachable loyalty and respectability, who had not the remotest idea that these words were top secret.

Considering that the branch U.S. Hydrographic Office in England delivered some 280,000 charts and 65,000 publications to ships before D-day, and that the British Admiralty must have given out

24 Pogue I 163.

From water color by Lieutenant Dwight Shepler USNR

Rehearsal at Slapton Sands

Two LSTs loading in the River Dart

Preparations

LCT loaded with troops

LST loaded with vehicles

Starting for the Far Shore

even more, it is astonishing that no leak occurred through care-
lessness. A general was sent home and cashiered because he hinted
at the date at a London cocktail party. "D-day," a standard military
symbol for the target date of any operation, became the subject of
so much speculation that it became synonymous with this particular invasion. Even after the lapse of years, the sixth of June 1944
is freshly remembered by millions of people, and it is likely to become one of the most widely known dates in the modern history of
the free Western nations.

On 8 May Admiral Ramsay reported to General Eisenhower that
5 and 6 June would be acceptable dates, and the Supreme Commander accepted the 5th as D-day, with the 6th and 7th as possible
substitutes in case bad weather required postponement.[25] Admiral
Ramsay on 9 May signaled his intention to "freeze" all naval plans
on the 12th in order to check the "spate of alterations" which
threatened to swamp the officers who had to study and digest them.

On 15 May a briefing conference was held in the Victorian
Gothic "model room" of St. Paul's School in London, where General Montgomery had set up his headquarters. The room, a circular
arena like a cockpit, with hard, narrow benches rising in tiers, and
a gallery supported by somber black columns, was packed with
rank. On the lower circular bench sat the King, with Prime Minister
Churchill on his right and the Supreme Commander on his left.
"Ike" had on his other side his deputy commander, Air Chief Marshal Tedder; next came Admiral Ramsay, "Monty," Air Chief
Marshal Leigh-Mallory and Admiral Creasy. On the P.M.'s right
were the First Sea Lord (Admiral Sir Andrew Cunningham), Admiral Stark and Field Marshal Sir Alan Brooke. Behind them, on
the second bench, were Admirals Kirk and Vian, Generals Bradley,
Bedell Smith, Dempsey, Morgan, Spaatz and Patton; and on the
back benches other naval task force commanders, commanding
generals of assault divisions and important air marshals. Although
the conference lasted all day, interest never flagged; for this was

[25] Pogue p. 167. Eisenhower confirmed this on the 23rd.

the first time that all commanders of important units had been together and that each learned in detail what the others were to do.

"As we took those uncompromisingly hard and narrow seats," wrote Admiral Deyo, who was present, "the room was hushed and the tension palpable. It seemed to most of us that the proper meshing of so many gears would need nothing less than divine guidance. A failure at one point could throw the momentum out of balance and result in chaos. All in that room were aware of the gravity of the elements to be dealt with.

"The first to rise and break the silence was the Supreme Commander himself. It had been said that his smile was worth twenty divisions. That day it was worth more. He spoke for ten minutes. Before the warmth of his quiet confidence the mists of doubt dissolved. When he had finished the tension was gone. Not often has one man been called upon to accept so great a burden of responsibility. But here was one at peace with his soul." [26]

Following Eisenhower, General Montgomery, an inspiring and effective speaker, gave the over-all plan for the Armies; Admiral Ramsay did the same for the Navies, and Air Chief Marshal Leigh-Mallory for the Air Forces; and by the time the conference rose for lunch the logistic and civil affairs people had had their say.

When the sessions were resumed at 1430, King George VI spoke a few words of greeting and Mr. Churchill made one of his extempore speeches which struck the Americans present with peculiar force. "Gentlemen, I am *hardening* toward this enterprise," he said — directed to those who knew of his earlier doubts and hesitations about a cross-Channel operation.

The next hour and a half were devoted to the American part of the assault. Admiral Kirk presented the Western Naval Task Force plan, General Bradley the First Army plan, and General Quesada the IX Army Air Force plan. Of their British opposite numbers who concluded the conference, Admiral Vian especially impressed the Americans with a forceful exposition of the plans and problems of his Eastern Naval Task Force.

[26] Vice Adm. Morton L. Deyo "Naval Guns at Normandy" p. 20.

All top commanders now visited every force and unit that they could reach. General Eisenhower and Admiral Kirk flew to Belfast on 19 May to inspect gunfire ships of the Western Naval Task Force. Again to quote Admiral Deyo: "One judged this to be a man whose abundant vitality and good spirits, whose awareness and gift of the common touch, protected by natural dignity, recommended him as a leader. It seemed that he belonged where he was and that, with earnest humility, he knew it."

The visit to Belfast was but one of the many inspections made by General Eisenhower and Admirals Ramsay and Kirk. King George VI was equally assiduous. On his visit to Portland, accompanied by Admiral Ramsay, he lunched as guest of Admiral Kirk on board *Augusta,* and afterward made a tour of the harbor in U.S.S. *PT–507,* commanded by Lieutenant (jg) Harold B. Sherwood USNR. The PT, all hands in dress blues and at action stations, darted among the assembled landing and beaching craft while high-ranking officers explained their duties and capabilities to the King. When they were returning to the dock, there was an encounter which His Majesty took in his stride, like the democratic monarch that he was. The chartroom door popped open before the startled admirals in the cockpit, and the beaming face of the boat's cook appeared to offer the hospitality of his craft, thus: "Would yer Majesty like a cuppa jamoke?" Eyebrows went up, but after this invitation had been suitably translated as "a cup of coffee," the King ducked into the charthouse and down the ladder to the tiny wardroom where, after a second cup, he extended his compliments to cook and skipper for "a most excellent cup of coffee." No complaints were ever again entertained by this particular sea cook as to the quality of his chow. "If it's good enough for the King of England it's good enough for youse guys!" silenced rank and file alike.[27]

Shoreline sketches to the scale of one to ten thousand were prepared and distributed to the smallest landing craft in the Western Task Force. These showed a photographic panorama, as seen from

[27] Lt. J. F. Queeny USNR "The Far Shore," a report to the writer in 1947.

the sea, with details of buildings and other landmarks, and included sunlight and moonlight data, beach gradient graphs, inshore current data and tidal curves. Each was overprinted with the names and limits of the assault beaches.

On 23 May the Supreme Commander decided that he could no longer delay confirming D-day, because the "corncob" ships to be sacrificed for the gooseberries needed six days to reach the Far Shore. So he set it for 5 June. This and the H-hours for the different groups of beaches were not announced to the commanding officers until 28 May, when Admiral Ramsay from Southwick House sent out the signal that started this vast operation in motion: "Carry out Operation NEPTUNE!"

All crews were now "sealed" in their ships and craft. The troops had already been placed behind barbed wire in their long marshaling camps called "sausages," with some two thousand men of the Counter-Intelligence Corps keeping a tight watch to prevent leaks and stifle loose talk. All mail of persons taking part in NEPTUNE was impounded on 25 May until further notice. And, to avoid the comment that would result if press correspondents accredited to the Expeditionary Force disappeared from their favorite pubs just before D-day, they were all rounded up one day in late May, sent to their assigned ships for a briefing, and returned to London.

These extraordinary precautions were brilliantly successful. There is no indication in any German record that the precious secrets of D-day and H-hour reached the enemy.[28] By contrast, Allied Intelligence, with two exceptions that we shall note, was nearly perfect.

In an earlier volume [29] we have related the successful efforts of the United States and Royal Navies to keep German U-boats at bay. In that operation Commodore W. H. Hamilton's Fairwing 7 played a notable part under Coastal Command R.A.F. That wing, now comprising Bombing Squadrons 103, 105 and 110 of Liberators especially equipped for antisubmarine work, was based at

[28] See above, end of Chapter III.
[29] Volume X 323-25.

Dunkeswell, Devon. It maintained an almost continuous air barrier across the "chops of the Channel" — the line from St. Alban's Head to Cape de la Hague, and from Ushant to Scilly. Every half hour, night and day, every part of the surface 50 miles on each side of the seaways was under the scrutiny of a Liberator. Seven planes per squadron were constantly in the air, with an additional standby or "rover" plane specially equipped to follow up a submarine contact. Additional patrols were flown to the south and west of Brest, and west of Lands End.[30] On D-day and for nine days thereafter, not one U-boat managed to get through this air barrier, which was only occasionally challenged by the Luftwaffe. Sightings of FW–190s, Ju–88s and FW–200s were fairly numerous on D-day, but there was only one combat, which an FW–200 lost. Fairwing Seven did not lose a single plane.

Although this antisubmarine patrol by Navy Liberators was essential for protecting the invasion fleet from enemy submarines, it was overshadowed by other air components of NEPTUNE — some of which, such as reconnaissance and the "transportation plan," we have already described. These were carried out by the R.A.F. and the VII and IX United States Army Air Forces. There was never any doubt about mastery of the air over the English Channel. That had been won by R.A.F. Fighter Command in 1943. Air supremacy, like sea supremacy, is seldom absolute, and in this instance the enemy was able to fly a limited number of reconnaissance sorties — only 125 in the Channel and 4 over the Thames Estuary and the East Coast — in the six weeks before D-day.[31] All he learned from them was that something very important was about to happen and much of what his aviators observed was deliberately planned to mis-

[30] Comnaveu Report to Cominch 17 Sept. 1945 in "Activities U.S. Naval Forces Europe," Supplementary Report on Normandy Invasion, Part I. Detachments of a searchlight-equipped Squadron 114 flew up from the Mediterranean, starting 19 June.

[31] Leigh-Mallory p. 55 gives the air order of battle, comprising 3361 U.S.A.A.F. powered planes, plus 1619 gliders, and 3258 R.A.F. powered planes, plus 972 gliders. The United States provided the bulk of the transport aircraft (1166 as against 462 British); but the R.A.F. provided 2172 fighters as against 1311 of the U.S.A.A.F. These figures do not include the 38 U.S.N. Liberators of Fairwing 7, augmented by 6 more on 18 June.

lead them. The Luftwaffe made several very feeble bombing attacks on the embarkation ports, which did little damage, except to the Royal Yacht Squadron clubhouse at Cowes; and it sent a few mine-dropping missions over the Solent which might have been lethal if the new pressure mine had been used; but the mines actually dropped were easily swept up.

6. *Misleading the Enemy* [32]

Not only was the enemy kept guessing about the date; he was deliberately and successfully deceived as to the target. Although the story of this important contribution to the Allied victory has already been told in detail by others, it is worth repetition here.

"The cover plan," writes General Bradley, "involved a monumental scheme of deception. It had been built around known enemy agents, phony radio nets, and a mock-up invasion fleet. Its objective was to delude the enemy into believing that we had collected a full-scale army group on the east coast of England for a *main* Channel assault through Pas-de-Calais. Dummy headquarters for this fictitious assault was to be the First U.S. Army Group." Lieutenant General George Patton, whose dashing tactics in Sicily had made him well known to the Germans, and whose arrival in England had been well publicized, posed as the phantom army group commander. Patton did not relish this ghostly rôle, but he was promised the command of a real army in France later, and well played the game. His fake headquarters was set up close to Dover. Dummy landing craft in great numbers began to appear in the Thames and the Medway; hundreds of dummy tanks were planted where the German planes could photograph them. After the British troops originally quartered here had moved out to embark for Normandy, smoke still rose from their cooking fires and trucks rolled to and fro along the deserted camp roads. "Those devices," writes General Bedell

[32] Bradley, pp. 344–45; W. Bedell Smith *Eisenhower's Six Great Decisions* pp. 25–26, 48; Col. Brenton G. Wallace *Patton and His Third Army* (1946).

Smith, "were largely the result of British ingenuity, and I came to recognize that the British are masters of this sort of deception." Other "camps," actually deserted tent cities, were left in East Anglia, and given enough semblance of life to register as real camps on high-level air photographs.

Patton's dummy army group was successful beyond our fondest hopes. It pinned down the German Fifteenth Army in the Pas-de-Calais for as much as six weeks after D-day, owing to the high command's belief that, any day, "First Army Group" would land there. The enemy fleeted up forces from Brittany and Southern France, "thinned Norway and stripped Denmark in his quest for troops" during June and the first half of July. "Yet, through it all, 19 German divisions waited idly on the bluffs of Pas-de-Calais." [33]

In addition to this major deception three minor ones were put on for the night before D-day. British aircraft and small naval vessels put on three feints: Operation GLIMMER directed at Boulogne, TAXABLE at Cap d'Antifer and BIG DRUM at Cape (Pointe) Barfleur. "Radio counter-measures were employed . . . to give an appearance to enemy radar similar to that presented by the real forces. We now know that these were very successful and were an instrumental factor in enabling our forces to continue for so long towards the enemy coast before their composition could be determined." [34]

By 1 June 1944 all England began to swarm with soldiers of Britain, Canada and America in battle uniform, with their weapons and field equipment, marching along country roads by day, rolling in their armor by night through blacked-out villages and towns. Countless columns of troops and convoys of steel vehicles converged on the embarkation ports between East Anglia and the Thames estuary, and along the South Coast and on the Bristol Channel. All night long no sound was heard but the clatter of army boots on paved streets, the "*Hup*, two, three, four; *hup*, two, three, four" of Army sergeants, the rattle of vehicles and the roar and putter of

[33] Bradley p. 345.
[34] Ramsay p. 2.

engines, as men marched and machines rolled to the water's edge, there to board beaching craft on the "hards" and landing craft and transports at the docks. Gunfire support ships converged from northern ports in England and Ireland, block-ships for the gooseberries lumbered southward from the Clyde; and at a score of airfields paratroops climbed on board transport planes and gliders. No music, no bands, no fluttering crowds to cry farewell; only women and old men offering a last drink or cup of tea and a hearty "God bless you!" to the soldiers. Thus, efficiently and in silence, supported by the prayers of the free world, began the great invasion to crush Germany and liberate France.

CHAPTER V

Crossing the Channel[1]

3–6 June 1944

1. *First Starters*

"FOR NOW SITS Expectation in the air . . ." By 3 June almost every vessel was in her assembly port awaiting the word to form convoys. Loading was nearly completed. Every available berth was filled in every port from Felixstowe on the North Sea to Milford Haven in Wales, and many vessels for which no room could be found in these harbors were moored in the Humber, the Clyde and Belfast Lough.

Admiral Moon's Force "U" loaded in five ports between Plymouth and Torcross, and sortied from eight ports between Plymouth and Poole, where it was organized in twelve convoys to cross the Channel. Admiral Hall's Force "O" assembled in Portland Harbor and Poole, to be organized in nine convoys. Commodore Edgar's follow-up Force "B" assembled at Fowey and Falmouth. The three British assault forces, "G" (16 convoys), "J" (10 convoys) and "S" (12 convoys) started from the Solent, Spithead and Portsmouth. Behind the assault forces those for the build-up were already assembling in the Bristol Channel, the Thames estuary and Harwich.[2]

---

[1] Ramsay, Harrison; and Rear Adms. Kirk, Hall, Moon and Deyo Action Reports.

[2] The question of numbers is difficult because it depends on what you count in or out. According to the one consistent tabulation that has been made, by the Admiralty, we have 931 ships for the Western Naval Task Force, and 1796 for the Eastern Naval Task Force. This includes everything that crossed the Channel on its own bottom, excepting landing barges of the ferry service, which for the most part did not cross on D-day. If one includes them together with landing craft carried on ships, the totals are 2010 for the Western, and 3323 for the Eastern.

Following the Western Naval Task Force in detail, the gunfire support and bombardment ships sailed from Belfast Lough 3 June. At noon the same day three minesweeping groups put to sea from Channel ports, and during that afternoon and evening the slow beaching-craft convoys of Force "U" sortied. As Force "O" had the shorter distance to go, it got under way later than Force "U."

Portland Harbor, an artificial port on the northeast side of Portland Bill, was the scene of tremendous activity during the loading of the LCT and LST, which had arrived from many places in the United Kingdom. The harbor was laid out in lanes with large mooring dolphins so spaced that three LCT could tie up at each and still swing with the wind and tide. Beaching craft were constantly moving to and from the shore to be loaded on the "hards," cement aprons extending into the harbor at the right slope to accommodate these vessels. Soldiers, tanks and vehicles were arriving in a continuous stream and the "hardmaster" and his crew were like policemen coping with an endless flow of traffic; but they managed to keep it moving, and into the right craft. It took about half an hour to load each LCT, which at the same time was topped off with fuel and water. Similar activity was going on all over the extensive harbor of Plymouth, and, in less degree, in the smaller ports of embarkation. Every vessel in Portland Harbor was supposed to get under way by 0315 June 4 and rendezvous outside to form convoys for the run across Channel. That was when D-day was still to be 5 June.

The vanguard of the assault had to be minecraft. In order to insure precise coördination and timing, Admiral Ramsay himself directed the first phase of the sweep for the Western as well as the Eastern Naval Task Force. Channels had to be swept along the English coast, in case the Luftwaffe and E-boats had peppered those waters with delayed-action mines; lanes had to be swept from the Isle of Wight through mid-Channel and up to the transport area off the Far Shore. During the night of 31 May–1 June, ten sonic underwater buoys were laid to provide accurate reference points for the start of the sweep of each channel. To each of the five assault forces, two adjacent channels about 400 yards wide were assigned. Each was marked by lighted dan buoys spaced at one-mile intervals, laid by Fairmile motor launches of the Royal Navy, which followed immediately behind the minecraft. To handle this mammoth sweeping job simultaneously required 245 vessels, with ten standbys in case of accident.

Just before the 14th Minecraft Flotilla, sweeping ahead of Force "U," received the order to turn back on the morning of 4 June, it discovered a clutch of mines. Although the weather was worsening, Commander George Irvine RNVR decided to sweep them up before turning back. H.M.S. *Campbell*, closing this group to make visual signal to return to port, suddenly found herself in the midst of "floaters," but the minecraft blew them and extricated her without damage. Admiral Ramsay, when he got word of this, ordered Commander Irvine next day to sweep and buoy a channel through the area; but in the rough water and foul weather that then prevailed, the minecraft were unable to locate and detonate every single mine. Hence, on the evening of 5 June, when U.S. Mine Squadron 7 (Commander Henry Plander) was sweeping near the place where H.M.S. *Campbell* got in trouble, *Osprey* hit a mine. The blast blew a large hole in her forward engine room, fires broke out, and the ship had to be abandoned at 1815. She sank soon after, with a loss of six men, first casualties for the United States Navy in Operation NEPTUNE.

2. *Weather and the Great Decision* [3]

On 1 June General Eisenhower arranged to meet twice daily, at 0400 and 2130, with ranking generals and naval task force commanders at Southwick House, Admiral Ramsay's headquarters, to hear the latest weather forecasts. These were presented by a "dour but canny Scot," Group Captain J. M. Stagg RAF, head of a meteoro-

---

[3] Chester Wilmot *The Struggle for Europe* (1952) pp. 220–26. Wilmot had access to Capt. Stagg's diary and conversed with other officers who were present.

logical committee which had every weather facility in the United Kingdom at its disposal. By Saturday, 3 June, the forecasts began to be highly unfavorable, even alarming. An unsettled westerly type of weather had set in, with anticyclones over Greenland and the Azores and depressions moving ENE across the Atlantic. It seemed more than probable that the state of wind and sea on Monday the 5th would rule it out as D-day. Nevertheless General Eisenhower confirmed sailing orders for the early sortie of Force "U," which had the greater distance to sail. Forecasts became grimmer as the day wore on, and when the generals and admirals met "Ike" at 0400 Sunday 4 June, the prospect appeared completely hopeless. The weather map looked like that of a December day. All experts predicted a low ceiling on the 5th, which would prevent the air forces from carrying out their part of the assault, and seas heavy enough to swamp landing craft. Under these circumstances the air commanders were unwilling to take off, and Admiral Ramsay, after being advised that the wind would reach Force 6 on Beaufort scale, feared that the Channel would be too rough for small craft. Only "Monty" wished to carry out the schedule. Eisenhower, after hearing what everyone had to say, decided to postpone the operation for 24 hours, to 6 June. Shaef sent out signals by 0500 June 4, recalling to their emergency postponement ports all ships and craft already at sea.

For the gunfire support ships, postponement caused no trouble; they merely countermarched up the Irish Sea all Sunday, and in the evening, turned south again. But small craft, receiving the order in the gray dawn after a rough, black night at sea, had a miserable time complying. One minesweeping unit was only 35 miles from the French coast when it received the recall. An LCT–LCM convoy of Force "U" long failed to get the word, and by 0900 was already 25 miles south of the Isle of Wight. Since strict radio silence was required, three destroyers were sent to turn this convoy back, but they could not locate it; finally a "Walrus" — a venerable Royal Navy pusher seaplane — made contact and reported that the convoy's course had already been reversed.

Royal Navy Official Photo

Southwick House and Park

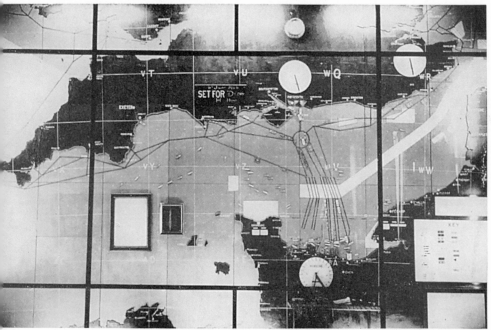

Royal Navy Official Photo

The wall map "frozen" for D-day, H-hour

Nerve Center of the Invasion

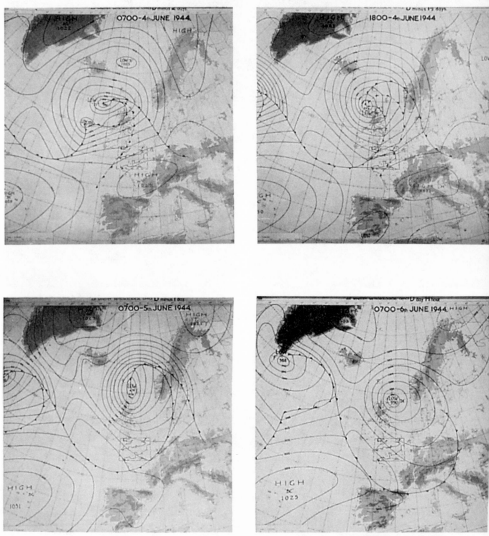

Four Weather Maps at Crucial Hours, 4–6 June 1944

According to Admiral Ramsay, "at one time it was thought that Force 'U' would have to return to Devonshire to re-form; but when it was pointed out that this would almost certainly result in the postponement of the operation to the next moon period, Rear Admiral Kirk, with characteristic verve, announced his readiness to proceed."

By 2240 Sunday June 4, all small craft were back in port except the LCT convoy already mentioned. No more berths were available when it returned to Portland and it had to churn about, off Portland Bill, near the dangerous Portland Race, "a chaos of pyramidical waters leaping up suddenly without calculation or rule of advance." [4] After midnight room was found for this convoy in Weymouth Bay; but in the meantime, *LCT-2498*, whose engine had broken down, drifted into the Race and foundered.

When General Eisenhower postponed D-day to Tuesday the 6th, Admiral Ramsay observed that no second postponement could be made to the 7th, because many of Admiral Kirk's ships would then have to fuel. Thus the Supreme Commander's choice was narrowed to 6 or 8 June, or to a fortnight's postponement until the 19th, when tidal conditions would again be favorable. Had he done that, the results might have been disastrous, for on 19-21 June a strong northeast gale raged over the Channel.

The 4th of June was a miserable day for the soldiers cooped up in little beaching craft under lashing rain, and one of intense anxiety for the top commanders watching ashore. By 1800 the two low-pressure systems had amalgamated off the Hebrides in the single low marked "D1" on the chart. The meteorologists predicted that "D1" would fill during the next 24 hours, with resulting moderation of wind in the Channel and a break-up of the cloud cover, essential for air operations.

At 2115 a dramatic meeting of the commanders in chief was held at Southwick House. The weather chart still looked bad, but Captain Stagg predicted a good prospect for a favorable break on the 6th, and for heavy bombers' being able to fly during the preceding

[4] Hilaire Belloc *Cruise of the Nona* p. 203.

night. The northwest wind, then blowing Force 5, was expected to moderate and back southwesterly, bringing lower seas and less surf on the Far Shore on the 6th; but nobody could hazard a firm prediction for the 7th and 8th.

Admiral Ramsay declared that Admiral Kirk must be informed within thirty minutes if his force was to meet H-hour on 6 June, and that any further postponement would have to be for at least 48 hours. Air Chief Marshal Leigh-Mallory, who within a week had protested against the entire air drop as a "futile slaughter" of two divisions,[5] now had the support of Air Chief Marshal Tedder. All commanders were appalled at the prospect of a fortnight's delay when every ship and military unit was fully briefed on the operation; even the tight security restrictions in force could hardly be expected to prevent leakage. To General Eisenhower, who had to decide, the question was, "Just how long can you hang this operation on the end of a limb and let it hang there?" "Ike," "Monty" and Ramsay were willing to give the word to go that night; but as Leigh-Mallory still hung back, they postponed the final decision to next morning, although starting the movement at once.

As far as the two Navies were concerned, 2300 June 4 was the moment of decision, since orders were then issued for all vessels to resume sailing to meet the 6 June D-day.

At 0330 Monday 5 June, General Eisenhower turned out for the final weather conference. His trailer camp was shuddering under the force of the wind, and the rain seemed to be driving horizontally; but the worst was over. The "D1" low north of the Shetlands was filling up; the weather front was clearing across southern England, and by 0700 had reached a line between Scandinavia and Paris. Captain Stagg predicted a fair interval of two days, starting the morning of 6 June, with moderating west to northwest winds backing southwesterly, an overcast with base at 1000 feet and two-foot waves off the Far Shore. He could not predict beyond the 6th, as

---

[5] *Crusade in Europe* p. 246. General Bedell Smith has told me that the toughest thing for "Ike" in the entire operation was watching the 101st Airborne Division take off around midnight of the 5th, after Leigh-Mallory had confidently assured him that their casualties would be 80 per cent.

there were signs of more foul weather to come; but even Leigh-Mallory now agreed that the risk must be taken.

"Ike" listened to final comments, paused a moment, and at 0415 June 5 made the great decision: —

"O.K. We'll go."

That afternoon Admiral Ramsay issued a special Order of the Day to every officer and man of the two Navies: —

"It is our privilege to take part in the greatest amphibious operation in history . . .

"The hopes and prayers of the free world and of the enslaved people of Europe will be with us and we cannot fail them . . .

"I count on every man to do his utmost to ensure the success of this great enterprise which is the climax of the European War. Good luck to you all and God Speed."

3. *The Crossing*

> . . . O, do but think
> You stand upon the rivage and behold
> A city on th' inconstant billows dancing;
> For so appears this fleet majestical,
> Holding due course for Harfleur. Follow, follow:
> Grapple your minds to sternage of this navy,
> And leave your England . . .

Thus Shakespeare in *King Henry V* exhorted his audience to imagine the cross-Channel operation of 1415. What words could he have found to describe that of 1944, what striking metaphors, what bold similes? For here was no mere "city on th' inconstant billows dancing," but the choice, picked men of three nations, in higher numbers than had any city of his day, borne by more vessels than there were in all the world when Elizabeth I was Queen of England. Majestical they are indeed, whether proudly advancing by day, or blacked out at night, endless columns converging, then parting, for their destinations in the Bay of the Seine.

Swept channels from the English coast were wide enough for two convoys to sail abreast up to Point "Z," 13 miles southeast of the Isle of Wight. Around this point was a circle of five miles' radius, nicknamed "Piccadilly Circus," through which almost every convoy for the Far Shore had to pass. Thence five swept lanes were provided, one for each task force.

About halfway across the Channel each lane became two, one for the fast and one for the slow convoys. So complex was this movement that Admiral Ramsay issued special "Mickey Mouse Diagrams," as they were called, showing predicted hourly locations of every convoy. Our chart is based on the "Mickey Mouse" for 0030 June 6.

Let us first follow the fortunes of Captain Lorenzo Sabin's slow convoy for the Omaha beach. This was one of those that had started on the morning of 4 June, reversed course owing to the decision to postpone D-day, and dashed madly back to Portland. General Eisenhower, as we have seen, gave the word "Go!" at 0415 June 5. About five hours later, Sabin's convoy made its final start, in four columns 100 yards apart. The wind was still strong and the sea became rougher the farther they sailed into the Channel. Under such conditions, LCT are not easy boats to handle. Built of three sections bolted together, with the heavy machinery in the stern and the bow both high and light, they are almost impossible to hold on a course in a strong wind.

Here is the story by one of the LCT officers: —

We were located in one of the inside columns and spent our entire time trying to keep station. We had the misfortune to have a British "lettered craft" behind us which had the ability to go ahead twice as fast as the Americans, but lacked the backing power that we had. We would pound along, the whole boat bending and buckling; then the one ahead would slow down. We would go into full reverse to keep from riding up its stern, then the Britisher would start to climb ours. To avoid collision we would go full speed ahead with full right rudder, and sheer off toward the other column. The vessels of different columns would close to about five feet or less, usually crashing together, then separating with one going full speed at right angles to the course of the

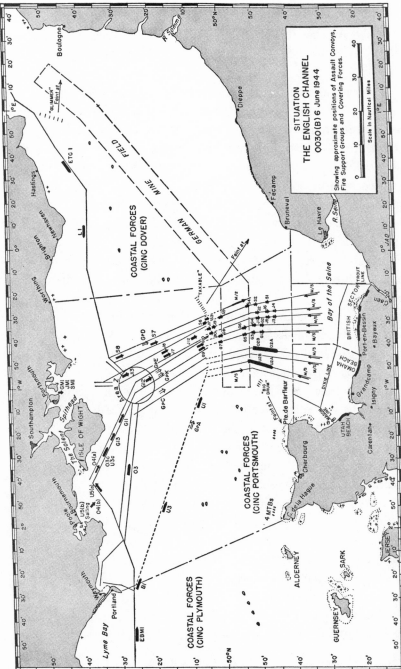

SITUATION
THE ENGLISH CHANNEL
0030(B) 6 June 1944

Showing approximate positions of Assault Convoys,
Fire Support Groups and Covering Forces.

Scale in Nautical Miles
0   10   20   30   40

convoy. All day there was always someone heading off by himself, having a wonderful time. Sleep was almost impossible, as you couldn't stay in your sack.[6]

Now let us turn to the heavy gunfire ships and transports, coming around Lands End and debouching from Plymouth. The bombardment group for Omaha, commanded by Admiral Bryant in *Texas*, forges ahead of Admiral Deyo's for Utah and makes a brave show off the Cornish coast as its signal flags snap in the breeze, lighted by a brief burst of sunshine. The "parade" forms up, each group in single column, in order to give minecraft the narrowest possible channel to sweep. Attack transport *Bayfield*, flying Rear Admiral Moon's two-star flag, slips into her place in the column off Plymouth at 1045. Three other transports for Utah join off Dartmouth. During the afternoon Deyo's column overtakes those of the beaching craft. He is impressed by "an air of cheerfulness, even jauntiness, in their crowded human cargoes." One Seabee, balanced precariously on the deck of a "Rhino ferry," [7] cups his hands toward the bridge of lordly *Tuscaloosa* and shouts, "How'll you trade your tub for this ship — about even?"

At 1800 June 5, off Portland Bill, Deyo's column changes course to SE. The sky is still overcast and the wind a fresh NW, but the sea is moderating. As far as the eye can reach, the Channel is covered with ships and craft "fraught with the ministers and instruments of cruel war," the small ones tossing and heaving, the great ones steadily advancing, all destined for a part on the great D-day. An hour before midnight battleship *Nevada*, veteran of the Pearl Harbor attack and behemoth of this fleet, observes the subdued blink of a control vessel's light on her port bow. She turns to starboard, followed by *Quincy*, *Tuscaloosa* and H.M.S. *Black Prince*. This is the entrance to swept channel No. 2, one of ten into which the approach lanes have now separated and through which the columns will pass to their initial positions for the landing. High overcast obscures the moon, but light filters through the clouds.

---

[6] Report to the writer by Lt. Stanley C. Bodell USNR, 1947.
[7] A barge composed of pontoon units, propelled by big outboard motors.

Now the gunfire ships begin to tick off the lighted dan buoys, red to starboard and white to port, emplaced by the careful sweepers and their attendant Fairmiles.

In Portland, as midnight 5–6 June approaches, the only assault forces left are the motor torpedo boats, which are to dash across after daybreak. The lighthouse on Portland Bill is the point of departure for transport planes carrying the paratroops who are to precede the seaborne assault. Aircraft, in groups of 18 flying at about 500 feet, come in with running lights on, the stripes on wings and fuselage still visible. As they converge on the darkened lighthouse tower, their lights are switched off and they alter course for the Far Shore, Normandy, streaming away from the towered headland like the wings on the Victory of Samothrace.

On board ships that have already reached the Far Shore, awaiting eight bells to usher in D-day, voices are instinctively hushed. Every bridge is dead quiet, but the atmosphere is alive with emotion. Men feel a quiet exaltation, something more than confidence, as though the Admiral of Heaven were directing and reassuring them.

There were indeed things so remarkable in this crossing as to suggest divine guidance. The crowded movement of these thousands of vessels and small craft ran off very close to schedule in spite of the foul weather. Small craft had a rough passage, and some strayed — but none foundered and few were seriously late. The other amazing circumstance was the enemy's complete unawareness of what was going on. Everyone was astounded to observe the light at Cape (Pointe) Barfleur, one of the world's tallest and most conspicuous lighthouses, burning brightly. No enemy reconnaissance planes had discovered anything unusual in the Channel. German E-boats had failed to make their routine patrol on the night of 5–6 June, because their commander thought that the weather was too foul both for them and for us, and because Admiral Krancke thought that the tides were "not right" for an invasion.

Not until 0309 June 6 did German search radar pick up anything, although many ships had reached their transport areas an hour earlier. Admiral Krancke promptly issued orders to repel an invasion,[8] but the shore batteries waited until first light, shortly after 0500, when they opened up on destroyers *Corry* and *Fitch*. At this unscheduled curtain-raiser to the battle for the Normandy beachhead, we may break off to describe another aspect of the operation which had direct bearing on the landings at Utah and was essential for the success of the main assault on the Cotentin Peninsula.

4. *The Air Drop* [9]

The northern part of the Cotentin Peninsula around Cherbourg is hilly, but opposite Utah the hills give way to low, flat pastures and the *bocage* of small fields divided by thick hedgerows or earth walls. The neck of the peninsula is almost cut in two by a series of swamps, rivers and drainage ditches which were devised by Napoleon, at least in part, for defense. The Douve and the Merderet Rivers join the Carentan, which empties into the Bay of the Seine in the angle between the Utah and Omaha beaches. When flooded, as these lowlands were by the Germans, they form a long, wide and shallow water barrier which forces all north–south traffic at the base of the peninsula through one of three well-defined routes. Behind the Utah beaches the Germans had also flooded the pastures which extend inland for about two miles. But there were nine causeways across these pastures, connecting the nearest north–south road with the beach exits. Prompt control by the United States Army of these causeways was essential for deploying the troops. Otherwise they might be pinned down on the beaches, unable to move across the flooded pastures, and at the mercy of German artillery. To ensure the one and prevent the other, two United States airborne divisions were assigned to assist VII Corps.

The plan for gaining prompt control of critical points was to

[8] Weichold "German Naval Defense Against Allied Invasion" pp. 12–13.

[9] Leonard Rapport & Arthur Northwood, Jr. *Rendezvous with Destiny* (1948), a history of the 101st Airborne Division, has the most detailed account of the drop. Also valuable are Harrison, Bradley, Leigh-Mallory, and Dept. of the Army *Airborne Operations, German Appraisal* (1951).

drop paratroops inland about five hours before H-hour of D-day. The 101st Airborne Division, Major General Maxwell D. Taylor USA, dropping southeast of Sainte-Mère-Église, would capture the land ends of the beach causeways and block the land approaches to the peninsula near Carentan. The 82nd Airborne Division, Major General Matthew B. Ridgway USA, Mediterranean veterans, were to land astride the Merderet River west of Sainte-Mère-Église, with the mission of seizing that crossroads village and guarding against counterattack from the northwest. The Germans had installed anti-paratroop obstacles consisting of *Rommelspargel* ("Rommel's asparagus"): tall wooden poles joined by barbed wire and mined. But most of these were in places which the paratroops did not use; the Germans expected the drops to be much farther inland than they were. When it turned out that the air drop came between their troops and the beaches, they were at a loss what to do about it.

H-hour for the airborne landings was 0130 June 6. Six regiments (approximately 13,000 paratroops), with attached artillery, engineers and naval shore fire control parties, were flown to the jump points in about 925 C–47 transport planes of the IX United States Army Air Force Troop Carrier Command. Reinforcements were scheduled to arrive by glider at dawn and at dusk on D-day. At 2215 June 5, the C–47s began to take off from 25 different airfields in the English West Country. Twenty Pathfinder aircraft flew half an hour ahead of them to six drop zones. The drops were widely scattered, a few "sticks" (plane loads of paratroops) landing as much as 25 miles from their intended spots. About 60 per cent of the equipment was lost, and it was exceedingly difficult to assemble the troops; but this wide dispersion did help to confuse the Germans. Reports began to flow into German Seventh Army headquarters as soon as the paratroops began to drop; and at 0215 the whole LXXXIV Corps was alerted. Even so, the German high command was so firmly convinced that the main assault would strike the Pas-de-Calais that these drops were estimated as diversions and nothing was done except to issue routine orders.

*   *   *

Let us first follow the action of General Taylor's 101st Airborne Division, which comprised the 501st, 502nd, and 506th Parachute Infantry Regiments. As the troops landed in the dark, the first step was to assemble in groups, the men identifying one another by the chirping of toy crickets. It was noon of D-day before Colonel Howard R. Johnson could collect 200 men of his 501st Regiment to seize or destroy two bridges over the Douve northwest of Carentan. A naval shore fire control party with Colonel Johnson called on cruiser *Quincy* to deliver 8-inch shellfire on enemy positions that were holding him up, one of the rare instances of naval gunfire supporting airborne troops. The 506th, which had the mission of seizing dry ground behind the inundated pastures that bordered Utah beach, and securing the left flank of the invading VII Corps, was badly dispersed in the drop, but by 0430 June 6 two battalions of partial strength were moving toward the exits. The 3rd Battalion wrested Pouppeville from the enemy at noon, and, shortly after, the paratroops made contact with the seaborne troops who had landed on the southernmost Utah beach. The 2nd Battalion also encountered strong resistance, but one company reached Beach Exit No. 2 by 1330, and cleared the way for troops and tanks of the 4th Division to use it. The 502nd Regiment had the mission of seizing the land ends of Exits 3 and 4, setting up perimeter defense, and linking up with the 82nd Division to the west. Most of the troops missed their drop zones and were widely scattered; but, as elsewhere, the battalion commanders collected such men as they could and set off for their objectives. One party of 15 men captured the village of Mésières and 150 Germans. The 3rd Battalion commander started out with about 75 men for the beach exits, and reached them without difficulty by 0730. Shortly after noon he linked up with troops of the 4th Division moving inland.

General Ridgway's 82nd Airborne Division, comprising the 505th, 507th and 508th Parachute Infantry Regiments, having dropped at the edge of the German 91st Division assembly area, had more fighting than the 101st, and attained its objectives only in part. One battalion of the 505th occupied the important cross-

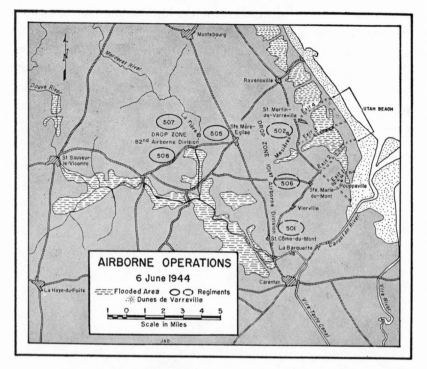

AIRBORNE OPERATIONS
6 June 1944

roads village of Sainte-Mère-Église by 0430, and successfully defended it against strong German counterattacks. Another battalion seized two bridges over the Merderet. The other two regiments made very scattered drops. By the end of D-day most of the 82nd Airborne were near and around Sainte-Mère-Église, under attack from three directions, having lost 156 men killed, 347 wounded, and 756 missing.

The glider build-up was not a success. Fifty-one gliders came in for the 101st Division and suffered many casualties and wrecks while trying to land on the small Normandy fields. A second echelon, arriving at twilight, made an even worse landing, and the 82nd Division, too, suffered heavy losses in troops and wrecked gliders.[10]

Plotting these air drops on the map — from which ours has been much simplified — makes it look as if it had been spattered by a

[10] Statistics of total efforts and losses in terms of aircraft are in Leigh-Mallory pp. 59–60.

paintbrush; yet this "airhead" drew the bulk of the German countermeasures around Utah on D-day. Although the paratroops did not immediately attain control of the zone behind the beaches, they dominated the country for about seven miles inland, drew the first counterattacks, and, by their gallant fighting, set the stage for what proved to be the easiest of the five major landings in the invasion of Normandy.

CHAPTER VI

Utah Beach[1]

6 June 1944

1. Before H-hour

THE TENSE SILENCE on the flag bridge of *Bayfield*, where Admiral Moon and General Collins were standing side by side, was broken at 0229 by the rattle of chain cable through the hawsepipe. "Anchor holding, sir, in 17 fathoms," came the word. It was the long-awaited D-day, and only 240 minutes to H-hour. An 18-knot westerly wind was blowing off the Cotentin Peninsula and the beaches, which lay eleven and a half miles in that direction. There was a heavy overcast, through holes in which moonlight occasionally burst, and the night seemed hot after the recent cool days in England. Sunrise was coming at 0558.

Bayfield and her attendant transports, guided through the mineswept channel by lighted dan buoys, had reached the exact point indicated by the plan, and on time. To seaward of them, LCTs loaded with tanks and vehicles were closing up. Between them and the beach were four control craft, two PC and two LCC (Landing Craft, Control) to guide the boat waves. Admiral Deyo's gunfire support ships, too, were mostly between the transports and the shore, ready to protect Force "U" if the enemy opened up, and in any case to cover the minecraft who were busily sweeping the boat

[1] *Utah Beach to Cherbourg*, Ramsay, Harrison; Action Reports and Operation Orders of Admirals Kirk, Moon and Deyo; Lt. Cdr. Leonard Ware USNR War Diary of Force "U" 31 May–25 June 1944, Aug. 1944 (corrected by Admiral Moon and members of staff). For the German reaction, German Naval Command West War Diary, Weichold "German Naval Defense against Allied Invasion of Normandy." The sprightliest account of the Utah landings yet to appear is Commo. J. E. Arnold USNR "N.O.I.C.Utah" in U.S. Nav. Inst. *Proceedings* LXXIII 671–81 (June 1947).

lanes. Everything had gone well so far, but there was the usual feeling of "anything may happen" that is characteristic of an amphibious operation. Everyone had been so impressed with the need for secrecy that sailors on deck spoke in whispers, as if the Germans could overhear.

There was no time to brood, and no need for Admiral Moon to give the classic order "Lower all landing craft!" He had already ordered each transport to "follow standard operating procedure," which meant that the lowering of boats would begin immediately. *Barnett's* boats for the first wave were waterborne within seven minutes of her anchoring — and the others were only slightly behind. In the waves that the offshore breeze and current had kicked up, it was impossible to prevent boats from banging against the steel sides of the transports. That made an ungodly racket, but it was not yet time to boat the troops.

At 0405 transports began to debark the 1500 to 1650 assault troops that each carried. They scrambled down the cargo-net ladders like veterans; but hitting the slippery deck of an LCVP rising on each wave crest, then falling in the trough, proved to be difficult. So well trained were the boat crews and so well disciplined the troops that the loading was done quickly and in complete silence, so far as the human voice was concerned; but there was a deep bass of naval gunfire — sweet music to the soldiers' ears — to accompany the harsh clanking of steel against steel.

Since 0200, 18 American and 16 British minesweepers had been busy in the transport area, in the boat lanes to within a mile of the beach, and in the approach channels and fire support areas for the bombardment ships. These complex sweeps were carried out under the overall command of Commander M. H. Brown RN, with exemplary skill. Unfortunately most of the mines in this sector were of the delayed-action type which come to life only after several sweeps, and others were later dropped by aircraft. These kept popping off for many days, and in the end the casualties from mine explosions exceeded those from all other causes.

There were an estimated 28 German batteries in the network of coastal fortifications defending the Utah sector. They comprised about 110 guns ranging from 75-mm up to a naval battery of 170-mm between Cape Barfleur and Saint-Vaast-la-Hougue. Four of these batteries and the one on Pointe du Hoc also covered Omaha, but most of them were two or three miles behind the east coast of the Cotentin Peninsula and north of Quinéville. Also ranging on the beaches were 18 batteries located inland, the largest having four 210-mm guns in casemates near Saint-Marcouf. The others comprised eight 152-mm, six 155-mm, eight 122-mm and sixteen 105-mm guns.[2] In addition, the Germans had a large number of mobile 88-mm guns.

General Bradley's headquarters issued a list of the batteries which he wanted neutralized in the preliminary naval bombardment, and this list was augmented when Admirals Deyo and Moon and General Collins put their heads together and, studying reconnaissance photos, found more strongpoints that needed attention. Deyo's plan for silencing these batteries was simple. The battleships and cruisers were to fire from about 11,000 yards off the beaches; the destroyers from 5000 yards. Since these ships would be unable to maneuver in the narrow swept channels of their assigned areas, they were directed to anchor before commencing counter-battery fire. At the same hour (H minus 40), the secondary batteries of *Nevada* and *Quincy* and the main batteries of H.M.S. *Enterprise* and destroyers *Hobson* and *Shubrick* would drench selected beaches with a high rate of fire. For ten minutes before the landing the main batteries of *Nevada* and *Quincy* also were to be turned on the beaches. On signal by the commander of the first boat wave, firing a black smoke rocket as he neared the shore, all gunfire was to be shifted to selected flank targets. Main battery shooting by *Nevada* and *Quincy* was especially requested by General Collins, who displayed complete confidence in the accuracy of naval gunfire in the hope that direct hits would knock gaps in the concrete seawall. And, in addition, rocket-equipped LCTs were to deliver 5000 five-inch rockets on the beaches just ahead of the leading boat wave.

[2] Harrison Map VIII supplemented from other sources.

The bombardment ships entered their assigned channels at 0140 June 6 and anchored. At 0505, as we have seen, a shore battery opened up on destroyers *Fitch* and *Corry*, and 20 minutes later the large-caliber battery at Saint-Vaast took under heavy fire the small minecraft which were sweeping 3500 yards off shore. H.M.S. *Black Prince* promptly replied, attracting the battery's fire to herself, while the YMS placidly continued their methodical sweep.[3] By 0536, when heavy shots were coming uncomfortably near his heavy cruisers, Admiral Deyo decided to jump the gun on the scheduled pre-landing bombardment, and in a moment every ship was shooting at her assigned target. At 0610 support planes, as planned, began to lay a smoke screen between Force "U" and the shore, but the one which should have protected *Corry* was shot down, leaving her in the clear to become the concentrated target of several German batteries. She maneuvered as rapidly as possible in the restricted waters, firing all the while, and in so doing had the misfortune to strike a mine amidships. The explosion almost cut her in two; both firerooms and the forward engine room were flooded. Lieutenant Commander Hoffman headed for sea by hand steering, but within four minutes all power was lost, the ship began to settle, and at 0641 he ordered Abandon Ship. *Hobson* and *Fitch* blazed away at the German batteries from one side while they lowered boats to recover *Corry*'s survivors on the other; and by 0830 the rescue was completed. *Corry* lost 13 killed and missing and 33 wounded.

Leaving the landing craft of the assault waves milling around waiting for the word to go, let us take a look at the section of the Far Shore which they were destined to invade. The nine-mile stretch of the Cotentin east coast then (and still) named Utah is about as featureless a shoreline as you could find. It might be any one of a hundred beaches on the East Coast of the United States between Maine and the Carolinas. The beach proper, the tidal part, is a gentle slope of yellow sand, crossed by numerous runnels, planted with several lines of anti-boat obstacles and about 300 to 400 yards

[3] Com YMS Squadrons (Cdr. G. W. Allen) Action Report 20 July.

wide at low water. After you cross that, there are a few yards of dry sand where driftwood, seaweed and shells are tossed up; and behind that, a 100- to 150-yard-wide belt of low sand dunes partly covered with beach grass, against which, on the seaward side, the Germans had constructed a low concrete wall. At the north end of that part of the beach which we actually used, the dunes rose a little higher than elsewhere, and were called after the nearest inland village, Varreville. Behind the beach, flooded pasture lands ran a mile or two inland. These (as we have seen when describing the air drop) were crossed by causeways which gave access to the beach by exits through the dunes.[4] About four miles off shore, and parallel to the shoreline, are two tiny islands called Saint-Marcouf [5] and two shoal-water banks, one of the same name, and the other the Cardonnet, with only nine to fifteen feet of water over them at low tide. The waters chosen for the transport area, where *Bayfield* and her consorts were now anchored, lay some six miles seaward of these, and eleven and a half miles from high-water mark on the beach. This writer, looking shoreward from the former transport area on a calm, clear day in 1956, could see the Saint-Marcouf Islands clearly, but the shore very faintly. Even as one approaches the beach, there are no steeples, buildings or distinctive hills visible to help a landing-craft coxswain to orient himself. The long beach was divided into eight lettered sectors, and each of these subdivided into a Beach Red and Beach Green. But only the two southernmost were actually used in the initial assault.

2. *The Landings*

Owing to the great distance at which the transport area was located from the beach, the run-in was long and rough for the troops,

[4] Because of deliberate flooding of this area by the Germans, only three of the 11 roads which crossed this marshy ground were dry on 6 June 1944.

[5] A detachment of the 4th and 24th Cavalry Squadrons, numbering 132, was landed on these islands at 0530 in order to deal with a suspected enemy observation post. They found none, but suffered several casualties from land mines and booby traps. Later, the islands made useful sites for antiaircraft batteries.

and landing-craft coxswains could not even see the beach until they were more than halfway.

A 173-foot PC acted as primary control vessel for each beach. Two LCC, 36-foot boats equipped with small radar and radio for guiding boat waves, assisted each PC. From the line of departure, 4000 yards off the beach and inside the line of the Saint-Marcouf Islands and the Cardonnet Bank, 26 scheduled waves were directed ashore in a movement planned to extend over a period of six hours.

The novel feature of all landings on D-day was an initial boat wave of eight LCT, each carrying four British-designed DD (dual drive) amphibious tanks, in order to afford the infantry artillery support as soon as they stepped ashore. These tanks were fitted with "bloomers," accordion-pleated canvas screens, which, when raised, were supposed to be sufficient to float the tanks ashore, after which they could be discarded. The DD tanks were to be launched at a point 5000 yards off the beach from their LCT carriers. These arrived in the transport area at 0430. *PC–1176* and *PC–1261* then undertook to guide four carriers each toward the beach. With almost nine miles to go before launching tanks, the craft made very slow speed against head wind and steep chop. Just as they were crossing the Cardonnet Bank, at 0542, *PC–1261* struck a mine, rolled over and sank. This deprived the four craft destined for Beach Red, as well as all later waves to that beach, of their primary control vessel. Fifteen minutes later *LCT–597*, en route to the other beach, exploded a mine and sank almost immediately, taking down the four DD tanks that she carried.[6]

The silence of early morning had now given way to a deafening racket — the fire support ships "belting away" at their designated targets raised an "almost continuous wall of sound"; the enemy batteries were replying briskly; and overhead was the drumming of aircraft engines of the flights returning to Britain to reload.

[6] CTU 125.4.6 (in *PC–1176*) Action Report. At the time it was assumed that these losses were due to direct artillery hits; but it is now certain that mines caused them.

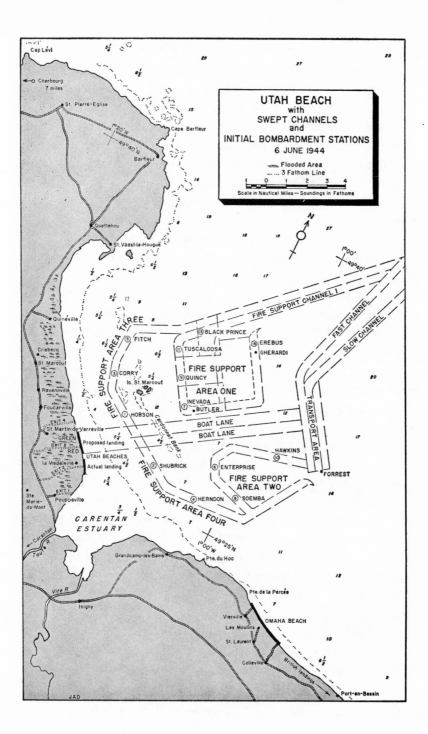

Lieutenant (jg) John B. Richer USNR, control officer in *PC–1176*, realizing that the rest of the DD tanks would be too late to support the first assault troops if launched according to plan, took it upon himself to lead their carriers closer in. At about a mile off shore, the tanks were launched in the relatively calm water. All 28 landed about ten minutes after the first troops, and went right into action.

After naval bombardment of the beaches lifted, 276 IX Army Air Force Marauders dropped 4400 bombs on enemy positions. Next, four LCG armed with 4.7-inch guns closed the beach on the flanks of the first boat wave to give close support. And, when the first wave was about 700 yards from the shore, clusters of rockets began to stream out of 17 specially equipped LCT(R).[7]

All this pounding raised a pall which completely obscured such few terrain features as there were. Nothing but smoke and dust could be seen from the sea, and radar was of no use for distinguishing one beach from another. The strong current threw everyone off, so that the LCCs set up the line of departure some 1500 yards south of where it should have been, and the leading boat waves, shaping a compass course for the beach, were swept another 500 yards farther south by the tidal stream.

Twenty landing craft of the first wave touched down exactly at H-hour, 0630. The men had to wade through about one hundred yards of water to reach dry land, but that did not bother them because there was no surf, and they were pleasantly surprised at receiving no enemy gunfire. But where were they? Nothing checked with their diagrams. Brigadier General Theodore Roosevelt USA, who had volunteered to land with the first wave, was the first to find out. He had so carefully studied the terrain from maps that, shortly after coming ashore, he ascertained that the entire landing had "slipped" about 2000 yards south of the designated point. He then helped two battalion commanders to reorganize their attack to conform to the terrain that actually confronted the troops.[8] Later in the morning, "Teddy" ducked into a foxhole on the beach where

[7] *Utah Beach to Cherbourg* pp. 43–47.
[8] Report of Lt. Col. John W. Merrill to General Barton, 1300 June 6.

Minecraft exploding mines across Cardonnet Bank, morning of D-day

U.S.S. *Augusta*, and *Ancon*, and a British Fairmile, off the beaches

D-day, 6 June 1944, Operation NEPTUNE

Navy beach party, Utah, examines German "Beetle" tanks

"Air raid!" Beach party ducks for a foxhole
(Note concrete seawall and horned scullies removed from boat lanes)

D-day

Captain Arnold, N.O.I.C. Utah, had set up temporary headquarters, and persuaded him to divert landing craft thither from a beach then under heavy fire.

A kind providence had thus corrected an error in the operation plan, which, if carried out, would have placed one assault battalion on a beach enfiladed by two casemated German batteries. At the actual landing place there were few and weak enemy positions, whose defenders were easily overcome.[9] It was accepted as the proper landing place, and the big colored screens and other identification marks meant for Tare Green and Uncle Red were there set up.

Beach obstacles at Utah were few and unformidable compared with those at Omaha, and were not mined. Within an hour and a half they were blown or uprooted by eleven UDTs (Underwater Demolition Teams) which landed in the second boat wave. These cleared 700 yards of beach for boat traffic by 0800, and another 900 yards in the afternoon. German artillery, mortar and machine-gun fire began to register on the beaches soon after the second wave landed, costing the Navy demolitioners four killed and eleven wounded.

Twenty-six assault waves (not counting the DD tanks) for both beaches — the first twelve consisting almost entirely of landing craft and the remainder all beaching craft — were scheduled to land at ten- to twenty-minute intervals until half an hour after noon. The first five waves for both beaches, and most of those for Beach Red, landed exactly on time; but, owing probably to the loss of control craft, and the rumor that Beach Green was being heavily shelled, Admiral Moon at the transport area delayed the departure

[9] The Red and Green beaches on our chart were the ones so redesignated after the landings, not those originally so called in the op. plan. Red Beach can now be reached by Route N13 from Carentan to Sainte-Marie-du-Mont, thence over one of the old causeways to a group of houses called La Madeleine, which is rapidly becoming a resort. This beach is marked by a monument to the 1st Engineer Special Brigade; Green Beach adjoins it on the NW. Following the new road just behind the dunes, you come to the exit at Les Dunes de Varreville, where there is a monument to General LeClerc and the 2nd French Armored Div. which landed there in August. This is the original Tare Green beach, and the concrete strong-points enfilading it, which were captured by the 22nd Infantry on 7 June, may still be seen.

of waves 6 through 12 for that beach, some for as much as two hours.[10] At 1015 he sent Colonel James E. Kerr USMC of his staff shoreward in *PC–484* to take over control and see what went on; and at 1045 he received a report from the beach, "Landings can be made anywhere on Red Beach . . . obstacles no longer obstacles." [11] Waves to Beach Green which had "piled up" in the transport area were then sent in, and later ones were less delayed.[12]

So rapidly did the tide rise that, as one LCI commander described it, no sooner did one drop ramp than the soldiers were plunged into water over their heads; he had to retract and beach five times before he could land one shipload. His wave of LCI had been ordered to stream barrage balloons; but, noticing that German gunfire was coming uncomfortably close, he gave the order, "Cut all balloons." They then floated slowly out to sea, followed by salvos from the puzzled German gunners.

The two Utah beaches were rapidly organized, dumps were quickly established inland so that there was little congestion at the water's edge, and the "beetles" or "doddlebugs" — remote-control miniature tanks, which the Germans here had intended to send against boats as they beached, to blow them up — failed to operate. Transports were unloaded on the double; *Empire Gauntlet* was discharged by 0830, *Dickman* and *Barnett* by 1243. By midnight all three were back in Portland Harbor. *Bayfield,* as the flagship, stood by. By 1800 of D-day, 21,328 troops, 1742 vehicles and 1695 tons of supplies had been landed on these beaches.

Noteworthy was the seamanship displayed by the much-battered small-craft convoy U–2A(1), commanded by Lieutenant Commander L. E. Hart USNR and consisting of 50 LCM, 37 LCT and

[10] Lt.(jg) H. Vanderbeek in *LCC–60,* and Lt. J. B. Ricker in *PC–1176,* Reports to Rear Adm. Moon 6 June. Owing to the narrow front, each wave was very small, an average of 7 LCM, 5 LCT or 6 LCI for Beach Red, fewer for Beach Green.

[11] Intelligence Officer Beach Red (Lt. Mark Dalton) Report to Rear Adm. Moon 6 June; info. from Col. Kerr in 1956.

[12] *PC–1176* and CTU 125.5.1 Action Reports; Rear Adm. Moon Action Report p. 4.

23 other small craft. This was the one which, after being turned back by the postponement of D-day, arrived off Portland Harbor near midnight 4 June, only to find most of the berths taken. It set forth again on the morning of 5 June, and arrived at the transport area precisely on schedule after passing three nights and two days at sea. "The performance of the leading groups of Force 'U' was particularly praiseworthy," reported Admiral Ramsay; "by H-hour their commanding officers had been on their bridges continuously for 70 hours." Out of the total number in this convoy, "only seven failed to take part in the assault, and this figure took account of engine failures, as well as the stress of the weather." Convoy U–2A(2), consisting of 136 LCT, did equally well.[18]

When General Roosevelt and the two battalion commanders of the 8th Infantry sized up the beach situation shortly after H-hour, they decided to mop up nearby strongpoints and push inland to the set objectives. Coastal defenses in the Utah sector were manned by one regiment of the German 709th, a "static" division composed largely of reservists and foreign volunteers. The gunners continued to shoot on the beaches as long as they could do so without risk to themselves, but gave up readily to attacking GIs. Their communications with higher German headquarters had already been severed by air bombing and the paratroops, so that it was not until late on D-day that General Dollman, commanding Seventh Army, realized that a seaborne landing had taken place on the Cotentin Peninsula. American troops cleaning up enemy fortifications near the beaches encountered slight resistance on their way to the several exits, the inland end of which, where they joined the north–south road, was being secured by the paratroops. By the evening of D-day most of the units had reached their first objective line on the main highway between Carentan and Sainte-Mère-Église. Hitler's Atlantic Wall had been pierced at remarkably low cost. The 4th Division had suffered only 197 casualties. We had no firm perimeter yet, but a penetration six miles broad and deep.

[18] Ramsay p. 6; Leonard Ware War Diary Force "U" p. 15.

3. *Naval Gunfire Support*

A principal factor in breaking down German resistance at Utah was abundant and accurate naval gunfire support, especially on the remote and large-caliber batteries that the assault troops could not get at. Following H-hour, *Nevada*, the United States heavy cruisers, and H.M.S. *Black Prince* and *Erebus* continued for 50 minutes to bombard heavy German batteries north of the beachhead in the neighborhood of Saint-Vaast-la-Hougue, using air spot. After completing these scheduled shoots, the big ships fired on targets of opportunity with air spot or direct observation, and on request of shore fire control parties. H.M.S. *Enterprise* and the destroyers, nearer inshore, took on targets of opportunity and supplied call fire.

A method of air-spotting for the bombardment ships had been improvised to meet enemy antiaircraft artillery. It would have been suicidal to use the slow Kingfishers and Seagulls from battleships and cruisers over a land whence abundant antiaircraft fire was to be expected. Consequently, these ship-borne planes had been "put on the beach," and the British had provided a pool of fast fighter planes — five squadrons of R.A.F. Spitfires and Mustangs, and four squadrons of Royal Navy Seafires.[14] Seventeen units were manned by United States Navy pilots taken off the SOCs; the rest by R.A.F. pilots who had had no previous experience in spotting. The Spitfires, in pairs, departed Lee airdrome on the Solent at fixed intervals. They had fuel for only 45 minutes over the target. While the wing man watched for enemy planes, the spotter pilot had to fly his plane, dodge flak, spot fall of shot, and telephone to the ship to which he was attached — a formidable assignment which these pilots executed remarkably well. While one pair of Spitfires was spotting, another would be coming from, and a third returning to England for refueling. That required six aircraft for each spotting mission — a costly

[14] Admiral Deyo "Naval Guns at Normandy" p. 18. A Seafire is a carrier-borne Spitfire. At that time the United States Atlantic Fleet had no carrier pilots trained to spot gunfire, except those who were to be used in Operation DRAGOON.

makeshift for want of long-range planes or carrier aircraft trained in this specialized form of combat aviation.

With the landing force on D-day were 18 shore fire control parties; and, with the airborne force, nine paratroop naval gunfire spotters, one to each battalion of the 101st Division. One s.f.c.p. (shore fire control party) was assigned to each infantry or field artillery battalion of the 4th Division.

Destroyer *Shubrick* (Lieutenant Commander William Blenman), directly off the beaches, got in touch with her s.f.c.p. as early as 0635, and directed her fire accordingly. Twice she obeyed orders to check gunfire when it was in danger of falling on friendly troops. Nothing could be seen through the thick cloud of dust and smoke which hung over the beaches until after 0700. *Shubrick's* combat information center then figured out that the landings had been made a mile south of where they should have been; this explained why she had endangered our troops. At 0740, she located a battery firing from the eastern side of the Carentan estuary, opened fire and silenced it; but at 0820 it came to life and landed a salvo close aboard. She then bombarded the battery for 25 minutes and silenced it once more. At 1026, after firing 440 rounds of 5-inch shell, *Shubrick* was relieved by *Glennon*, which received only one call for gunfire support during the rest of D-day.

Although the mistake in locating the beaches was immediately fortunate, it did bring the landings about a mile nearer enemy batteries on the eastern side of the Carentan estuary, and these, after vainly trying to hit the boat waves, began at noon to pound both landing beaches.[15] *Herndon*, the venerable H.M.S. *Hawkins*, and H.N.M.S. *Soemba* — designated to take care of these batteries — found plenty to do. The Dutchman fired her 5.9-inch guns on call from an s.f.c.p. which was with the Rangers on Pointe du Hoc. Initial targets for *Hawkins* were a battery of four 155-mm and one of four 75-mm, a mile or two southwest of Grandcamp, in the V

[15] Intelligence Officer Beach Red (Lt. Mark Dalton) Report; Beach Green Assault Group Commander Report, both to CTF 125.

Corps sector. These were reported neutralized after repeated hits. *Herndon* thrice, between 0655 and 0815, blasted and silenced batteries near Grandcamp which she had observed firing on the boat channels.

Nevada distinguished herself, as we have seen, by supporting the paratroops — for which she received the thanks of General Ridgway and the congratulations of Admiral Deyo; and no wonder, for she had destroyed a group of tanks and field artillery, and caused a German assembly point to be shifted. This grand old battlewagon expended 337 rounds of 14-inch and 2693 rounds of 5-inch ammunition on 6 June. *Tuscaloosa* made 16 shoots during the day and expended 487 rounds of 8-inch and 115 of 5-inch ammunition. Most of her targets lay far inland and were spotted from the air; others were hit as the result of direct observation. At 0711 she silenced a battery about two and a half miles south of Quinéville that was shooting at stricken *Corry*. That and other batteries at the north end of the beachhead were very troublesome, as they were able to range on the beaches. Thrice during the day *Tuscaloosa* was taken under fire, but the closest shots missed by 300 yards. *Quincy* at 1120 established communication with an s.f.c.p. operating with the 101st Airborne Division. That afternoon and evening she answered eight calls for fire on troop concentrations along the Carentan–Sainte-Mère-Église highway, and was told that all eight shoots were successful. Between calls she pounded troublesome batteries north of the beaches. On D-day, she expended 585 rounds of 8-inch, 660 rounds of 5-inch and 53 rounds of 5-inch white phosphorus shell.

H.M.S. *Enterprise*, subsequent to 0716, fired 145 rounds of 6-inch at coastal strongpoints northeast of Pouppeville, in response to six calls from her s.f.c.p. H.M.S. *Black Prince* fired rapidly with her 5¼-inch guns on several troublesome targets.

The experience of a German naval battery of three 210-mm guns in concrete casemates, just north of the village of Saint-Marcouf, illustrates the devastating effect of naval gunfire. As early as 0630, one gun was already out of action from a direct hit. By 1557 a second had been knocked out, and at 1830 the commander reported that all three were *kaput*.[16] H.M. monitor *Erebus* was responsible for dropping a 15-inch shell on No. 2 gun, which thereafter was of no further use to the enemy.

Admiral Deyo observed, respecting this counter-battery fire: "Direct hits observed by spotting planes did not permanently disable the batteries, which within a few hours or a day were able to resume fire, though at greatly reduced volume and effectiveness. Never before has it been attempted to silence with naval gunfire so extensive and elaborate a system of coast defenses as found here. The surprising thing is that more losses were not sustained by our force in this stage of the operation." [17]

This international bombardment force had every reason to be proud of the support it gave to VII Corps in the Utah area on D-day.

4. *Situation at End of D-day*

At Paris, Admiral Krancke admitted in his war diary at 0800 June 6: "The enemy have certainly succeeded in surprising to a certain extent the whole machinery of German defense organization; and not least by the clever choice of a period to land when the weather appeared to be unfavorable, but kept improving." Grossadmiral Doenitz acknowledged on 11 June: "The enemy's surprise attack was not only a tactical but a strategic success." [18] Weight and breadth of the assault were so vast that the German high command obtained no clear picture of what was happening until the close of D-day. Their only naval craft in a position to counterattack when the alert was sounded at 0309 June 6 were 15 E-boats based at Cherbourg. These headed for the Bay of the Seine; but, according to Krancke's war diary, were forced by the weather "to give up the task at first light," without their seeing hide or hair of Force "U." Before the invasion, 36 U-boats based at Brest, L'Orient,

[16] German Naval Command West War Diary 6 June. The battery claimed a hit on a cruiser, but none was made.
[17] Action Report p. 13.
[18] Weichold "German Naval Defense" p. 13.

Saint-Nazaire and La Pallice, eight of them with snorkel, had been designated to operate against any seaborne assault.[19] These were alerted to be ready to proceed into the Channel, and three German destroyers were ordered up to Brest from Royan to stand by.

Underwater mines proved to be the most effective enemy defense at Utah. In order to reach the beaches, landing craft had to pass directly across a minefield laid along the Cardonnet Bank. None of these mines were detected before H-hour, since they were of the type that require successive sweeps. Destroyer *Corry* and *PC–1261*, three LCT and two LCI were sunk by them on D-day. *LCI–232* was retracting at 1235 when she struck a mine and blew up, with the loss of an officer and 16 men.

Beach organization kept pace with other developments on D-day. The 1st Engineer Special Brigade organized the beaches rapidly and blew gaps in the concrete seawall, which made it possible for the troops to use Exits 1 and 2 leading across the flooded pastures. Both unloading and build-up were well synchronized with the landing of troops, and the wall of uncleared supplies that we had learned to look for on assault beaches was conspicuously absent.

The IX Air Force and IX Tactical Air Command maintained such a strong umbrella of fighters over assault sectors that the Luftwaffe never got into the picture until after dark, when it attacked in a desultory fashion, producing more pyrotechnics than damage. In the meantime, the IX Engineer Command had sent ashore during the morning an engineer aviation battalion which under enemy fire reconnoitered a site at the dry-land end of Exit 3; and, after the fighting had surged beyond that point, constructed a sod landing strip. This was ready for emergency landings at 2115 June 6. Three days later, a second strip was ready near the village of Beuzeville. [20]

The ease with which the Utah landings were made surprised everyone, especially the 4th Infantry Division, which was having its first battle experience in World War II. But the German defense

[19] See Volume X 319–25.
[20] Craven & Cate III pp. 564–65.

was very feeble. The strongest opposition, apart from the exploding mines, came from coastal artillery — which, despite frequent shoots by alert bombardment ships, placed accurate fire on the beaches from time to time. Admiral Moon reported, almost apologetically, that there was "little to write about the assault," except that it went "essentially according to plan." To the war correspondents, before noon on D-day, Admiral Moon said: "The initial action has been won. Next phase will be a race between the build-up of the Allied forces and movement by the enemy reserves." He had well grasped the essence of this operation: that the most successful assault would avail the Allies naught unless they could maintain momentum.

Events here were in sharp contrast to the bloody battle on the Omaha beaches only a few miles away.

CHAPTER VII

Approach to Omaha[1]

6 June 1944

1. Terrain and Defenses

OMAHA BEACH — there's a name that will live, like Tarawa and Guadalcanal, as long as men prize valor and feel for suffering. It was merely a code name given to a stretch of French *plage* selected by the planners as landing beaches in Operation NEPTUNE. Yet the fame of Omaha has eclipsed that of every other amphibious landing in World War II, because it marked the return of the Allies to the continent of Europe, and the beginning of the liberation of France. It was defended by every device and weapon that a resourceful enemy could think up, and that withering defense called forth the highest qualities of courage and decision on the part of the attacking force — Force "O" United States Navy, commanded by Rear Admiral John L. Hall, and the 1st and 29th Divisions of V Corps United States Army.

From the base of the Carentan estuary, the Norman coast trends easterly and takes on a very different character from the shores of the Cotentin Peninsula. The land, instead of sloping very gently to meet the sea, is a bold, high plateau which the sea has abruptly chopped off, leaving either precipitous, rocky cliffs or steep, sandy bluffs. At the foot of the cliffs the beach is very narrow and pebbly;

[1] CTF 124 (Rear Adm. Hall) Op-Order; Rear Adm. Kirk Gunfire Support and Intelligence Plan and Shoreline Sketches with Defense Overprint; O.N.I. Photo Intelligence Summary "Invasion of Normandy." Provisional Engineer Special Brigade Group "Operation Report NEPTUNE" pp. 62–73 has the best account of obstacles, beach gradients and the like. Action Reports of Commander Bombardment Group (Rear Adm. Carleton F. Bryant) and Commander Gunfire Support Craft (Capt. Lorenzo Sabin) are particularly useful for the approach.

but at the foot of the bluffs there are wide sandy beaches of the same character and width as at Utah, access to which from the land is obtained by a series of eroded ravines. La Côte du Calvados, as the French call this shore, is named after a reef off Arromanches, which in turn was named after the galleon *Salvador* of the Spanish Armada which struck there and broke up in 1588.

As one sails along the coast today, approaching Omaha Beach from Cherbourg, it presents a grim and desolate aspect from Pointe du Hoc past Pointe de la Percée. There the cliffs give way to bluffs, the beach widens, green pastures extend to the lip of the plateau up to a point near the village of Saint-Laurent, where the land suddenly appears to have blossomed with Easter lilies. Upon closer inspection these prove to be the white marble crosses and six-pointed stars of the Normandy American Cemetery and Memorial. That beach fringing the bluffs for three miles is the one, nameless before 1944, which shall forever bear the name Omaha.[2]

About three miles east of the Omaha beaches, there is a break in the plateau where nestles a small fishing village, Port-en-Bessin. Here begins the "Gold" area of the British sector, where the cliffs rise again; they are not unscalable, but for the most part have no break at the foot until one reaches Arromanches, where the plateau once more slopes evenly to the sea.

The Omaha beach, though offering a better chance for the attacker than the high, rocky cliffs on either side, would have been easy to defend even with rifles and hand grenades. Invading troops, after debarking at low water, had to tramp over some three hundred yards of wet beach interspersed with runnels and planted with mined obstacles; then cross a few yards of dry sand above the high-water mark, and climb a seawall of big, smooth pebbles, which the French call *galet* and we call "shingle," "cobble" or "popplestone."

---

[2] It is so called today on National Geographic Society and French maps, and the Michelin Guide says, "This name, which up to 6 June 1944 existed only in the secret Allied code, well deserves to be applied to the beaches of St. Laurent, Colleville and Vierville-sur-Mer, as homage to the American soldiers of the 1st Division who fell in the most costly battle of D-day." In the cemetery, dedicated 19 July 1956, 9385 Americans are buried; but only a small part of these were killed in the Omaha assault.

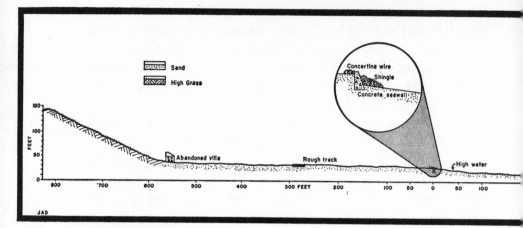

Above this was a ruff of "concertina" barbed wire, against an artificial seawall, concrete for about half the length of Omaha and
piling the rest of the way. Having surmounted that, the GI found
himself on a level, grassy area 100 to 150 yards wide at the western
end, and up to 300 yards wide near exits D–3 and E–1. It was de-
void of cover, except for the remains of two small seaside villages,
Hamel-au-Prêtre and Les Moulins. Each contained a dozen to fifteen
substantial stone and brick villas, which had either been demolished by the Germans or turned into strongpoints commanding the
beach. On the inland side of the level shelf was a line of bluffs, too
steep to be climbed by wheeled or even tracked vehicles, and
through which there were only four exits, deep ravines eroded
through the plateau. Through each ravine a narrow unsurfaced road
connected the beach with a village on the main road which ran
parallel to the shore, about one to two kilometers in the rear.[3] These
sandy ravines, which are generally referred to in the American accounts as "draws," since they resembled the dry beds of our Western watercourses, were to play an important part in the assault, and
to be the end of the road for many a GI.

[3] The main road from Port-en-Bessin and Colleville in 1956 makes a 90-degree
turn at Saint-Laurent and follows the old road down to Omaha Beach at Les
Moulins, then continues along the shore to Vierville, where it heads inland again.
In 1944 this was a narrow dirt road, and along the rest of Omaha Beach there was
a mere wagon track.

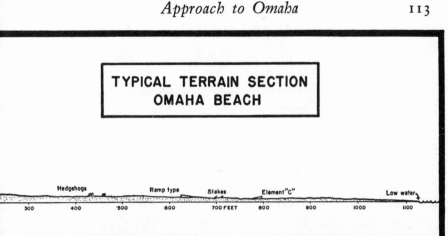

**TYPICAL TERRAIN SECTION
OMAHA BEACH**

Hedgehogs   Ramp type   Stakes   Element "C"   Low water

300   400   500   600   700 FEET   800   900   1000   1100

The four villages called Vierville, Saint-Laurent, Colleville and Sainte-Honorine, strung along the road which runs behind the bluffs, were quiet little communities of farmhouses, each built with thick stone walls in a hollow square — an admirable defense position. Between the edge of the bluffs and the villages were green pastures, and at the road begins the terrain that the French call *bocage* — tiny fields often no more than a few acres in extent, separated by heavy earthen walls surmounted by hedges and trees.

Even so, Omaha might have been no harder than Utah if the Germans had let it alone. The major mistake of Allied Intelligence was the assumption that this and the British sector were defended by only one static German division, the 716th, with no armor or wheeled transport. One of the persistent myths about Omaha is the story that all the trouble was created because a first-line, tough German division "just happened" to have been sent there for a tactical exercise when our troops landed. This yarn makes a good cover for faulty Intelligence, but there is nothing to it. What actually happened is that, in mid-March 1944, Generaloberst Dollman, commanding Seventh Army, sent the 352nd Division to take over the western half of the sector. One regiment of the 716th, already opposite Omaha, was attached to the 352nd; and one regiment of the 352nd, together with a fusilier battalion, was held in corps reserve near Bayeux — only a few miles from the beach. Thus, instead of being opposed by only one regiment of a low-grade division, the American assault forces on D-day encountered better than two regiments of first-line German troops.[4]

The other bad surprise for the Allies was the strength and character of German fixed defenses, which Intelligence had observed only in part. The intensive arming of this sector had begun only in the spring of 1944 after Rommel had inspected the Norman coast, given all local commanders a "kick in the pants," and procured for them the necessary weapons and matériel. And, although Omaha was not nearly as heavily armed as the Pas-de-Calais or the coast of Picardy, where the Germans expected the main landing to take place, it was armed heavily enough to inflict about 2000 casualties on the 34,000 troops who landed there on D-day.

Here is a brief description of the defenses. The first was the beach itself, which slopes at the low gradient of one foot in 190 for most of its width above low-water mark, and increases to one in 47 as it nears high-water mark.[5] The local range of tide, 22 feet in the morning and 23 feet in the afternoon of D-day, meant that a width of at least 150 yards was bared at low water. The inshore half of this entire area had, by June 1944, been planted thick with underwater obstacles of the most formidable kind, in three rows. First, the attack force would have to encounter a row of "Element C" or "Belgian barn doors" or "gates" — steel frames 7 by 10 feet with waterproof teller mines lashed to the uprights. About 20 yards inshore of these were 8- to 10-foot-deep *chevaux de frise* consisting of sharpened wood or concrete poles angled toward the sea, with about every third one mined. The inner row of obstacles consisted of "hedgehogs" (also known as "horned scullies"), each consisting of three six-foot steel bars welded together at right angles, like a giant jackstone. These were interspersed with curved steel rails and V-shaped wooden ramps, all mined. Since 9 April, Allied reconnaissance planes had been observing the assembling of these obstacles and their emplacement with the aid of stout draft-horses.

[4] Harrison pp. 257, 319. The "defense exercise" yarn apparently originated from G–2 just before D-day.
[5] CTF 122 "Revised Gradients Omaha Beach" 24 Mar. 1944.

Concrete tetrahedra had also been built, but few had been planted by D-day. The local peasants, faced with the alternative of working here for the Germans at good wages or being deported to Germany as slave laborers, generally chose the easier horn of the dilemma.[6]

The level shelf between the seawall and the bluffs was crossed by antitank ditches and heavily mined. Clustered around each beach exit were strongpoints, and along the edge of the bluff were trench systems, machine-gun emplacements, and mobile 88-mm guns, together with many 75s. Most dangerous to the troops were gun emplacements so cunningly dug into the bluffs as to enfilade almost the entire length of beach, and protected from offshore observation and gunfire by three-foot concrete shields. According to Admiral Ramsay the failure of Allied photo interpreters to spot these emplacements in reconnaissance photos was a serious failure of Intelligence. While none of the guns that they contained were larger than 88-mm, there were believed to be 155-mm coastal batteries on Pointe du Hoc and near Port-en-Bessin, which together were capable of spraying the entire beach with high-caliber gunfire. Many 47-mm turrets stripped from French tanks had been sunk flush with the ground, and infantry mortars up to 90-mm caliber were sited in sunken concrete pits, with panoramas of their field of fire painted on their interiors.

Altogether, the Germans had provided the best imitation of hell for an invading force that American troops had encountered anywhere. Even the Japanese defenses of Iwo Jima, Tarawa and Peleliu are not to be compared with these. Moreover, the protective works

[6] Engineer Shore Battalion "Operation Report NEPTUNE" pp. 353–56. The Norman population along the coast, cut off from the rest of the world, had come to believe in German invincibility and did not relish being the victims of their country's liberation; they were naturally not pleased to have their horses and their cattle destroyed in the process, and many believed what the Germans told them, that this was another "hit and run" raid like Dieppe, which would be promptly liquidated. Those in the coastal zone seemed sullen and uncoöperative to British and American soldiers, in contrast to the people in other parts of Normandy, encountered as the armies advanced. An officer of one of the French cruisers told the writer about sending a boat ashore laden with provisions to Port-en-Bessin shortly after it had been captured by the British. His reception by a delegation of the natives was so cool that he inquired whether naval gunfire had killed many people? "Only four or five," he was told, "but your ships killed over fifty of our cows — you ought to be more careful!"

for Omaha had hardly been touched before D-day, because Allied air power had concentrated on isolating, not pounding, the beachhead. This "sealing off" of the combat area was very effective and essential for victory; but — owing to the imperative need for tactical surprise — very little had been done to bomb the immediate beach defenses and the Navy was not given time enough to do it.

2. *The Approach*

The 4th Minesweeping Flotilla (Commander John S. Cochrane RN in H.M.S. *Kellett*), having swept and marked with dan buoys 27 miles of Approach Channel No. 4, laid the last buoy eleven miles off the Omaha beach at 0008 June 6 and had the transport area swept and buoyed by 0055. It was assisted by the 31st Canadian Minesweeping Flotilla (Commander Anthony H. G. Storrs RCNR in H.M.C.S. *Caraquet*), which had swept Approach Channel No. 3. Not one mine was found.

A second British sweeper flotilla, the 104th of ten YMS, had trailed the 31st along Approach Channel No. 3, much to the exasperation of Rear Admiral Bryant in *Texas*, whose gunfire support group was treading on its heels. When the 31st peeled off to sweep the transport area, this YMS flotilla kept straight on to sweep and mark with dan buoys a channel for the western fire support area, right up to the ten-fathom line, 4000 yards off shore. They found not one mine nor received one shot from the enemy, although the sweep was completed a quarter hour after sunrise.

A similar service was later performed for the eastern fire support area by the Canadian flotilla, assisted by the 167th British. Each flotilla was escorted by two American destroyers to cover it in case shore batteries opened up. Throughout this sweep the enemy kept silent, to everyone's astonishment. Finally the British 104th Flotilla of 10 YMS, which accompanied the big transports, swept the boat lanes up to the beach and had at least one of them buoyed by 0355.

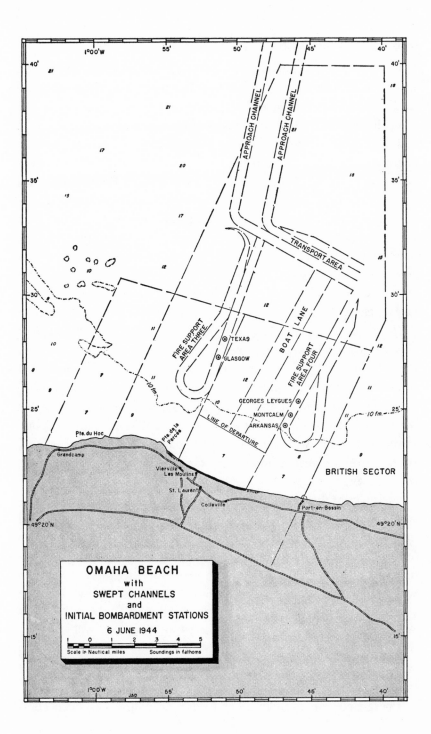

OMAHA BEACH
with
SWEPT CHANNELS
and
INITIAL BOMBARDMENT STATIONS
6 JUNE 1944

Scale in Nautical miles   Soundings in fathoms

Force "O," floating the assault elements of V Army Corps, crossed the Channel in two convoys through swept Channels 3 and 4. The bombardment group led the convoy, which was under the immediate command of Rear Admiral Hall in *Ancon*. Astern of the cruisers, in one column, steamed 16 big transports, 33 LCI, and escorting destroyers. Captain Lorenzo S. Sabin's slow convoy comprised eleven LST towing Rhino ferries, 161 LCT and a large assortment of small craft. After vicissitudes which we have already described, it arrived at the designated point off the transport area almost on time. There, it had to await the arrival of the big-ship convoy which had been practically chewing the fantails off the sweepers. While Sabin waited for the big fellows to execute a left turn and cross his bows en route to their anchorages, his own convoy piled up in confusion astern. Captain William D. Wright in *LCH–86*, in complete darkness, pulled out of the confused mass such craft as were urgently needed in the assault, and sent them to their stations. LCTs carrying DD and other tanks, LCT and LCM with demolition units on board dodged among *Ancon, Chase, Empire Anvil* and other slow-moving transports, scaring the daylights out of their deck officers; but there was no collision. Captain Sabin, in the meantime, was rounding up the laggards — some of whom, for want of properly compensated compasses, had completely lost their bearings.

Fortunately the fire support ships had got in ahead of this confusion. Arriving in the transport area around 0220, they had divided into western and eastern groups. Heavy cruiser H.M.S. *Glasgow* led the column to the western fire support area, followed by Admiral Bryant's flagship *Texas*. The procession to the eastern area was led by *Arkansas*, oldest battleship in the Navy, who in her youth had served with *Texas* as part of Admiral Rodman's famous 6th Battle Squadron in the Grand Fleet. She was followed by French light cruiser *Montcalm*, flagship of Contre-Amiral Jaujard; and by *Georges Leygues*, known to American signalmen as "George's Legs."

These two cruisers, like other French warships, had been completely overhauled and modernized in American naval shipyards. Since they had had few replacements in three years, the sailors knew their ships thoroughly, and were prepared to give a good account of themselves. "You may well imagine," Admiral Jaujard told this writer after the war, "what emotion was aroused when we were ordered to bombard our home land! But it was part of the price we had to pay for defeat in 1940." Through long association with the United States Navy the French officers were familiar with American signals and communications. And "to be under Admiral Bryant," said the French admiral, "was a blessing for us; for he was ever mindful of us, and kept us *au courant* with his wishes."

In addition to the cruisers and battleships, eight United States destroyers and three British of the "Hunt" class ranged along a line extending from near Pointe du Hoc almost to Port-en-Bessin.

The 16 transports, starting with *Ancon* at 0251, anchored in their designated area in two lines parallel to the beach, eleven miles off shore. The distance — chosen largely to keep the transports out of range of the Pointe du Hoc guns — turned out to be a big mistake. That roadstead, even more than the one off Utah, was exposed to the elements. The northwest wind had over eighty miles of Channel in which to raise a nasty chop, which made it difficult for all small craft, and impossible for some, to make the long run to the beach. Waves were three to four feet and some even six feet high, right in the transport area.[7] And there were no big guns on Pointe du Hoc after all!

Transports *Chase*, *Henrico* and *Empire Anvil* rail-loaded their landing craft. *Jefferson* rail-loaded some but not all. *Empire Javelin* used "helter-skelters," a sort of canvas fire-escape chute, down which the troops shot into waiting landing craft with a loud thud.

By 0430 assault landing craft were on the way to the beach, and those for later waves were circling. Everyone, without exception, was wet; many were seasick, and most were unhappy. One very

[7] Report of Lt. D. W. Pritchard in *Ancon*; and that of 1st Lt. Charles C. Bates USA, who was at London headquarters correlating all weather reports.

green-faced GI in an LCVP about to beach was heard to mutter, "That s.o.b. Higgins — he hasn't got nothing to be proud of, inventing this boat!"

So far there had been no enemy reaction; not one ship had been fired upon. It was too quiet to be healthy!

3. *Break of Day*

Let us take an imaginary bird's-eye view of the ocean off Omaha at 0426 June 6, with an hour and a half to go before sunrise. On both edges of a rectangle four miles by ten, parallel to the beach and extending eleven miles off shore, minesweepers are heading back to sea, relieved that their mission has been accomplished without loss. The battleships and cruisers in columns, "Arky" in the van, are moving into their gunfire support areas, 5000 to 10,000 yards off the beach. Eight miles inshore of the transports, a line of subchasers is supposed to be stationed, but not more than half of them are there; and, a mile farther in, PCs are waiting to act as primary control vessels. Columns of LCT carrying tanks are approaching the subchaser line. Astern of them, other LCT and LCG are plowing along. At the edge of the transport rectangle about 50 landing craft are circling, ready for the word to go. At 0430 it comes; the circles straighten out into five columns, each heading for its designated beach. Big LCMs carrying the demolition teams are killing time until their hour, 0455, to start. Later waves are being loaded into boats alongside the transports; many LCT and LCI are marking time nearby.

Had you been in a helicopter when day broke, around 0515, you would have seen something very different from the neat diagrams in operation plans which show all boats steaming along their prescribed lanes and hitting precisely at H-hour, 0630. You would have assumed that something was going wrong, and you would have been right.

*   *   *

Now let us shift attention to the bombardment ships closer inshore. First enemy gun, from a light battery near Port-en-Bessin, opened up on *Arkansas* at 0530, about as early as a ship could be seen from the shore that day. Five minutes later, other batteries on the east flank fired on the destroyers. As air spot had arrived, the "cans" replied promptly. *Arkansas* followed and by 0552 these batteries had been silenced, temporarily.

In the meantime, at 0550, the scheduled pre-landing bombardment of assigned targets had started. *Texas* directed her 14-inch guns to Pointe du Hoc. While her spotter plane circled overhead, the old battlewagon dug huge craters in the cape and tumbled great chunks of cliff into the sea. But the Pointe du Hoc battery, regarded by Intelligence as the "most dangerous battery in France," was silent — for a very good reason.

There were other cliff strongpoints on both sides of Pointe du Hoc. Destroyer *Satterlee* pitched in on the machine guns and pillboxes on the western flank, while H.M.S. *Talybont* fired on the radar station near Pointe de la Percée and on machine guns between it and Pointe du Hoc.

On the 120-foot cliff at Pointe de la Percée, overlooking the western end of the Omaha beaches, were several enemy strongpoints and machine-gun nests. Destroyer *Thompson*, lying 2200 yards off shore, fired 163 rounds before and after H-hour and extracted a large part of the sting from the batteries in that vicinity.

From the western end of Omaha, an exit road led up a ravine to Vierville. Strongpoints on both sides of the road, and an antitank wall, were assigned to *Texas*. The volume and accuracy of naval fire would largely determine how tough a time the 1st Battalion 116th Regiment would have to secure this exit after H-hour. At 0550, *Texas* began to work over enemy positions on the western side of the road with her secondary battery, which shortly was aided by the 4.7-inch guns of *LCG–424*. Destroyer *McCook* shot at pillboxes and antitank guns on the other side of the road. *Texas* fired 190 rounds, and both *PC–568* and *LCT–464* joined in; but the

volume here and elsewhere was not enough to attain the desired results, because not enough time was allowed for the bombardment
— the Army did not wish it to start before daylight.

The next exit road, about 2000 yards east of the Vierville one,
led to Saint-Laurent. The 2nd Battalion 116th RCT was to land
here, where there was a small beach resort called Les Moulins. The
bluff between the Vierville road and Les Moulins was lightly defended, and did not require much attention. Destroyer *Carmick*
spread 250 rounds over the machine-gun pits and pillboxes on the
edge of the bluff; and *LCT–423*, just before H-hour, loosed 1000
rockets at Hamel-au-Prêtre, a string of villas, some of which were
strongpoints, midway between the two exits. *PC–567* peppered a
pillbox behind the seawall with 3-inch shells, and two tanks in
LCT–2050 added 300 rounds.

Les Moulins received the compliment of the heaviest pre-landing
fire in the Omaha area, because it was supposed to be the site of a
formidable strongpoint. *Arkansas*, after counter-battery fire on the
German guns on the eastern flank, at 0552 shifted her fire to Les
Moulins. In this, her first performance against an enemy, the "old
gal" neutralized a radar station, a machine-gun position and a fortified house. H.M.S. *Glasgow*, at the same time, expended 219 rounds
on the bluff above Les Moulins.

From the eastern half of Omaha, two additional roads led inland to Saint-Laurent and Colleville. These exits also were well defended, and Admiral Hall had planned heavy bombardments for
both. French light cruiser *Georges Leygues* and H.M.S. *Tanatside*
covered the bluffs where the military cemetery is now located, with
6- and 4-inch shells respectively, while *LCG–811* and *PC–553* fired
at pillboxes. During the last few minutes before H-hour, tanks fired
from the "armored" LCTs in which they were carried, and *LCT
(R)–447* fired a thousand rockets over their heads onto the bluff
that dominated this sector.

The fourth (easternmost) exit road led inland to Colleville from
Fox Green beach; this was the landing sector for the 3rd Battalion
16th Regiment. Fox Green curves seaward, and the German guns

there raked the entire area. Several of 75-mm caliber were in casemates, and the hillside was studded with pillboxes and machine-gun pits. Four destroyers, the 5-inch battery of *Arkansas*, and a number of craft were to fire on Fox Green before H-hour in order to open the easterly exit and quench the raking fire from the enemy guns.

Destroyer *Doyle* laid 300 rounds on the easternmost strongpoint of this group. Her target was wreathed in smoke, but her skipper, taking no chance of letting the Germans get away with anything, continued "blind" firing until H-hour. *Emmons, Harding* and *Baldwin* had to avoid the line of fire of other vessels and cope with a heavy smoke pall. *Emmons* fired 258 rounds, 65 of them hand-loaded after a casualty to one mount. *Arkansas*, preoccupied with a battery two miles inside the British zone that had been assigned to her, did not shoot on Fox Green. *LCG–687* fired 220 rounds on the eastern flank, while three specially equipped LCT loosed nearly 3000 rockets on the beach and nearby strongpoints between 0623 and 0632. And several tanks fired on beach pillboxes as LCTs brought them in to a landing. But there was simply not time between daylight and 0625 for strongly defended Fox Green beach to receive the naval gunfire it deserved. And the thick pall of dust and smoke that obscured all targets from view by air and sea, made it difficult to remedy this state of affairs after the landings had begun.

East of Fox Green, the bluff that lies behind the beach gives way to a sheer cliff rising 150 feet from the water's edge. The Germans had no need for defenses here. But at the village of Sainte-Honorine, where the highway skirts the cliff, there were a number of machine guns, and possibly a few of medium caliber. *Montcalm* and *Doyle* fired several precautionary rounds after the Germans in that vicinity opened fire at 0530. H.M.S. *Melbreak* then began a steady fire on this erstwhile quiet hamlet that lasted well past H-hour, while *Montcalm*, after firing for ten minutes on Port-en-Bessin, shifted to six specific targets behind the western end of the beach. The enemy guns at none of those places covered the beaches; the naval bombardment was intended primarily to freeze the German garrisons and prevent them from reinforcing the beach.

German counterfire was neither severe nor dangerous. *Satterlee, McCook, Carmick* and *Baldwin* were shot at, and so was Captain Sabin's *LCT–520,* but no Allied ship was hit. Up to H-hour, not a single ship of Force "O" had been damaged by enemy action. Mines, too, were mercifully absent off Omaha; all losses of small craft were due to swamping in the heavy sea.

At 0600, ten minutes after the scheduled naval bombardment had begun, 480 B–24s of the VIII United States Army Air Force were to sweep in from the Channel and drop 1285 tons of bombs on 13 German targets, including all major strongpoints on the Omaha beach. H-hour passed, but not one bomb fell on Omaha, for a very good reason. The night before, VIII Air Force headquarters had anticipated a low cloud ceiling on the 6th. This meant that the B–24s would have to bomb blind through an overcast. To avoid the possibility of hitting landing craft approaching the beach, bombardiers were ordered to delay their drops 30 seconds. The result was that all bombs fell inland, up to three miles, destroying only crops and cattle. Soldiers and sailors alike watched the beach in amazement as H-hour drew near and they saw no bombs exploding. No one at Air Force headquarters had thought to tell them what to expect.

In the last minutes before H-hour, 0630, the naval bombardment reached its peak. Shells crashed on strongpoints, nearly 10,000 rockets whistled in flaming arcs, tank and machine-gun fire cracked at beach pillboxes. As this uproar died down, a new and ominous noise was heard. From Pointe de la Percée to Port-en-Bessin, German automatic weapons and artillery began belching fire on landing craft at the water's edge.

From the 35-minute naval bombardment too much had been expected. It was no failure; on the contrary, naval gunfire probably reduced enemy resistance by half to three quarters; but it could not reach the targets protected from the sea, nor hit targets not spotted beforehand. No more ships could have been used — there was too much crowding as it was — and, under the hazy and smoky conditions, the shooting was excellent. In retrospect: H-hour at Omaha should either have been set for around 0400, as Admiral Hall wanted, in order to give the underwater demolition teams time to clear the obstacles, or postponed to 0730 to give naval gunfire more time to play on beach defenses. As in most operations, the plan was a compromise between the ideal and the possible.

4. *The Rangers at Pointe du Hoc* [8]

An appropriate subtitle for this section might be "The Battery That Wasn't There." For the enemy battery on Pointe du Hoc — the threat of which had caused the transport areas for the American beaches to be located so far off shore, and the capture of which took as much ingenuity and courage as anything that happened on D-day, turned out to be temporarily absent. Nevertheless, the very gallant action that took place became in the end a real contribution to victory.

Pointe du Hoc is a blunt, triangular cape rising a sheer 117 feet from a narrow rocky shore about three and a half miles west of the nearest Omaha landing beach, and two miles east of Grandcamp. Its name — old French for "jib" — is derived from a conspicuous knife-edged outcrop.[9] The Germans had mounted there a six-gun 155-mm coast defense battery with concrete observation and range-finding stations, and two of the guns were casemated. This battery, with an estimated range of 25,000 yards, dominated both sets of American beaches. None of the planners believed that the American

[8] CTF 124 (Rear Adm. Hall) and CTG 124.9 (Rear Adm. Bryant), Action Reports; and those of ships participating. A detailed account of this action, by Col. Charles H. Taylor, is in *Small Unit Actions* (1946) in the American Forces in Action series. Lt. George M. Elsey USNR obtained more details by personal inspection of the terrain on 10 June 1944, and by conversations with survivors, with Rear Adm. Bryant and other officers. W. C. Heinz in *Collier's* (11 June 1954) tells of a visit by Col. Rudder to this Point ten years later.

[9] It is consistently misspelled "Hoe" in most of the Action Reports and even in books.

landings could succeed unless Pointe du Hoc was neutralized or captured.

The VIII and IX Army Air Force Bomber commands had raided it thrice since 14 April, battleship *Texas* dropped some 250 fourteen-inch shells on it before H-hour on D-day, and *Satterlee* and H.M.S. *Talybont* joined in the final shoot, which terminated at 0645. But neither Admiral Kirk nor General Bradley dared to assume that these attentions would knock out the battery; and they were right. So an early assault was planned. The Pointe du Hoc mission, which General Bradley considered the toughest ever handed to soldiers under his command, was given to 200 men of the 2nd Ranger Battalion United States Army, under Lieutenant Colonel James E. Rudder USA. Their task was to land on a rough shingle beach covered by several machine-gun positions, then to scale an almost perpendicular cliff as high as a ten-story building, and capture the battery. When the initial plan reached Admiral Hall's headquarters, his Intelligence officer snorted: "It can't be done. Three old women with brooms could keep the Rangers from climbing that cliff."

Yet — done it was. Under Colonel Rudder's supervision, six LCAs were fitted each with six rocket launchers. The first pair of rockets trailed ordinary three-quarter-inch lines; the second had similar lines fitted with toggles for hand grips, and the third pair trailed rope ladders. Each line or ladder was fitted with grapnels to catch fast in the earth over the cliff edge. The LCAs also carried lightweight sectional ladders, which could be assembled quickly into a 112-foot length; and they were accompanied by four dukws fitted with 100-foot extension ladders borrowed from the London Fire Department. All these gimmicks had been tested on a cliff near Swanage in England, and found workable. Destroyer *Satterlee*, attached to this tough outfit to furnish fire support, trained with them; and a shore fire control party, commanded by Lieutenant P. C. Johnson USNR, was assigned to climb the cliff with them. The Rangers were full of confidence that they could swarm up Pointe du Hoc and take the big guns before "Jerry" woke up.

The Rangers crossed the Channel in H.M.S. *Amsterdam* and *Ben My Chree*, from which they were to land in 12 British LCA. U.S.S. *LCT–46* carried the four dukws. Two small British support craft, *LCS–91* and *LCS–102*, and the British Fairmile *ML–304* acted as escorts to the beach. En route from the transport area, the LCAs shipped so much water that the Rangers had to bail with their helmets, and one troop-carrying boat foundered. All her passengers and crew were rescued, but one LCA carrying supplies went down with all hands.

The C.O. of the guiding Fairmile mistook Pointe de la Percée for Pointe du Hoc. Fortunately, when the boats were just short of Percée, Colonel Rudder (in *LCS–102*) asserted himself and, true to the promise of his nautical name, changed course for the Hoc and ordered all boats to follow him. But the initial mistake now forced them to buck both wind and a strong tide-rip, the Raz de la Percée, close to the cliffs and under German machine-gun fire. H.M.S. *Talybont* came to their rescue until relieved by *Satterlee* at 0700; but one dukw was hit and fell out, and the two support craft could make little headway against the current. *LCS–91* flooded forward; her stern rose so that her propellers churned the air, and at that juncture she was holed by machine-gun fire. Some of her crew were washed overboard; but her skipper, Lieutenant N. E. Fraser RNVR, replied with his 0.5-inch Vickers and managed to recover the swimmers. This game little vessel had to be abandoned and sunk.

The 35-minute delay occasioned by the mistaken course gave the Germans that much time after naval gunfire was lifted to get ready; but they failed to profit by it. Men on *Satterlee's* deck, as she closed Pointe du Hoc, could plainly see men preparing to "repel boarders" at the cliff edge. She dispersed them by gunfire, and also silenced a small gun on the cliff that was firing at her.

All boats grounded about 0708 in full daylight on a steep, rocky beach under the eastern face of the cliff. The few Germans on top who had withstood *Satterlee's* shots tossed down hand grenades and fired with small arms, wounding 15 men as they were crossing the 30-yard strip of shingle between the water's edge and the foot of the cliff. *ML–304,* eager to atone for her earlier mistake, closed range to 700 yards and fired vigorously at the edge of the cliff. This, coupled with *Satterlee's* fire, kept the Germans from being too obnoxious.

The shingle beach was too steep for dukws, so they were unable to hoist their firemen's ladders; but the LCA rockets actually worked. All but two boats managed to hook at least one line on the cliff edge, the extension ladders were put together in a jiffy, and, within half an hour of landing, 150 Rangers were climbing over the top. The "three old women with brooms" failed to materialize.

In small squads the Rangers fanned out promptly over the Point. There they made the astounding discovery that the only guns present were wooden dummies made of telephone poles! The Germans had removed their pieces to the rear some time before D-day, intending to replace them as soon as casemates were completed for all six. But the gunners were still there, underground, where they had excavated a number of chambers with connecting tunnels that neither planes nor naval bombardment could reach.

Now Rudder's Rangers were isolated. Reinforcements to the number of several hundred men under Colonel Max Schneider had been standing by; but, since nobody radioed the situation to him, the Colonel assumed that Rudder's mission had failed and, following his orders for that eventuality, landed his men on the western-most Omaha beach.

Rangers were plenty busy atop the Point. Germans kept popping out of craters, and from tunnels connecting the former gun emplacements, to shoot at them. While some of the Rangers engaged in mopping up these nuisances — a process not completed until next day — others pressed through to the Grandcamp–Vierville road, where, at about 0830, they set up a roadblock and defense perimeter. One of their patrols discovered four of the six 155-mm guns that had been removed from the Point — sited in a field to cover the Utah beaches, well camouflaged, and with heaps of ammunition on hand. The Rangers spiked them with thermite grenades and so accomplished their mission after all.

Throughout the day *Satterlee, Barton* and *Thompson* gave the Rangers fire support. But at 2100, Rudder was still in a critical situation, with one third of his men killed or wounded, and ammunition running low. The last of three German counterattacks launched against his perimeter that night broke through, and he had to withdraw to the Point. Next day, 7 June, the Colonel had fewer than a hundred men left who were fit to fight, and very little food. *Thompson,* which had been firing on call from the Rangers since daybreak, was relieved by *Harding* at 0606. A whaleboat sent in to evacuate casualties was so damaged by grounding on the rocky beach in a heavy sea and current that it was unable to retract. Around noon, Admiral Hall sent reinforcements in landing craft, and Admiral Bryant contributed both food and ammunition from *Texas* to keep the Rangers fighting.

The worst was now over. On 8 June they were relieved by the 1st Battalion 116th RCT, which approached by land, supported by destroyers as they advanced. And at 1130 that day the Stars and Stripes went up on Pointe du Hoc.

This gallant action, in which the Navy was proud to assist a group of superb fighting men, was out on the western flank of Omaha. We shall now take up the principal actions within that sector.

CHAPTER VIII

Landings at Omaha[1]

6 June 1944

1. *Bloody Morning*

LANDING PLAN and troop deployment plan were tailored to
fit the special conditions that were believed to exist at Omaha.
The initial landing force was a composite division, under Major
General Clarence R. Huebner USA, commanding general of the 1st.
Its main components were as follows: —

Force "O," Rear Admiral Hall and Major General Huebner.[2]

Assault Group O–2, Captain W. O. Bailey. To land 116th RCT
29th Division (Colonel Charles D. W. Canham USA) at 0630, between Vierville and Les Moulins on Beaches Dog Green, White
and Red, and Easy Green, covering the two western exits.

Assault Group O–1, Captain E. H. Fritzsche USCG. To land 16th
RCT 1st Division (Colonel George A. Taylor USA) at H-hour, on
Beaches Easy Red and Fox Green, covering the three eastern exits
to Saint-Laurent, Colleville and Cabourg.

*Divisional Headquarters, Engineer Special Brigade and Naval
Beach Battalions.* To begin landing at 0700.

115 RCT 29th Division. To remain afloat as V Corps reserve
until called.

18th RCT 1st Division. To follow the assault waves.

[1] *Omaha Beachhead* contains more details than does Harrison, but the latter
incorporates fresh material. Principal Action Reports are those of Admiral Ramsay,
Rear Adm. Kirk and Rear Adm. Hall; Cdr. Francis D. Fane USNR *The Naked
Warriors* (1956) contains some of the most vivid firsthand accounts of the landing.
[2] Force "B," arriving off the beachhead in three convoys at 1530 and 1630
June 6, and 0600 June 7, consisted of remaining elements of 1st and 29th Divisions,
V Corps First U.S. Army, 26,000 troops (Maj. Gen. C. H. Gerhardt USA).

Each regimental front in the assault was about 3000 yards long. Four battalions (eight companies) were to land abreast. Each infantry company — every boat team, in fact — had a definite point assigned where it was supposed to land, after which it would proceed through a beach exit to a designated assembly area in the rear. This scheme was a little too neat. Its success depended on every boat's beaching within 50 yards of the right spot, and on there being not-too-stout defenses on the roads leading to the assembly areas. The first was too much to expect of landing-craft sailors who had eleven miles of rough water to cover before hitting the beach. They had control vessels to guide them, but these were little better than the blind leading the blind.

H-hour was set for 0630, one hour after low water. The leading boat wave, carrying the eight assault battalions, was due to touch down at 0631. Two minutes later, 14 underwater demolition teams would land to blow lanes through the obstacles, so that the flood tide would enable landing craft to beach. In order to afford each UDT half an hour to work at its vital job without interference, the second troop wave was not scheduled to land until 0700. Thereafter, boat waves were timed for every ten minutes until 0930.

The line of departure, where the boat waves assembled and circled until they got the word to go in, lay about 18,000 yards inshore from the transports and 4000 yards off the beach. It was marked by a line of patrol craft (PC) which anchored very nearly in the planned positions. A mile seaward of them was stationed a line of 110-foot subchasers (SC), as secondary control vessels to keep the boats in order. These, however, proved to be a weak link in the chain. The SC and PC were the "little lost sheep" of American Naval Forces Europe, with no type commander or squadron organization. They had been too busy escorting beaching craft from Belfast, Liverpool and the Clyde to the Channel ports to take part in the big rehearsal, but were merely informed toward the last of May that they were to be control vessels. Although their mission was vital, they were given only the briefest of briefings before Operation NEPTUNE started.[3] Notwithstanding this, all PC and SC were on or near their stations at 0500, the hour set. They were not responsible for the first tragedy of the invasion, the drowning of DD tanks.

Scheduled to land five minutes in advance of the first infantry wave were the DD tanks, counted upon to render fire support as soon as the first wave of troops landed. The poor seagoing qualities of these tanks, which (as we have seen at Utah) were floated by canvas "bloomers," were well known. After Admiral Hall had discussed their employment with divisional and corps commanders, it was decided to launch them from the LCTs in which they were carried, between 6000 and 1000 yards off shore if sea conditions were favorable, but from the beach if it was too rough; the final decision to be left to the senior officer of each unit, who would be best fitted to judge.

Captain Sabin, in whose convoy these tank-laden LCTs crossed, divided them into two groups as they approached the transport area, and sent them on their way. *PC–568* escorted eight LCT under Lieutenant D. L. Rockwell USNR, which were assigned to the western, the 116th RCT half, of Omaha; *LCC–20* guided the eastern, the 16th RCT half. One of the former group strayed, but the others stretched out in a thin wavy line. Lieutenant Rockwell, upon approaching the point three miles off the beach where the tanks were supposed to go overboard, felt that the sea was far too rough for a safe launching and, after conferring by tank radio with the Army commander, obtained his agreement to beach instead of launch. In order not to ground too early, Rockwell's group milled around until the first wave of LCT, carrying standard tanks,[4] caught up, and joined forces with them two miles off shore. The two LCT waves then dashed in to the beach together, tank guns blazing away over the bow ramps. Lieutenant (jg) Phil Bucklew USNR, whose LCT was in the lead, when about a mile from shore made out through the smoke that they were heading for the wrong

[3] Information in 1956 from Cdr. Joseph W. Philippbar, who was C.O. of *SC–1361* in 1944. This applies equally well to Utah.

[4] These were LCT(A)s laden with two tanks and a tank dozer each.

Rangers at Pointe du Hoc

The Omaha beach, D-day afternoon

Omaha

U.S.S. *Arkansas* delivers gunfire support

U.S.S. *Ancon*, PC–564, and other ships, off Omaha

Omaha

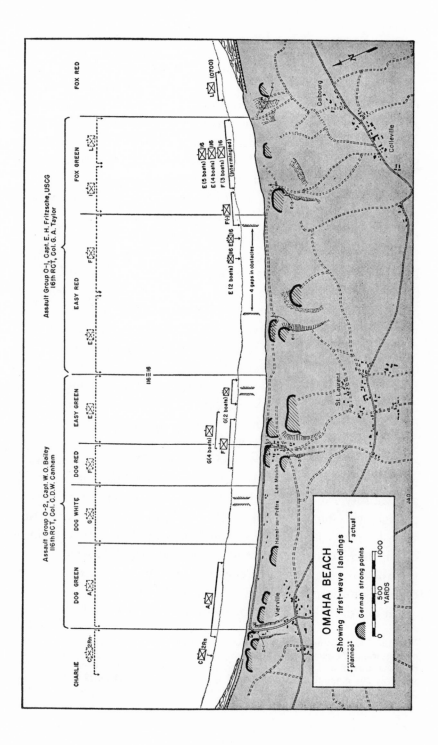

Assault Group O-2, Capt. W.O. Bailey
116th RCT, Col. C.D.W. Canham

Assault Group O-1, Capt. E.H. Fritzsche, USCG
116th RCT, Col. G.A. Taylor

CHARLIE — DOG GREEN — DOG WHITE — DOG RED — EASY GREEN — EASY RED — FOX GREEN — FOX RED

Vierville

Hamel-au-Prêtre Les Moulins

St. Laurent

Colleville

Cabourg

4 gaps in obstacles

E (2 boats)   116   116   E   116
F(+)
E (5 boats)   116
E (4 boats)   116
F (3 boats)   116
Intermingled

G(4 boats)
F   G(2 boats)

L (0700)

OMAHA BEACH

Showing first-wave landings

planned‡   ‡actual

German strong points

0   500   1000
YARDS

J.A.D.

beaches and waved the whole unit to the right ones. At precisely one minute before H-hour, 28 DD tanks began waddling up Beaches Dog White and Green, firing furiously at the enemy; and 14 standard tanks, landing at the same time on Easy Green and Dog Red, added to the din. The Germans were not slow to counterfire; two LCT were holed by shells before they could retract, and several tanks, stopped dead, burst into flames.

All this in the western sector of Omaha. The DD tanks destined for the eastern sector (Easy and Fox beaches) were far less fortunate. The Army captain in charge delayed his decision until the LCTs were 5000 yards from shore, when he gave the word to launch. Overboard went the tanks; their canvas "bloomers" began to collapse in the choppy sea, and some went straight to the bottom; others managed to reach the line of departure for Fox Green beach, where all but two foundered. It was pitiful to see them disappear one after another. Control vessel *PC–552* was busy for the next 45 minutes picking up survivors. The skipper of *LCT–600* (Ensign H. P. Sullivan USNR) showed good judgment by pulling up his ramp after the first tank went down and landing the remaining three on the beach. Thus, only five of the 32 tanks destined for the eastern sector of Omaha survived.[5]

The first wave of LCVP and British LCA carrying infantry made the long run to the beaches on a course which put the wind and sea forward of the starboard beam. That meant a wet, rough passage, with some straggling. There were six boats for each of the six color-designated Dog, Easy and Fox beaches — each carrying, on the average, one officer and 31 enlisted men. They passed the control vessels at the line of departure, two miles off shore, almost on time, and were waved on toward the beach.

All this time the fire support vessels were shooting at shore tar-

[5] Com LCT Group 35 (Lt. Rockwell) Action Report; *PC–552* Action Report; conversation of Captain Bern Anderson with General Gerow in 1948. The General then said that more DD tanks landed than he ever expected. The wind at the time was only force 3, and the sea not too bad; it is clear that DD tanks could be expected to swim only in relatively calm and protected waters.

gets over the boats. Ernest Hemingway, who was in one of them, wrote that the soldiers who had not turned gray with seasickness "were watching the *Texas* with looks of surprise and happiness." (I have seen that look, off Fedhala and at Okinawa; the men's faces lighted by the orange-colored flashes of the guns. It is one of the most gratifying things to a sailor, in an amphibious assault.) "Under their steel helmets," wrote Hemingway of the GIs, "they looked like pikemen of the Middle Ages to whose aid in battle had suddenly come some strange and unbelievable monster." [6]

What happened next is confused by the fog of war. A dense pall of smoke and dust over the beaches obscured landmarks from the wave leaders, and cleared but slightly as the boats approached. An easterly-flowing tidal current, augmented by the westerly wind, threw the LCVPs off, and some control craft which had not anchored also drifted eastward. At about 500 yards off shore, the landing craft were brought under fire from small arms, mortar, artillery and converging automatic weapons. They began to beach at 0630, but by that time the continuity and order of the first wave were lost. As the boats grounded and dropped ramps, the soldiers floundered into three or four feet of water and came under intense gunfire. They had to wade through 50 to 100 yards of water, dodging the obstacles, and then cross 200 to 300 yards of beach under fire to the protection of the concrete seawall; and on the Fox beaches there was no concrete, only the shingle seawall and short wooden piling. Many didn't make it, since with the heavy equipment on their backs a man could drown after one stumble or a wound. A large proportion of the company officers were killed or wounded. All these men were brave or they would not have been there; but some, less bold or resolute than the rest, crouched behind beach obstacles, hoping for the gunfire to lift; and that was usually fatal because they were right in the enemy's field of fire and the flood tide soon put an end to their sufferings. Those who got

[6] Hemingway "Voyage to Victory," *Collier's* 22 July 1944, p. 12; the best account yet written by a passenger in an LCVP. His boat was in the 6th wave for Beach Fox Green.

across the beach huddled under the seawall, almost leaderless. This state of affairs occurred in varying degrees along the three-mile length of the Omaha beach.[7]

Starting on the western end, Company A 1st Battalion 116th Infantry landed in six LCA from British transport *Empire Javelin* on the correct beach, Dog Green, at 0635. One boat hit a submerged obstacle 100 to 150 yards off shore and sank, losing many of her passengers. One boat from *Prince Charles*, landing a company of Rangers to the right of Company A, received four direct hits and disintegrated. Three boats managed to beach behind the protection of a broached LCT of the tank wave. Many men of this company were unable to cross the sand under a withering fire from a strongpoint on the Vierville exit, and returned to the water for such protection as they could find behind the obstacles. Estimates of casualties for the day run as high as 66 per cent.

Next eastward, Companies G, F and E from *Thomas Jefferson* were supposed to land from 18 boats on Beaches Dog White, Dog Red and Easy Green. They did land at 0634, but not on these beaches. An LCVP, with slightly higher freeboard than the British LCA, took the sea comparatively well, but something went wrong after leaving the line of departure. Company G, intended for Dog White, skipped one whole beach and landed on Easy Green, while Company F landed on the wrong side of Company G, straddling the beach exit at Les Moulins between Dog Red and Easy Green. Fortunately, grass fires kindled by the bombardment concealed this foul-up from the Germans, and the troops had a comparatively easy time making the seawall. It was lucky for Company G that it did miss Dog White, which was viciously swept by a strongpoint located in a villa of Hamel-du-Prêtre. The troops who landed opposite Les Moulins beach exit came under heavy fire and required 45 minutes to reach the shelter of the seawall. Company E, supposed to land on Easy Green, ended all strung out, a mile and

[7] *Omaha Beachhead* pp. 43–49 has full details on where each company in this first infantry assault wave landed. A vivid description of crossing the body-strewn beach under fire, and spending the morning under the seawall, is Gordon Gaskill "Bloody Beach" in *American Magazine*, Sept. 1944.

more eastward. Most of the DD and other tanks destined for this sector of Omaha got through, but the infantry assault companies were all but decimated before they could get off the beach.

Turning now to the eastern, or 16th RCT, sector of Omaha: the initial infantry assault units from *Henrico* and the British *Empire Anvil* made even more confused landings than those of the 116th. Companies E and F of the 2nd Battalion landing team were supposed to be set down on Easy Red, but only two of the twelve boats managed even to find this mile-long beach, and they hit it on the eastern edge, along with two boats carrying 116th RCT units from *Jefferson*, which should have been on Easy Green. The soldiers in these four boats were lucky, because there were no strongpoints along that part of Easy Red. But the rest of Companies E and F were landed on Fox Green, intermingled with four boatloads of Company E of the 116th from *Jefferson*, which were two miles east of where they should have been. Exit E–3 from this beach to Colleville was heavily defended, and many a GI who landed there ended up in the Saint-Laurent cemetery that now overlooks the beach. Fox Green was equally inhospitable to ten boats from *Henrico* carrying Company F and the rest of E (16th RCT), who should have been landed on Easy Red. To make matters worse, they were met by heavy fire from a 75-mm gun concealed in the exit leading to Colleville, and from a casemated 88-mm on their left flank. Many were killed or wounded in the water, and by the time the survivors managed to crawl up the beach they were shaken and exhausted. On Fox Green even the slight protection of a concrete wall was wanting; the men who reached the dry part of the beach lay "like a human carpet" along the shingle seawall above the high-water mark, sitting ducks for the two German pieces which enfiladed that part of the shore. And anyone who stuck his head over the big pebbles became a target for machine-gun and mortar fire.[8] Company E of the 116th lost its captain and 104 others on D-day, mostly in the morning. Only two officers of Com-

---

[8] Lt. Henry Watts USNR, then commanding one of the LCIs, letter of 18 July 1944 and conversation in 1956.

pany F survived,[9] and one boat lost 23 men out of 30. Survivors of
the first wave on Fox Green consisted of one lonely DD tank,
dazed by its good luck in being high and dry, a few M–4 tanks, 14
boatloads of infantry that didn't belong there, and a Navy beach
party. Those that did belong there, Companies I and L of the 3rd
Battalion 16th Infantry, were nowhere to be seen. Company L, minus two boatloads which swamped off shore, landed on Beach Fox
Red to the eastward, which was not supposed to be used at all;
Company I's boats carried it to a point off Port-en-Bessin before
discovering the error but finally landed the company on Fox Green
90 minutes late.

All along Omaha there was a disunited, confused and partly
leaderless body of infantry, without cohesion, with no artillery support, huddled under the seawall to get shelter from withering fire.
There were two long stretches of beach where nobody had landed.
Only two companies out of eight were on the beaches where they
were supposed to be. German gunners concentrated on each tank
as it came ashore and disabled or exploded many of them before
they could afford the infantry any support.

The busiest people in this phase of the assault were the 16 underwater demolition teams of seven sailors and five Army Engineers
each, who blasted boat channels through beach obstacles before
these were submerged by the rising tide. They, too, were landed
"all over the place," but quickly organized and set to work. One
team was wiped out by an enemy salvo just as it was landing.
Another had its charges all set to blow when a direct hit set them
off and killed every man but one. Before the rushing flood, rising
twelve inches every eight minutes, forced them to vacate, these
brave men had blown five big channels and three partial ones
through the hideous array of murderous obstacles.[10] Unfortu-

[9] Total strength of a company was then 180 officers and men.

[10] C.O. NCDU Force "O" (Lt. Cdr. Joseph H. Gibbons USNR) Action Report;
Cdr. Fane (*The Naked Warriors* chap. v) tells of their work in detail, and the
quick thinking and bright courage of men like Lt. (jg) Lawrence L. Heideman
USNR, and Gunner's Mates Wm. R. Freeman and R. W. Bass. One third of the
Navy members of these units were killed and their total casualties were 52 per
cent.

nately there was too little time to mark the gaps before the tide covered them. Coxswains of landing craft could not see where the gaps were until the obstacles were exposed by the afternoon ebb.

As the second wave of landing craft approached the beach at 0700, the flood tide reached the seaward line of obstacles, and an hour later it covered the entire field. This second wave met heavy and accurate gunfire from a variety of weapons, and the troops were badly sprayed with lead and steel as they struggled up the beach. Most of the landing craft were set eastward of their destinations, but neither so far as those of the first wave, nor outside the limits of their assigned beaches. Colonel Canham of the 116th RCT landed at 0730 together with Brigadier General Cota, Assistant Division Commander of the 29th. Subsequent waves landed about on schedule, at ten-minute intervals, until 1015.

Most of the waves after the 8th consisted of LCI, LCM and dukws which carried army artillery. Boats and craft destined for beaches where no gaps had been blown in the obstacles had to be waved away to others, where there were gaps; and, as a result, wave organization was broken up.[11] *LCI-91*, a veteran of Sicily and Salerno, bearing the alternate headquarters organization for the 116th RCT, was hit by artillery fire as she was beginning to worm her way among obstacles. Her skipper, Lieutenant (jg) Arend Vyn USCGR, backed her out and made another try, but was stopped by a "Belgian barn door." A shell hit her cracked deck and passed through a troop compartment, from which no man escaped alive. She burst into flames. The surviving troops, many with burning clothes, jumped into the sea, where some drowned and others were blasted by mines. A few moments later, *LCI-92* met the same fate nearby, and both craft burned for hours. Over at Fox Green, *LCI-85*, carrying a large part of the 16th RCT's medical corps, stuck on a "barn door" and was hit by a shell and set afire; her gangways were shot away, and two freak fires broke out; but the skipper, Lieutenant (jg) Coit Handley USCGR, backed her away,

[11] Deputy Commander Assault Force "O-2" (Capt. W. D. Wright) Action Report p. 3.

quenched the flames, and managed to transfer his casualties to another vessel before his ship went down.[12]

As vehicles landed, many drowned out because the water came over their engines; others were damaged by shellfire and their survivors joined the GIs under the seawall. By 0800, an hour and a half after H-hour, not a man nor a vehicle had moved off the beaches in the western sector. General Cota and Colonel Canham were busy stirring up officers and non-coms to lead their men out from under the seawall and move inland. At 0830 the Navy beachmaster for Omaha signaled all control vessels to suspend the landing of vehicles.

At length machine guns began to be set up to answer the Germans. Army Engineers blew gaps in the concertina wire. Under the initiative of company and platoon commanders, some patrols by 0830 were scaling the bluffs. Colonel George Taylor of the 16th RCT, who hit the beach at 0815, established his command post under the edge of the bluff, organized patrols and sent them inland under the nearest non-coms he could find. They found a bowl-like depression in the sand which was protected from German gunfire; into it men cautiously infiltrated, two or three at a time; and by the early afternoon they were strong enough to take nearby German strongpoints from the rear.[13] By noon, there was also an inland penetration at the western end. Strongpoints were still spattering the beaches, but by 1100 tanks were getting into action, and the press of soldiers on the beach was beginning to thin out.

Most of the artillery scheduled to land between 0800 and 0900 was boated in dukws — amphibious trucks — which were unable to cope with the choppy seas. Only five of them made the shore, and only one Army battery managed to get into action on D-day. The place of the drowned Army artillery was proudly taken by the 5-inch guns of Admiral Bryant's destroyers.

At 0830, when the beachmaster ordered that no more vehicles land, there were about 50 LCT and LCI off shore searching for

---

[12] *Omaha Beachhead* p. 56; Report of Loss of *LCI–85*.
[13] Information from Lt. Henry Watts.

A German Sketch of Beach Obstacles Lined Up on D-day

Rear Admiral Carleton F. Bryant USN

gaps in the obstacles. For two hours they searched in vain, but at 1030 the initiative of two young skippers broke the stalemate. *LCT-30* (Lieutenant [jg] Sidney W. Brinker USNR) crashed through the obstacles opposite the Fox Green exit leading to Colleville and beached, her automatic weapons blazing at a German strongpoint in an isolated villa that was holding up the troops. She managed to silence the enemy guns, but they riddled her with 88-mm and machine-gun bullets and she had to be abandoned. At the same time, *LCI-554* (Lieutenant E. B. Koehler USNR) was ramming her way through obstacles with all guns firing that would bear, and one of the infighting destroyers closed to cover her. She landed her troops and retracted with no loss, after accelerating the movement of troops off the beach.[14] Other beaching craft followed. Troops were landing almost continuously, and the exit from Fox Green to Colleville became the focal point of later operations by, and on behalf of, the 16th Regiment.

Captain M. H. Imlay USCG in *LCI-87* and Captain W. D. Wright in *LCH-86*, deputy commanders of Assault Groups O-1 and O-2, checked the progress of unloading troops from the transports and dispatching boat waves, and at about 1100 went in to the line of departure. There they found beaching and landing craft milling around between them and the beaches, their original wave organizations inextricably confused. Imlay and Wright made the sensible decision to order these craft to retire to the line of departure and there reform. As yet there were too few gaps through the obstacles and too much enemy gunfire on the beaches to permit orderly landings. Craft were sent in as space became available, mostly on the Easy and Fox beaches where opposition was less formidable than on the western half of Omaha.

Until well on in the morning, the Army commanding generals on board ship, helpless to direct events, believed that the issue was in doubt; an attitude still evident in General Bradley's *Story*. General Gerow, V Corps commander, had a colonel of his staff in a

[14] Provisional Engineer Special Brigade "Operation Report NEPTUNE"; *Omaha Beachhead* pp. 90–93.

dukw close to shore, sending him a succession of alarming reports by radio. General Huebner of the 1st Division was exceedingly worried over the outcome. But Admiral Hall, who was responsible for the entire Omaha assault, retained his customary calm and confidence. He reminded the generals that the aspect of beaches in an opposed amphibious operation always looks hopelessly confused, that company and battalion commanders were straightening things out, and that although the assault might falter, there was such power behind it that it could not fail.

A vivid description of the situation on the eastern flank (Easy Red and Fox Green) around 0930 is given by Lieutenant W. L. Wade USNR, commanding troop-laden LCI Group 28.[15] When this group arrived at the line of departure, the waters off the beach were cluttered with landing and beaching craft trying to find channels through the obstacles, or waiting to take the places of boats about to retract. "Enemy fire on the beaches was terrific — 105-mm, 88-mm, 40-mm, mortars, machine guns, mines — everything apparently," reported Lieutenant Wade. "Very few shells fell to seaward. The enemy would wait until the craft lowered their ramps and then cut loose with everything they had. Someone was lucky to get ashore with an FM set (radio-telephone) and was sending back instructions and ordering the craft in. He was doing a marvelous job. Destroyers were almost on the beach themselves, firing away at pillboxes and strongpoints. Rocket boats and gunboats did not faze the enemy in the least; they were too far underground. The soldiers, the battleships, the cruisers and the destroyers did the good work. It seems a miracle this beach was ever taken."

2. *Naval Gunfire Support* [16]

For the prelanding bombardment nine U.S. destroyers and three British of the "Hunt" class were given stations inshore of the heavy

[15] Com LCI(L) Group 28, Action Report 25 July 1944, with commendatory endorsements by Com LCI Flotilla Ten (Capt. Imlay USCG) and Rear Admiral Hall.
[16] Deputy Cdr. DD Force Support Group (Comdesdiv 36, Cdr. Wm. J. Mar-

ships and 5000 to 7000 yards off the beach. Five occupied a line from Pointe du Hoc to the western edge of the boat lanes; six made a second line, extending east of the Fox Green boat lanes to the British sector. The mission of these destroyers was to fire on designated targets before H-hour, to deliver close supporting fire on targets of opportunity during and after the landings, and to deliver call fire as requested by shore fire control parties assigned to the battalions of the assault force. *Satterlee* and H.M.S. *Talybont*, as we have already related, engaged in an isolated action at Pointe du Hoc, and the others made such an important contribution to the success of D-day at Omaha that their action must also be told in some detail.

At about 0800 individual destroyers began closing the beach to fire on targets of opportunity on their own responsibility. An hour later Captain Harry Sanders (Comdesron 18), who had done close-in fighting in the Mediterranean,[17] entered Fire Support Area No. 3 and promptly sized up the situation. Concerned over the growing number of wrecked tanks and vehicles and wounded men ashore, he ordered all destroyers to move in as close as possible to the beach to support the troops. Admiral Bryant at 0950 called all gunfire support ships over TBS: "Get on them, men! Get on them! They are raising hell with the men on the beach, and we can't have any more of that! We must stop it!"[18] Magnificently they complied, although hampered by the want of s.f.c.p.'s (which had been shot up or their radios drowned out), and by extreme care lest they hit friendly troops. In their eagerness to help they incurred the risk of running aground time and again; and several of them did scrape the bottom, but got off.

Here are some individual stories. *McCook* (Lieutenant Commander Ralph L. Ramey), from 0830 onward, fired almost contin-

---

shall) Action Report; conversations with Rear Admiral Sanders in June 1955, and with several COs in 1956; Action Reports of all destroyers.

[17] See references in Volume IX to *Woolsey*, his flagship at Salerno and Anzio.
[18] Recorded by Martin Sommers on board *McCook*, as he relates in *Sat. Eve. Post* 8 July 1944 p. 98.

uously on targets in the vicinity of the Vierville exit and on the face of the cliff toward Pointe de la Percée — gun positions, pillboxes, buildings and dug-in cliff positions. Two guns set into the cliff, which were enfilading the beaches, were taken under fire at 0933; 15 minutes later one of the emplacements was seen to fall off the cliff onto the beach and the other to blow up. By 1030 "Rebel" Ramey, as he is known in the Navy,[19] had closed almost to the three-fathom line, within 1300 yards of the beach between Vierville and Pointe de la Percée, where he spent the rest of the day firing at targets of opportunity, since his shore fire control party never got in touch with him.

At 1625, when he was firing at cliff positions, German soldiers appeared waving a white flag and trying to signal the ship by semaphore and flashing light. For the next hour, efforts were made to establish intelligible communication in German or English. After *McCook's* signalman had blinked in English that the ship was resuming fire immediately, a prompt answer — "Ceize fire!" — came from the beach. Ramey then ordered the Germans to move along and surrender. He shifted fire to a still active gun, but kept a watchful eye on the Germans until they were seen surrendering to the Rangers. *McCook* then concluded her shooting for the day, after having expended about 975 rounds.

Carmick (Commander Robert O. Beer) ranged the shore from Pointe de la Percée to Beach Fox Red, firing at targets of opportunity. Her s.f.c.p. at 0810 gave her a target well inland, but after firing one ranging salvo she was unable to raise them again. Someone in that team had left the transmitter key of its radio open and so it was unable to receive messages; but the conversation between members of the party itself was clearly audible in *Carmick*. "Their remarks were quite detailed and to the point. We could also hear the whine of enemy machine-gun bullets over their foxhole, which they were rapidly digging deeper. Their situation was certainly appreciated by the men listening to the SCR–608 receiver in C.I.C.,

[19] For his record in the Pacific see references to U.S.S. *McKean* in Volume VI 351.

but unfortunately there was nothing we could do to help them."

Carmick, ranging the beaches up to only 900 yards off shore, managed to keep visual communication of a sort with the troops. Early in the forenoon a group of tanks was seen to be in trouble near the Vierville exit. When one tank fired a single shot at a certain bluff, Commander Beer took it as a signal and blasted the same spot. On another occasion a group of soldiers appeared to be pinned down behind a house at Les Moulins. Observing a spot on the bluff at which they were shooting with their rifles, *Carmick* laid 5-inch shell on the same target; and, when she had finished, the troops moved out of their cover and advanced. She continued to fire at targets of opportunity — concentrating on the Vierville exit, where the opposition appeared to be stiffest. Early in the afternoon she was called over to the Colleville exit to assist *Frankford* (Lieutenant Commander James L. Semmes) in clearing out an emplacement that was holding up our troops. After they finished combing the right side of the ravine, the troops were seen to advance up the exit; and about half an hour later sailors in the destroyer could see a party of German prisoners being escorted to the beach. *Carmick* expended 1127 rounds during D-day.

Frankford got into the act at 0920 after throwing an antisubmarine screen around the transport area, whither she had to return at 1755, after expending 343 rounds of 5-inch shell. She patrolled and fired in shoal water up to 800 yards off the beach, often with but a few inches between her keel and the sand.

Emmons (Commander Edward B. Billingsley), for her initial bombardment, took station 3000 yards off Port-en-Bessin, on the eastern flank of Omaha. At 0537, as day was breaking, a German battery on a bluff opened fire on her and made several straddles and near misses. *Emmons* silenced that battery with 18 rounds of 5-inch, and then milled around some 1000 yards off Port-en-Bessin to cover any batteries in that vicinity that might prove troublesome.[20] At 1238 she spotted for *Arkansas's* 12-inch fire on an em-

[20] This little port was in the British sector, but no British forces were yet present.

placed gun east of that village; and, when enemy troop movements were observed, she strafed them with shellfire. At 1537 a mortar battery that had been firing on the beaches all day, concealed in a hedgerow behind Fox Green, exposed its position by smoke puffs and was promptly silenced by *Emmons* with 44 rounds. Next, Admiral Bryant sent word that Germans were spotting from the eleventh-century tower of the Colleville church; he wanted the tower knocked down without hurting the rest of the sacred edifice. That was a little too fine an order, even for *Emmons*. Her 12th shot was so near a miss as to shake the tower, and the 13th clipped it off obliquely a few yards above the arch of the west portal; part of the tower fell in the churchyard and part crushed in the nave.[21] Thereafter the Army requested no more shooting at Colleville, as troops were approaching. *Emmons's* expenditures that day were 767 rounds of 5-inch.

Doyle (Commander James G. Marshall) had been taken under fire at dawn by a 75-mm battery west of Port-en-Bessin, and had silenced it before her scheduled bombardment. Thereafter she worked over batteries observed to be firing from positions west of that little seaport. At 0901 she and *Emmons* used direct fire and air bursts on a German patrol boat observed behind the breakwater in the port. At 1048 she was ordered to close the beach to support troops unable to advance inland. Taking station off Easy Red, she fired on every enemy gun observed to be shooting, and, on the request of her s.f.c.p., on German troops. *Doyle* closed the day's work with an expenditure of 558 rounds of 5-inch, after finally disposing of the German patrol boat in Port-en-Bessin.

Harding (Commander George G. Palmer) also patrolled close in, but her expenditure was only 457 rounds, as she was ordered to carry Rear Admiral Arthur B. Cooke and Major General Thomas T. Hardy, passengers from Washington in *Ancon*, close inshore to observe the fighting.

[21] As offshore estimates varied between 3 and 66 salvos for this shoot, I have taken pains to obtain local data from people who saw it fall, through Médecin en Chef Hervé Cras. Nobody was killed, and the one wounded, an aged miller hit in the foot, was promptly flown to the American hospital at Netley.

Thompson (Lieutenant Commander Albert L. Gebelin), after taking apart a German radar station west of Pointe de la Percée around 1100, moved over to Beach Easy Red and commenced firing on a villa from which gunfire appeared to be holding up troop movements. She then shifted to a rocket battery which was firing on the beach, and silenced it shortly after noon. Observing that troops were being held up at Les Moulins, she moved over there — and made things uncomfortable for the German usurpers of that small beach resort. Thirty-five minutes of fire were required to silence the intruders. At 1311 she established communication with her s.f.c.p. and was told to stand by; at 1403 she resumed firing at the Les Moulins exit. About four hours later she closed her day's work with 12 rounds on an observation-post slot on the face of Pointe de la Percée, ceasing fire when the face of the slot caved in and the post was sealed. After expending 638 rounds of 5-inch ammunition, she relieved *Satterlee* off Pointe du Hoc.

Baldwin (Lieutenant Commander Edgar S. Powell) had the distinction of being the only ship of the bombardment group to be hit by enemy gunfire on D-day. At 0820, when lying 2700 yards off shore, she was struck by two shells from a battery east of Port-en-Bessin. They exploded on impact and did only superficial damage. For the rest of the day, and until complete darkness fell at 2230, she stood by off the Easy beaches firing at targets of opportunity, getting rid of 660 rounds of 5-inch ammunition.

This destroyer action against shore batteries has been set forth at some length because their fire afforded the troops the only artillery support they had during most of D-day. They filled the breach created by the terrific loss of tanks and of dukws carrying Army guns. Captain Lorenzo Sabin's gunboats were eager to help, but could contribute little for want of direction and because targets were obscured by smoke. Shore fire control parties, which landed early in the morning, suffered many casualties and lost so much equipment that only late in the day did that system of control begin to function. This meant that the heavy ships, drawing too much water to close the beach, were not so useful as Captain Sanders's bold little "cans"; and even the destroyers had to lay off several apparently profitable targets because they did not know where our troops were. Their commanding officers, in fact, were unduly modest about the effect of their shooting. Commander W. J. Marshall in *Satterlee* reported that, owing to want of information, only about 20 per cent of the destroyers' fire support capabilities were used.

"It was most galling and depressing," he wrote, "to lie idly a few hundred yards off the beaches and watch our troops, tanks, landing boats and motor vehicles being heavily shelled and not be able to fire a shot to help them just because we had no information as to what to shoot at and were unable to detect the source of the enemy fire." [22]

Bombardment by the heavy ships, though less spectacular than that of the destroyers, helped to seal off the beachhead and prevent enemy troop movements. Battleships and cruisers had one advantage over the destroyers — air spot from Spitfires operating from English bases, as we have described for Utah — and very keen they were to find suitable targets for the naval guns. *Texas* made five shoots at inland strongpoints and batteries before noon, when Admiral Bryant brought her closer in to get in touch with the situation. Between 1223 and 1230 she put six 14-inch shells into the German strongpoints at the Vierville exit, helping to clear that troublesome ravine. On three other occasions, with air spot, she fired on enemy troops and vehicles near Longueville and Formigny, several miles inland. Her expenditure on D-day of 421 rounds of 14-inch and 254 rounds of 5-inch ammunition is good evidence of her zeal.

A Spitfire pilot gave *Arkansas* at 0800 a mobile antiaircraft battery on the Bayeux-Isigny road and reported a successful shoot. "Arky" then turned her guns on German batteries at Port-en-Bessin and between that port and Colleville, using both plane and top spot. She expended 350 rounds of 12-inch ammunition — pretty good for a thirty-year-old battleship.

[22] Comdesdiv 36 Action Report p. 7.

From water color by Lieutenant Dwight Shepler USNR

U.S.S. Emmons *Delivers Gunfire Support, D-day*

88-mm gun emplacement blasted by naval gunfire

Troops landing from *LCI–412*, afternoon of D-day

Incidents

H.M.S. *Glasgow*, after completing her scheduled fire on a villa at Les Moulins, was coached by her plane spotter onto targets south of Grandcamp-les-Bains, and expended 505 rounds of 6-inch ammunition on these and other targets. Of the two French cruisers, *Montcalm*, subsequent to her scheduled pre-H-hour shoots, fired 174 rounds of 152-mm (approximately 6-inch) shell at 10 different targets, and *Georges Leygues* did even better.[23]

Colonel S. B. Mason USA, chief of staff of the 1st Division, wrote the following letter to Rear Admiral Hall after an inspection of the German defenses at Omaha. They should, he said, have been impregnable. "But there was one element of the attack they could not parry. . . . I am now firmly convinced that our supporting naval fire got us in; that without that gunfire we positively could not have crossed the beaches."

The Omaha landing, he observed, differed from those earlier experienced by his division at Oran and Gela, "in that we were met on the beach. I looked over the destruction of German pillboxes, fortified houses and gun positions, and in all cases it was apparent that naval guns had worked on them. . . . If ever we have to do another of these jobs, we will all hope for the good fortune of being teamed with the XI Amphib, for planning and execution.

"General Huebner concurs in the above. . . ."[24]

3. *D-day Afternoon*

Now let us turn to the beaches and resume the story of the landings.

A few minutes after noon, the rest of the troop-laden LCI group that had been milling about the line of departure for more than three hours, were ordered in. It was now an hour after high water, the ebb was running so fast that it became difficult for an LCI to avoid stranding, so they discharged troops into landing craft, which

[23] From their Action Reports, examined in Paris.
[24] Col. S. B. Mason to Rear Adm. John L. Hall 8 July 1944, Adm. Hall's files.

shuttled between them and the shore. The Germans caught on to this and began to spray the transfer points with shellfire. Boats being at a premium, *LCI–490* traded a load of her troops to an LCM for an unwanted load of high explosives, to which she promptly gave the "deep six." [25]

Off shore, Admiral Kirk in *Augusta* and Admiral Hall in *Ancon* were trying to piece together a picture of the situation from the fragmentary messages received. To Admiral Hall it was apparent that opposition was stiff, that little or no progress had been made ashore, and that the entire landing schedule had been delayed. Admiral Kirk sent his gunnery officer and one of General Bradley's staff in a PT boat to observe conditions at the beaches. Their report was discouraging. General Bradley was especially concerned because Commodore Edgar's Force "B" was due to arrive with reinforcements for Omaha that afternoon. Unless conditions improved very rapidly, it would be necessary to transfer them either to Utah or to the British sector, where successful landings had been reported. Either would disrupt the Army's scheme of maneuver.

The first good news from the beach reached Admiral Hall at 1137 — Germans were coming out of their positions and giving themselves up. Three minutes later, General Gerow's observer in a dukw reported that troops, "thanks due destroyers," were moving up the west slope of the Easy Red exit toward Saint-Laurent. That village, where the Germans had converted the stone-walled farmhouses into a series of strongpoints, held out until 1600. Vierville had been captured before noon, but a strongpoint on the exit thence to the beach pinned down troops until 1300, when *Texas* and a destroyer knocked it out. At 1630 General Gerow's observer reported a general advance up the bluffs and through the exits on the eastern half of the beaches.

Conditions ashore had improved greatly by the time Commodore Edgar's follow-up Force "B" landed. It arrived off Omaha on schedule, but was ordered not to begin landing until 1630 be-

[25] Com LCI(L) Group 28 (Lt. W. L. Wade USNR) Action Report.

cause higher-priority troops and equipment were still waiting to get ashore. At 1705 Major General C. H. Gerhardt USA of the 29th Division, who was with Edgar, left destroyer escort *Maloy* to establish his command post ashore.

German artillery and automatic weapons continued to fire on the beaches during the afternoon, but with diminished intensity. Shore party engineers blew more gaps through the seawall, bridged anti-tank ditches and cleared mine fields. As the tide receded the under-water demolition teams made a fresh onslaught on the obstacles. Enemy fire still harassed them but by late afternoon five large and six small boat channels had been cleared and marked, mostly lead-ing to the exit from Easy Red toward Saint-Laurent. The engineers did not wait for the last house of that village to be captured, but "dozed" out a bypass to the Bayeux–Isigny highway. And by 2000 they had made a new road inland from the edge of Fox Red on the extreme east, making a fifth exit, and started on the one from Fox Green to Colleville. There was now a steady flow of traffic from the beach inland. Unloading never caught up to the planned schedule on D-day, but by late afternoon order was be-ing restored, and the momentum of the assault had not only been regained but was being sustained. Casualties and matériel losses of the afternoon, though still high, were much lower than in the morning.[26]

Tanks began to move inland during the afternoon and evening. Late in the day, Army artillery began to come ashore in strength, but, owing to difficulties of control and observation, only one bat-tery got into action on D-day. By dark the greater part of five reg-iments of the 1st and 29th Divisions was ashore. The troops had reached an almost continuous line, a mile to a mile-and-a-half in-land, extending from southwest of Vierville to a point east of Colleville.

The Atlantic Wall had been penetrated but troops were far short of their D-day objectives, and there were pockets of resistance still left between the beaches and the advanced line. Germans in Colle-

[26] Cdr. Force "B" (Commo. Edgar) Action Report 22 June.

ville resisted stoutly, fighting from house to house, and were not completely cleared out until next day. Nevertheless, the situation was encouraging.

Admiral Kirk, thinking over D-day ten years later, said, "Our greatest asset was the resourcefulness of the American sailor." Through all the confusion, the heavy enemy fire on the boats and the explosion of mined obstacles, the bluejackets kept their heads, found means to beach (not always on the right beach), retracted, brought in another load under fire, never flinched, never failed. Destroyer sailors risked grounding and being pounded to pieces by shore batteries to help the troops. Battleship sailors did their best to knock out strongpoints. Minecraft sailors were in there first, sweeping. UDTs, the "naked warriors," sacrificed themselves to help the others. Courage there was in plenty; but, as the Admiral said, it was the resourcefulness of young sailors, coxswains, junior boat officers, and the skippers and gunnery officers of the "cans" that made courage and training count.

Major General Huebner established his 1st Division command post ashore at 1900. Within an hour, General Gerow left *Ancon* to establish V Corps headquarters on the beach. His first message to General Bradley, on board *Augusta*, was: —

"Thank God for the United States Navy!"

Nevertheless, a good deal of petulant criticism was directed at the allegedly meager air and naval support to the troops. Why did not the planners for NEPTUNE provide several days' bombing and bombardment of German strongpoints, as later at Iwo Jima and Okinawa, instead of a scant half-hour at break of day? Why didn't bombers and naval guns pulverize the German defenses? Hadn't the Navy learned the value of its own support? Did there have to be all that carnage on the beaches?

The answer (we repeat) is that the Allies were invading a continent where the enemy had immense capabilities for reinforcement and counterattack, not a small island cut off by sea power from sources of supply. They had to have tactical surprise, which a long pre-landing bombing or bombardment would have lost; they had to establish the beachhead so firmly on D-day, and provide so powerful a follow-up, that the Germans could never wipe it out. Even a complete pulverizing of the Atlantic Wall at Omaha would have availed us nothing, if the German command had been given 24 hours' notice to move up reserves for counterattack. We had to accept the risk of heavy casualties on the beaches to prevent far heavier ones on the plateau and among the hedgerows.

The Germans were indeed surprised, but for them the Omaha sector was only part of a much bigger problem; their greatest efforts on D-day were directed against the British sector, because they regarded Caen as the key to the situation. At 0600 Seventh Army headquarters reported heavy naval gunfire all the way from Grandcamp to the Orne, but at 0645 General Dollman was still doubtful of Allied intentions; the gunfire might be a diversion to cover a main effort elsewhere. Not until 0900 did General Marcks of LXXXIV Corps report to Seventh Army that landings had been going on for two hours, with the heaviest concentration near Caen. General Kraiss, whose 352nd Division bore the brunt of the Omaha assault, expected to pin down the Americans indefinitely on the beach — since he ordered his reserve regiment to counterattack in the British sector. By 1100, in consequence of a fresh estimate, he diverted one battalion and a tank company of the reserve regiment to the Colleville sector. At 1335 he reported that as soon as the Americans in Colleville were disposed of, his corps commander might consider the Omaha assault liquidated. By evening this overconfident General Kraiss was singing a different tune: he reported that Americans had overrun his strongpoints and reached the Colleville–Asnières line. After more alarming reports had reached him, Kraiss at midnight reported to Marcks that his entire division was committed and suffering heavy losses; it might be able to hold out another day but must have reinforcement. He was told that he would have to hold on with what he had.

It was already too late. The Germans had based their tactical plans on mowing down the Allied assault on D-day, to gain time for deployment and counterattack at the crucial point. But, by the end of D-day, to quote an early communiqué of General Montgomery, "the violence, power and speed of our assault" had "carried us right over the beaches and some miles inland"; and although he added that at some points on the Omaha beaches the leading troops were "hanging on by their eyelids," [27] that was no longer true. The British and American forces had established not only three beachheads; they had the makings of a continuous bridgehead, big enough to contain their built-up maximum strength, and no possible shifting of German forces could dislodge them. It would only be a matter of time before Eisenhower's army broke out into the open country of Northern France.

[27] Quoted in W. B. Courtney "The 100 Hours," *Collier's* 12 Aug. 1944, p. 72.

CHAPTER IX

Supporting the American Beachhead[1]

7–18 June 1944

1. Events in the American Sector, 7–9 June

NAVAL PLANNERS expected the German Navy to react to the landings with everything at its disposal. Its forces that could immediately be committed amounted to only five destroyers, about ten torpedo boats, 50 to 60 E-boats, 50 to 60 minesweepers and other miscellaneous small craft. U-boats were expected to concentrate in the western approaches to the Channel, and there were midget submarines and "human torpedoes" in Le Havre and Cherbourg. Not an imposing force, to be sure, but capable of doing considerable damage.

Admiral Ramsay was responsible for the naval defense of the actual assault areas, both American and British; but the main part of the Channel, north of latitude 49°40′N (which passes through Capes Barfleur and d'Antifer), was divided among C. in C. Plymouth, C. in C. Portsmouth and Flag Officer, Dover.

South of this line, and west of the British assault area, Admiral Kirk established defense sectors. At about 1700 on D-day he set up an area screen, after most of its components had been rendering the spirited close gunfire support which we have already described. Initially it consisted of nine destroyers, three DE, nine PC and six British gunboats. They patrolled stations about 600 yards apart on the "Dixie" and "Mason" lines, one at each end of the Omaha

[1] Ramsay; the Action Reports of all flag officers and ships concerned; and the usual printed books. One of the most useful reports on this phase of the operation is Provisional Engineer Special Brigade "Operation Report NEPTUNE."

area, augmented by groups of PTs. Area screen, skillfully handled by Captain Harry Sanders in *Frankford*, was one of the important naval contributions to NEPTUNE–OVERLORD. Maintained for 28 days at almost full strength, it prevented enemy surface forces from penetrating the assault waters. The Germans left it severely alone after their E-boats had been badly mauled during their few attempts to penetrate, shortly after D-day.

Neither surface nor submarine attack was made in the American sector during the night of 6–7 June. Admiral Krancke, commanding Naval Group West at Paris, suspected by 0300 June 6 that a major landing was in progress. He ordered small craft to patrol coastal waters, and alerted the 36 U-boats of Group "Landwirt," then held in readiness in Biscay ports.[2] Several torpedo boats, ordered out of Le Havre to reconnoiter toward Grandcamp, ran into the British gunfire ships [3] and sank the Norwegian destroyer *Svenner*. Apart from this attack, Operation NEPTUNE was not threatened by a single enemy vessel for twenty-four hours.

The Luftwaffe, Goering's vaunted "Spearhead of the Anti-Invasion Forces," proved to be putty under the Allied air blanket. On D-day, his Air Fleet Three had 815 aircraft in France, Belgium and Holland, but fewer than 500 were ready to counter the Allied landings, and the long-range and torpedo bombers flew less than one hundred sorties. At about 2220 June 6 scattered attacks began against shipping in the British sector and continued along the invasion front. *Ancon* sighted three enemy planes shortly before midnight, and two were shot down.

On the seventh of June began the consolidation of the beachhead and the beginning of the massive build-up. Although the troops had scanty artillery and tank support from their own elements that day, they enjoyed ready and accurate naval gunfire support, which frustrated the enemy's attempts to counterattack.

In VII Corps sector, behind Utah beaches, General Collins de-

---

[2] See Volume X 319–25 for the fate of these U-boats.
[3] See Chapter XI.

voted his efforts that day to cleaning out pockets of resistance and to consolidation. The 4th Division extended its line about two miles to the north, where it was held up by German strongpoints at Azeville and Crisbecq. Admiral Deyo's gunfire support group had another busy day. Enemy artillery fire continued to fall upon Utah beach intermittently, and fortified positions outside the troop perimeter came to life from time to time. *Quincy*, at 0500 June 7, began a long day of bombardment on bridges over the Douve near Carentan; during the day she fired 302 rounds at these and other targets including motor transport columns and troop concentrations. When she withdrew from the fire support area at 1720, she had only 35 rounds of high-capacity ammunition left. *Tuscaloosa's* first target was taken under fire at 1536. An hour later, after she had fired on German infantry in front of the 4th Division, her s.f.c.p. reported, "Mission successful, resistance is heavy, you knocked hell out of them." At 1837 she was called upon to fire on the persistent high-caliber coastal batteries near Saint-Vaast, which at the time were popping at destroyer *Jeffers*. *Nevada* had 14 different targets, mostly batteries located by her plane spotter, during the 7th. At 1604 she broke up a troop concentration north of the 4th Division with 43 rounds of 14-inch shell; her spotter reported, "Perfect hit in the middle of four guns."

The destroyers also contributed to fire support in Utah sector. *Walke* answered numerous calls for fire on a left flank counterattack, which her s.f.c.p. reported as "fiercest in the area." *Glennon* at the hot corner of the fire support lanes west of the Saint-Marcouf islands, supported troops advancing north toward Quinéville. *Butler*, after contributing 430 rounds, was relieved by *Jeffers* at 1530, which, between 1832 and 1856, became the target of 155-mm batteries near Saint-Vaast. German salvos pursued her relentlessly despite violent maneuvers, and she had to call on *Nevada* for help. After the battlewagon had fired 34 rounds of 14-inch, her s.f.c.p. reported, "Target demolished. Waste no more ammunition on this target." [4]

[4] *Nevada* Action Report. She expended 358 rounds of 14-inch on 7 June.

In the Omaha sector on 7 June the position of V Corps greatly improved. Landing of troops and equipment was still behind schedule, the beaches were not yet fully organized, some beach obstacles were still intact, but order was emerging from the initial chaos. The 1st Division continued its attack southward and eastward. The 29th Division, on the west flank, launched a drive with the object of relieving the Rangers at Pointe du Hoc and linking with VII Corps at Utah to form a solid First Army perimeter. By the end of the day the 1st Division had cut and crossed the Bayeux–Isigny highway, but the 29th Division was short of Pointe du Hoc by about a mile.

German artillery fire continued to harass the Omaha beaches on 7 June, and gunfire support ships fired on all observed targets. As early as 0252, *Baldwin* was called upon to silence a battery near Formigny. During the day she answered several more calls. At noon, after bombarding Trévières, she spotted two German landing barges in Port-en-Bessin but was unable to hit them behind the breakwater. At 1458 she answered an emergency call on the village of Etreham, southwest of Port-en-Bessin, after which s.f.c.p. reported: "Area cleared. Thanks." *Thompson* got in several bombardments in the early morning hours before she ran out of ammunition and was relieved by *Harding*, which spent the day helping the Rangers at Pointe du Hoc. *McCook* fired at targets of opportunity and answered a few calls.

Five times *Texas* was called upon to fire on targets at Formigny and the nearby village of Trévières, which were then reported by her spotter as "laid waste"; and on a troop and vehicle column, which she dispersed. *Arkansas* had four calls, on one of which she destroyed a railway train, and tracks and overpass at La Plaise on the Caen–Cherbourg line. Her other targets were a battery southeast of Trévières and troop concentrations on the main road south of Vierville. H.M.S. *Glasgow* received 13 calls during the day to fire at enemy batteries, troop concentrations and vehicles, for a total of 423 rounds of 6-inch. French light cruiser *Montcalm* had 11 calls on 7 June and fired 309 rounds from her main

152-mm battery; *Georges Leygues* had five calls and fired 59 rounds.

General Eisenhower, making his first visit to the beachhead with Admiral Ramsay in H.M.S. *Apollo* on the afternoon of 7 June, was concerned over the wide gap between V and VII Corps from Carentan to east of Isigny, and left orders that it be closed as soon as possible. During the following night, Army commanders ashore began to worry about their ammunition supply. A large quantity of reserve ammunition had already been ordered to the Far Shore in barges whose peacetime duty had been lightering freight cars across New York Harbor. Four LCIs were ordered to tow two barges each to the beach, each barge carrying about 600 tons of explosives. It was imperative that they land at high water, 0100 June 8. Exactly at midnight the LCIs received an order to stand by, as a bombing raid by the Luftwaffe was going on, and the beach was "too hot." At 0045 came the order "Take barges in anyway, got to have the ammo." That's what they did, while bombs burst all around them. By 0200 the barges were beached and their lines cut. In one instance the Navy beachmaster signaled "Barge don't belong there — take it away! " To which *LCI–490* replied, as she hastily retracted, "It's your baby now!" [5]

The gap in the Carentan estuary between V and VII Corps might have been serious if the Germans had been able to do anything about it. Hitler, Rundstedt and Rommel still believed that a second and heavier attack would be directed toward the Pas-de-Calais. On 7 June the situation began to clarify at German headquarters. Rundstedt decided that the British sector near Caen was the vital point for the Allies, and ordered I SS Panzer Corps to counterattack there. General Dollman of the German Seventh Army, lulled by relatively small gains by his enemy in the American sector, also turned his attention to the British. Rommel in the meantime sensed the threat to Cherbourg, and on the 7th ordered forces up from Brittany toward the Cotentin Peninsula. Free-ranging Allied aircraft pounced on every troop movement that exposed itself, with

[5] Com LCI Group 28, Action Report 25 July.

the result that no German reinforcements reached the battle area before 8 June. By that time, the original defenders had been all but obliterated.

Although unloading at the Omaha beaches was still behind schedule, troops continued to pour ashore and, by the morning of 8 June, V Corps was prepared to occupy the planned beachhead line with three divisions abreast. The 29th Division drove toward Isigny and made junction with VII Corps.

Naval gunfire continued to support the troops. *Arkansas*, anchored off Port-en-Bessin, began to answer calls at 0644 June 8 from her s.f.c.p., then seven miles inland. During the day she expended 138 rounds of 12-inch, on troops, tanks, batteries and vehicles. *Texas* delivered effective fire on Isigny in the morning, and on troop concentrations approaching that town in the afternoon, expending 130 rounds of 14-inch shell. She also landed a few rounds of 5-inch on a tank concentration which was firing into our troops near Grandcamp.[6] H.M.S. *Glasgow* supported American troops advancing toward Isigny with 270 rounds, until they passed out of range. French cruisers *Montcalm* and *Georges Leygues* also contributed to the shooting on 8 June, firing 60 and 152 rounds respectively.

Destroyer *Ellyson* on 8 June supported the Rangers at Pointe du Hoc until they were relieved. At 1805 she was called upon to fire on German artillery near Rubercy, from a range of 14,200 yards. After firing 185 rounds, she heard from s.f.c.p., "Mission successful." On 9 June she contributed the final destroyer shoot of the Omaha sector at a road junction near Rubercy, range 18,100 yards.

In the Utah sector, most of the firing on 8 and 9 June was done in deep-support missions. *Nevada* between 0557 to 0940 June 8 shot at five casemated batteries and strongpoints. At 1023 she was called upon for an exceptionally juicy target, a concentration of about 90 tanks and 20 vehicles in the woods along a road half a mile west of Montebourg. She expended 70 rounds of 14-inch from 23,500

---

[6] *Texas* went to Plymouth on 9 June to replenish ammunition, but was back at Omaha on the 11th.

yards' range, and her spotting planes reported that all tanks and trucks were destroyed or damaged — none got away. By the time *Nevada* retired to Plymouth for replenishment, she had expended 926 rounds of 14-inch and 3491 rounds of 5-inch ammunition.

Tuscaloosa had a long day's work on 8 June, expending 352 rounds of 8-inch shell in response to 18 calls between 0630 and 2241. Most of these were deep-support missions at ranges upward of ten miles. After the final fire on a defended post at Montebourg, her s.f.c.p. reported, "Good shooting, raising hell in town!" On 9 June, before leaving for Plymouth to replenish, she took on eight more targets at ranges out to 23,900 yards. H.M.S. *Hawkins* and *Enterprise* also supported the advance of VII Corps. *Quincy* received eight calls on 9 June, fired 138 rounds of 8-inch, and retired to Plymouth for replenishment.

Destroyer fire on 8 and 9 June was directed at troop concentrations and at coastal batteries not yet overrun by our troops, which had an annoying habit of coming to life and lobbing shells onto the landing beaches after they had supposedly been silenced. *Jeffers* fired at three of these batteries, including a pillbox north of Saint-Martin-de-Varreville. After ten salvos had been fired a white flag was raised, *Jeffers* checked fire, and the garrison surrendered to American troops in the vicinity. *Laffey* on 8 June was called upon eleven times to help the 4th Division advance toward Montebourg; she expended 610 rounds of 5-inch in the process. The s.f.c.p. reported, "We are lying on our stomachs in a ditch under enemy fire, unable to spot.". . . Later: "Whoever was shooting at us has stopped, so you must have done all right." On 9 June *Laffey* was called upon twelve times to pound coastal strongpoints. When she reported at the end of the day that her ammunition was almost exhausted, Admiral Deyo ordered her to fire a few "farewell salvos" at two troublesome targets.

The aviation engineers assigned to Omaha were unable to get themselves and their equipment ashore until June 7. For an emergency landing strip they chose the site of the future military cemetery at Saint-Laurent-sur-Mer and by 2100 June 8 had built a

3500-foot earth runway capable of taking transport planes. This became the first operational American airfield in France.

2. *Follow-up and Unloading* [7]

Unloading at Utah proceeded in an orderly fashion, the chief distractions being an intermittent shelling of the beaches, and air raids in the small hours of the morning. No serious congestion developed, no mountain of stores piled up as had usually occurred in amphibious operations; on one occasion the beachmaster clamored for more work! Admiral Kirk, accompanied by General Bradley, arrived in the transport area in *Augusta* on 7 June, and held a conference with Admiral Moon on board *Bayfield*. During the morning the surf was too high for LSTs to be "married" to Rhino ferries for unloading, but at 1400 the weather moderated, and shortly afterwards Admiral Moon ordered all LCT and LST to close the beach and discharge. He also moved *Bayfield* to an anchorage about five miles off the beach. On the night of 7–8 June, when the Luftwaffe put on its first raid on Utah anchorage, *Bayfield* was ready with a smoke screen. *Somers* and H.M.S. *Enterprise* and *Hawkins*, which had no provision for making smoke, were near-missed; and destroyer *Meredith* (as we shall see presently) was sunk by a glide-bomb.

At 1030 June 8 a convoy of 17 Liberty ships arrived off Utah carrying the 90th Division; and by the evening of the 9th all the men with most of their equipment were ashore. Shuttle control of convoys between England and the Far Shore went into effect at 1100 June 8. By the evening of June 10, 62,550 troops, 4133 vehicles and 9986 tons of supplies had been landed on Utah beach.

Admiral Ramsay made no attempt to schedule cross-Channel convoys beyond the first four days, hoping that a rhythm would then be established to feed troops, supplies and equipment to the

[7] Admirals Hall and Moon, Commander Gunfire Support Craft (Capt. Sabin), and Provisional Engineer Special Brigade Group, Action Reports; also Leonard Ware's War Diary Force "U."

Far Shore as fast as they could be handled. This, as it turned out, was a mistake, because "Buco," the Build-up Control Organization, excellent in theory, almost broke down in practice.[8] Nevertheless, on an average day during the first month of OVERLORD, nine transport types, 20 LCI, 25 Liberty ships, 40 LST, 75 LCT and 38 British coastal freighters arrived at the assault area from England. The total figures for 7–30 June at both British and American beaches are even more impressive: 180 transport types, 570 Liberty ships, 372 LCI, 905 LST, 1442 LCT and 788 coasters. Admiral Ramsay estimated that in supplies alone the daily tonnage handled in France during this period was one third of the normal import capacity of the United Kingdom.[9]

The really brisk time off Utah was the small hours of the morning, which the Luftwaffe chose for raiding. Plenty of warning was given to the invasion fleet by radar. The Luftwaffe ritual was to have a reconnaissance plane drop a line of float lights as a guide to the bombers. As soon as the first flare was seen, patrolling PTs began to shoot them out one by one and every vessel that could make smoke did so. In a few minutes the bombers were overhead. The Army ashore and the ships afloat opened with antiaircraft fire, tracers crisscrossed the sky, burning planes plummeted into the ocean, exploding 1000-kilogram bombs sent up immense geysers. After half to three quarters of an hour the pandemonium ceased and the amphibious forces tried to grab a little sleep before unloading was resumed at daylight.

[8] Ruppenthal I 422–25, and tables on pp. 416–21.

[9] Ramsay Op. Order ON-13 and Report, Appendix 9, p. 95. No convoys from the United States were routed directly to the beaches during the first month. The following table from Ruppenthal I 457 gives the date of the arrival of U.S. Army divisions at the beaches in June:

6 June: 1st, 4th and 29th Infantry; 82nd and 101st Airborne dropped.
8 June: 2nd and 90th Infantry.
10 June: 2nd Armored.
12 June: 9th Infantry — one day ahead of schedule.
14 June: 79th Infantry.
16 June: 30th Infantry — 3 days behind schedule.
21 June: 83rd Infantry — 9 days ahead of schedule.
22 June: 3rd Armored — 5 days behind schedule.

Seven more U.S. Army divisions arrived in July; and by a curious coincidence the millionth Allied soldier to land in France did so on the 4th.

By the close of 17 June, 110,227 troops, 14,907 vehicles and 42,298 tons of supplies had been landed in the Utah sector.[10]

At Omaha, where the major facilities for First Army build-up were established, unloading problems were more difficult. On 7 June the beaches were littered with wreckage from the preceding day's heavy resistance, and German artillery and mortar fire continued intermittently all morning. Casualties and loss of equipment delayed the complete clearing of beach obstacles by the UDTs until the afternoon of 10 June. In the meantime, ships and craft were streaming cross-Channel according to plan, with troops, equipment and supplies to be discharged. On 8 June unloading fell so far behind schedule that Admiral Hall became deeply concerned.

Although the follow-up convoys were routed on schedule, the method of handling their cargoes at the beach broke down. It had been planned to send copies of each ship's manifest, embarkation roster and stowage plan by fast boat or plane to the beachhead in advance of each convoy. It had been agreed that ships arriving off the beaches would occupy pre-assigned berths. But First Army for several days insisted on unloading according to priorities fixed by itself. The two deputy assault group commanders, Captains Wright and Imlay, were supposed to direct the unloading until a port organization under a Naval Officer in Charge (N.O.I.C.) could take over. N.O.I.C. Omaha, unavoidably delayed in landing men and equipment, had to assume control before he was really ready to function, making the unloading situation worse.[11] Early on 10 June, Admiral Hall sent for his favorite trouble-shooter, Captain Lorenzo S. Sabin, and gave him oral orders to take charge ashore and "get the ships unloaded." What he observed is best told in his own words: —

The reason for the delay in unloading ships was apparent five minutes after the first conference. The Army was insisting that ships be unloaded on a priority basis when not only were manifests not available, but the names of ships in the harbor were not known. Captains Wright

[10] Force "U" War Diary p. 47.
[11] Admiral Hall Action Report pp. 13, 115.

and Imlay had the almost impossible job of going around in small boats with all available officers, finding out what ships were present and what cargo they had. This information then had to be taken to the Army, who in turn would indicate the ships they wanted unloaded. Ferry craft would have to be assigned, ships spotted off the beaches, and stevedores sent by the Army. It was a ridiculous situation. I requested the Army again and again to lift the priorities.

Captain Sabin soon had the opportunity to tell his troubles to Admiral Ramsay, who visited the beachhead 10 June. He was ordered to "empty the ships and priorities will take care of themselves." General Bradley finally came around to the same common-sense view. Within 36 hours the backlog of ships had been cleared,[12] and thereafter the rate of cargo discharge rose rapidly. Under pressure for speed, "drying out" LSTs — beaching them shortly after high tide and unloading them directly on the beach as the waters receded — was tried and found practicable.[13]

While the beach tangle was being unraveled at Omaha, the artificial harbor was being constructed.[14] On 7 June parties from Captain A. Dayton Clark's force began to survey sites for the gooseberry breakwaters and for Mulberry A and buoyed spots where the units were to be sunk. The first blockships arrived that afternoon and three were sunk in place the same day. Work was temporarily suspended and crews removed when German batteries began to straddle the immobile vessels. At Utah several blockships for the local gooseberry were emplaced under fire on the 8th, and on the same day "phœnixes" — the big concrete caissons for Mulberry A — began to arrive off Omaha. These were promptly sunk in place. The Omaha gooseberry was completed 10 June, and the Utah one next day. German gunners, mistaking these blockships for transports, fired on them from time to time.

Mulberry A, the artificial harbor for Omaha, began to function

---

[12] Capt. Sabin Action Report pp. 9, 19–20.

[13] Admiral Hall Action Report pp. 14, 116; Admiral Moon Action Report p. 34. This had been urged by the Americans in the planning stage, but was rejected by Admiral Ramsay because he feared the LSTs would break their backs.

[14] A detailed account of the placing of these artificial harbors is contained in Cdr. Alfred Stanford USNR *Force Mulberry* (1951) chaps. viii–xi.

at 1630 June 16, when an LST dropped its ramp on the first completed Lobnitz-whale runway. No fewer than 78 vehicles rolled off and ashore in 38 minutes flat. Eleven LST docked that day and the next, taking an average time of one hour and four minutes to discharge, as against ten to twelve hours "drying out" on a beach. A second whale pontoon runway was connected with its Lobnitz pier on 17 June, when the "bombardon" outer floating breakwater was also completed. Work on a third pier-runway was going well, when Boreas intervened.

The contrast between Omaha on 6 June and twelve days later was amazing. This lonely three-mile stretch of beach, where nothing bigger than a small fishing boat had ever landed, was now a major port of entry. Through 18 June it had received 197,444 troops, 27,340 vehicles and 68,799 long tons of supplies.[15] With the aid of Mulberry A, Omaha had now become the most active port in northern France, with the greatest capacity. And for the moment it was the most active port of Europe, with British Beach Gold a good second.

3. *Naval Gunfire Support, 10–18 June*

Significant gains were made ashore between 10 and 18 June. In V Corps sector, the Germans held out stubbornly at Trévières until the night of 9–10 June when their 352nd Division, now mustering but 2500 men, was withdrawn to a river three-and-a-half miles from Saint-Lô to form a new defensive line. There was little fighting in V Corps sector while the troops rested, reorganized and prepared for a new attack, which was launched on the 12th. Steady advances were made against increasing resistance as the Germans began to get up reinforcements. Limited attacks were launched on 15 June toward Saint-Lô. By 18 June, V Corps line was two-and-one-half miles north of that unfortunate town, running easterly

[15] Ruppenthal I 421.

from the Vire River. These positions were held for the next two weeks.

There were more calls in VII Corps than in V Corps sector, because the entire Cotentin Peninsula was within naval gunfire range. The troops reached Montebourg by 10 June, but the coastal strongpoints at Saint-Marcouf, Crisbecq and Quinéville, which continued to shell the beaches intermittently, held out and had to be reduced one by one by ground forces. *Nevada*, back on duty 11 June, had five calls for shoots on artillery positions near Quinéville Ridge. On 12 June she had five more calls, one of them on a group of about 40 tanks which her air spotter had seen northwest of Saint-Vaast. *Quincy*, back from Plymouth that day with a brand-new camouflage that made her look like a British battleship, on 14 June fired her final shoot on an enemy pillbox near Quinéville with the satisfying report from her s.f.c.p., "Mission successful, our troops advancing." "Tusky," too, was back off Utah. On 12 June she had three calls for fire on Quinéville, and two days later she demolished some German pillboxes at the same place, allowing the troops to advance. Destroyers promptly pounced on all coastal batteries that came to life and began to harass the beaches. Quinéville fell on 14 June and a new front line was established on the ridge behind it. *Arkansas* was active that day and the next. In the center, a drive spearheaded by the 90th Division had heavy going for a few days but made more gains westward. On 14 June, the 9th Division took over, and on the 18th reached the west coast, isolating the Cotentin Peninsula. General Collins was then ready to launch the drive for Cherbourg.

As troops moved inland, fewer targets suitable for naval gunfire were available, but the cruisers and battleships, rotating in order that some might return to England for replenishment, continued to support V Corps whenever called upon. Early on 9 June, H.M.S. *Bellona* set part of the Camembert cheese town of Isigny on fire with her shelling; and H.M.S. *Glasgow* fired on a position southwest of it later in the day. On 10–11 June there was a lull while the troops regrouped. *Arkansas* was in touch with her s.f.c.p. on 13

June, but had only one call, to fire on tanks at a position southwest of Isigny.

On 15 June Admiral Kirk placed all gunfire support ships off Omaha and Utah under Admiral Deyo's command, as a support group for both sectors. That day, *Texas*, H.M.S. *Glasgow* and *Bellona* closed out the firing in support of V Corps, now advancing beyond range. Naval gunfire support for First Army was suspended on 18 June.

It is impossible to assess accurately the contribution of naval gunfire support to the establishment of the American First Army ashore in Normandy. The Army histories scarcely mention naval gunfire after D-day, and the Navy made no attempt after the campaign to check results. But, as we have seen, naval gunfire remained an important part of the Army's support on 7 and 8 June, before its own artillery had landed in large numbers, and warships were dishing it out every day to the 15th. The heavy concentrations of fire on Trévières and Quinéville certainly helped to clear the way for our troops to occupy them; and Montmartin-en-Graignes, a troublesome German strongpoint for three days, was so thoroughly pounded by naval guns on 15 June that troops of the 30th Division were able to occupy it with only 20 casualties.[16] According to Admiral Kirk, the First Army became so enamored of naval gunfire support that he had to warn General Bradley not to overdo it; the naval guns were being worn out, and the ships would have to be used shortly in the Mediterranean. Tributes also came from the receiving end. On 16 June, a German military journal yielded the following excerpts, a translation of which was promptly relayed by Shaef to the gunfire ships:—

The fire curtain provided by the guns of the Navy so far proved to be one of the best trump cards of the Anglo-United States invasion Armies. It may be that the part played by the Fleet was more decisive than that of the air forces because its fire was better aimed and unlike the bomber formations it had not to confine itself to short bursts of fire. . . .

[16] Harrison pp. 377–78.

Fire power of warships must not be underestimated. . . . Battleships carrying 38-cm or 40-cm [14- or 15-inch] guns have a fire power which to achieve in land warfare is difficult, and only possible by an unusual concentration of very heavy batteries. . . .

Repeatedly, strong formations of warships and cruisers are used against single coastal batteries, thus bringing an extraordinarily superior fire power to bear on them. Moreover, time and again they put an umbrella of fire over the defenders at the focal points of the fighting, compared with which incessant heavy air attacks have only a modest effect.[17]

Generalfeldmarschall von Rundstedt, commenting after the war on the effect of Allied air bombing, stated: "Besides the interference of the Air Forces, the fire of your battleships was a main factor in hampering our counterattacks. This was a big surprise, both in its range and effect." [18] General Blumentritt, his chief of staff, remarked that Allied Army officers who interrogated him after the war did not seem to realize the serious effect naval gunfire had on the German defenses. Admiral Krancke noted in his war diary on 16 June 1944: "The very heavy bombardment of the rear of the German line Montebourg-Quinéville which has been carried out continuously by naval units lying off the east coast of Cotentin, and the fierce, unopposed air attacks, represent more than any forces can stand without any relief." [19] Rommel, in a review of the situation written on 10 June, said: "Our operations in Normandy are tremendously hampered, and in some places even rendered impossible, by the following factors: (*a*) The immensely powerful, at times overwhelming, superiority of the enemy air force . . . (*b*) The effect of the heavy naval guns. Up to 640 guns have been used. The effect is so immense that no operation of any kind is possible in the area commanded by this rapid-fire artillery, either by infantry or tanks." Even Hitler, in his directive of 29 June, "made it clear that he regarded the destruction of the enemy's battleships as of outstanding importance." [20]

[17] Appended to Admiral Bryant's Action Report.
[18] B. H. Liddell Hart *The German Generals Talk* (1948) p. 244.
[19] Naval Group Commander West War Diary 16 June 1944 (p. 65 of trans.).
[20] Liddell Hart ed. *The Rommel Papers* (1953) pp. 476–77, 480. The other two factors were American matériel and the employment of airborne troops.

CHAPTER X

Counterattacks by Air, Sea and Weather

8–22 June 1944

1. *Mines and Air Raids* [1]

THE LUFTWAFFE promptly flew in reinforcements from Germany and Italy, to the extent of about a thousand aircraft of all types, mostly fighters but including 45 torpedo-carrying Ju–88s. Beginning 7 June, it made one or two air raids nightly, shortly after midnight, to strafe troops on the beaches and to bomb shipping lying off shore. Some of these planes carried radio-controlled glide-bombs; others sowed mines. During the night of 7–8 June, about a hundred sorties were flown against shipping off the beaches, and on that night their one success with a glide-bomb was achieved.

Destroyer *Meredith*, patrolling three and a half miles from the Saint-Marcouf Islands, felt a violent explosion at 0152 June 8. A glide-bomb from a He–177 had hit her near the waterline. She lost all power, went dead in the water, and was prematurely abandoned at 0250. Protracted efforts to save her by Captain Albert C. Murdaugh of Desron 17, in *Jeffers*, were unavailing. *Meredith* at 1010 June 9 suddenly broke in two and went down so quickly that the tug alongside had to cut lines to get clear.[2]

The destruction of this unlucky destroyer was the most serious

---

[1] Action Reports of C.O.s and ships concerned; War Diary Naval Group Command West (Admiral Krancke) June 1944; Weichold "German Naval Defense against the Invasion of Normandy"; O.N.I. "The German Air Force and the Invasion of Normandy 1944"; Peter Scott *The Battle of the Narrow Seas*.

[2] Report of Loss of *Meredith*; Comdesron 17 and *Jeffers* Action Reports.

damage inflicted by the Luftwaffe, which flew 1683 bomber and torpedo-plane sorties against shipping during the first week of Operation NEPTUNE.[3] Early on 10 June Liberty ship *Charles Morgan* off Utah was hit aft by a bomb, and her stern settled to the bottom, but she was salvaged.

The German weapon that gave Admiral Ramsay the greatest concern, and rightly so, was the mine. And one of the most fortunate things that happened to the Allies, as we have seen, was the enemy's delay in planting the oyster or pressure mines that he had developed. Most of those that did the damage off the beaches were delayed-action magnetic or sonic mines, laid before D-day. At 0820 June 7, transport *Susan B. Anthony* exploded one of these while approaching Omaha, and went down quickly. Her troops were taken off by small craft, *LCI–496* alone embarking 434 men in 15 minutes.[4] Next day saw the loss of destroyer escort *Rich*, and a desperate struggle of destroyer *Glennon* to survive. Efforts to save the latter were of the quality that old sailors respect – the sort of story they like to hear even though it has no happy ending.

Glennon (Commander Clifford A. Johnson) was approaching her gunfire support position at 0803 June 8, about three miles northwest of the Saint-Marcouf Islands, when her stern struck a mine. A sailor standing on the fantail was tossed 40 feet into the air before he splashed into the water, both legs broken. After a quick check of the damage, Commander Johnson passed this word over the loudspeaker: "The ship will not sink; all hands remain on board, repair parties proceed with rescue and salvage work." He lowered the whaleboat to pick up men in the water, and requested assistance from Admiral Deyo. Within half an hour, minesweepers *Staff* and *Threat* were on hand. Passing a towline to one, while the other swept ahead, Commander Johnson was ready to be towed when a salvo from a German battery landed about 200 yards astern. He requested a nearby cruiser to fire on two suspected targets, which she did; but two more salvos splashed close aboard *Glennon* before

[3] Weichold p. 19.
[4] Com LCI(L) Group 28, Action Report 25 July.

the offending battery was silenced. Destroyer escort *Rich* (Lieutenant Commander E. A. Michel USNR) closed in the wake of the minesweepers, and asked *Glennon* if she needed assistance. Johnson answered, "Negative; clear area cautiously; live mines." At about 0840 *Rich* was slowly rounding *Glennon's* stern to take station ahead of the towing minesweeper when she felt a heavy explosion that tripped her circuit-breakers. Three minutes later a second explosion blew off a 50-foot section of her stern. Less than two minutes after that, a third mine exploded under the forecastle. The commanding officer, although badly injured, calmly supervised the transfer of survivors to motor torpedo boats and other small craft. The exec. of *PT–502*, which was standing by, reported: —

> With her back broken, with bodies and parts of bodies draped from her radar mast, her gun tubs and what remained of her funnel, the destroyer escort was a scene of holocaust. . . . As the vessels lay dying in the water like wounded monsters with their spawn of tiny offspring frantically trying to resuscitate them, astonishing examples of individual heroism took place. . . . As *PT–508* backed off at last from the sinking after-end of *Rich*, a lone figure bobbed by under the overhanging bow of the boat. The bow line was rapidly coiled to rescue this last living survivor, but before it could be tossed the man raised his face to the sailors on deck staring down at him, and in a firm, calm voice, said, "Never mind; I have no arms to catch it." Lieutenant Calvin R. Whorton USNR, the skipper of *PT–508*, was over the side by this time; but death was faster, for by the time he reached the man he had turned and sunk.[5]

The wreck that was *Rich* sank within 15 minutes of the first explosion; and, out of her crew of 215, twenty-seven were killed, 52 were missing, and 73 were wounded.

As the destroyer escort was going down, *Staff* reported that she could not budge *Glennon*, whose fantail was apparently firmly anchored to the bottom by her starboard propeller. The minesweeper took off most of the ship's company and proceeded to the transport area. Those remaining on board *Glennon* busied themselves lightening the stern by pumping fuel forward and jettisoning depth

[5] Queeny "The Far Shore" pp. 14–15.

From water color by Lieutenant Dwight Shepler USNR

A "phoenix" being emplaced

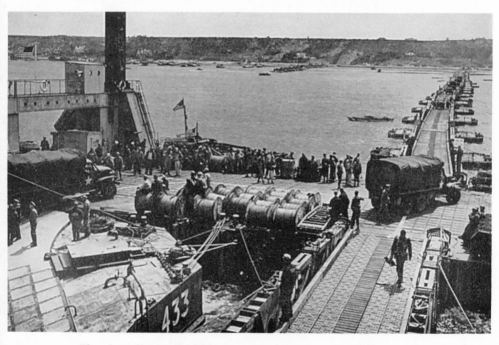

Trucks rolling off LST alongside Lobnitz pier and runway

"Mulberry A"

"Mulberry A" after the Great Storm

From water color by Lieutenant Dwight Shepler USNR

LSTs "drying out" and unloading on Omaha beach

"Mulberry A"

charges and topside gear. Tug *Kiowa*, preceded by two minesweepers which detonated two mines en route, came alongside about 1100. The sailors remaining on board *Glennon* rushed forward, "sallying ship" according to the old-time method for getting clear, but even with their assistance *Kiowa* could not move her.

June 9 was spent in planning salvage operations, assembling the necessary equipment, and placing some 60 officers and men of *Glennon's* crew back on board. On the morning of the 10th, just as Commander Johnson was about to resume efforts to save his ship, a German battery near Quinéville found her range. Its second salvo hit *Glennon* amidships and cut off all power. After a third salvo had registered, the C.O. gave the order to abandon ship, and the men were taken off in an LCM. *Glennon* stayed afloat until 2145, when she rolled over and sank. Twenty-five of her crew were lost, and 38 wounded.

Minesweepers kept busy every day. On 7 June, 30 mines were detonated near the boat lanes for Utah. Sweeper *Tide* herself became a victim of a mine near the eastern end of Cardonnet Bank. She sank while under tow. *LST-499* was badly damaged by a mine, and British netlayer *Minster* was sunk by one when escorting mulberry units to Omaha. Minecraft worked continually expanding the swept areas off the beaches and enlarging the mid-Channel shipping lanes. Up to 3 July, a total of 261 mines were swept up in the American sector and 291 in the British.

On 20 June the first pressure mine was recovered close inshore, less than two weeks after its use had been approved by Hitler. The Luftwaffe had already dropped 216 of them between 11 and 14 June, and went right on dropping them.[6] Since these mines lay on the bottom and exploded from the pressure exerted by a ship's hull passing over or near them, vessels had to slow down to four knots in shoal water. Orders to that effect were issued and the invasion fleet suffered no more pressure-mine casualties. Admiral Ramsay in his report paid tribute to the courage and tenacity of the minecraft crews: "The strain on officers and men of daily sweeping

[6] Naval Command West, War Diary June 1944, and Admiralty documents.

followed by nights on the patrol line or mine watching was undoubtedly severe, and in bad weather ships' complements must have at times been near the limits of endurance."

2. *E-Boats and Destroyers*[7]

During the night of 7–8 June five German E–boats departed Cherbourg to make torpedo attacks on the Western Naval Task Force. They claimed to have reached a point north of the Saint-Marcouf Islands at about 0130, to have fired three spreads of torpedoes at destroyers and a cruiser, and to have made three hits; but of all this the Allied Navies were completely unaware. An hour later these boats ran afoul of British MTBs of the Portsmouth command, supported by two frigates, on routine patrol off Cape Barfleur; they suffered some damage and returned to port.[8]

The following night was a busy one in the western English Channel. Admiral Krancke ordered the Cherbourg E-boats to lay mines around the Saint-Marcouf Islands, and also to raid the convoy lanes in mid-Channel. Ten E-boats departed Cherbourg at 2330. The sky was overcast, moon just past full, and wind and sea moderate from the southwest. Before long they encountered destroyers *Frankford*, *Baldwin* and *Hambleton* of Captain Sanders' area screen. The two last-named opened fire on radar contact at 0036, range 7500 yards. The E-boats promptly reversed course, turned up 30 knots, and escaped.

Admiral Krancke, however, was well pleased with that night's work, since other boats that raided the convoy lanes in mid-Channel sank two vessels, *LST–376* and *LST–314*, part of a five-ship convoy under escort of H.M.S. *Beagle*, and in waters under the

---

[7] Weichold, War Diary Naval Group Command West; Scott *The Battle of the Narrow Seas*. E-boat was an Admiralty term used by the Allied Navies for any small fast craft of the enemy. Generally an E-boat was a 105-ft. *Schnellboot*, a type similar to our PT or the British MTB, but it might be what is more properly called an R-boat (*Räumboot*), an inshore minesweeper.

[8] War Diary Naval Group Command West 8 June 1944 p. 22.

jurisdiction of C. in C. Portsmouth. *LST-314* lost half her crew.[9]

Allied aërial reconnaissance on 7 June revealed the presence in Brest of the four German destroyers which had moved up from Royan. Admiral Leatham RN, Commander in Chief Plymouth, reasoned that they would make for Cherbourg, which is exactly what Admiral Krancke had ordered. Accordingly on the night of 8–9 June he sent the 10th British Destroyer Flotilla (Commander B. Jones RN in H.M.S. *Tartar*) then patrolling 20 miles south of Lands End, to intercept. They did so, and between 0127 and 0526 there took place a confused running night action. *ZH-1*, a former Netherlands destroyer captured by the Germans, and *Z-32* were sunk. *Z-24*, heavily hit and seriously damaged, returned with the fourth destroyer to Brest.[10]

Every night the Cherbourg E-boats were ordered out to attack any vessel they encountered in the Bay of the Seine. On 11 June, fleet tug *Partridge* steamed into trouble. She and four other tugs were towing a pontoon runway, one of the heaviest mulberry components, from England to Omaha. At 0215, when about 10 miles from the Far Shore, she was torpedoed by an E-boat, and sank in less than a minute, taking down 32 officers and men, almost half her crew. The E-boats now turned to attack a nearby LST convoy. *LST-538* dodged one torpedo and was hit by another; yet she managed to make the beach, unload, and retract after making emergency repairs.[11]

The E-boats scored another success the following night, blowing the fantail off destroyer *Nelson*; she had to be towed to Portsmouth for repairs.

By 14 June the Germans had begun to block and demolish the harbor of Cherbourg, transferring their E-boats to Saint-Malo and Le Havre. Coastal forces under C. in C. Plymouth patrolled the waters between Brest and Cherbourg so thoroughly that all sea com-

[9] Admiral Hall Action Report "Summary of Battle Damage"; C.O. *LST-314* Report of Loss of Ship.
[10] War Diary Naval Command West 9 June pp. 29, 30. The British call this "The Night Action off Ile Vierge."
[11] *Partridge* and *LST-538* Action Reports.

munication between them was cut off, and Cherbourg was isolated. A supply run to Saint-Malo on the night of 22–23 June ended the German Navy's effort to interfere with the Western Naval Task Force on that flank. But it took several more cracks at our British allies off the Bay of the Seine.

3. *The Great Storm* [12]

By D plus 12 day, the flow of men and supplies over the beaches was running smoothly; and, although the planned amounts and rates had not been attained, the deficiency was more than balanced by lower combat losses and less consumption of matériel than had been expected. By the end of 18 June, 314,514 troops, 41,000 vehicles and 116,000 tons of supplies had been landed over the American beaches. Figures for the British beaches are almost identical: 314,547 troops, 54,000 vehicles and 102,000 tons of supplies.[18]

Then Nature intervened with the worst June storm in 40 years.

[12] Stanford *Force Mulberry* chaps. xii, xiii. Valuable data on this storm were collected by 1st Lt. Charles C. Bates USAAF at London headquarters, and placed at the writer's disposal in 1956; the data collected by 21st Weather Squadron IX A.A.F., recorded in Engineer Special Brigade "Operation Report NEPTUNE," is almost identical. The relevant data may best be expressed in a table: —

WEATHER CONDITIONS OFF OMAHA BEACH 19–22 JUNE

Date	Hour	Wind Direction	Wind Velocity, Knots	Wave Height, Feet	Scope of Wind, Miles
19 June	0100	NNE	13	2	90
	0700	NNE	19	6½	90
	1300	NNE	22	7	90
	1800	NE	21	?	105
20 June	0100	NE	19	7	105
	0700	NE	23	7½	105
	1300	NExN	21	8½	125
	1800	NNE	27	8	90
21 June	0100	NNE	26	?	90
	0700	NNE	25	8	90
	1300	NNE	19	?	90
	1800	NNE	17	7½	90
22 June	0100	NNE	16	8	90
	0700	NNE	15	6	90

[18] Harrison p. 423.

At midnight 18–19 June, a strong northeast wind with heavy rain began to blow on the assault beaches, which happened to be in a funnel between low and high pressure areas. During the day the wind increased to 22 knots with gusts up to 32, and the sea built up so rapidly that by midafternoon 19 June unloading had to stop.[14] This was particularly distressing to all hands, because on the 18th the western pontoon runway had just been married to its Lobnitz pier, and two streams of traffic were rolling rapidly from ship to shore. The NE to NNE wind, accompanied by very high tides, continued throughout the 20th and 21st, with a force no greater than 6 on the Beaufort scale except in gusts; but it had a scope of 90 to 125 miles from the cliffs of Dover to build up those short, steep waves that are characteristic of the English Channel. Heavy surf pounded the beaches, small craft took shelter behind the block-ships, all work stopped, the ships anchored off shore dragged their anchors and fouled one another. Many LCT, landing craft and barges were driven ashore and smashed; and, worst of all, the Omaha Mulberry A began to break up. On the 20th, a drifting United States salvage barge and five LCT banged into the center pontoon runway, which was already buckling in the swell. Captain Clark ordered all craft to keep clear, but many LCT, which had only stern anchors and insufficient fuel to ride out a gale, became unmanageable and barged in. Seabees and other sailors who were working under dangerous conditions to save the mulberry shouted, screamed, cursed and even fired small arms at the LCTs; but nothing could stop them. By the evening of the 20th all the British Fairmiles which had been used to place the pontoons had been sunk or abandoned, and only one tug was operating; but it managed to pull all derelict vessels away from the piers and the pontoon roadways. Tows of phœnix caissons for the still uncompleted breakwater now approached. Captain Clark ordered them to return to England, but the tugs could make no headway against

[14] Lt. Bates states that his forecasters gave the people on the beach 18 hours' warning, but, having no storm bill or instructions as to what to do, they went right on unloading. The Admiral Ramsay, Admiral Hall and Army Engineers' Reports agree that all weather forecasts received by them were favorable.

wind and sea and the great clumsy caissons had to be beached or scuttled. By dark on the 20th, three of the four Lobnitz piers were being precariously held by their steel legs against seas which rushed in through breaches in the breakwater. Worst of all, the 200-foot steel "bombardons" of the outer floating breakwater began to part their mooring cables and drift to leeward, battering like giant rams into the phœnix caissons. These had been planted so far out that the heavy seas broke over their tops, and in such soft sand that the rough water scoured around their bottoms; many capsized and some rolled toward the beach; 21 to 25 out of the 35 were destroyed. During the night more LCT, together with LCVP and other small craft, piled up against the pontoon runways.

All day 20 and 21 June the wind shrieked, rain fell in torrents, surf pounded and Mulberry A continued to disintegrate. The crash of beaching and landing craft, dukws, vehicles and derelict units grinding together was heard above the din of war. When the wind abated on 22 June, the Omaha beaches were a shambles of stranded and wrecked craft, coasting vessels, barges and mulberry fragments. General Bradley was "appalled by the desolation." Yet, even before the wreckage was surveyed, unloading had to be resumed, since almost nothing had been landed during those three days; it had been necessary to ration ammunition among the troops ashore. Unloading soon recovered its momentum; on 24 June, 15,525 troops, 3321 vehicles and 11,562 tons of supplies were landed over the Omaha beaches alone.[15]

Mulberry A was so thoroughly broken up that Admiral Kirk, on

[15] Ruppenthal I 416–21. The following figures are from Stanford Appendix 5: — biggest day's unloading before the storm, 15 June, 9008 tons at Omaha and 5736 at Utah. Worst day during the storm, 22 June, 494 tons at Omaha, 865 at Utah. Best June day, the 29th, 14,869 tons at Omaha and 8171 at Utah. Apparently no figures exist as to what part of the Omaha unloadings were in Mulberry A. Were the mulberries an indispensable factor in the success of NEPTUNE? Captain Harold Hickling RN, chief of staff to Rear Admiral W. O. Tennant RN, who had overall charge of their construction and assembly, is reported to have said that they were of only 15 per cent value in the landings; the official British Report to the Chiefs of Staff states that it is probable that the invasion would have been successful without them; and Admiral Hall believes that they consumed more steel and labor than they were worth. General Bedell Smith, on the other hand, strongly disagrees. "That 15 per cent," he said, "was crucial."

the advice of Admiral Hall and Commodore Sullivan, decided to make no attempt to repair it. Such pontoon units as had survived were towed to the British artificial harbor off Arromanches. "B" had been far less damaged than "A," owing to partial protection by the off-lying Calvados Rocks, and by the capes which jut out into the Channel north of Le Havre.[16] Most of the gooseberry breakwaters of sunken ships at Omaha and Utah held firm and protected several hundred landing craft from destruction during the storm.

[16] The breakwater components of the British Mulberry B were still in place in 1956, and in the adjacent Arromanches museum there is a complete model of the original. Another model, presented by Mr. Churchill to F.D.R., is in the Roosevelt Library at Hyde Park, New York.

CHAPTER XI

The British Sector[1]

6 June–8 September 1944

1. D-day on Gold, Juno, and Sword

ALTHOUGH we cannot relate the history of the Eastern Naval Task Force commanded by Rear Admiral Sir Philip Vian RN in the same detail as we did that of the Western Naval Task Force, the Eastern is a vital and essential part of the picture. Many beaching craft of the United States Navy participated in the British landings, just as British landing craft, minecraft and support ships were used in the American sector.

The British assault area extended from Port-en-Bessin, where Omaha ended, about 25 statute miles eastward to Ouistreham at the mouth of the River Orne. Although the three sectors into which it was divided were coterminous, the assault landing beaches (Gold and Juno three miles long, and Sword two miles long) were separated from one another by Calvados and other reefs which prevented access to the shore. High rocky cliffs similar to those around Pointe du Hoc extend about four miles east of Port-en-Bessin, where sandy bluffs begin again, with a gentler slope than those at Omaha, and less elevation; they rise to only about 50 feet above sea level.

This region has close historic ties with England. Caen was the favorite seat of William the Conqueror. There he and Queen Mathilda are buried in the famous monuments of Norman architec-

[1] Reports of Admirals Ramsay, Vian and Talbot, and Commodores Douglas-Pennant and Oliver; Field Marshal Montgomery *Normandy to the Baltic* (Cambridge 1948); Col. C. P. Stacey *The Canadian Army 1939–45* (Ottawa 1948); John North *Northwest Europe 1944–45* (London 1953); Brigadier John D. Slater *Commando* (London 1953); Lt. Cdr. Peter Scott *The Battle of the Narrow Seas* (1946). For the German side see Chapter III of this volume, note 1.

ture, L'Abbaye-aux-Hommes and L'Abbaye-aux-Dames, which they built. William's invasion of England in 1066 was launched from nearby Dives, which the receding sea has left high and dry. Bayeux, six miles inland from Port-en-Bessin, gives its name to the famous contemporary tapestry which depicts the Norman Conquest of England.

In comparing the British assault with the American one at Utah and Omaha, three factors must be kept in mind. First, it was a bigger assault — a three-division affair as compared with a two-division landing. Second, Caen roadstead, eastern part of the Sword sector, although outside the range of the powerful German coast defenses to Le Havre, was very close to it, and within range of other batteries between the Orne and the Seine. And Caen, from the enemy point of view, was the key to the defense of Normandy. It was here, after the initial assault, that the Germans launched their major counterattacks.

The mission of the Eastern Naval Task Force was to land and support the British Second Army, Lieutenant General Sir Miles C. Dempsey. The scheme of maneuver was as follows: —

Gold (Western) Area: Force "G," Commodore Cyril E. Douglas-Pennant RN. To land assault elements of 50th (Northumbrian) Division, Major General D. A. H. Graham.

Juno (Center) Area: Force "J," Commodore Geoffrey N. Oliver RN. To land assault elements of 3rd Canadian Division, Major General R. F. L. Keller.

Sword (Eastern) Area: Force "S," Rear Admiral Arthur G. Talbot RN. To land assault elements of 3rd British Division, Major General R. G. Rennie.

Follow-up Force "L," Rear Admiral William E. Parry RN. To land various elements on all three beaches.

The 6th Airborne Division. To be dropped northeast of Caen during the night of 5–6 June, at the same time as the American paratroops on the Cotentin Peninsula, with the mission of seizing bridges over the Orne River and the Caen Canal.

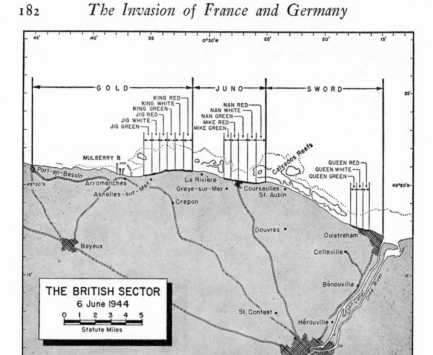

THE BRITISH SECTOR
6 June 1944
0 1 2 3 4 5
Statute Miles

A feature of the British assault was the use of seven commandos of 500 to 600 men each, one of them French in part, for special missions independent of the other troops. One brigade of four commandos was to land at Ouistreham in the Sword sector, make for the bridges over the canal and river at Bénouville, and cross to link up with airborne troops on the right bank. Other commandos were assigned to capture strongpoints in the coastal defenses, such as the heavily bunkered radar station at Douvres. One Royal Marine Commando was assigned to land at Arromanches and capture Port-en-Bessin from the rear.

After the final rehearsals Forces "G" and "J" assembled at Southampton, the Solent and Spithead; Force "S" between Portsmouth and Shoreham; Force "L" at the Nore and Harwich. The Eastern Naval Task Force, having a shorter distance to sail cross-Channel than the Western, was not so much upset by the postponement of D-day from 5 to 6 June.

All British assault convoys, like the American, made first for "Piccadilly Circus," the ten-mile circle around Point "Z." Thence they crossed through six swept channels, preceded by minesweepers. Each force reached its lowering point (as the British call a transport area) very close to the planned hour. Lowering points were located only seven to eight miles off shore, which made the landing much easier than in the American sector, although sea conditions were about the same.

Sword, easternmost assault area, provided the only instance of interference by German surface vessels with Operation NEPTUNE on D-day. When Admiral Krancke's naval command was alerted by reports of the air drop in the early hours of June 6, he ordered units of his Western Defense Force out to patrol. At 0430, torpedo boats *T–28*, *Jaguar*, and *Möwe* departed Le Havre to sweep the Bay of the Seine. An hour later they passed through a smoke screen laid by Allied aircraft to shield the approach of the Eastern Task Force from the Le Havre batteries, and found themselves within range of a number of large and tempting targets. They launched 18 torpedoes, one of which hit Norwegian destroyer *Svenner* amidships, and sank her; another narrowly missed Admiral Talbot's flagship *Largs*. The torpedo boats turned away into the smoke screen and made port with only minor damage.

Because the Calvados reefs and foul ground off the western British beaches were bare at low water it was necessary to postpone H-hour until the flood tide had been running between 60 and 90 minutes. This gift of time was well improved by the Royal Navy to bombard selected strongpoints with high-caliber shell for almost two hours by daylight — four times as long a bombardment as the U.S. Navy had time to deliver at Utah and Omaha. *Warspite* was straddled by salvos from coastal batteries guarding the mouth of the Seine, but changed station and evaded further harassment. The bombardments by this veteran of the Battle of Jutland were particularly admired; here, as in the American sector, aged battleships covered themselves with glory.

Force "G" arrived off the Gold beaches at 0530; H-hour there was set at 0725. Destroyers, LCGs and rocket craft drenched the beaches between 0545 and 0725, and the 50th Division landed on time. A coastal battery opened on Commodore Douglas-Pennant's flagship *Bulolo* at 0557 and caused her to shift her berth seaward. Because of the choppy sea, the wise decision was made to beach every LCT carrying a DD tank. Demolition units found beach obstacles more numerous than the air photographs indicated, and the tide rose so quickly that several landing craft of the initial wave were damaged. Troops landed at Gold in good order and quickly overran the immediate beach defenses, meeting slight resistance from the "static" enemy 716th Division, about one quarter of which was Polish and Ukrainian.

This did not apply to all enemy strongpoints. Those at Asnelles and La Rivière, sited to enfilade the beaches and not neutralized by the initial bombardment, soon came to life and interfered with the landings. Close support fire by destroyers and gunboats finally reduced them. The first troops to land bypassed strongpoints that did not yield promptly, leaving them to be mopped up later. The British Army had naval gunfire support parties which they called FOBs,[2] and the larger ships also used plane spot. A number of calls for fire on batteries, mortar positions, vehicles and troops, chiefly on the right flank, were answered during the day by cruisers and destroyers.

The D-day objective of the 50th Division called for the occupation of Bayeux, Port-en-Bessin, and the highway between Bayeux and Caen. Bayeux was not taken on D-day, but the Division pushed four miles inland and almost reached its objective line. Royal Marine Commando No. 47 landed at 0930 with the mission of capturing Port-en-Bessin, but as it lost all but two of its landing craft, with radio and other equipment, that port was not taken until the evening of 7 June.

Turning now to Juno, the center beach: Force "J," lifting the 3rd Canadian Division, reached its lowering point without inci-

[2] Meaning Forward Officers, Bombardment. (Compare Volume IX 165–66.) Because of difficulties in establishing communication with FOBs, there were few calls for naval gunfire support on D-day.

dent. Rough seas so delayed the beaching craft carrying the demolition teams for this force that H-hour was postponed to 0755 for
some units. The landings were preceded by a bombardment by
H.M. light cruiser *Diadem* and eleven destroyers. German guns so
sited as to enfilade the beaches were temporarily silenced but came
to life soon after the leading assault troops moved inland.

At the last minute the DD tanks for the 7th Brigade were
launched 1000 yards off shore; eight went down in the rough sea,
but the remainder beached well ahead of the infantry and gave a
good account of themselves. The first infantry waves for both brigades actually landed at 0810, but the 8th Brigade's DD tanks arrived ten minutes later. Because of these delays, the obstacle-clearance men were hampered by the rising tide and managed to blow
fewer gaps than had been planned. Fortunately the obstacles at
Juno were so widely spaced that landing craft were able to thread
their way between them. The leading assault troops moved rapidly
inland and were delayed only by fire from fortified stone houses in
the villages. They penetrated about four miles at a cost of 335
killed and 611 other casualties, and armored patrols of the 3rd Canadians reached a point on the Caen-Bayeux highway, ten miles
from the sea.[3]

In Sword, the eastern sector, Force "S" had a tricky navigational
problem, since the assigned beaches were very narrow. Adjoining
them on the east were the Merville sandflats at the mouth of the
Orne, which extended a mile out to sea; on the west the shore is
backed by low cliffs. So the 3rd Division had to land on a single-
brigade front. To insure that no mistake would be made, it was
decided to station a midget submarine 7000 yards off the beach,
to act as picket ship.

First French troops to take part in the liberation of their country
were 171 *fusiliers-marins* of Commando 4, under Lieutenant de
Vaisseau Kieffer. They were landed at 0700 from two LCIs on the
beach before Ouistreham, promptly captured that town, and made

[3] Stacey *The Canadian Army 1939–1945* pp. 176–80.

contact with the British paratroops who had dropped several hours earlier.

Although the sea off Sword was rough for DD tanks, 28 out of a total of 40 made the beach safely by 0730 and went into action promptly against guns enfilading the beaches. Within 15 minutes they had silenced most of the enemy weapons. LCTs carrying obstacle-clearance units passed between the DD tanks and beached five minutes ahead of them; and landing craft carrying the first wave of infantry made the shore at 0730. Succeeding waves beached under increasing mortar and small-arms fire, and there were some casualties from mined beach obstacles; but these were less numerous than in the other British sectors. Assault elements of the 3rd Division moved steadily inland against infantry, mortar and artillery fire. At 0930 eight Ju–88s made the only daylight air attack of D-day on the entire invasion front, bombing the Sword beaches with slight effect. Here, as in the other British landings, the initial phases were much less bloody than those at Omaha. Except for the torpedo-boat raid, the assault of Force "S" was "unbelievably unopposed," reported Admiral Talbot. A sailor of an LCT returning from launching DD tanks shouted to inbound craft, "It's a piece of cake!" Not for long, however.

General Rennie's troops turned back the only serious counterattack in the British sector on D-day. Von Rundstedt's first order to the I S.S. Panzer Corps to get into it was quickly countermanded by Hitler, who granted permission for their commitment only in the late afternoon, so sure was he of an attack on the Pas-de-Calais. But the 21st Panzer Division (Generalleutnant Feuchtinger) already had a tank regiment and division headquarters southeast of Caen and two Panzer Grenadier regiments north of that city on both sides of the Orne. The 6th Airborne Division jumped into the midst of one of them. Shortly after the seaborne landings began, General Marcks of LXXXIV Corps attached them to 716th Infantry Division. Rommel's headquarters had released 21st Panzer Division to Seventh Army at 0500, but it was not turned over to LXXXIV Corps until about 1000. In the meantime, Feuchtinger organized his remaining elements and moved northward with the intention of attacking down the east bank of the Orne. At about 1300, Marcks ordered him to shift his attack west of the Orne, but three hours elapsed before he was ready to jump off.[4] He made little progress along the river, owing to strong resistance by the 3rd Division; but farther west one German battalion managed to send some elements right down to the beach. When darkness fell, Feuchtinger dug in on the line Saint-Contest–Hérouville, linking up with the German 716th Division east of the Orne. The first counterattack had failed.

By the end of D-day the 3rd Division had reached a line about four miles inland, had secured the Orne bridges at Bénouville, and had made contact with the British 6th Airborne Division. On its western flank, the 21st Panzer Division had driven a wedge between the 3rd British and the 3rd Canadian Divisions.

The British landings were very successful, but the extent of penetration inland was disappointing. There had been hopes of entering Bayeux and Caen on D-day, and the first fell on 7 June; but Caen was to be captured only after more than a month of heavy fighting. For there, the Germans committed their principal reserves and made their bitterest stand against the invasion, to block the road to Paris.

2. *The Build-up*

Unloading fell behind schedule in all three British sectors. By the morning of 7 June there were about a hundred LST waiting off shore to beach; and, as the number of Rhino ferries which acted as causeways had been reduced by shell damage, Admiral Vian ordered the LSTs to "dry out," as was later done at Omaha. That enabled the congestion to be cleared by the end of 8 June. Damage to LCTs delayed the unloading of transports and freighters for which they acted as lighters; on 7 June only 19 of them out of 64 were operating.

[4] Harrison p. 332 and Geyr von Schweppenberg Essay p. 20.

After the initial landings there was confusion about what ship unloaded where, and when; similar to the state of things in the American sector that we have already described. The story of the skipper of an American LCI may illustrate this point. After landing American troops at Utah on the afternoon of D-day, he was sent back to the Solent, where he received orders to load British troops at one of the local hards. Having done so he awaited orders, but none came. Observing an LCI convoy making up in the Solent he decided to join it, lest his passengers run out of food while waiting. As he was passing the Isle of Wight a signal station blinked to him, "Where do you think you are going?" to which the skipper replied, "I don't know!" After an interval came the answer, "Proceed!" Upon his arrival at the Far Shore a British beachmaster told him where to land the troops, and everyone was happy. By 10 June most of the initial confusion had been cleared, and unloading proceeded smoothly, although not yet up to schedule.

A gooseberry artificial harbor for small craft was provided for each of the three British sectors. The one for Juno was incorporated into Mulberry B off Arromanches, which was still incomplete when the great storm broke. It suffered relatively little damage in comparison with Mulberry A, owing partly to a tighter construction, but mostly to the protection afforded by out-jutting capes. Mulberry B continued to serve as a harbor throughout the winter, and the core of it was still there in 1956, figuring as a harbor of refuge in the French Coast Pilot. Port-en-Bessin, captured 8 June, was being used to unload coasters on the 10th, and the tiny port of Courseulles in the Juno sector was opened for small craft on the 8th.

For over a month after D-day the Germans held both banks of the Orne down to a point five to six miles from the sea. The Sword beaches were within range of mobile German batteries located in thick woods east of the river. These guns, mostly 88-mm, followed the pattern, already familiar to our troops in Italy, of firing only a few rounds at a time and then moving to a new position. They were so difficult for the fire support ships to locate that Admiral Talbot believed they were directed by well-placed forward observers. And they found good target practice on a number of U.S. Navy LST.

LST–226, –307, –331, –332 and –350 crossed the Channel in a convoy, peeled off as ordered, and beached on Sword at 0945 June 16, on a falling tide. About 15 minutes later, when they were hard and fast aground, German shellfire began to "walk" up the beach toward them. They continued unloading under fire, since their cargoes were badly wanted by the Army, and all five vessels were hit. The feeling of their crews, hopefully awaiting the rising of the tide, was well expressed by the flotilla commander: —

One who has not experienced it can scarcely understand the feeling of complete inadequacy which comes over the mariner when he finds his ship stranded, by his own design, and at once under fire to which he cannot retaliate. Such a situation established on a falling tide affords plenty of time to consider a misspent life and to lay up a generous catalogue of virtuous acts which you will surely perform if, God willing, your ship should ever be waterborne again. At long last, marking the passage of the century and at least the thousandth shell, the tide floods, the ship is alive once more, and in that heroic moment you are convinced that there is no natural phenomenon under heaven to compare with a flood tide.[5]

Fortunately the German gunners were inexplicably bad shots on these stationary targets; they scored only 15 hits and the LSTs lost but five killed and 26 wounded.

The British front line remained substantially as on 7 June for over a month, except on the west flank, where it advanced a few miles to link with the American V Corps. This was due in part to General Montgomery's over-all plan to use the British Army as an anchor, and to draw upon it the bulk of German counter-effort, giving the United States Army time to capture the port of Cherbourg. And it must be admitted that the Germans did exactly what "Monty" wanted. During the first few days, considering the threat to Caen and the road to Paris their most immediate danger, they concentrated their efforts there in hope of throwing the British into the sea. Fortunately, owing to the conviction of the German high

[5] Com LST Flotilla 4 (Cdr. Terence W. Greene) Action Report 8 July 1944.

command that another major landing was coming in the Pas-de-Calais, the bulk of its Fifteenth Army was kept away from the fighting area for more than a month. Thus, while General Bradley's First Army was expanding its beachhead and sealing off the Cotentin Peninsula, General Dempsey's Second Army took the brunt of the German offensive. It appeared to some observers to be a static battle, but actually was a most interesting campaign of attack and counterattack, maneuver and countermaneuver.

We cannot attempt to relate this month-long battle for Caen in detail. But we must observe that the Royal Navy was as busy delivering gunfire support in that area as the United States Navy was in its own sector. There was not a day and hardly an hour after 6 June when one or more British battleships, cruisers or destroyers were not supporting Second Army.[6]

3. *Small Craft and Secret Weapons* [7]

British experience with German aircraft was similar to the American, except that for the first few days there were a few daylight attacks. H.M.S. *Bulolo*, flagship of Commodore Douglas-Pennant RN, was hit by a bomb at 0600 June 7, but the fire that it kindled was quickly quenched, and there were few casualties. In the Juno sector, H.M. frigate *Lawford* was bombed and sunk at 0515 June 8. Night raids continued in all sectors, and the night bombers began to drop pressure mines. On 23 June Admiral Vian's flagship *Scylla* struck a mine, and was towed to England for repairs. Destroyer *Swift*, two small craft and merchant vessel *Derry Cunahy*, in which there was heavy loss of embarked troops, also were destroyed by mines off Sword.

The Germans moved up naval reinforcements from various places

[6] Field Marshal Montgomery makes no mention of naval gunfire in his *Normandy to the Baltic*, but there is a picture of him in Edwards *The Royal Navy 1943–44* p. 268, on board H.M.S. *Rodney*, thanking her crew for their "splendid help."

[7] Sources mentioned in Note 1 to this Chapter; War Diary Naval Group Command West, June 1944.

along the North Sea to Le Havre, which they held until 8 September. This resulted in some spirited night actions off the mouth of the Seine.

The protection of this east flank from surface attack was the task of Captain P. V. McLaughlin's Coastal Forces. The 55th Flotilla of British and the 29th Flotilla of Canadian motor torpedo boats bore the brunt of it at first. Admiral Vian's eastern flank area was protected also by a line of small gunfire craft anchored 600 yards apart in what was called the "trout line," running north from the mouth of the Orne. At night, two or three divisions of MTBs were stationed northeast of this line, and pairs of destroyers operated north of it in the mineswept channels.

During the night of 6–7 June German torpedo boats *Jaguar* and *Möwe* sortied from Le Havre to attack British shipping. At 0338, so they reported, each boat fired a spread of six torpedoes at three different destroyers, one of which they left in flames; but no Allied ship was damaged that night — the presence of the torpedo boats was not even detected! There was an even more formidable sortie from Le Havre the following night, in search of a British southbound convoy, which was effectively protected by the area screen. Two coasters carrying ammunition were sunk on the night of 9–10 June; on the following night H.M.S. *Halstead* had her bow blown off by a torpedo, but was successfully towed to Portsmouth; she was avenged by R.A.F. bombers, who sank three E-boats and an R-boat in the early morning. That showed the way to deal with the Le Havre nuisance fleet. At Admiral Ramsay's request, Bomber Command hit the harbor with 2000 tons of bombs shortly before midnight 14 June. The effects were catastrophic. Torpedo boats *Falke, Jaguar* and *Möwe*, 10 E-boats, 15 R-boats, several patrol vessels and harbor defense vessels, and 11 other small craft were sunk; others were badly damaged. And at dusk 15 June, the R.A.F. hit Boulogne with a similar raid, sank 25 R-boats and small craft, and damaged 10 others. Thus, within two days, the German surface fleet threatening the Allies in the Bay of the Seine was wiped out; but there was more to come.

Fresh E-boats began to arrive from the North Sea on 18 June, but the ensuing four-day storm prevented them from operating. Two days later, the long-heralded secret naval weapons began to arrive at Le Havre. The first of these, the "human torpedo," [8] appeared during the night of 5–6 July. No fewer than 26 sortied. They sank minesweepers *Magic* and *Cato* at the cost of nine of themselves; but the German version of this battle was the sinking of a cruiser, two destroyers, one freighter and six LSTs. A second attack, by 21 human torpedoes, came during the night of 7–8 July. All were lost, but they sank H.M. minesweeper *Pylades* and so badly damaged the old cruiser *Dragon* that she was added to the gooseberry rather than be salvaged.

These did not empty the German bag of tricks. They employed a long-range, slow-speed, pattern-running torpedo that was set to circle in search of a target at the end of its run. Probably these were what damaged H.M.S. *Frobisher*, two destroyers and a repair ship. The third secret weapon was a remote-controlled motor boat with an explosive charge in the bow. These were first used in an attack coördinated with midget submarines during the night of 2–3 August. "Hunt"-class destroyer *Quorn*, a small minesweeper (*Gairsay*), two small transports and one landing craft were torpedoed and sunk, but 58 of the boats were lost or destroyed before they could inflict further damage. Other attempts followed, but, aside from harassment, the German secret weapons were hardly worth the effort.

In the meantime British Coastal Forces had established a close blockade of Le Havre, set up patrols to protect the cross-Channel routes, and searched for German coastal traffic east of Cape de la Hêve. Through the remainder of June, July and August, there were almost nightly brushes between the E-boats and MTBs or destroyers and frigates, and some really tough battles at close range.

---

[8] This type of craft was, in effect, one torpedo suspended from another. From the upper one, for propulsion only and capable of a top speed of 4 knots, was hung the detachable missile torpedo. The operator sat astride the upper torpedo, enclosed in a watertight casing with his head above the surface in a transparent plastic dome 18 inches in diameter. (Bulkley "PT History" p. 437.)

On 4 August, four boats of American MTBron 35, veterans of the Pacific who had been working with British forces out of Portsmouth, were sent to join the Le Havre patrol. On the way across their escorting frigate, H.M.S. *Stayner*, made a submarine contact and, with H.M.S. *Wensleydale*, after a series of depth-charge attacks extending over five hours, sank *U–671*. On the night of 8–9 August three PTs, under the command of Lieutenant Sidney I. Saltsman USNR, attacked a small German convoy off Cape d'Antifer, and were rather roughly handled. PTs of Squadron 30, which had been operating off Cherbourg, also joined the patrol off Sword. On the night of 8–9 August three of these, led by Lieutenant Lawrence F. Jones USNR, drove four R-boats back to Le Havre with gunfire, and repeated the performance on the following night. Between 23 August and 1 September, Coastal Forces, backed by several destroyers and frigates of the Royal Navy and French destroyer *La Combattante*, repeatedly attacked small craft entering or departing Le Havre. The American PTs engaged E-boats four nights in succession.

The final German attempt to reinforce Le Havre came on the night of 26–27 August. A task group of British MTBs and American PTs, under the tactical command of Lieutenant Saltsman, vectored by destroyer escort H.M.S. *Retalick*, broke up a convoy of lighters. United States PTs had their last brush with R-boats off Fécamp the following night. Le Havre, sealed off ashore by the Canadian Army, was captured on 8 September.

Great credit is due to the British support craft which manned the area screen off Sword for weeks and months. Daily they bombarded German positions, and nightly they protected the line. And the gallantry of the motor torpedo boat crews, who never flinched, was outstanding.

These events on the east flank of the British sector are an interesting commentary on Admiral Mahan's doctrine of the ineffectiveness of special devices and a mosquito fleet against a seagoing navy. Here were the British shuttling thousands of men and hundreds of ships between the English coast and the Far Shore every day and night, right under the noses of the Germans at Le Havre — a city that had land, sea and air communications with Germany. The enemy had plenty of torpedo boats, small craft and secret weapons; but they availed him naught. But we must not forget to give high marks to the R.A.F. bombers, which really "did a job" on the enemy fleet at Le Havre.

We have now proceeded far beyond important events which had occurred in the American sector — the capture of Cherbourg and its rehabilitation as an invasion port.

CHAPTER XII

Cherbourg[1]

June–September 1944

1. *The Bombardment Is Laid On*

THE THIRTEENTH DAY of the invasion, bringing the
storm that smashed Mulberry A and much besides, warned
soldier and sailor alike that our hold on Normandy was precarious.
Until the Allies could capture Cherbourg, the nearest major port,
they would be at the mercy of tricky English Channel weather.
"We've *got* to get to Cherbourg in a hurry," was the theme of
every staff conference at First Army headquarters in the apple or-
chard behind Pointe du Hoc. General Bradley had hoped to have
this port by D plus 8 but it was already D plus 16 when the storm
abated on the 22nd. On the previous day General "Lightning Joe"
Collins issued orders for the final drive and informed his divisional
commanders that the capture of Cherbourg was to be their first
major effort.

From 18 June, when the Cotentin Peninsula was sealed off by the
Americans, the east flank and center of the Allied front was fairly
static. Dempsey's Second Army joined the eastern flank of Bradley's First Army at Caumont, about 15 miles south of Port-en-
Bessin. Thence the American line ran northwesterly through a
point about three miles short of Saint-Lô to Saint-Sauveur-le-Vi-
comte, and thence to a point on the west coast. During the follow-

[1] Comcrudiv 7 (Rear Adm. Morton L. Deyo) message file, "Action Report on
Bombardment of Cherbourg 25 June 1944" July 6, and "Narrative" written in
1956; Combatdiv 5 (Rear Adm. C. F. Bryant) "Report of Action off Cherbourg"
15 July 1944; Action Reports of ships engaged. From the French point of view,
Raymond Lefèvre *La libération de Cherbourg* (Cherbourg 1946) is most informing.

ing month this line was little changed, except on the Cotentin Peninsula.

That peninsula has a very peculiar topography. It is shaped roughly like the head of an ox, with Cherbourg in a depression on the forehead, Cape de la Hague as the western horn, and Cape Barfleur as the eastern and crumpled horn. The southern part — the muzzle, as it were — is low, marshy and easily inundated; but the northern third — the brow — is rocky, rugged and easily defensible.

Most of the German forces which the Americans had been engaging since 6 June remained on a stabilized line after the peninsula had been sealed off, but "Fortress Cherbourg" contained a formidable garrison of over 40,000 men.[2] The garrison commander, Generalleutnant Karl von Schlieben, had been charged by Hitler to make Cherbourg impregnable. The Fuehrer well knew the Allies *must* have a port to supply their armies, and thought he could thwart the invasion by denying it to them.[3]

By 22 June General Collins's VII Corps, now swollen to four infantry divisions, the two original airborne divisions, two squadrons of motorized cavalry and two tank battalions, was ready to advance. Three divisions did the bulk of the fighting. They lost over 2800 killed and 13,500 wounded in liberating Cherbourg. But it will not detract from the Army's glory to point out that the United States Navy delivered an important Sunday punch on 25 June.

Why this naval bombardment was not planned before the operation began has never been explained. Rear Admiral Morton L. Deyo, under whom Admiral Kirk placed all bombardment and gunfire support ships in the American sector on 15 June, offered his services to General Collins a few days later. The General declared that he wanted the Navy to neutralize the coastal guns on the northern and eastern horns of the Peninsula, where there were 20 casemated batteries, 15 of them of 150-mm or greater caliber, including three of 280-mm. In addition there were many batteries of 75-mm

[2] Exact figures of the German garrison lacking. *Utah Beach to Cherbourg* p. 199 states that 39,000 were taken prisoner, but does not report the killed and wounded.
[3] Hitler's speech of 20 March 1944, quoted in *The Rommel Papers* p. 465.

and 88-mm guns, some of which could be trained inland as well as seaward.

Immediately after this conference the great gale struck in. On 20 June, while the storm-devils were shrieking and no boats could be lowered, Admiral Kirk ordered Admiral Deyo in *Tuscaloosa* to anchor within visual signaling distance of his flagship *Augusta*. Admiral Ramsay had just signaled him to instruct Deyo to plan a bombardment — Bradley had asked for it. Deyo sent his outline plan to Kirk by blinker that afternoon, but observed that he could not execute the plan before Saturday the 24th, owing to the fact that the storm had scattered his bombardment group, and to the necessity of his discussing the plan with the Army before gunfire was laid on.

Deyo ordered all units of his task force, then in various ports between Plymouth and Portsmouth, to assemble at Portland as quickly as possible, and reached the Bill himself on the 22nd. Lieutenant Colonel Fred P. Campbell usa, artillery liaison officer from VII Corps, was flown across Channel to discuss the plan with General Collins, who by that time began to think he would need no naval bombardment. For, on 19–20 June, the VII Corps had swept five to ten miles northward with virtually no opposition, in hot pursuit of German forces which appeared to be disorganized, but actually were falling back according to plan and digging in. General Collins learned that interesting fact when his advance was stopped cold at the defense perimeter, a belt of field works and fortifications that extended in an arc seven miles west, four miles south and eight miles east of Cherbourg. The General then changed his mind about naval bombardment. Around noon he signaled Admiral Deyo that he needed his help quickly — next day, the 24th, if possible.

The 24th was impossible. Battleship *Arkansas* and the nearest minesweeper squadron were at Plymouth, and other bombardment ships had not yet reached Portland. So Deyo replied by sending an outline bombardment plan which, regretfully, he would be unable to execute before sunrise Sunday, June 25.

At about noon on the 24th, Admiral Kirk conferred with General Bradley at First Army headquarters ashore. They agreed, in view of the meager portion of the Peninsula now left in enemy hands, that Deyo should not commence firing before noon on Sunday the 25th, that he must shoot for 90 minutes only, instead of the three hours that he had planned; and that he must take under fire only targets designated by the Army and cleared through Colonel Campbell, who was now back on board *Tuscaloosa*. Deyo, although somewhat mystified as to what really was wanted, continued to brief his task force.

In the meantime the Army had been moving into the environs of Cherbourg; 9th Division on the left flank, 79th in the center, 4th Division on the right. By the night of 24 June, forward elements of VII Corps had reached a semicircle about a mile from the edge of the city. German forces on the capes had been pushed into isolated pockets.

After more backing and filling by the higher command, Deyo's gunfire ships departed Portland at 0430 Sunday June 25, in two groups: Group 1, *Tuscaloosa, Quincy, Nevada,* H.M.S. *Glasgow* and *Enterprise,* and six destroyers; Group 2, under Rear Admiral Bryant in *Texas,* with *Arkansas* and five destroyers. United States Mine Squadron 7 and British 9th Minesweeping Flotilla swept a lane ahead of them, directly to Cherbourg. And General Quesada of IX Army Air Force, at little more than a moment's notice, provided fighter protection.

Bombardment Force passed the morning watch of 25 June in an uneventful crossing of the Channel, now dead calm after the storm. The sea was glassy smooth under light airs, which barely increased after daylight. There was a light haze which, as the ships approached the French coast, was enhanced by smoke from artillery fire and demolished bomb targets, blown over the water by an 8-knot southwest breeze. Liberators and Avengers flew antisubmarine patrol westward, P–38s from fields in southern England provided combat air patrol. As the ships approached the coast, the O.T.C. received a request from General Collins to belay all previously planned long-range shoots on coastal batteries lest

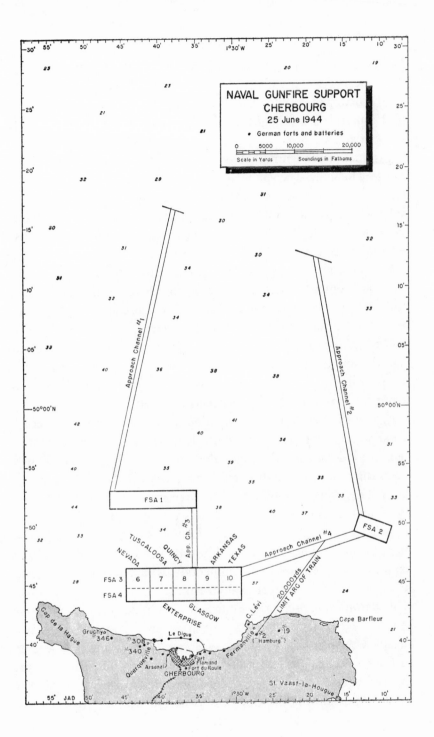

shellfire fall on friendly troops, and to deliver call fire only. In reply, Deyo pleaded for the General's permission to shoot at five specific enemy batteries. Collins signaled back that he could have three of them, and any others that fired at him; but to leave the rest to the Army.

Group 1 made landfall at 0940, about 15 miles north of Cherbourg. The minesweepers were in the van, clearing approach channels to the fire support area for both groups. Bryant's Group 2 steamed in a parallel column several miles to the eastward. Admiral Deyo now startled his skippers by imparting the request he had just received from Collins: They must not fire before noon unless fired upon; but from 1200 on, they were to take on targets designated by shore fire control parties, as well as enemy batteries firing on them. For nearly an hour, in the butt end of the forenoon watch, Bombardment Group 1 steamed in circles in Fire Support Area 1 without being fired on or receiving a call. *Quincy's* spotter plane, working the western part of the peninsula, reported that two top-priority targets on Cape de la Hague were completely destroyed, apparently by the Germans themselves.

Eight bells struck, but still nothing happened. Shore fire control made no requests, the enemy kept silent, and Deyo's group continued to plod shoreward behind the sweepers. Five or six minutes later, the suspense was broken. There were flashes on the beach from the village of Querqueville, three miles west of Cherbourg, and about 15,000 yards from Deyo's group. Four 150-mm shells whistled over H.M.S. *Sidmouth*, leading sweeper for Bombardment Group 1. These were quickly followed by another salvo that exploded between two of the minecraft, which could make only 5 knots' speed with sweeper gear streamed.

Reaction came promptly. Four Fairmiles peeled off to lay a dense smoke screen. And, before the spray from the second salvo had subsided, Admiral Deyo ordered Captain C. P. Clarke RN, leading in *Glasgow*: "Engage with direct fire the batteries firing on the minesweepers." At 1214 she opened fire on the distant flashes. The Spitfire spotting for her flew low over Querqueville to mark the fall of shot, but the shells kicked up so much dust that the pilot had trouble finding the target. H.M.S. *Enterprise* joined in. Soon so many shells were falling around Querqueville that the spotter could not tell whose they were. By 1230 the enemy salvos had straddled nearly every minecraft; and although not one was hit, Admiral Deyo decided that it was time to dismiss them, both for their own safety and to get them out of the way of his gunfire ships. During the rest of the action they lay-to out of range while the column of heavy ships steered elliptical courses in Fire Support Area No. 3, dodging salvos. The destroyers laid smoke to protect the heavy ships and closed the range to use their main batteries effectively.

This spirited duel between Deyo's ships and a Querqueville battery (designated "308") continued for another half hour. The German guns concentrated on H.M.S. *Glasgow* and *Enterprise*. At 1251 a 150-mm shell crashed into *Glasgow's* port hangar, and four minutes later another exploded in her after superstructure. She turned quickly away, increased speed, and checked fire while Captain Clarke surveyed damage. Having ascertained that her propulsion was not affected, he requested and obtained permission to rejoin. Shortly thereafter *Enterprise* learned from her spotting plane, and reported to the Admiral, that two German guns at Querqueville were out of action. But the two still firing were two too many. By 1440, when *Enterprise* ceased firing, "308" was silent. It had taken 318 rounds of 6-inch shell to neutralize one Germany battery, temporarily.

Air spot followed the same pattern as at the landing beaches — pairs of Spitfires, a few of them manned by United States Navy pilots from the heavy ships' Kingfishers, but most of them by R.A.F. pilots; each pair timed to spend 45 minutes over the target. More than 50 Spitfires were briefed to spot for the Cherbourg naval gunfire, but only half that number actually did so. The rest failed to report to their assigned ships, owing to flak or engine trouble or plain failure to find the target.

Simultaneously, Deyo's group was answering requests from shore fire control parties for help to VII Corps. In answer to the first call, *Nevada* at 1212 opened with her 14-inch battery on a target about two and a half miles southwest of Querqueville. Using range corrections supplied by the s.f.c.p., her 14-inch shells began to land squarely on the target. "You are hitting in there and digging in," said fire control at 1229; and after five minutes had elapsed and 18 rounds of 14-inch had been delivered: "Nice firing. You are digging them out in nice big holes." At 1237, after 25 minutes of fire: "They are showing a white panel but we have learned not to pay any attention to that. Continue firing." Continue she did, and with the aid of *Quincy*. After a few more rounds she shifted to a new target between Querqueville and La Rivière, using plane spot, then to a third target nearby on s.f.c.p. call, then on targets of opportunity, finally ceasing fire at 1525. Her expenditure for the day was 112 rounds of 14-inch and 985 rounds of 5-inch.

In the meantime, *Tuscaloosa* was distributing her fire among several targets. At 1236 her s.f.c.p. asked for a brief shoot on an unidentified target one mile west of Querqueville. The cruiser obliged with seven 8-inch shells. "You are walking salvos around the target," reported s.f.c.p.; and at 1315 she made direct hits on a casemate. Two Spitfires that were spotting for her were hit by flak and forced to retire.

During the first hour of the bombardment, while Deyo's group had been concentrating on strongpoints near Cherbourg, and VII Corps was at the point of breaking into the city streets, the Navy had had to give some attention to enemy fire from the western horn of the Cotentin Peninsula where, at 1207, *Ellyson* had reported gun flashes from target "346," four 150-mm guns near the village of Gruchy. *Glasgow* sent her spot over, and at 1311 commenced firing. After 54 rounds, which apparently silenced the guns, it was time for *Glasgow* to retire with the rest of the group.

The destroyers of Group 1 were feeling neglected. They made smoke as required and did their best to stay out of the way of the big ships. *Emmons* did take on Fort de l'Est, a pinpoint on one of the harbor breakwaters. She had fired 64 rounds at this tiny fort by 1308 when a shore battery which she could not locate began to pay her marked attention. Commander Billingsley, observing that each salvo came closer than the last, decided it was time to retire behind a few smoke pots that *Rodman* obligingly dropped. But *Emmons* had done a good job from a range of 15,000 yards; Fort de l'Est did not fire again.

As the 90-minute firing period established by his superior officers drew to its end, Admiral Deyo was well aware that the bombardment had fallen short of expectation. In no mood to retire at the exact time prescribed, he signaled to VII Corps at 1320, "Do you wish more gunfire? Several enemy batteries still active." General Collins somewhat tardily replied at 1405, "Thanks very much — we should be grateful if you would continue until 1500."

Without waiting for this answer, Deyo turned *Tuscaloosa* inshore and pitched in on the Querqueville battery which had come to life with a sudden burst of attention toward *Murphy*, a destroyer notorious for attracting enemy gunfire.[4] *Murphy* had kept quiet so far and had just made contact with an s.f.c.p. at 1327 when the Querqueville battery found her range and straddled her four times in 20 minutes. Splashes and splinters from near-misses covered her deck as she dodged behind a smoke screen. *Tuscaloosa* came to her aid at 1342 with 8-inch salvos on Querqueville. She fired 17 rounds and scored a direct hit, which brought a burst of flame from the target. The German guns still fired, although more slowly; so *Ellyson* and *Gherardi* joined in, the latter contributing 110 rounds of 5-inch. Next turn was *Quincy's*. She fired for half an hour; but one of the German casemates at Querqueville was still shooting at 1445. *Nevada's* s.f.c.p. then called for 14-inch fire, and the battleship's fourth salvo fell squarely on what appeared to be the one active German gun. S.f.c.p. called "Rapid fire — no change." After *Nevada* had thrown eight more 14-inch shells, her spotter reported, "I do not see any need for further firing." But target "308" at Querqueville had a charmed life. After the combined efforts of a

4 See Volume II 58–64.

battleship, four cruisers and several destroyers, it came to life as the task force retired, and defiantly tossed a few more shells in its direction.

Even more astonishing than the endurance of this battery was its failure to score. Everyone topside in Deyo's force was amazed at the large number of near-misses, and the absence of hits. As a sailor of *Quincy* remarked, "It's just like throwing rocks at a bottle — no matter how many you throw, you can't hit it."

Of more immediate importance than that battery to the troops assaulting Cherbourg were the fortifications near the city. Fort des Flamand, at the eastern end of the inner breakwater, had eight dual-purpose 88-mm guns which were holding up a regiment of the 4th Division. After an s.f.c.p. called for naval aid, *Hambleton* at 1432 began to shoot at the fort from a range of 14,250 yards; but after eight salvos, large-caliber shells from Battery No. 2 ("Hamburg") began to drop around her and she was glad to retire and let *Quincy* take on the fort with heavier stuff. That did the trick.

There were other shoots by the group after 1330. Target "346" near Gruchy came to life again; at the request of an s.f.c.p., H.M.S. *Glasgow* fired 57 rounds of 6-inch, to which *Rodman* added 36 rounds of 5-inch; but "346" was shooting with undiminished vigor and accuracy when *Rodman* pulled out of range at 1510. Smoke and haze were so dense, and the fire of Batteries "2" and "346" so persistent, with other guns near Cherbourg giving tongue whenever ships closed range to within 15,000 yards, that it sometimes seemed as if every hummock housed a battery, and ships' spotters saw gun flashes where there were no guns.

At 1500, the new deadline set by General Collins, Admiral Deyo ordered his group to cease fire, and called Admiral Bryant over TBS to follow him out of the bombardment area. So reluctant was he to quit while coastal guns were still active that he allowed flagship *Tuscaloosa* to answer a fresh call. This came from an s.f.c.p. covering the city, wanting target "322" (75-mm field guns in casemates, on the dock at the entrance to the naval arsenal) to be pounded.

U.S.S. *Texas* under fire from Battery Hamburg

U.S.S. *Quincy*

Bombardment of Cherbourg, 25 June

Cherbourg from the air, 21 June

Rear Admiral John Wilkes USN

Bombardment of Cherbourg

Tuscaloosa, already on her way out, opened at 1515 when her range was 25,400 yards, and continued until 1540 when range had opened another mile and a half. Nevertheless, those Parthian shots were among the best of the day. The heavy cruiser scored a direct hit by an 8-inch AP shell on one casemate and damaged another by a near explosion.

Nevada did not cease firing until 1525, and for four more minutes the batteries on the west side of Cherbourg continued to shoot at her, as one or another had been doing almost continuously since 1206. Over twenty times she was straddled by large-caliber shells. One missed her as close as 25 feet; two passed right through her superstructure and splashed close aboard on her disengaged side. But *Nevada* seems to have had a charmed life. She suffered no casualties and received only superficial damage from shell fragments.

2. *Duel with Battery "Hamburg," 25 June*

While Admiral Deyo's group was battling to a draw with German batteries west of Cherbourg and within the city, Admiral Bryant's smaller group, consisting of *Texas, Arkansas,* and five destroyers, dueled with Target "2." Battery "Hamburg," as the Germans called it, was located on a hill near Fermanville, a short distance inland from Cape Levi and some six miles east of Cherbourg. Manned by sailors, this battery was the most powerful German strongpoint on the Cotentin Peninsula. Four 280-mm (11-inch) guns, well separated, were protected by steel shields similar to naval gun turrets, and by reinforced concrete casemates. Clustered around them were six 88-mm, six heavy and six light antiaircraft guns.

The two distinguishing features of Battery Hamburg were its long range — 40,000 yards — and the arc of train. Sited to cover the sea approaches to Cherbourg, they could not fire east of a line running about 35° true. Admiral Deyo, taking these facts into account, planned to charge *Nevada*, whose major battery carried almost as far as the Hamburg guns, with the mission of neutralizing them from extreme range. In the meantime *Texas* and *Arkansas*, whose guns ranged only 20,000 yards, would sneak in from the eastward, stay within the "blind" arc of the battery until *Nevada* had silenced it, complete the destruction, and then pass through the arc of fire to join Bombardment Group 1 off Cherbourg. But that is not the way it worked out. *Nevada*, as we have seen, had more urgent missions on the other side of the city.

Texas, followed by *Arkansas*, preceded by Commander Plander's Minron 7 (*Pheasant*, flag) and screened by destroyers *Barton*, *O'Brien*, *Laffey*, *Plunkett* and *Hobson* (Captain Freseman commanding), entered Fire Support Area 2 at 0955 June 25. Admiral Bryant expected *Nevada* to commence firing on No. 2 while he worked over other batteries east of Cherbourg. His spotting planes were over their targets and his two battlewagons were all ready to speak when he was handed Deyo's flash at 0955 that the earlier long-range bombardment plan was canceled. He was not to fire until noon, and then only at the request of an s.f.c.p. or in self-defense against active batteries. And his group was to join Admiral Deyo's off Cherbourg at 1200.[5]

This radical change left Bryant breathless, for it meant that his two antiquated ships would have to pass directly through the arc of fire before it had been softened up. However, this bad news was mixed with good. Plane spotters for *Texas* reported no activity around her first target, and the second was "surrounded by dead Germans." (Neither of these was the "Hamburg.") American troops had overrun both of them. So, at 1034, Admiral Bryant, much cheered, headed WSW toward Fire Support Area 3 north of Cherbourg, Minron 7 leading as usual. Three destroyers screened the sweepers, while two stayed with the battleships.

The minecraft made slow headway against the strong current, which set them inshore of the planned Approach Channel No. 4; the battleships plodded slowly toward Cherbourg, falling further and further behind schedule. By 1130 Bryant had given up hope

[5] Bryant's Report p. 5.

of joining Deyo in Fire Support Area 3 at noon. He still had to pass the big battery.

Arkansas's s.f.c.p., on a hill overlooking Battery Hamburg, sent in a call as soon as it established radio contact with the ship. She slowly closed the range to 18,000 yards, and at 1208 opened up. *Arkansas* was fitted with hand-me-down fire control equipment, some of which had originally been installed in *Tennessee*. Her gyrocompasses, taken over from *Tuscaloosa*, had always given trouble and were inadequate for rapid maneuvering. So Captain Richards kept her on a steady course and fired slowly at Hamburg, still silent. *Texas*, out of touch with her s.f.c.p., steamed behind the sweepers as though she were a yacht idly cruising on this beautiful June day.

The German naval gunners were merely biding their time. Unperturbed by the salvos from *Arkansas*, they deliberately ranged on the slowest ships, waiting until they came well within the battery's arc of fire, and then let fly. The first salvo landed among the sweepers; the second straddled destroyer *Barton*. She and *O'Brien* opened counter-battery fire. A shell which hit the water on *Barton's* shoreward side ricocheted into her hull, crashing into the after diesel engine room, slashing through bulkheads and coming to rest after traveling a considerable distance inside the ship. It was a 240-mm (9.4-inch) shell from another battery, fortunately a dud; no one was hurt. *Barton* returned fire on this other battery without air spot or s.f.c.p. All the sweepers were splashed by near-misses, but it was another destroyer that caught the next hit. At 1232, *Laffey* took a 240-mm shell on her port bow near the anchor. This too was a dud; the damage control party pried it loose and threw it overboard.

Firing now became general. *Plunkett* and *O'Brien* pitched in on Battery Hamburg, together with *Arkansas*, *Barton* and *Laffey*. *Texas* fired three 2-gun salvos at it from a range of 19,200 yards; but neither she nor the plane saw the results, since the target was completely obscured by smoke. Captain Baker was in no mood to fire very long at unseen targets; he was having too hot a time to indulge in that luxury. *Texas* took a 3-gun straddle across her bow and swung to starboard with full right rudder just in time for three shells to whistle over her stern. Straddles began to fall at intervals of 20 to 30 seconds. They seemed to come from a knoll 400 yards northeast of Battery Hamburg; and at 1245 Captain Baker shifted his main battery fire to this new target.

Despite the feeling of *Texas* sailors that their ship was the enemy's only target, they were getting comparatively small stuff; Hamburg's 280-mm guns, strangely enough, were not firing at her, but concentrating on destroyers and minesweepers, then "churning about like loony ants" (as it seemed to the battleship's sailors) to evade. Hamburg's next victim was destroyer *O'Brien*. At 1251 a shell sheared away the ladder to her bridge, scattered her signal flags over the deck, and caromed into the after corner of combat information center. There, in the ship's nerve center, it exploded. Thirteen men were killed and 19 wounded. Her skipper, Commander Outerbridge, turned north immediately to investigate damage and found that all radar was out of commission. This was not pleasant, since her smoke screen, made to cover her retirement, was so dense that all other ships were out of sight. Like a blind man escaping a forest fire, *O'Brien* felt her way through the smoke to comparative safety in waters north of the approach channel.

Three hits in quick succession on his destroyers, near-misses all around the battleship, and no letup in the enemy's fire convinced Admiral Bryant that it would be healthier to turn north to open the range. During the next two hours (1300 to 1500) his two battle-wagons fired 228 rounds from their main batteries. At the same time, the Admiral ordered Commander Plander to belay sweeping and retire. The minecraft, much relieved to get out of the middle of this high-caliber duel, turned north while *Barton* and *Laffey* made smoke astern of them; *O'Brien*, also laying smoke, limped along too. The three destroyers, under the stern hand of their squadron commander, kept shooting until the batteries were beyond their range. Captain Freseman knew that 5-inch bullets fired at extreme range could not do much to casemated batteries, but he kept it up in hope of distracting the enemy from firing at other targets, and of bothering the German ammunition parties. A gallant gesture and valiant hope; but the enemy was a little too tough.

Admiral Bryant's group now concentrated on other German guns near Fermanville. *Arkansas*, between 1255 and 1325, trained her main battery on four German 105-mm field howitzers in casemates, and silenced them with 22 rounds, guided by her s.f.c.p. and a plane. The enemy repaid her efforts with a few more near-misses which scattered shrapnel over her forecastle. *Texas*, at the same time, took on Battery Hamburg, destroyers *Hobson* and *Plunkett* making smoke for her. With heavier shells and better fire control equipment, she was a more evenly matched contestant than 30-year-old *Arkansas*. Her spotter plane was on the job, but her s.f.c.p. had not yet made contact. When a sudden gust of wind cleared the destroyers' smoke from *Texas*, the German gunners took full advantage of her naked state. At 1316 a 280-mm shell skidded across the top of her conning tower, knocked a fire director periscope into the fire control tower (where it barely missed killing the gunnery officer), hit a supporting column of the pilot house, and there exploded. The bridge was wrecked, the helmsman was killed and eleven men were wounded. Captain Baker, checking splashes on a wing of the bridge, was thrown to the deck but not injured. His exec. in the conning tower took over control, and *Texas* continued to fire without pause.[6]

In the midst of this hullabaloo, *Texas* scored a direct hit on Battery Hamburg. One of her shells pierced the iron shield and knocked one gun out for keeps. But three more were still active.

At this point the task force commander, at Admiral Bryant's request, assigned *Quincy* to help his hard-pressed group. She plugged away at Hamburg from 1330 to 1410, directed by an s.f.c.p. and by plane spot; but when Deyo called her off at 1410 to resume fire on the old troublemaker near Querqueville she had no hits to report. Deyo thought that too many ships were engaging this battery for accurate spotting.

[6] *Texas* was hit also by a 240-mm dud at 1234, and by fragments from a near-miss.

Texas was now joined by *Arkansas*, who divided her fire for the rest of the afternoon between Hamburg and a nearby 105-mm battery. From then on the afternoon was relatively quiet for Admiral Bryant's group. The two battleships stayed about 20,000 yards off shore, too far for their screening destroyers to do any shooting. Neither side scored direct hits, though not for want of trying. Between 1401 and 1407 *Arkansas's* s.f.c.p. reported Battery Hamburg to be a "mass of rubble," to which her spotting plane promptly retorted, "Maybe so, but they are still shooting!" The ships knew better, too; and when *Texas* strayed back into the arc of fire of the remaining three Hamburg guns at 1447, she was greeted by a furious burst of fire; the nearby 105-mm battery at the same time tried to sink *Arkansas*. Both battleships maneuvered violently, *Hobson* and *Plunkett* made smoke, and all escaped with no damage.[7]

At 1501 Admiral Deyo signaled Admiral Bryant to head back to Portland, by the same course that he had followed in the crossing. *Texas* had fired 206 fourteen-inch shells; *Arkansas* had fired 58 twelve-inch shells, and five destroyers had fired 552 five-inch shells at Battery Hamburg. The ground was scarred and furrowed for acres around, the concrete casemates were pocked and cracked; but only one of the four guns was out of action — that was owing to the *Texas* hit at 1335.

What, then, was the contribution of this bombardment to the capture of Cherbourg? General Collins wrote to Admiral Deyo on 29 June: "I witnessed your Naval bombardment of the coastal batteries and the covering strongpoints around Cherbourg. . . . The results were excellent, and did much to engage the enemy's fire while our troops stormed into Cherbourg from the rear."[8] And

[7] At the height of this flurry, one of *Texas's* officers discovered a 280-mm shell nestled cozily against his bunk. It was another dud, which had crashed into the ship earlier in the day. The crew had been too busy dodging near-misses and straddles to notice that one of them was a hit after all. Details of *Texas* action from article by Martin Sommers, who was on board (*Sat. Eve. Post* 16 Sept. 1944).

[8] Quoted in CTF 129 endorsement on Combatdiv 5 Report. General Collins added in his letter, "Fortunately we did not ask the Navy to shell Fort du Roule — fortunate in that it contained among other things a well-stocked wine cellar."

Lieutenant Colonel Campbell, the liaison officer, who returned to VII Corps, wrote to Admiral Deyo on 20 August that all Army officers he had talked with agreed that the bombardment broke the back of the German defense of the city. "I took a look for myself, and am convinced that you did tremendous damage to those batteries. Some were never active after the bombardment, and still pointed out to sea when the city fell, even though they could have been turned." And the Supreme Commander wrote, "The final assault was materially assisted by heavy and accurate naval gunfire." Similar testimony comes from the enemy. General von Schlieben, reporting to Feldmarschall Rommel on the morning of 26 June, referred to the "heavy fire from the sea" as one of the factors that made resistance useless; and Admiral Krancke in his war diary, after the fight had ended, referred to "naval bombardment of a hitherto unequalled fierceness" as one of the contributing causes to the loss of Cherbourg.[9]

Just before the two bombardment groups entered Portland Harbor on Sunday night, Captain Clarke of H.M.S. *Glasgow* called Admiral Deyo over TBS and said he hoped to have the honor of holding the captains' conference on board his ship. Deyo took the hint; and, as he writes, "We all trooped on board about 2100, a little haggard and very thirsty, and spliced the main brace in the Captain's cabin, which was well ventilated by shell fragments. It was a nice touch."

Admiral Ramsay, who visited Portland next day, personally thanked both flag officers and each C.O. of a bombardment ship.

"This operation," he wrote in his Despatch on OVERLORD, "was carried out with skill and determination by Rear Admiral Deyo, but it is considered unfortunate that it was not found possible to adhere to the original plan, which provided for the initial neutralization of the enemy long-range batteries, as, had better fortune attended the enemy gunners, they might well have inflicted heavy

[9] *Crusade in Europe* p. 260; Harrison p. 434; War Diary Naval Command West, 30 June.

damage to our ships at the relatively close range at which they were firing."

The 25 June bombardment was instructive in the domain of naval gunfire *vs.* shore batteries. Before World War II, it had been naval doctrine that warships could not with impunity expose themselves to the fire of coast defense guns of nearly equal caliber. Events up to June 1944 in the Mediterranean and the Pacific had considerably shaken this doctrine; time and again, gunfire support ships had closed the coast and knocked out coastal batteries. The catch was that nowhere in the Mediterranean had the shore batteries been well and resolutely served, and that Japanese coast defense gunners were inadequately trained. Consequently the United States Navy had become somewhat confident on the subject. The Cherbourg shoot did much to redress the balance, without upsetting previous experience to the effect that a casemated gun is exceedingly difficult for a rapidly maneuvering warship to destroy with a direct hit, although a shower of salvos around the coast defense position will silence the guns temporarily.

3. *Cherbourg Liberated, 26 June — 1 July*

At the very hour when Admiral Deyo's ships were pounding batteries at Querqueville and Fermanville, American soldiers captured from the rear Fort du Roule, which overhangs Cherbourg like a veritable rock of Gibraltar. On 26 June the 9th and 79th Divisions penetrated the city itself. The Army closed in, fighting from street to street, and isolated the German garrison in small pockets. That day, which the Cherbourgeois call their Day of Liberation, Von Schlieben (who had been ordered by Hitler to defend the city to the last man) and the naval commander, Konteradmiral Hennecke, surrendered. The Admiral was subsequently consoled with a high German decoration, on the ground that his sailors manning Battery Hamburg had sunk two heavy cruisers.

When he surrendered, Von Schlieben had no communication

with isolated units of his command, holed up in a number of strong-points which had to be reduced one by one. The most formidable of these was the Arsenal or *Port Militaire* on the western edge of the inner harbor; a fortress in itself, some 1500 meters square, walled and moated, and enclosing four wet basins. Its artillery was mounted to cover land as well as sea approaches, and the garrison, fortunately divided into several units, was provided with enough food and ammunition to withstand a long siege. A French engineer who knew the terrain well made contact with VII Corps staff before the city was entered, and gave exact information about armament and angles of fire. On the morning of 27 June, an American psychological warfare unit in a truck delivered a ten-minute harangue to the garrison; soon after, white flags appeared on the walls. Colonel G. W. Smyth of the 47th Infantry went forward and received the surrender of General Sattler, the garrison commander, with 400 of his troops, while a mass of ragged men and disheveled women, slave laborers from Eastern Europe, made a dash for liberty from an adjoining hangar.[10] But this surrender did not include either the strong Fort du Hamet, at the northern angle between the Arsenal and the inner harbor, or other small resistance pockets throughout. The Army seems to have forgotten about them, and left them to the Navy to mop up, through the brilliant improvisation of a Coast Guard officer.

Commander Quentin R. Walsh USCG commanded a small United States Navy port reconnaissance party which had been organized to report what needed to be done to make Cherbourg usable for vessels. At 0800 June 28, Commander Walsh took Ensign Daniel Laner USNR and a squad of 15 sailors armed with sub-machine guns and hand grenades to reconnoiter the Arsenal and the adjacent waterfront. After picking up as guide, a German sailor who knew a little English, this party penetrated deep into the Arsenal. Then a machine gun opened up on them. The guide informed them that there were pockets of "no surrender" Nazis, most of them drunk,

[10] Lefèvre *La libération de Cherbourg* ch. xx; *Utah Beach to Cherbourg* pp. 194–96.

all over the place. After waiting to silence the machine guns, the Navy party resumed its reconnaissance. A German came toward them with hands raised to say that a captain and 200 men had decided to surrender. This they did, and the entire lot were marched to the main gate by a detail of four sailors. Within the next hour, the remaining two officers and eleven men of Walsh's party killed several snipers and took about 200 more prisoners, who were marched under escort of four more sailors to the gate. Commander Walsh, Ensign Laner and the seven remaining sailors calmly examined the German demolitions on the edge of the inner harbor, and incidentally received the surrender of 85 more Germans who filed out of a bunker. One of the prisoners, who had lived in the United States, informed them that some 50 American paratroops were still imprisoned in Fort du Hamet in charge of fanatical Nazis who refused to surrender. The two American officers then approached to within 150 yards of the fort and waved a piece of a white parachute. In reply, a German officer appeared with a white flag and conducted them into a room on the second deck of the fort, where the German commander and six other officers were sitting. The Oberst, incredulous that his superior officers had given up, refused to surrender or to release the paratroops, until Walsh informed him that he had 800 men outside the Arsenal ready to rush in and take Fort du Hamet by storm. The bluff worked; the fort's entire garrison surrendered; and the American paratroops, who belonged to the 101st Airborne Division and had been dropped near Cherbourg by mistake, were happily released.[11]

The forts on the *digue*, the big outer breakwater of Cherbourg, and some of the coastal batteries too, held out for another day. Admiral Kirk, on information that enemy guns were still bothering the Army, sent *Shubrick* and six PTs to deal with them, around sundown June 27. While the destroyer and four boats maneuvered five miles off shore, Lieutenant Commander J. D. Bulkeley, riding *PT-510*, with *PT-521* in company, was detached to deal with the

[11] Cdr. Walsh's account in *The Coast Guard at War. Landings in France XI* (official mimeographed publication, 1946) pp. 193-207.

forts. He zigzagged for some 35 minutes as close as 150 yards to the *digue*, spraying the forts with machine-gun fire and drawing a shower of 88-mm shells, one of which closely missed and damaged *PT–521*. For five long minutes she lay dead in the water, while the motor machinist's mate made emergency repairs. Bulkeley's boat ran a tight circle around her, concealing her by a smoke ring. *Shubrick* in the meantime had been collecting straddles from a battery at Macqueville west of Querqueville, and had seen flashes from or near Battery Hamburg. Recalled at 2117 by the squadron commander, she ascertained that the PT boats were retiring in good order, and turned away herself, still pursued by straddles.

Repeated bombings by P–47s of the IX A.A.F. finally persuaded the forts on the *digue* to surrender. At about 1101 June 29, Fort du Centre (the big circular one at the harbor entrance) gave up; and the rest followed suit. Captain Norman Ives went out in a small sailboat, the only craft he could find, to take the surrender.

By this time some 39,000 Germans had surrendered in and around Cherbourg, but about 6000 more had retreated toward Cape de la Hague. The task of bagging them was entrusted to the 9th Division and the 4th Cavalry, with the aid of the IX A.A.F. By 1 July that cape, as well as the entire Cotentin Peninsula, had been secured.

On the same date, we may consider the NEPTUNE part of OVERLORD concluded. The two attack force commanders, Rear Admirals Moon and Hall, were relieved on 25 and 27 June respectively by Rear Admiral Wilkes. Moon proceeded to the Mediterranean to take part in Operation DRAGOON, as did Deyo, Bryant and Jaujard, with their gunfire support ships. Admiral Kirk's Western Naval Task Force was dissolved 10 July; *Augusta* went to the Mediterranean to be the flagship of Rear Admiral Davidson, and Kirk two months later became Commander U.S. Naval Forces, France. Admiral Ramsay, however, remained Allied Naval Commander under Eisenhower until his death the following January.

In the meantime the Twenty-first Army Group, which (except on the Cotentin Peninsula) had been almost stationary since 18

June, regained its momentum. On 25–26 June Montgomery opened a drive to take Caen, which fell on 9 July. The American First Army launched a general assault across the Taute-Vire Canal on the 7th. After eleven days' heavy fighting in the *bocage* country, American troops entered Saint-Lô on 18 July.

On 1 August, the 18 divisions of the United States Army in Normandy were formed into the Twelfth Army Group under General Omar Bradley. Lieutenant General Courtney B. Hodges now took command of the First Army on the east flank adjoining the British, and Lieutenant General George S. Patton, who had finished playing his deceptive rôle as commander of a phantom "Army Group" in England, took over the Third Army on the west flank. Everything then began to move rapidly.

4. *Cherbourg Cleared, July–September* [12]

The Germans, in obedience to Hitler's orders, left Cherbourg a demolished, ruined and booby-trapped port. An entire freight train of explosives was blown to convert the Gare Maritime, the railway station where boat trains from Paris connect with the transatlantic liners, into a mass of twisted steel and burning wood. The adjacent Darse Transatlantique was a basin of scuttled ships, thickly sown with mines. All big cranes and other harbor works which could have been useful were destroyed.

Clearing was begun by the Navy reconnaissance party, of which Captain Norman Ives took command on 28 June, Commander Walsh becoming his chief of staff. Commodore William A. Sullivan and part of his famous salvage outfit arrived shortly after. Rear Admiral John Wilkes, now Commander United States Naval Bases, France, arrived 14 July with his capable staff,[13] a few hun-

---

[12] Com U.S. Ports and Bases, France, War Diary for 1944; Ruppenthal II ch. ii of mimeographed draft; Lucius D. Clay *Decision in Germany* (1950).

[13] Capt. W. M. Percifield, deputy chief of staff; Capt. Charles Quinby, who succeeded Capt. Ives as base commander; Capt. J. E. Forsyth, matériel and repair officer; Capt. R. B. Hunt and Cdr. N. W. Lowrie, logistics officers. Capt. V. E. Korns, chief of staff, now became Comlancrabeu at Plymouth.

dred Seabees and two "Drews," to operate the port. Clearance of mines in the harbor was his responsibility, unless they were attached to a sunken ship; these were attended to by Sullivan's crew. Six British and three American salvage vessels, 20 United States Navy coastal minesweepers, two flotillas of similar British craft and four flotillas of British motor minesweepers were allocated for the clearance. Commodore Sullivan, who had already salvaged North African ports, Palermo and Naples, found that German sabotage and demolition, commended by Hitler as "exemplary," had been well executed as far as it went; but, planned by men who knew little of harbor operations, it was more spectacular than effective. This deficiency was more than made up by an unprecedentedly intricate and thorough mining of both outer and inner harbors. Many of the mines were of the repeatedly delayed-action kind which required a number of passes before being neutralized. Eight magnetic and eight acoustical sweeps had to be made every morning for 85 days from the day they were laid, in order to render the harbor reasonably safe. In addition to these anchored mines, there were the concrete shoal-water kind, which could only be dealt with by divers, or by vessels "sitting down" on them — which was not good for the vessels.

"I cannot say too much," writes Commodore Sullivan, "of the courage and ability of Lieutenant Commander James L. Harries RCN who did this work in Cherbourg." Commander John B. G. Temple RN of the minesweeper flotilla also received his high praise. A total of 133 mines was swept by 13 July,[14] and in the meantime a score or more of merchant ships that had been scuttled to obstruct channels and docks were removed. In addition to the minecraft casualties already mentioned, three American and one British small craft were mined and sunk by 12 August.

The first freight was landed at Cherbourg on 16 July when dukws began discharging the cargoes of four Liberty ships on a

[14] Lefèvre *La libération de Cherbourg* p. 81. According to Commo. Sullivan about 86 of these were magnetic or acoustical, and the 133 figure does not include the small concrete mines, which we called "Katies," and whose removal extended into September.

specially cleared beach. By the end of July, 12 to 14 Liberties could be discharged at once, together with six LST, two car ferries and one sea train. Within a few days, the anticipated goal for daily cargo discharge, 8500 tons, was reached; [15] and in September the daily total reached a figure more than double that. The arsenal basins, not completely cleared until 21 September, alone could handle eleven Liberty ships and five coasters. This excess over the predicted figures was both fortunate and necessary, because the abandonment, in early August, of plans for capturing and utilizing the Breton ports of Brest and Lorient, and for building an artificial harbor in Quiberon Bay, deprived the Army of an estimated 8000 to 14,000 tons of daily cargo discharge.[16]

The first "Pluto" pipeline from England was completed 12 August, but shortly after was broken through being fouled by a ship's anchor. Two more went into operation near the end of September, but they too failed. Eventually 17 pipelines, which were laid across the Strait of Dover to Boulogne, proved very useful for supplying the Allied Armies as they advanced into Germany.

By autumn, Cherbourg had become second only to Marseilles as a port of logistic supply to the United States Army in Europe. Between 16 July and the end of the war, 2137 vessels entered; 2,826,740 tons of cargo were unloaded; 130,210 passengers were landed and 307,939 were embarked, including 124,206 German prisoners and 148,753 Allied wounded. Proudly the Cherbourgeois refer to their city as the first French port to be recovered, and the starting point of the *chemin de la libération* which led to Paris, and, eventually, to Berlin.

[15] About the same as the daily landings at Omaha and Utah in July. Adm. Wilkes also used Barfleur, Saint-Vaast, Isigny, and Grandcamp for entries, and their figures are combined with those of Cherbourg. Monthly unloadings at Cherbourg alone, according to a table at the museum in the Fort du Roule, rose to 433,000 tons cargo and 164,000 tons oil in November 1944. Top day at Cherbourg was 19,955 tons on 4 November.

[16] Figures in *Infantry Journal* March 1948 p. 8.

PART II

Southern France: Operation DRAGOON

CHAPTER XIII

High-level Wrangling[1]

October 1943–August 1944

OPERATION ANVIL–DRAGOON, the landings on the coast of Provence, was in some respects unique. An almost perfect performance which contributed heavily to victory over Germany was preceded by a difference of opinion between the British and American high commands as to whether it should or should not take place; a controversy which still continues in the histories of the war.

Tentatively adopted at Quebec in mid-1943 as a desirable southern jaw of the pincer on German-held France, authorized by the C.C.S. at Teheran in December, Operation ANVIL, because of Mr. Churchill's opposition, did not get the final green light until five days before its D-day. For the first time in the Mediterranean the Army allowed the Navy to lay on an extended pre-landing bombardment, and to land assault waves in daylight. The aviators co-operated perfectly. Events unrolled almost "according to plan" with only negligible foul-ups. If Tinian in the Pacific was the "perfect amphibious operation" on a small scale, DRAGOON was the nearly faultless one on a large scale.

"In order to contain the maximum German forces away from the Caen area, diversionary operations should be staged against other areas, such as the Pas-de-Calais and the Mediterranean coast of France." [2] This inconspicuous paragraph in General Morgan's overall Cossac plan of 30 July 1943 seems to have been the germ of

---

[1] Ehrman V chaps. v–viii and Appendix vii, and Pogue chaps. vi and xii give detailed accounts of the strategic discussions; Sacmed Report is essential and "Revised Draft of SAC Despatch" gives other details.

[2] Harrison p. 453.

ANVIL–DRAGOON. General Marshall brought it up at the first Quebec Conference, where the C.C.S. proposed "to establish a lodgment in the Toulon–Marseilles area and exploit northward to create a diversion in connection with OVERLORD." At the same time, they suggested that the expedition include the French forces then being trained and newly equipped in North Africa. Mr. Churchill doubted whether the French would be ready, and growled over using good divisions to invade Southern France instead of Italy or the Balkans; but Mr. Roosevelt was enthusiastic, and the Combined Chiefs directed General Eisenhower to submit an estimate and outline plan for Operation ANVIL, as it was named shortly after.

The respective attitudes of these important people remained constant. Churchill never overcame his misgivings; Roosevelt occasionally wavered, like a compass needle over a sunken ship, but always returned to the Provençal target when he had passed over it, especially if General Marshall or Admiral King had the conn. The General brought up ANVIL at the Cairo Conference in November 1943, where the Combined Planners produced a scheme for it to be launched on the Normandy D-day. From Cairo the Combined Chiefs, together with Churchill and Roosevelt, flew to Teheran to meet Stalin. There, as we have seen in Chapter II, the Prime Minister proposed to leave ANVIL to one side and shape a course for the Ægean or points East. Stalin, whom Roosevelt (after a brief fluctuation of the needle) supported,[3] insisted that the invasion of Southern France was a logical concomitant of OVERLORD. And Churchill, apparently won over, gave his approval to it after the conference had returned to Cairo.

At Cairo, the C.C.S. "urgently" directed General Eisenhower to prepare an outline plan, which his staff produced as early as 17 December. This was promptly communicated to Cincmed, Admiral Sir John Cunningham RN, who on 28 December designated Vice Admiral H. Kent Hewitt Commander Western Naval Task Force to invade Southern France. In Cincmed's directive Hewitt's mission was defined as establishing a beachhead on the coast of Provence

[3] *Closing the Ring*, p. 405.

on the Normandy D-day, and maintaining an army there, in order "to support the invasion of Northern France." He was told that ground forces would probably consist of three or four United States and six or seven French divisions, of which two or three would probably be in the assault. With this slender information Eighth Fleet staff began to plan.

Before the end of 1943 it looked as if NEPTUNE–OVERLORD would crowd ANVIL off the map. General Eisenhower, as we have seen, insisted that the Cossac plan for invading Normandy must be broadened from a three- to a five-division front. General Montgomery agreed, but pointed out that in order to obtain enough troops and troop-lift, ANVIL would have to be dropped. A large part of Eisenhower's difficulty in keeping it on the books stemmed from his insistence on the broad landing in Normandy. But there were other contestants for the forces that he wished to commit in Southern France: General Wilson, who hated to diminish Allied strength in Italy; Mr. Churchill, who wanted to advance on Vienna from the Adriatic. Everything depended on how one cut the pie of strategic resources. It looked as if ANVIL would get a thin slice at best, and on 6 January 1944 Cossac proposed that it get none.

General Eisenhower, however, believed that ANVIL was necessary, not so much to keep Germans in Southern France off his back, as to extend the southern flank of his Expeditionary Force and to make best use of Allied resources in the Mediterranean. The French Army was being rebuilt in North Africa and, like the French Navy, was eager to take part in the liberation of their country. What better way could they be employed than to land in Provence and thrust northward toward the Belfort Gap?

Mr. Churchill's initial distaste for this operation was strengthened by the bog-down at Anzio. On 4 February 1944 he proposed that ANVIL be scrapped. The B.C.S. promptly passed the word to the J.C.S., but failed to move them; it became a matter of jest between Marshall and Eisenhower that we Americans had at long last become "Mediterraneanites"! For a time, the American view prevailed. The basic C.C.S. directive of 12 February 1944 to General

Eisenhower declared that the Allied Commander in Chief, Mediterranean Theater (General Wilson), "will conduct operations designed to assist your operation, including the launching of an attack against the South of France at about the same time as OVERLORD."

General Wilson, however, did not take this very seriously. "Even if the C.C.S. should find the resources," he wrote, "I was now opposed to their expenditure in this way." On 22 February he signaled both the B.C.S. and the J.C.S. that even a two-division assault on Southern France "would have a most serious effect on the operations in Italy," and he recommended "that the projected operation be canceled." [4]

Stalemate on the Italian front at Monte Cassino caused the J.C.S. to weaken. On 26 February they yielded to British objections to the extent of agreeing to consider postponing ANVIL if the situation in Italy had not improved by 1 April. Eisenhower gave his consent to the postponement on 21 March, but even he considered the prospects for a Southern France invasion very doubtful. [5]

Next, the Americans tried to make a deal in which the chips were those indispensable workhorses of the Fleet, the LSTs. Admiral Lord Mountbatten's Indian Ocean amphibious forces had already been cannibalized in order to obtain LST for Anzio. In December 1943, when that operation was coming up, 56 American LST were scheduled to depart shortly for British waters to train for OVERLORD, leaving a mere 30 for the entire Mediterranean, and there was no denying that there was not enough vehicle-lift for Anzio. President Roosevelt consented to Wilson's keeping the 56 ships on the understanding that "OVERLORD remains the paramount operation" and "that Rhodes and the Ægean," two of Mr. Churchill's pet schemes, "must be sidetracked." In March 1944, when Anzio beachhead was still a drain on our resources, Wilson asked that all LST then in the Mediterranean be kept there indefinitely, the United States to provide new ones to replace those earmarked for OVERLORD. The

---

[4] "Revised Draft of SAC Despatch" p. 5; Ehrman V 231.
[5] Ehrman V 247.

J.C.S. then proposed that, in return for a firm commitment for ANVIL, they would consent (1) to postpone it for about two months after Normandy D-day, so that some of the assault shipping could double for both operations; and (2) to supply additional beaching craft for the postponed ANVIL.

Sounds fair enough; but the British refused to "buy." After two weeks' more dickering, the C.C.S. on 19 April could agree only to direct General Wilson (*a*) to go all-out in Italy; (*b*) to develop the most effective threat possible to contain German forces in Southern France; and (*c*) to plan for the "best possible use" of his remaining amphibious lift, "either in support of operations in Italy, or in order to take advantage of opportunities arising in the South of France or elsewhere for the furtherance of your objects."[6] About as "woolly" a directive as one can imagine. But ". . . or elsewhere" meant a bottle or two for Mr. Churchill's brainchild, Ljubljana, which he was trying to nurse from a somewhat puny baby to a lusty brat.

Implicit in this debate was the fundamental difference which had bedeviled Anglo-American strategic plans since 1942. The Americans, who had the Pacific war on their hands, were anxious to carry out decisions once made, for which they had to make long-term logistic plans. The British hated rigid commitments which might prevent us from exploiting a sudden break in the enemy armor. The Americans wished to go all-out for a direct attack on the heart of Germany by obtaining more than one lodgment in France; the British wished to use in Italy "or elsewhere" forces not required for Normandy. The Americans had concluded that the Italian campaign, which they never liked, would never get us anywhere; the British still felt that the Germans could be pushed out of Italy if Wilson were given a few more divisions. Monte Cassino fell on

---

[6] Pogue p. 117. General Wilson in "Revised Draft of SAC Despatch" p. 26 states that on 22 March the British Chiefs of Staff proposed that the projected operation (ANVIL) be canceled as an operation but retained as a threat, and on 19 April the U.S. Chiefs of Staff agreed to this proposal. I do not think that this is a correct inference from the C.C.S. directive of 19 April quoted above; but it did encourage General Wilson to expect nothing to be done that would weaken him in Italy.

11 May, but it was highly probable that if American and French divisions were now withdrawn from the Italian front to train for ANVIL, another Italian stalemate would occur.

A glance at the map of France will show why Marshall and Eisenhower continued to insist on ANVIL, even after it was postponed two months and so could no longer directly support the invasion of Normandy. Their first consideration was to secure, for the forthcoming advance across the Rhine, another major port where French and American troops could enter to support Eisenhower's right flank, and through which they could be supported. There was a "backlog" of trained infantry divisions in the United States which could not be handled through inadequate Channel ports or over the beaches of Normandy. Marseilles, "the mother city of Western Europe," filled the bill perfectly. It is about a hundred miles nearer the German frontier at Belfort than Cherbourg is to the Saar; it is served by a major railway, excellent roads and the navigable Rhone. Marseilles and the Rhone with its connecting canals are to France what New York City, the Hudson and the Erie Canal are to the northeastern United States. The only practical alternative was Bordeaux; but the only way to wrest Bordeaux from the Germans would be to land near Marseilles or Cette, and roll about 200 miles cross-country to the Bay of Biscay.

Although Marseilles was in the picture from the first, as a port of Army supply, its importance relative to other objectives increased after ANVIL was postponed; and in the end the wish to use Marseilles as a major port of entry dominated American strategic thinking on the subject. There was also the political and sentimental value of using French troops to liberate Central and Southern France, where the F.F.I. was already very strong. And it was desirable to eject the German U-boats from their last Mediterranean bases, at Toulon and Marseilles, where, in the summer of 1944, they were constructing submarine pens with concrete roofs 23 feet thick.[7] Yet Mr. Churchill's attitude, right up to 10 August, was "anything but ANVIL." He saw no need of it and wanted no part of it.

[7] Heinz Eberbach "Last German Submarine in the Western Mediterranean."

Dislike it as he might, ANVIL was still on the Allied program. On 7 June, three days after the fall of Rome, General Wilson declared that he would be ready to launch it on 15 August.[8] General Eisenhower renewed his plea to have this date firmed up, and ANVIL became a leading subject of discussion at the meeting of the C.C.S. on 11–15 June. General Marshall and the other American members pressed for it, but the British brought out that lusty young baby ". . . or elsewhere" whom the Prime Minister had been nursing. They proposed that all Allied forces in the Mediterranean concentrate on pushing the Germans right up the Italian boot into Venetia Giulia and Istria, whence the drive should continue up via the Ljubljana Gap through Yugoslavia into the Hungarian plain. Budapest or, even better, Vienna, might be secured in time for the next high-level conference; the war might even end there, with a second Congress of Vienna.

Since hindsight strategists argue that if the Allies had done what Churchill wanted they could have prevented the "Iron Curtain" from falling outside Austria, Hungary and the Balkans, we must take a quick look at the Ljubljana Gap. Unless the Allies managed to push the Germans beyond the Po, this operation would have had to start with an amphibious landing on the Istrian peninsula near Trieste. All naval planners, as well as the French and American generals, looked upon that with dismay. It would have meant thrusting a naval force up the long, narrowing and heavily mined Adriatic between enemy-held shores. The distance from Gibraltar to Trieste is one thousand miles more than the distance from Gibraltar to Marseilles, and a Trieste operation would require about threefold the shipping to support the same number of troops as an invasion of Southern France.

Even if the Germans were routed out of Italy so that no amphibious landing near Trieste were necessary, the obstacles to sending a military force from the Adriatic to the Hungarian plain were tremendous. The so-called Ljubljana Gap is an area between the Julian and the Dinaric Alps where the mountains are not quite so

[8] "Revised Draft of SAC Despatch" p. 30.

high as they are to the north or the south. A route through it had been developed by Austria in the nineteenth century to link Vienna with Trieste. Between them, passing through Ljubljana (Laibach), a double-track railway and a 20-foot-wide road had been constructed. The highway was very winding and poorly surfaced, with gradients up to one in ten, and it crossed two 2000-foot passes dominated by much higher mountains. The region is one of heavy rainfall, and the roads, frequently blocked by winter snows, run through gorgelike defiles, heavily forested, which leave no room for vehicles to maneuver. The railway also passes through narrow gorges and over high passes during the first 185 miles of the 370-mile stretch from Trieste to Vienna. Mr. Churchill in his arguments against ANVIL, and even the official historian of British Grand Strategy,[9] stressed the "rugged nature" of the Rhone valley up which troops there committed would have to march; but the route north from Marseilles is an open speedway compared with the Ljubljana route to Vienna, which Mr. Churchill seems to have viewed as a sort of Sherman's march through Georgia in reverse. Kesselring was ready to set up a defense against a landing near Trieste, just as he did against the one at Anzio, and later he began constructing defense positions on each side of the Ljubljana Gap.[10] Tito probably — though by no means certainly — would have helped the Allies, but if forces allocated to ANVIL had been diverted to that region, it is extremely unlikely that they would have passed Ljubljana before the summer of 1945. Russian armies reached Bucharest on 31 August 1944, and any army would have had to make an amazingly quick rush through the Gap to have beaten them to Vienna. One may further observe that the conquest of enemy territory by Anglo-American forces did not necessarily save it from going behind the Iron Curtain — witness Montgomery's advance to Lübeck and Patton's to the outskirts of Prague in April and May 1945.

The London meeting of the C.C.S. at which this Ljubljana proj-

[9] Ehrman V 239, 249.
[10] Kesselring *A Soldier's Record* (1954) p. 261.

ect was discussed ended on 15 June without coming to any decision. Generals Marshall and Arnold and Admiral King then flew to the Mediterranean to obtain the views of the theater commanders. On the 17th, Marshall and Arnold conferred with General Wilson; with his deputy, General Devers USA; with Air Chief Marshal Slessor and other high British commanders at Caserta. Marshall pointed out that the many United States infantry divisions which were being readied for the European theater must have a better port of entry for themselves and their logistic supply than Cherbourg, and Wilson appeared to be impressed. Nevertheless he recommended to the C.C.S. on 19 June that ANVIL be given up; that "the continuation of General Alexander's land advance to the Po valley and the Ljubljana Gap, with the assistance of amphibious operations against Trieste in September, would be the best way to help General Eisenhower's operations in Northern France." [11]

"Ike" naturally did not see how a Balkan safari would help him. On 23 June he replied indirectly to "Jumbo" Wilson, urging that, if ANVIL could not be launched by 30 August, all French divisions then in the Mediterranean, and one or two American divisions as well, be committed to France by whatever ports were then available. This brought Churchill again into the fray. In a dispatch to Roosevelt on 28 June he begged his support on "doing justice to the great opportunities" in the Mediterranean. "Let us resolve not to wreck one great campaign [Italy] for the sake of another." He enlarged upon the "very great hazards, difficulties and delays" of an advance up the Rhone valley; "the country is most formidable." The President firmly replied:

As to Istria, I feel that Alexander and Smuts, for several very natural and human reasons, are inclined to disregard two vital considerations: the grand strategy firmly believed by us to be necessary to the early conclusion of the war, and the time factor as involved in the probable duration of a campaign to debouch from the Ljubljana Gap into Slovenia and Hungary. The difficulties in this advance would seem far to exceed those pictured by you in the Rhone valley, ignoring the effect

[11] "Despatch" p. 34; conversations with General Marshall and Sir John Slessor in 1956.

of organized resistance groups in France and proximity to OVERLORD forces. I am informed that for purely logistical reasons it is doubtful if, within a decisive period, it would be possible to put into the fighting beyond the Ljubljana Gap more than six divisions. Meanwhile we will be struggling to deploy in France 35 United States divisions that are now in continental United States. . . . I cannot agree to the employment of United States troops against Istria and into the Balkans, nor can I see the French agreeing to such use of French troops.

He reminded the Prime Minister that Eisenhower considered ANVIL "of transcendent importance," that plans for it were well developed, that ANVIL had been firmed up at Teheran, and that Stalin must be consulted before it could be abandoned. "My dear friend, I beg you to let us go ahead with our plan."

Finally, for purely political considerations over here, I should never survive even a slight setback in OVERLORD if it were known that fairly large forces had been diverted to the Balkans.[12]

Although "deeply grieved" by this telegram,[13] the Prime Minister was neither silenced nor convinced. Nevertheless, on 2 July the C.C.S. instructed General Wilson to launch ANVIL "at the earliest possible date," preferably 15 August. This was the best the Americans could do toward getting a firm date.

As a precaution against possible compromise of this code name, Churchill, it is said, made the humorous suggestion that the name DRAGOON be substituted, because he had been "dragooned" into accepting it.[14] And that it became.

Mr. Churchill continued to snipe at ANVIL–DRAGOON. He wished the Americans to know "that we have been ill-treated and are furious."[15] On 12 July the B.C.S. informed the J.C.S. that neither the British government nor themselves considered the operation "correct strategy." And on 5 August, after the Allied breakout in Nor-

[12] Ehrman V 353-4, *Triumph and Tragedy* pp. 722-3. General Marshall drafted this document.

[13] To F.D.R. 1 July (Ehrman V 355-57); to which F.D.R. replied next day that he believed in God and remembered his Euclid — "A straight line is the shortest distance between two points."

[14] At least this was the reason for the change according to rumor in the Mediterranean.

[15] Ehrman V 361.

mandy, the Prime Minister had a long talk with General Eisenhower in which he proposed that the forces then being assembled for DRAGOON make a quick shift to Brittany, or even to French ports in the English Channel. The reason for this proposal was the fact that General Patton's troops had already invaded Brittany, whose outports were expected shortly to fall into our hands, and where the building up of a new port of entry in Quiberon Bay was still on the cards. In the discussion, General Bedell Smith joined the First Sea Lord (Sir Andrew Cunningham RN) on the side of the "P.M." He felt that, since the Expeditionary Force was already two thirds of the way across Northern France, the German divisions in Southern France would pull out without a fight; that Cherbourg which we already had, and the Brittany ports which we expected to capture shortly, could take care of logistic supply; and that Patch's and De Lattre's Armies could be deployed just as well from Brest or Cherbourg as from the shores of Provence. Admirals Ramsay and Tennant, however, favored DRAGOON, and General Eisenhower insisted on going ahead with it. As Captain Butcher relates it, "Ike said 'No,' continued saying 'No' all afternoon, and ended saying 'No' in every form of the English language at his command." [16]

The British Chiefs signaled General Wilson to be alert for a shift to Breton ports, and to stand by for the word from them. That was too much for "Jumbo," even though DRAGOON was little to his liking. He replied somewhat crisply that 5 August, ten days before D-day, was too late to shift targets; 42,000 U.S. soldiers who had already embarked in beaching craft for Provence would have to be reëmbarked in bigger ships if, instead of a short run across the Mediterranean, they were to be sent through the Strait, around Portugal and across the Bay of Biscay to Brittany. [17]

Although the top people did not seem to know it, the situation in Northern France had been radically changed by General Brad-

[16] Butcher *Three Years with Eisenhower* p. 634; *Crusade in Europe* pp. 281-84.
[17] Revised Draft of SAC "Despatch" p. 49. Ehrman (V 364-5) represents Wilson's reply as being "not entirely hostile" to the Brittany shift; my reading of the despatch is that Wilson said in effect that he could do it if the C.C.S. insisted, but it would cause all kinds of trouble and the target date would have to be postponed at least two weeks.

ley's decision to throw the weight of Patton's Third Army eastward, which meant that no harbors in Brittany would be available.[18] And Cherbourg was far from ready to take in an additional
load. Marseilles was now a "must."

The Prime Minister was still obdurate; he appeared to think it as
easy to shift targets for DRAGOON as to postpone the 80-mile crossing
of the English Channel. President Roosevelt, in the Aleutians, could
not be reached, but Churchill conveyed his misgivings to Harry
Hopkins and urged him to obtain presidential consent for the switch
to Brittany. Hopkins replied that he was certain Roosevelt would
not consent; nor did he, when he got the word.[19] On 9 August
Churchill made his last plea to Eisenhower, who was adamant; and
next day — D-day minus five — the British Chiefs directed General
Wilson to proceed with DRAGOON as planned.

Despite his inveterate opposition to this operation, Churchill made
one of his genial appearances off the landing beaches in Provence on
the afternoon of D-day, on board H.M.S. *Kimberley*. Sailors and
GIs heading for shore recognized the familiar cherubic face, long
cigar and "V" sign on the bridge, and were duly cheered and impressed. He would have been set ashore, but for strict orders to the
contrary from Cincmed, but he "had at least done the civil to
ANVIL." [20]

Through all this indecision, and uncertainty in the high command, Eighth Fleet staff went quietly ahead with its planning.

[18] This will be further considered in Chapter XVIII.
[19] Sherwood *Roosevelt and Hopkins* pp. 812–13; *Triumph and Tragedy* pp.
66–71.
[20] Same, p. 95, but see pp. 101, 107, and 120 for his disparaging remarks about
the operation even after it had been proved a success.

CHAPTER XIV

Planning and Training[1]

January–August 1944

1. The Plan, Forces and Defenses

GENERAL EISENHOWER'S joint planning staff at Algiers had an "appreciation" or "estimate of the situation" [2] for ANVIL ready on Christmas Eve, 1943. The objectives there stated were "in conjunction with the invasion of Northern France to establish a Mediterranean beachhead and subsequently to exploit towards Lyons and Vichy." Directives were promptly issued to Admiral Hewitt and Commanding General Seventh Army. Detailed planning began early in the new year at the École Normale in Bouzarea, a suburb of Algiers. To Admiral Hewitt's staff were joined representatives of Seventh Army (Brigadier General Garrison H. Davidson USA) and the Allied Mediterranean Air Forces (Brigadier General Gordon P. Saville USA commanding XII Army Air Force).

The experienced Captain Robert A. J. English headed Admiral Hewitt's planners. The French Army shared in the planning after 15 April 1944, when De Gaulle appointed Général d'Armée Jean de Lattre de Tassigny to command the French II Corps in the landings, and eventually, the First French Army. Contre-Amiral Lemonnier, chief of staff of the French Navy, a great enthusiast for DRAGOON, assigned one of his officers to Admiral Hewitt's staff.

[1] Naval Commander Western Task Force (Vice Adm. H. K. Hewitt) "Report on Invasion of Southern France" 15 Nov. 1944, an unusually comprehensive Action Report; also his article "Planning Operation ANVIL–DRAGOON" in U.S. Naval Institute *Proceedings* LXXX (July 1954) pp. 731–45; *Seventh Army Report*, Vol. I (Heidelberg, 1946) and Sacmed "Despatch."

[2] The first is the British and the second the American term.

There is magic in the very name of Provence, but its fascinating history did not detain the task force planners. The ancient Provincia Romana, one of the "three parts" of Gaul, it was fought over for centuries by Frank, Visigoth, and Saracen; and in the eleventh century, under the Counts of Provence, became famous for the troubadours and their poetry in the Provençal language. Annexed to France in 1486, Provence became one of the seats and source of French sea power, and Toulon a great naval port. Since 1839, when Lord Brougham "discovered" the beauties of Cannes, that eastern part of the Provençal coast, the French Riviera, had become a favorite winter playground of English lords, Russian grand dukes and American millionaires.[3] Straight from this Riviera rise the snow-capped Alpes Maritimes, with picturesque hill towns like Vence, and Grasse, from which the great French sailor who won the naval battle off the Chesapeake Capes in 1781 took his title. Behind the western half of the coast the Massif d'Esterel and the Massif des Maures make an equally impressive background for deeply indented shores, pine-clad, rocky headlands and yellow beaches.

Captain Leo A. Bachman, Admiral Hewitt's Intelligence officer, probably came to know more about the beaches of Provence than anyone in the long and vivid history of that region. The reader may remember a call from Naval Intelligence in 1942 for photographs of European and African beaches. These now came into play. Thus, over the shoulders of a smiling couple in bathing suits taking the sun on the Île de Porquerolles, one observes a pier suitable for tying up PT boats. The man who snapped Mademoiselle standing on the ramparts of an old fort inadvertently chose a background which helped an Intelligence officer to make a panoramic sketch of that part of the coast. A bather standing waist-deep in the waters of Baie de Bougnon tells us that an LST may beach there dry-ramp. But the aërial verticals taken by the Army Air Force

[3] The term French Riviera, originally applied to the coast between Cannes and Mentone, has been extended westward to take in Saint-Raphaël, but is rejected by the resorts farther west. *Côte d'Azur* is a tourist-office term which the true Provençaux reject.

over several months supplied the main grist for photo interpretation. British Admiralty and French official charts contributed solid information on depths, shoals and reefs. Many French naval and military men at Algiers knew the coast intimately from residence or maneuvers of other days. The F.F.I., who were very strong in Provence, and with whom we had excellent communications, were the most important source for enemy defenses.

Selection of assault beaches was the first problem. There were several hundred possible ones between Marseilles and Nice. The choice had to be determined not only by hydrography, vehicle exits, enemy defenses and the like, but also by their possibilities for a rapid movement of troops northward and a prompt capture of Toulon and Marseilles. "Only Marseilles could be developed to serve as a major supply base," stated the staff estimate of 12 January 1944. This was always a principal objective before the planners, even though it did not loom large in the foggy atmosphere of London. Topography and the 240-mm guns guarding Toulon ruled out the 45-mile stretch of rugged coast between Marseilles and the Îles d'Hyères, and the beaches of the Rade d'Hyères; the landings must bracket the Golfe de Fréjus. There an important river valley, the Argens, cuts between two mountain chains, offering the invader a choice of routes to Toulon, Marseilles and the Rhone valley, as well as flat ground for an inland parachute drop. Along the coast on each side of the Golfe de Fréjus are several good landing beaches with easy exits; although these shores were not neglected by the Germans in their scheme of coast defense, they had been provided with weak coastal batteries compared with those installed around the large cities. Additional advantages of landing near Fréjus were the shorter distance from the nearest Allied base in Corsica, and access to a second road to the heart of France, the Route Napoléon taken by the Emperor after his return from Elba. Eventually five beaches between Cavalaire and La Calanque d'Anthéor, within a 45-mile stretch of coast, were selected for the main landings.

Planning for DRAGOON involved diplomacy. Admiral Hewitt was

under Admiral Sir John Cunningham,[4] the Allied Naval Commander in the Mediterranean, and the relationship was not always easy. The Royal Navy, which had been used to supremacy in that sea, did not relish being outnumbered by the U.S.N., and some American naval officers in the theater thought that the tactful and gentlemanly Hewitt did not stand up strongly enough for their rights. That he did so, nevertheless, may be inferred from a subsequent remark that Sir John Cunningham made to Admiral Stark in London: "I never wholly like a man until I have had a fight with him, and now that Hewitt has had it out with me, I love and respect him!"

After the fall of Rome the 3rd, 36th and 45th U.S. Infantry divisions were detached from the Fifth Army in Italy and incorporated in the Seventh Army, Lieutenant General Alexander M. Patch, which was to invade Southern France. The 45th (Major General William W. Eagles) and the 36th (Major General John E. Dahlquist), veterans of Sicily and Salerno, were ordered to the Salerno plain for retraining, while the 3rd (Major General John W. O'Daniel), veterans of Morocco, Sicily and Salerno, trained at Pozzuoli on the Bay of Naples. These, with attached engineer, antiaircraft, tank and service units, were to form the VI Corps under Lieutenant General Lucian K. Truscott — the assault force. Two veteran French divisions, the 1st Infantry, motorized (General Brosset), and the 3rd Algerian Infantry (General de Monsabert), were withdrawn from Italy in mid-June as nucleus of the French II Corps.

General de Lattre de Tassigny was eager to share in the initial assault, but Admiral Hewitt persuaded him that there was enough confusion in amphibious operations without adding the language difficulty. A French tank and motorized infantry brigade was, however, joined to the VI Corps.

General Wilson's Mediterranean theater headquarters moved from Algiers to the ancient royal palace of Caserta, twenty miles from Naples, in early July, 1944. Seventh Army and Eighth Fleet

---

[4] Not to be confused with his predecessor, Admiral of the Fleet Sir Andrew Cunningham, who at this time was First Sea Lord.

headquarters followed on the 8th, most of the planners making the trip in Admiral Hewitt's command ship *Catoctin,* so that they could continue working at sea. In an office building on the Naples waterfront, near the Castel dell'Ovo, Army, Navy and Air Force planners on all levels worked in close juxtaposition. At last Hewitt had fulfilled his dream of how an amphibious operation should be planned. "The Admiral had only to walk out one door and in the next to be able to consult with the General and vice versa."

On 8 July General Wilson issued an order to all ground, naval and air commanders to carry out the operation; nobody below his level knew about the subsequent tergiversation in London. Wilson's directive provided a three-division assault, supported by an airborne troop-lift and an ultimate build-up to at least ten divisions, to establish a beachhead as base for the capture of Toulon and Marseilles, and to exploit toward Lyons and Vichy. He retained overall command of DRAGOON until General Eisenhower could assume operational control and responsibility for the logistic supply of the armies in France.

In the meantime Admiral Hewitt had been given three attack force commanders, each to be responsible for landing an Army division. For "Alpha" Force on the west flank, Rear Admiral Frank J. Lowry, who had commanded the assault on Anzio; [5] for "Delta" Force in the center, Rear Admiral Bertram J. Rodgers, who had made his reputation in the Pacific; [6] and, for "Camel" Force on the east flank, Rear Admiral Don P. Moon, who had commanded the Utah assault in Normandy.[7]

[5] For biography see Volume IX 325*n.*

[6] Bertram J. Rodgers, b. Pittsburgh 1894, Naval Academy '16, served in *South Carolina* World War I, submarine service until 1926. Qualified as a blimp officer and served in *Los Angeles, Akron* and *Macon,* 1928-34. C.O. *Blakeley* and *Selfridge* 1934-40; senior course at Naval War College, duty in CNO's office until 1943, when became C.O. of *Salt Lake City* and as such participated in the Battle of the Komandorskis (see Volume VII 22-36). Late that year assigned to Admiral Mountbatten's staff; CTF 85 for DRAGOON. His amphibious group in Dec. 1944 was transferred to the Pacific and took part in capture of Iwo Jima and Okinawa. Commander Amphibious Forces Pacific Fleet 1948-50; Com 12th Naval District 1950; Com Naval Forces Germany 1954.

[7] See Chapter VI and Preface to this Volume.

After much discussion, H-hour was fixed at 0800 on 15 August. A full daylight landing was an innovation in the Mediterranean. Owing to the Army's insistence on tactical surprise, all earlier landings in this theater had been made under cover of darkness. Admiral Hewitt had always been against night landings, with their inevitable foul-ups; at last he had won the Army over to his way of thinking. Intelligence reports showed that coastal defenses along this shore were formidable, though lacking the depth and volume of those in Normandy, and one of the lessons of NEPTUNE was that daylight landings would permit intensive prior aërial bombing and naval bombardment of beach defenses. These considerations did not apply to commando raids on the flanks, for which darkness was a necessity. The last-quarter moon, rising at 0315, would give enough light for them and for the paratroop drop.

The assault plan for the main force was to push rapidly inland, link up with the paratroops and drive toward the D plus 2 "blue line," a semicircle extending about 15 miles inland. Beginning on D plus 1, the French II Corps would begin landing over the west-ernmost beaches and fan out to capture Toulon and Marseilles, while Seventh Army pushed up the Rhone valley.

Rear Admiral Davidson, experienced in gunfire support in Sicily and Italy, was the natural choice for overall command of naval gunfire. He and his staff gunnery officer visited Normandy on 16 June and made a thorough study of the German defenses and Allied experience in overcoming them.

As the Eighth Fleet included nothing larger than light cruisers *Brooklyn* and *Philadelphia*, Admiral Hewitt asked Admiral King to order more fire support vessels to be sent to him from the English Channel, which was done. Five battleships were finally made available: *Nevada, Texas* and *Arkansas;* H.M.S. *Ramillies*, and French *Lorraine*. Heavy cruisers *Augusta, Quincy* and *Tuscaloosa* and many destroyers and beaching craft also moved south from the English Channel in late June and early July. The destroyers assigned to the Western Naval Task Force included a number manned by

Polish and Greek sailors and flying the flags of these countries.[8] For close air support, and to provide spotting planes for naval gunfire, an aircraft carrier force was assigned, under Rear Admiral Troubridge RN. It comprised seven British and two American escort carriers, screened by four antiaircraft cruisers and thirteen destroyers, divided into two task groups, one of which was commanded by Rear Admiral Calvin T. Durgin in *Tulagi.* The XII Tactical and Bomber Commands were partly fleeted up to Corsican airfields in order to prepare for the preliminary bombing and protection of the convoys.

Lieutenant Commander S. M. Barnes's PT boats had the task of screening the assault from surface attack by light German craft. Barnes and his boys, who had been conducting a sea-borne vendetta against German coastal traffic since the fall of 1943, were now based on Bastia, Corsica.

The Western Naval Task Force, in contrast to the floating part of the Normandy assault, was predominantly American in composition as well as in command, but the Royal Navy made a substantial contribution, including a battleship, seven light cruisers, over 25 destroyers, several transports, and a number of minecraft, tugboats and LCT. The French Navy contingent included most of the ships that had been in OVERLORD, and several others. The Canadian Navy provided two fast converted transports.

Generaloberst Johannes Blackowitz, commanding Army Group G (First and Nineteenth Armies), was responsible for the defense of Southern France, corresponding to Rommel in the North. It was he who directed the German retirement from the Mediterranean to the Vosges. Under General Wiese, four divisions of the Nineteenth Army were located between the mouth of the Rhone and the Spanish border; two were garrisoned at Marseilles and Toulon; and one, a reserve division, was charged with coast defense east of Toulon. On D-day the 11th Panzer Division of the First

[8] See Appendix II for complete list. Lt. Cdr. Barnes, the PT commander, took care to parade his boats past H.H.M.S. *Themistocles* in daylight; said he didn't want the Greeks to mistake them for Germans — or Persians!

Army was rolling from the vicinity of Bordeaux toward the Rhone, having been ordered thither when air reconnaissance spotted convoy movements on 13 August. Germany had about 30,000 troops in the assault zone and over 200,000 near enough to be committed, if the coastal defense could manage to hold up the invaders for a few days. A vain hope, indeed.

Coastal defenses in Provence, including many served by German naval gunners, were fairly formidable, but not in a class with those of Normandy. The Germans made maximum use of railroad guns, heavy coast artillery, field pieces, old French and Italian guns, and heavy naval guns transferred from French warships. Many were emplaced in heavy concrete casemates. There was the usual crust of local defenses behind the beaches — concrete blockhouses, antitank walls and tank traps, pillboxes, barbed wire, minefields, tank turrets mounted in concrete and villas camouflaged to conceal big guns. Thousands of land mines were planted on the beaches and behind them, with a density found nowhere else but in Normandy. Underwater obstacles were much less formidable than in Normandy, and after the experience at Omaha beach the Navy was better prepared to cope with them.

2. *Training and Rehearsal*

In March 1944 a joint Army-Navy Obstacle Board was set up to work on the problem of clearing beach obstructions. In Salerno Bay an experimental beach was rigged with copies of the German underwater obstacles to test the special devices developed at Fort Pierce, Florida. A particular problem was the slight tide in the Mediterranean, eight inches on D-day, which meant that underwater obstacles remained submerged and difficult to get at. On 20–21 June a demonstration of equipment and techniques was conducted on the experimental beach. The Air Force hit the beach with showers of small bombs rigged with special fuzes to detonate a few feet above the ground, for cutting wire obstacles and exploding land mines, and the Navy tried out its own chamber of horrors to cope with German devices. These were the "Woofus," a rocket-equipped LCM carrying 7.2-inch rockets with a range of 300 yards; the "apex" drone boat, remote-controlled landing craft filled with tons of high explosives, to be detonated over underwater obstacles; "Reddy fox," a pipe filled with explosives to be towed into obstacles, sunk and detonated. The demonstration proved that none were dependable, and that ultimate reliance would have to be placed upon underwater demolition units. In August no fewer than 41 teams of the "frogmen" were available for the assault. Each team consisted of one naval officer, five sailors and five enlisted Army Engineers.

The Army's Invasion Training Center was moved from North Africa to Salerno in the spring of 1944 and, in June, when the infantry divisions for the assault were released, it was placed under Seventh Army. The 45th and 36th Divisions, with their corresponding Naval attack forces, trained at Salerno; the 3rd Division trained at Pozzuoli and conducted landing exercises in the Gulf of Gaëta. The 1st Special Service Force practiced commando-like landings from fast destroyer transports off Agropoli and conducted a full scale rehearsal 6 August, on the islands of Ponza and Zennone, which were similar in character to their targets in the Rade d'Hyères.[9] Exercises for Navy beach battalions, Army shore parties and shore fire control parties were conducted jointly. Battleships, cruisers and destroyers laid on a three-day bombardment exercise, using shore fire control parties, at Camerata south of Salerno. The training period was topped by full-scale rehearsals off beaches near the training areas between 31 July and 6 August.

A tragic event now occurred. Rear Admiral Moon, last of the attack force commanders to arrive in the Mediterranean, plunged at once, with his usual conscientious vigor, into the trainings and rehearsals. Already worn out by the strain of commanding the Utah landings, he worried over the DRAGOON plan, and what he believed to be the unreadiness of his force. On 4 August, after a succession of sleepless nights, he begged Commander Western Task Force to

9 H.M.C.S. *Prince Henry* Report of Proceedings 18 Sept. 1944.

have D-day postponed. Admiral Hewitt tried to reassure him that things were not as bad as they seemed. He promised to observe the final rehearsal himself and, if it proved unsatisfactory, to take up the matter of postponement with General Wilson. Admiral Moon was apparently satisfied with this assurance; but the following morning he took his own life, a victim of extreme physical and mental fatigue.[10]

To replace him as attack force commander, Hewitt appointed his own chief of staff, Rear Admiral Spencer S. Lewis,[11] who was familiar with the plans. Captain Francis P. Old, Lewis's able deputy, then became Hewitt's chief of staff.

One late arrival who took things in his stride was Rear Admiral Theodore E. Chandler.[12] Detached temporarily from his command of Crudiv 2, he turned up at Naples 6 August to command a group of converted British and Canadian merchant ships which were to float a temperamental force of French, Canadian and American commandos to the Rade d'Hyères.

All participants agree that the training for DRAGOON was very thorough. Admiral Lowry said that all hands were so thoroughly indoctrinated in their respective tasks that they "could have made the landing without an operation order." "Seldom has an army moved from combat into training and then into combat again with so little loss of time," said General Patch.[18] Timing is indeed vital to the success of an amphibious assault, and well-nigh perfect timing was obtained in DRAGOON because all troops landed by the Western Naval Task Force were trained by that Force, thus breeding confidence and mutual respect.

[10] Hewitt in U.S. Naval Institute *Proceedings* LXXX (July 1954) p. 744; information from Cdr. Frank P. Morton USNR and Lt. Cdr. Rupert N. Allan USNR in 1944.

[11] Spencer S. Lewis, b. Texas 1888, Naval Academy '10, C.O. *Patterson* in World War I and of *Herbert* 1921; staff of Com Scouting Fleet 1922–23, exec. *Cleveland* 1925–28, gunnery officer *Wyoming* 1930–31; office of C.N.O. until 1935, exec. *Northampton* to 1937; Naval War College senior course; C.O. *Cincinnati* 1939–41; chief of staff successively to Rear Admiral Fletcher during Battle of Midway, to Admiral Hewitt, and to Admiral Stark 1945–46; retired 1947.

[12] Biography in Volume X 204*n*.

[18] *Seventh Army Report* I p. 89.

3. *Aërial Bombing; Mounting and Approach*

A highly important phase of DRAGOON was the preliminary aërial bombing, heavier and more prolonged than anything hitherto tried in the Mediterranean. The purpose of this effort was not only destruction of strongpoints but deception of the enemy as to the intended target. Everyone agreed that strategic surprise was impossible to obtain; the enemy must know that a big Mediterranean operation was impending when fleets and armies were assembling in many ports. But tactical surprise — keeping the Germans ignorant of the exact set of beaches where we would land — might be achieved by bombing several areas and landing in only one of them.

This pre-D-day bombing, accordingly, was aimed at four different stretches of coast in Southern France and one in Italy: (1) the region around Cette from Cap d'Agde to Montpellier; (2) Marseilles and Toulon; (3) the actual assault area; and (4) the Italian Riviera from Cape Mele to Genoa.

Strategic bombers of the Mediterranean Allied Air Forces began their softening up on 29 April 1944 with a raid on Toulon harbor. Up to D-day, Strategic had flown 5408 sorties, which had dropped 6407 tons of bombs, aimed mostly at railways and bridges. Every bridge over the Rhone, Durance and Var rivers was destroyed, with the exception of the famous Pont d'Avignon, which hardly mattered as it had fallen in years ago. But this was only about half the tonnage dropped; in the meantime Tactical went after coast defense batteries and radar stations, bringing the total bomb tonnage up to 12,500.[14] The number of targets selected in each of the three non-assault areas was approximately the same as in the intended assault area, so that the Germans could not guess which one we had actually selected for the attack. Daily entries in the German war diaries testify to the large number of guns and radar stations that were being put out of business by the repeated bombings.

[14] This was about one sixth of the bomb tonnage dropped on Northern France by Normandy D-day (Pogue p. 132).

This equal distribution of gifts was kept up from 5 to 15 August. On the 12th the war diary of the German Naval Staff at Berlin noted that a large-scale landing, either near Genoa or in Southern France, was imminent. A "dependable agent" at Naples having signaled to Berlin the presence there of *Augusta*, enemy Intelligence inferred that General Eisenhower would not have released so powerful a ship merely to bombard the Italian coast. The last entry in the War Diary of Konteradmiral Ruhfus at Toulon for 12 August declared that the whole coast was "in great danger. . . . It can hardly be hoped that an invasion can be beaten off by our forces, which are much too weak." Admiral Krancke at Paris jotted down his opinion on the 13th that the assault would start two days thence; and on the 14th he added that it would probably be "in great strength on the Rhone delta," with landings on a smaller scale between Nice and Toulon. Thus, the deceptive measures failed to deceive the enemy. He was unable to pinpoint the landings, but he had a fairly accurate idea of their locality.

During the last day or two of the air bombardment the XV Army Air Force, based on Southern Italy, which for some time had been working over the Ploesti oil fields in Rumania, got into action over Provence. Night bombers hit the coast at first light 14 August, and an air group, each plane carrying ten 500-lb. bombs, plastered the Îles d'Hyères and the coast eastward at 1615 that day. The same group took part in the pre-H-hour bombing on D-day. This operation was distinguished by good timing and execution by well-trained aviators, against negligible opposition from antiaircraft batteries and none from the Luftwaffe,[15] and in perfect weather conditions. Enemy air strength in Southern France had been greatly overestimated by Allied Intelligence.[16] On D-day there were only 14 Do–217 glide bombers, 65 Ju–88 torpedo bombers and a few dozen fighter planes within range of the beaches.

Although the strength of the DRAGOON assault fell short of NEP-

[15] Report to writer by Capt. William M. Taussig USA, navigator of 451st Bombardment Group. He observed that if there had been any antiaircraft opposition on D-day, many bombs would have been released prematurely and hit our own ships.
[16] Hewitt p. 36.

Official Bureau of Aeronautics photo

Left to right: Contre-Amiral Lemonnier, an aide, Vice Admiral
H. Kent Hewitt USN, General Sir Henry Maitland Wilson, Admiral
Sir John Cunningham RN, Captain R. A. J. English USN

DRAGOON *Commanders on Board U.S.S.* Catoctin,
Examining Models of the Shore of Provence

The Bay of Naples before Fleet Sortie

LSTs loading at Nisida

Just before Operation DRAGOON

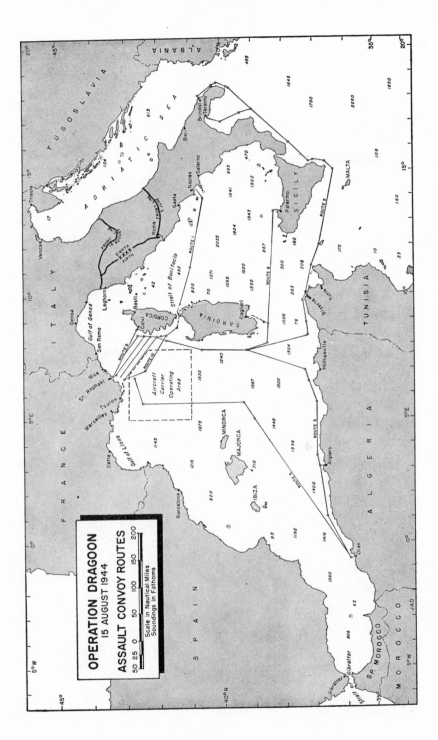

OPERATION DRAGOON
15 AUGUST 1944

ASSAULT CONVOY ROUTES

Scale in Nautical Miles
Soundings in Fathoms

TUNE, and of three later amphibious operations in the Pacific, it was indeed a major operation. A total of 880 ships, vessels and beaching craft reached the assault area on their own bottoms, and the landing craft carried on decks and in davits numbered over 1370. The aircraft engaged were more numerous than in any previous assault, excepting NEPTUNE.

The most important loading and embarkation points were included in the bay and harbor of Naples. Attack transports and freighters and Liberty ships embarked American troops from the Naples docks; beaching craft loaded at Nisida, Baia and Pozzuoli. Commandos for the predawn assaults assembled at Agropoli; the two assault French divisions were mounted at Taranto and Brindisi. Malta sheltered the escort carriers and the "Alpha" gunfire support force. The "Delta" support force under Rear Admiral Bryant, including the French cruisers, assembled at Taranto; [17] the "Camel" support force started from Palermo. Oran in Algeria was headquarters for most of the French Army build-up. Corsica was a godsend for the Western Task Force not only for mounting and staging beaching craft convoys, but for fleeting up supplies.

Logistics were well taken care of. By D-day eight British ammunition issue ships were at Propriano and La Maddalena and several American ammunition ships were at Oran, Bizerta and Palermo. Corsican harbors were studded with recently erected fuel tanks, YMSs were prepared to ply between them and the beachhead, and four United States fleet tankers were waiting at Palermo, Naples and Oran in case of need. The general stores issue ship *Pleiades* was at Augusta; *Yukon*, third "reefer" to arrive in the Mediterranean since 15 July, had just discharged 2750 tons of provisions into ships and warehouses at four principal ports.[18]

Convoy routes to the destination, which may be seen graphically on the appended chart, were worked out with regard to air cover, escort and proper timing. Main convoys from Naples passed through the Strait of Bonifacio and along the west coast of Corsica.

[17] Except the *Fantasque* class, which started from Bizerta.
[18] W. R. Carter & E. E. Duvall *Ships, Salvage and Sinews of War* (1954) chap. xvi; Hewitt chap. vi.

After passing Cap Corse the assault convoys lunged eastward, in the hope that German reconnaissance planes would conclude that they were heading for Genoa. By nightfall 14 August every ship so routed changed course and headed straight for her destination.

Never before had an amphibious force embarked so fit, ready, and full of *élan* as this one for the invasion of Provence. From H.M.S. *Kimberley*, holding station north of Corsica where the convoys divided and headed for their destinations, Admiral Sir John Cunningham sent a signal to Admiral Hewitt in *Catoctin:* "All convoys have passed at the planned moment. An operation so well organized must succeed."

CHAPTER XV

Night Landings in Provence[1]

14–15 August 1944

MAIN LANDINGS were timed for 0800 August 15, but there was plenty of "dirty work in the dark" before that: deceptions, diversions, commando raids and parachute drops. Operation DRAGOON opened at 2200 August 14 when Admiral Davidson arrived off Hyères roadstead in *Augusta* to supervise raids on the western flank. Shortly after midnight the reference vessels — destroyers, patrol craft and subchasers — began to take stations off the Alpha, Delta and Camel beaches, and shortly after that the predawn air operations began. No fewer than 396 transport planes of Provisional Troop Carrier Air Division, carrying over 5000 paratroops,[2] took off from ten different airfields near Rome shortly after midnight. Preceded by a squadron of Pathfinder planes and escorted by night fighters and radar jammers, they made for Cap Corse, the northern promontory of Corsica. Thence to the French coast, three beacon ships, stationed at 30-mile intervals, directed the formation north of the convoy lanes to a point on the coast south of Cap d'Antibes, whence it was only a few minutes' flight to the selected drop area on high ground near Le Muy. The Pathfinders made the target at 0315 August 15, just as the last-quarter moon

[1] Hewitt pp. 47, 181–2, 275; Craven & Cate III 427–8; *Seventh Army Report* I 110–15; CTF 86 (Rear Adm. Davidson) Action Report 21 Oct. 1944; CTG 86.3 (Rear Adm. Chandler) Action Report 30 Aug. 1944; Lt. Col. Robert D. Burhans *First Special Service Force* (1947) pp. 257–70; Joseph Schull *The Far Distant Ships* (Ottawa, 1950) pp. 362–65; C.O. of *Prince Henry* (Capt. V. S. Godfrey RCN) "Report of Proceedings" 18 Sept. 1944, same by C.O. of H.M.C.S. *Prince David* (Cdr. T. D. Kelly RCNR) with "Narrative Sitka-Romeo Force," in Canadian Naval Archives; information from Service Historique de la Marine, Paris.

[2] Mostly U.S. Army but included a British brigade, the only British troops except commandos in Operation DRAGOON. Maj. Gen. Robert T. Frederick USA commanded.

rose to light their way; the troop carriers completed their "spill-out" at 0514; and at 0926 seventy-one aircraft towed in a fleet of gliders with reinforcements.

Although the weather was far from perfect — a heavy mist had gathered over the land — this paratroop drop was one of the best in the entire war. Almost all men and equipment came down where they intended, and so compactly that they could organize quickly. Every plane returned safely to base. These airborne troops repulsed German counterattacks and captured the town of Le Muy in the early afternoon. They even accomplished something not in the plan — seized a German Army corps headquarters at Draguignan, depriving the troops in that region of leadership and communications. Before the end of D-day they had taken almost 500 prisoners and made contact with the 45th Division.

Earliest of the deceptive measures was a simulated attack on the Baie de la Ciotat, a break in the rugged coast between Marseilles and Toulon where the Germans believed a major landing to be possible. At 0155, five C–47s expelled 300 dummy paratroops rigged with demolition charges near La Ciotat, and flew back to Ajaccio, dropping "window" at frequent intervals to register phantom planes on enemy radar screens. The Germans were taken in, for a time. Some who made the mistake of trying to jab a "paratrooper" with a bayonet were unpleasantly surprised by the resulting explosion. Although the Germans were past masters at booby-trapping everything from fountains to fountain pens, they regarded this ruse as dastardly. Radio Berlin denounced it as a deception which "could only have been conceived in the sinister Anglo-Saxon mind."

Following this air preliminary, a division of the Special Operations Group commanded by Captain Henry C. Johnson in destroyer *Endicott*, together with eight motor torpedo boats, a dozen air-sea rescue craft and some British Fairmiles, came tearing along within radar range of Baie de la Ciotat, streaming reflector balloons and making a terrific din to simulate the motions of a major landing. Plenty of enemy fire was drawn, but there is no evidence that this gag worked; the Germans had been "had" more than once in similar deceptions. It merely gave Radio Berlin the opportunity to claim that a major landing had been bloodily repulsed.

At the other extremity of the assault area, another division of the Special Operations Group, commanded by Lieutenant Commander Douglas E. Fairbanks USNR in person, consisting of gunboats H.M.S. *Aphis* and *Scarab*, a fighter-director ship and four PTs, had been steering toward Genoa and simulating a big task force. This diversion was known as "Rosie." The PTs debarked the Groupe Navale d'Assaut de Corse (67 commandos under Capitaine de Frégate Seriot) in rubber boats off Pointe de l'Esquillon, about halfway between Cap Roux and Cannes. Their object was to cut the Corniche road so that the enemy could not move troops into the main assault area from Nice and Cannes. They landed at 0140 August 15 at the foot of a steep cliff, and while scrambling up to the road had the misfortune to run into a land-mine field, whose explosions attracted the Germans. After suffering several casualties, the survivors reëmbarked, only to encounter two friendly planes which machine-gunned their boats. The commandos jumped overboard and swam ashore, where they were taken prisoner.[3]

Gunboats *Aphis* and *Scarab*, in the meantime, fired a few shells along the Riviera eastward, and the fighter-director ship made enough racket to simulate an entire task force. Lieutenant Commander Fairbanks was rewarded by hearing from Radio Berlin that the Allies had landed near Cannes, and that Antibes and Nice had been bombarded by "four or five large battleships."

Heaviest of the raider groups, with the most important mission, was dignified by the status of a force with the name "Sitka." Its objectives were to land French commandos on Cap Nègre for cutting the two roads from Toulon into the main assault area, to knock out enemy batteries, and to capture the two easternmost Îles d'Hyères.

Something had to be done about the Îles d'Hyères. These beauti-

[3] CTU 80.4.2 (Lt. Cdr. Fairbanks) Report; Compte rendu 34 G.N.A. du 30-8-44 du Capt. de F. Seriot, French Naval Archives. A tablet on the wall of the Corniche road close to the Pte. de L'Esquillon marks the spot. The prisoners were liberated next day by F.F.I. and a unit of the 36th Division.

ful, pine-clad islands, recalling by their outline and their many indentations Isle au Haut or Mount Desert off the New England coast, had not been ignored by the Germans. A three-gun 164-mm battery on the easternmost island, Île du Levant, dominated all approaches to the Alpha landing beaches. The only way to be sure of it before H-hour was to land troops and take it.

Although everything in the Sitka area came under Rear Admiral Davidson, the "Sitka-Romeo" force, charged with capturing the islands, was commanded by Rear Admiral Chandler, who flew his flag temporarily in a converted Canadian vessel similar to our destroyer transports: H.M.C.S. *Prince Henry*. The four other transports in this force, British or Canadian "Princes," carried about 2300 men of the First Special Service Force, half Canadians and half Americans, commanded by Colonel Edwin A. Walker usa, together with 800 French commandos. All were provided with rubber boats, electric-motored surfboards, kayaks, razor-edged knives for slitting the throats of German sentries, and other weapons dear to raiders. Five United States destroyer-transports acted as escorts and gunfire support vessels.

The "Princes" anchored four or five miles off the Îles d'Hyères in the last hours of 14 August and had their boats in the water before eight bells sounded the beginning of D-day and the midwatch. Low-profiled British LCAs towed the rubber boats, crammed with troops, and cast them off a thousand yards from shore. Ahead of them, scouts in one-man kayaks or prone on electric surfboards checked the target beaches and discreetly coached in the boats by hooded lights. A selected portion of these raiders landed on the Levant and Port Cros islands between 0135 and 0200.

There was little resistance; the Germans were completely surprised, and most of them surrendered. But their surprise was nothing to ours when it was ascertained that the 164-mm battery on Île du Levant, occasion of all this fuss and mystery, was nothing but a few wooden guns manned by dummies. For a second time in three months, the Allies had fallen for one of the oldest ruses in the art of war — the "Quaker gun."

Rear Admiral Davidson's flagship *Augusta* had been maneuvering in her offshore station since 2200. Suddenly a flash shot up from the calm sea "like a torch suddenly thrust over polished basalt," as an onlooker described it, followed by the rumble of gunfire. All eyes stared out to sea. What was going on?

Destroyer *Somers* was enjoying a brief fight. At 0347 while patrolling south of Île du Levant, she had picked up on her radar two strange ships heading toward the assault area. Having been cautioned by Admiral Davidson not to "give away the show" by premature gunfire, Commander W. C. Hughes shadowed these ships for an hour, challenged them with searchlight, and fired only when they failed to reply. One, a German auxiliary named *Escaburt*, burst into flames with a hit from the first salvo — that was the torch seen from *Augusta*. She was promptly abandoned by her protector, *UJ–6081* (ex-Italian corvette *Camoscio*), which turned southeasterly at high speed. Passing within radar distance of *Augusta*, this 565-ton ship bemused the sailors in the flagship's combat information center — "Maybe it's the *Tirpitz!*" exclaimed a young ensign. The German sailors, unfortunately ignorant of this compliment to their vessel, abandoned ship after daybreak had deprived them of all hope of escape. A boarding party from *Somers* ascertained that she had taken more than 40 hits and could not be salvaged. They picked up some useful charts and left her to sink at 0722 August 15. *Escaburt*, burning and exploding in the meantime, had illuminated the entire Alpha area and alerted every German ashore.

Colonel Walker, who reported before dawn that Île du Levant was secured, soon learned better. About 50 Germans with mortars and machine guns were holed up in a cave on the northwestern end. H.M.S. *Lookout* tried gunfire on them, but could not penetrate the cave. As General Patch, with Admiral Hewitt in *Catoctin*, was unable to get in contact with Colonel Walker by radio, he decided in the late afternoon to send an officer ashore to find out what was going on. A distinguished passenger in *Catoctin*, the Honorable James Forrestal, Secretary of the Navy, went along "for the ride." Landing on Levant near the close of twilight, they found that the

Colonel had an entire regiment deployed around the strongpoint, which surrendered shortly after the party had returned on board ship, at 2300 August 15.

Île de Port Cros put up more of a fight than Île du Levant. The main German garrison had occupied three old stone forts built in the Napoleonic era; one of them had 12-foot walls, and overheads topped by 20 feet of earth. To take this required some effort, and when day broke things were at a standstill. The shore fire control party called for gunfire from *Augusta*, but her 8-inch shells "bounced off the heavy forts like tennis balls." Two forts surrendered around noon August 16; the third succumbed to 12 rounds of 15-inch shell from H.M.S. *Ramillies* on the 17th. As *Ramillies* was 28 years old, H.M.S. *Dido* sent her the saucy signal: "Many a good tune can be played on an old fiddle!"

East of the Rade d'Hyères, between Cap Bénat and Cap Nègre, lies the Rade de Bormes. This was the objective of the commando force known as the "Romeo" group.[4] Theirs was a four-nation enterprise — British, American, Canadian and French. The same "Princes" that brought in the troops for the islands debarked the "Romeos" into low-profiled Canadian LCAs. The waters were calm and starlight enabled one to see from three to six miles, but there was a ground mist on the shore and an unanticipated set of current. A unit of 75 French commandos under Lieutenant Colonel Bouvet cast off from an LCA in four rubber boats a few hundred yards from the coast and landed on a beach east of Cap Nègre at 0153 August 15. It was the wrong beach — Canadel instead of Rayol; but within a few minutes of landing the commandos had spread havoc along the shore. Scouts waiting below on surfboards could see flickering lights and hear the screams of enemy sentries being put to the knife.

The mistake in beach identification looked serious at 0300 when LCMs carrying jeeps arrived, as the land between Canadel beach

[4] Same sources as Note 1 to this chapter, plus Capt. Norris's Report to CTG 86.3 (Rear Adm. Chandler), with whose Action Report it is enclosed; conversations with Lt. L. E. Johnson USNR shortly after the event, and Bouvet *Ouvriers de la première heure* pp. 83–84.

and the road was too steep even for them; but they were waved over to Rayol where the road came down to the shore, and there the main body of "Romeos" landed about daylight. They assembled on the Corniche road, beat off a German counterattack, set up a roadblock, marched quickly over a pass in the coastal range to the inland road from Toulon, and blocked that too. Their shore fire control party got in touch with H.M.S. *Dido* when they first encountered stiff resistance. She at 0742, and *Augusta* at 0950, dropped a few salvos on the German defenses, then checked fire while the French pressed forward and the enemy surrendered. Lieutenant-Colonel Bouvet reported to Admiral Davidson around 1300 that he had not only blocked both roads but made contact with advanced units of the 3rd Division near the Baie de Cavalaire. A mission smartly and quickly accomplished.

CHAPTER XVI

The Main Landings

15–17 August 1944

1. *Minesweeping, Bombing and Bombardment* [1]

ALTHOUGH we have carried the reader from darkness into daylight in order to follow the fortunes of the paratroops and the commandos, we have yet to deal with three important operations that preceded the main landings: the minesweeping, the air bombing and the naval bombardment.

Admiral Hewitt's flagship *Catoctin*, with General Patch of the Seventh Army and Admiral Lemonnier of the French Navy embarked, arrived in the waters off the assault beaches at 0455 August 15. Day was already breaking, and although a bank of mist concealed the beaches, the French officers could orient themselves by the high capes and mountain peaks. "What happiness," wrote Lemonnier, "to return to this coast of Provence, the most lovely and beautiful shore of France!" By sunrise – 0638 [2] – clouds were gathering, it was pleasantly cool and only the lightest of light airs played over the water, smooth as a mirror. During the day the clouds disappeared and the temperature rose.

We expected to find plenty of mines in the roadsteads of Provence. Fortunately that coast is steep-to, unlike Normandy, and the

---

[1] Hewitt pp. 207–11, 252–6; CTF 86 (Rear Admiral Davidson), CTF 84 (Rear Admiral Lowry), CTF 85 (Rear Admiral Rodgers) and CTF 87 (Rear Admiral Lewis) Action Reports with those of the bombardment ships enclosed; Rear Adm. E. D. McEathron "Minesweeping History" in Administrative series.

[2] Double daylight saving time (Zone B, two hours later than Greenwich), which the Allies used in the Mediterranean as in Normandy.

100-fathom line, beyond which mines cannot profitably be laid, is, on an average, only three miles from the shore. It was unnecessary to sweep transport and fire support areas, but one could not afford to neglect the boat lanes or the shallows near the landing beaches. A large minesweeping force had been provided: 25 U.S.N. and 17 R.N. fleet sweepers, 32 U.S.N. coastal minesweepers (YMS) and 21 British of corresponding size, 30 U.S.N. subchasers and landing craft fitted for shoal-water sweeping close to the beaches, and a few British converted trawlers and motor launches for laying dan buoys. These were divided among the three main attack forces, with a few for "Sitka."

Sweeping of boat lanes to the three sets of beaches began at 0515, shortly after first light, destroyers standing by to cover. The smaller minecraft swept up to within 150 yards of the beach. "It was grand," said one observer, "to see the . . . sweeps running well and in good formation, with guns pointing and barking shoreward, followed by . . . the 'danners' planting their dan buoys, and then the boat sweepers . . . running well and true." Baie de Bougnon was swept prior to naval bombardment and, as the land there had not been bombed, these minecraft encountered a certain amount of machine-gun fire, which they silenced without aid from the destroyers. The boat lanes to the Camel beaches also were swept, between 0450 and 0615, and no mines were encountered, except Teller mines in a foot or two of water, which the UDTs took care of. Plenty could have been found in the Golfe de Fréjus; but there the sweep did not begin until around 1000, since no landing was planned until the afternoon.

After the sweepers, the "Apex" drone boats were sent in to explode underwater obstacles. Their performance was better than in the rehearsal at Salerno. They did show a tendency to weave in and out of obstacles instead of exploding on top of them, and one accidentally popped off so close to a subchaser as to put her *hors de combat*. But they took out nine obstacles at Cavalaire Beach and six at Pampelonne.

At 0550, an hour after first light, 1300 land-based bombers with escorting fighters began a massive pounding. The squadrons, flying from Italy, Sardinia and Corsica, relieved each other at intervals of only five minutes, so that the bombing seemed almost continuous until 0730, when it broke off to give the ships a chance. Not an enemy plane was seen, largely because of the intensive bombings of their airfields before D-day.[3]

Target selection and timing had been planned in close coördination with the staff of Admiral Hewitt, who admitted that the results could not have been better if naval gunfire alone had been employed. Communication between flight commanders and the joint control and operations room in *Catoctin* was continuous and excellent. Cloud cover, reported over certain targets by reconnaissance planes, frequently required the controllers to shift flights to alternate targets, or even to new ones.

The last four bomb waves were overlapped by naval bombardment. H.M.S. *Ajax* had fired the first shot at 0606, and firing became general 45 minutes later. On this calm, misty morning, the air bombing raised a cloud of dust and smoke that hung heavy over the land. French cruiser *Gloire* reported that at 0551 the summits of the Alpes Maritimes were just appearing out of the haze, and from the deck of H.M.S. *Ramillies* very little could be seen ashore at 0606, though she then lay only four miles south of Cap Camarat. Consequently for some time the ships had to practice "blind firing" – which does not mean banging away indiscriminately at a shore dimly seen, but indirect fire, with the ship's position and the gridded shore map used for pointing the guns, but with no opportunity to correct the solution by observing fall of shot. All pre-H-hour firing was on known batteries and strongpoints, so sited as to harass landing craft and soldiers on the beach. As soon as targets became visible the old SOCs from cruisers *Philadelphia*, *Brooklyn* and

[3] The Luftwaffe was saving its remaining fighter planes for an "emergency" and all bombers suitable for use against assault shipping had retired to the interior. The 14 Do–217s and 65 Ju–88s within range of the beaches made about 140 sorties on 16 and 17 August against shipping (the retiring torpedo-bombers complaining of "lack of suitable targets"), but by 21 August their bases had been evacuated and all German air activity in Provence ended. (Dr. Tessin of Bundesarchiv in letter of 28 June 1956.)

Quincy which were hovering about, spotted for the bombardment ships.[4]

H-hour is now approaching. Aërial bombing stops at 0730, to let the Navy give the final licks. At that moment the first troop-laden LCVP are speeding down the boat lanes. Fire support destroyers open a heavy drenching fire on the land behind the beaches. Rocket-equipped LCT spout missiles onto the beaches themselves, just ahead of the landing craft. The *cr-a-a-ck!* of the rockets sounds as if the beaches were being lashed with a mighty whip. Then comes comparative silence when the gun and rocket fire has been lifted, and one hears only the hum of landing-craft engines, like the buzzing of gigantic bees. This lasts but a moment. Now the first wave of landing craft begins hitting the beaches on the 30-mile front. One minute after H-hour, at 0801, signals begin to reach Admiral Hewitt that assault troops have landed on one beach after another, all the way from Baie de Cavalaire to Calanque d'Anthéor.

2. *Alpha Area* [5]

We shall take up the main landings in sequence from west to east, although all were made simultaneously. Briefly they were as follows: —

West Flank: Alpha Force (Rear Admiral Lowry) — 3rd Division, at Cavalaire and Pampelonne.

Center: Delta Force (Rear Admiral Rodgers) — 45th Division, Baie de Bougnon, or La Nartelle.

---

[4] CTG 84.7 (Rear Admiral Mansfield) pays a gracious tribute to the last-named, which did the spotting in his area. "I was particularly happy to have Capt. Senn and his fine ship *Quincy* under my command . . . I wish especially to record the fine work done by her aircraft, both as spotting planes and also on reconnaissance sorties when information was lacking."

[5] CTF 84 (Rear Admiral Lowry) Advance Action Report 10 Sept. and Final Action Report 16 Nov. 1944; *Seventh Army Report* I 119–27.

East Flank: Camel Force (Rear Admiral Lewis) — 36th Division, East of Saint-Raphaël.

The immediate object of Rear Admiral Lowry's Alpha Force was to capture Saint-Tropez and secure the southwest sector of the "blue line." Major General John W. O'Daniel's veteran 3rd Division was landed on two beaches, 13 miles apart by sea, Red on the Baie de Cavalaire and Yellow on the Baie de Pampelonne, to put a bite on the Presqu'île de Saint-Tropez.

This rugged little peninsula, about six miles each way, is a yet unspoiled bit of old Provence, with narrow, winding roads. Except for the areas immediately behind the two beaches, it is a region of rocky pine-clad hills, between which small fields, tiny vineyards and olive groves are tucked in. On a calm, sunny day, such as 15 August 1944 became around noon, boats approaching this peninsula can make out the ancient hill town of Ramatuelle in the center; while on the east the eye is caught by ruddy Cap Dramont near the eastern extremity of the DRAGOON area, and to the westward the îles d'Hyères look like floating clouds suspended between sea and sky.

Cavalaire Beach (Alpha Red), westernmost of the two, is of firm, dark yellow sand with the right gradient for landing craft, and on its edge there were no buildings or trees, except a tiny restaurant and a few discouraged-looking palms of the kind that they plant along this coast to suggest the tropics. The headlands that enclose this bay were planted with picturesque umbrella pines, most of which the Germans had felled to open up fields of fire. As this beach is deeply embayed and the German batteries were well placed for enfilading, the landing could have been a bloody one but for the efficient air bombing and naval bombardment, which drove the defenders into dugouts, or caused the batteries to be completely abandoned.

Each unit of the Alpha approach convoy reached its transport area on time. Admiral Lowry's flagship, U.S.C.G.C. *Duane*, arriv-

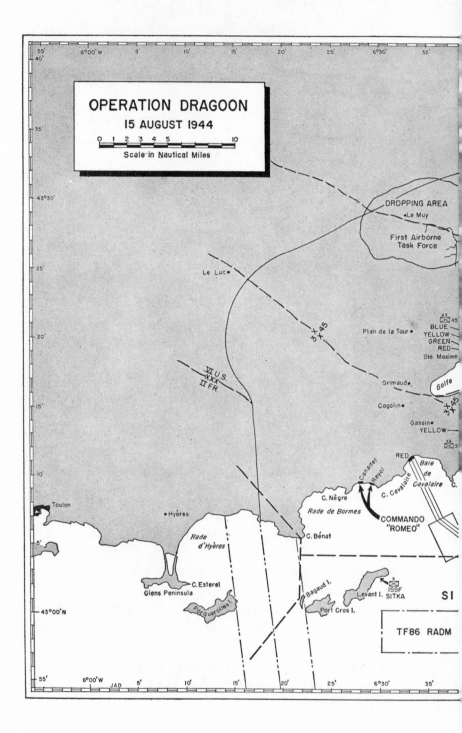

OPERATION DRAGOON
15 AUGUST 1944

0 1 2 3 4 5   10
Scale in Nautical Miles

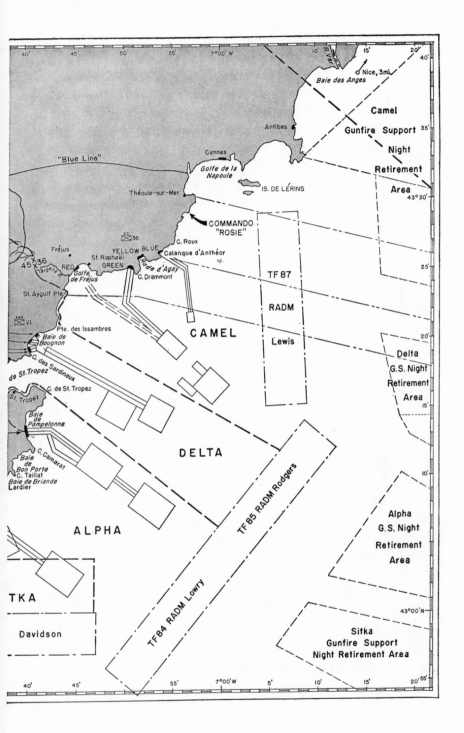

ing at 0451, was nine minutes early. The outer transport area for the big ships lay ten miles off shore, the inner one for beaching craft at half that distance. There was plenty of time for lowering and manning the boats, and no rough water to hamper their movements, as in Normandy.

The 7th RCT of the 3rd Division landed, two battalions abreast, on Cavalaire. The first wave of 38 troop-carrying LCVP, accompanied by two LCT with DD tanks and numerous smoker, rocket and small gunfire-support craft, touched down promptly at H-hour. Rocket craft were supposed to have drenched the beach to explode land mines, but rockets are difficult to aim and there were a number of misfires, so that the eastern half of Cavalaire was still full of mines when the troops came ashore. Naval combat demolition teams, arriving at 0810, went to work on shoal-water obstacles. These were so generously spaced and so clearly visible in the clear water that landing craft had little difficulty passing between them. By 0825, when the bolder Germans began to emerge from their bombproof shelters and to open small-arms and mortar fire, there were enough DD tanks ashore, together with many dukw-loads of field guns and howitzers, to discourage them.

While Army Engineers cleared roads through the heavily mined terrain,[6] and the UDTs blew up underwater obstacles, infantry patrols began fanning inland. At 0850 ships caught the violet-colored smoke signal indicating that all beach defenses were neutralized and that the divisional reserve, the 30th RCT, could land. Seven waves were already ashore, and German prisoners were being evacuated in LCVPs.

It seemed almost too easy. Nothing went wrong except that *LCI-588* and *LCI-590*, in one of the later boat waves, exploded land mines on the portion of the beach where they grounded, lost two of their passengers and were unable to retract. General O'Daniel and staff went ashore from *Duane* at 1044. By that time it had become an average summer day in Provence, not too hot but dusty,

[6] When the writer visited Baie de Cavalaire in January 1945 more than half the terrain was still mined, and German prisoners were busy exploding the mines under the watchful eye of a French sergeant.

with the cicadas chattering like mad except when a shellburst nearby made them stop for a moment.[7] By 1330 one battalion of the 7th RCT had made contact with the French "Romeos" who had landed near Cap Nègre, and the other had reached the village of La Croix, two miles inland. By dark the 7th had driven six miles inland to a road junction near La Mole on the inland road.

It was much the same story around Cap Camarat at Pampelonne, a long, firm, yellow sand beach, at one end of which were a few bath houses, locally known as "Le Tahiti." The 15th RCT, which landed here, had overcome all local resistance by 0840. Engineers placed pontoon causeways in position for the LSTs, as the gradient was too gentle for vehicles to be discharged directly.

An innovation for the Mediterranean, already tried in the Pacific, was to convert one LST for each attack force into a baby airplane carrier by constructing a runway amidships from stem to stern; four or five light observation planes could be accommodated on each side. One, which took off at H-hour to reconnoiter, reported the Golfe de Saint-Tropez to be empty of enemy craft, and no sign of a coastal battery in sight. Word came later from the F.F.I. that the town of Saint-Tropez was almost clear and the people eager to welcome Americans. A battalion of the 15th RCT reached the outskirts at 1500, to find those American paratroops who had dropped in the wrong place helping the F.F.I. to mop up the last pocket of resistance. By nightfall the Germans had been cleaned out of the entire peninsula, all land mines had been cleared from Cavalaire, and a convoy of Liberty ships which arrived in the afternoon were unloading cargoes into trucks brought out to them in LCMs.[8] On D-day some 16,000 men, 2150 vehicles and 225 long tons of supplies were landed on the two Alpha beaches, Cavalaire

[7] Temperatures noted in logs of fire support ships range from 80° to 82° at noon, and up to 90° in the afternoon.

[8] *Seventh Army Report* I 126 says seven out of ten Liberty ships due D-day didn't show up on time; but CTF 84 Action Report says Convoy SM–2, 50 Liberties, arrived off Beach Red at 1542 Aug. 15, 20 minutes ahead of schedule. Nine more arrived 0800 Aug. 16 and started unloading immediately, and five more at 0800 Aug. 17 – all according to plan. Ships carrying supplies for an amphibious operation are not all expected to arrive on D-day.

and Pampelonne.[9] The casualties of the 3rd Division on D-day numbered only 264, and it took 1600 prisoners. A battalion of the 15th, in the meantime, had combed the hills north of Ramatuelle without running into trouble.

Pampelonne, which had poor exits, was closed down after a few days, but Cavalaire remained a major port of entry for about three weeks.

3. *Delta Area* [10]

Rear Admiral Rodgers landed the 45th Division on Delta area, keystone to the assault arch; a wedge narrowing to a width of 10,000 yards between Alpha on the left and Camel on the right. It included the beautiful Golfe de Saint-Tropez and the resort town of Sainte-Maxime. All landings took place outside the gulf on an almost continuous 5000-yard beach between Pointe des Sardinaux and Pointe de la Garonne, called Baie de Bougnon on the charts that we used.[11]

Major General Eagles's "Thunderbirds" — the famous 45th Division composed in large part of Apache and Cherokee Indians — here found themselves in what had been a fashionable resort, very different from the dingy towns formerly encountered in Sicily. Numerous stucco-walled villas, once painted a gay pink, green or yellow, had been converted by the Germans into strongpoints, and so had had plenty of air let into them by the bombing and naval bombardment. At the eastern end of the bay was a recent real-estate development adjoining the prominent Pointe des Issambres. Here there was a 220-mm gun (made by Bethlehem Steel for the French in 1918) camouflaged to look like the garden of a nearby villa, with rosebushes carefully painted on the concrete. It had

[9] By 1800 Aug. 17, 48,200 men, 6438 vehicles, 1060 tons cargo (same source), but CTF 84 Action Report p. 23 gives 51,870 men, 8070 vehicles, 19,394 tons for 15–16 Aug.

[10] CTF 85 (Rear Admiral Rodgers) Action Report 25 Aug.; CTG 85.12 (Rear Admiral Bryant) Action Report 28 Aug.; *Seventh Army Report* I 127–35.

[11] This name seems to have become obsolete. The local people call the bay La Nartelle after its principal village.

been well pounded before the troops landed, but not altogether put out of business. The smaller Pointe de la Garonne, between the beaches and Issambres, had a 75-mm gun and numerous machine-gun positions. Pointe des Sardinaux on the west was also well provided with defenses.

Admiral Rodgers, in *Biscayne,* had 221 ships and craft under his command. These included six big transports which had been in almost every Mediterranean amphibious operation since TORCH, two British transports, 25 LST, 47 LCT (23 of them British), 41 LCI, 9 PC, 40 minecraft and a number of miscellaneous vessels. It takes all that, in modern amphibious warfare, to lift, land and support a reinforced infantry division.

The strongpoints on the limiting headlands, and a concrete casemate on the edge of one beach, might have been serious threats to the landing. Hence Delta Force was provided with an unusually strong gunfire support group, under Rear Admiral Bryant in *Texas.* Good old *Nevada* was there, too; rapid-firing "Philly"; French *Georges Leygues* and *Montcalm* and three small light cruisers,[12] under Contre-Amiral Jaujard. These ships opened counter-battery fire at 0640 and continued until 0815, closing to 3000 yards off the beach. According to Admiral Rodgers, "Inspection on D plus one showed that the men manning their guns were either dead when the 45th Division hit the beaches, or that the pre-H-hour aërial bombardment and Navy shell and rocket fire was so intense that it frightened the defenders out of the ground and away from the guns."

Because of the close-coupled nature of this Delta landing, the large number of ships and craft carrying troops and matériel had to concentrate in two small transport areas, respectively seven and a half miles and eleven miles off shore. Gunfire support ships crowded these areas and the boat lanes, and the landing plan had to be intricate. Yet there was no confusion. The first seven waves touched down exactly on time or even a few minutes early; the

---

12 *Le Fantasque, Le Terrible,* and *Le Malin,* 2600-tonners. The French called them light cruisers, and we, destroyer leaders.

seventh wave was all ashore by 0910. Without enemy opposition, it was a "dream landing." On D-day Delta Force unloaded here the contents of all the transports and over a hundred beaching craft, carrying some 33,000 men and 3300 vehicles. No loss of landing or support craft, and no casualties. The only contretemps was the knocking out of four amphibious tanks which made the mistake of waddling up Beach Blue in line abreast before land mines had been sprung. Their crews later obtained standard tanks and caught up with the infantry.

Upon landing, the two regimental combat teams carried out their plan, deploying in opposite directions. One battalion of the 157th RCT bypassed Sainte-Maxime and turned northwesterly, and by nightfall was at a crossroads village called Plan de la Tour, on the "blue line" about ten miles from the beach. The other battalion, which landed on the extreme left, made straight for Sainte-Maxime, where it had a lively house-to-house fight with Germans. After mopping the place up and taking prisoners it proceeded westward along the Corniche road, made contact with elements of the 3rd Division (the Alpha force) at 2100, and joined the rest of the regiment for the night at Plan de la Tour.

The 180th RCT, which landed on the right flank, had the double mission to clear the enemy from heights overlooking the beaches and to assist Camel Force in securing Beach Red at the head of the Golfe de Fréjus. One battalion by next morning had reached Roquebrunne on the Le Muy-Fréjus road. Another moved coastwise toward the town of Saint-Aygulf, which it took after a sharp fight. General Eagles came ashore at 1100 D-day, and in the afternoon Commander VI Corps, General Truscott, set up headquarters in a villa near Sainte-Maxime and committed the reserve regiment, the 179th. Casualties for D-day were only 109 for the 45th Division and none for the Navy.

Naval gunfire support in this area was exceptionally abundant and precise, despite the fact that visibility was poor — it decreased to only two miles during the morning, owing to dust, smoke and haze, with no wind to dispel it. Visibility improved a little at 0800.

Le Malin, known in the French Navy as "the one-legger" since she had lost a propeller to a mine off Tripoli, began the post-landing bombardment three minutes later on a pillbox a mile north of Pointe des Issambres. Thickening mists made it impossible to observe results after she had fired 18 rounds. At 0836 the order was issued to all ships to fire only on call, but there was not a quarter-hour of the day when they were not doing it.[13] The honors, by general agreement, went to Admiral Bryant's gunfire support ships. Admiral Rodgers sent him a blinker signal to the effect that the success of the assault was mostly due to the "terrific pounding" they had given to the enemy, and Contre-Amiral Jaujard informed Admiral Rodgers "It is particularly agreeable to me to assure you of the profound satisfaction that we have experienced in serving under the orders of Admiral Bryant. By his pluck, his perfect knowledge of his profession and his leadership, he has won our admiration and our gratitude."[14]

4. Camel Area[15]

Camel Force was the only one that did not find Operation DRAGOON a pushover. It drew the only section of the target coast that was thoroughly mined and well defended.

This area extended from Pointe des Issambres on the edge of Delta to a point on the Golfe de la Napoule, facing Cannes. On the west flank the shores of the Golfe de Fréjus, overlooked by the town of Saint-Raphaël, were badly wanted by the Army. Here the sluggish Argens River flows into the sea, and here the French before the war had built a small airfield and seaplane base behind the beach: the only one on the water's edge in Provence. As the Argens valley is a natural invasion route to the interior — had been so used for at least 1500 years — the Germans guessed that we

---

13 CTG 85.12 (Rear Adm. Bryant) Letter Sept. 17.
14 The letter, here translated, is attached to Bryant's of 17 Sept. to Admiral Hewitt, forwarding French Action Reports.
15 CTF 87 (Rear Adm. Lewis) and CTG 87.7 (Rear Adm. Deyo), Action Reports; *Seventh Army Report.*

would land there if anywhere on this part of the coast, and had prepared a hot reception. Since Intelligence predicted this, Admiral Hewitt's staff selected beaches east of Saint-Raphaël for the
initial assault, but postponed landings at the head of the gulf until
the afternoon in order to allow time for coast defenses to be
pounded and mines to be swept.

Rear Admiral Lewis, in *Bayfield*, was charged with the Camel assault. He had two beaching craft groups for landing on the small
Agay beaches, and seven transports and cargo vessels, from which
the main body was to land at the head of the gulf. The gunfire
support group, under Rear Admiral Deyo, included battleship *Arkansas*, heavy cruiser *Tuscaloosa*, and five light cruisers. The 36th
Division (Texas National Guard, Major General John E. Dahlquist), which was landed here, had the vital mission of securing the
eastern flank of the assault force and the main road for a northward
advance.

The coast here is mostly cliffs, and the beaches are merely short
stretches of *galet* or shingle at the feet of valleys that have been
carved through the cliff line by the freshets of a million years. The
larger of the two beaches, Green, we nicknamed "Quarry Beach"
because a large quarry of graystone is nearby. Immediately east of
this spot there is an abrupt change in the geology. The gray cal-
careous rock which has extended all the way from Marseilles here
gives way to a red sandstone of astounding brilliance when it
catches the sun, a spectacular contrast to the blue Mediterranean.
The main line of railway and the road, here called the Corniche
d'Or, cut across the neck of ruddy Cap Dramont and circle the
1000-yard-wide Rade d'Agay. That roadstead was not selected for
an initial landing, because aërial reconnaissance had indicated that it
was closed by a net and appeared to be heavily defended, many elaborate villas in this fashionable part of the Riviera having been converted by the Germans into strongpoints. The Rade d'Agay is
bounded on the east by the high, rocky Pointe d'Anthéor. East of
that point the line of sandstone cliffs is broken only by a few deep
coves with pebbly beaches at their heads, called in the local dialect

PT–212 with German survivors from *Escaburt*

Alpha Red beach, D-day

Operation DRAGOON, *August 1944*

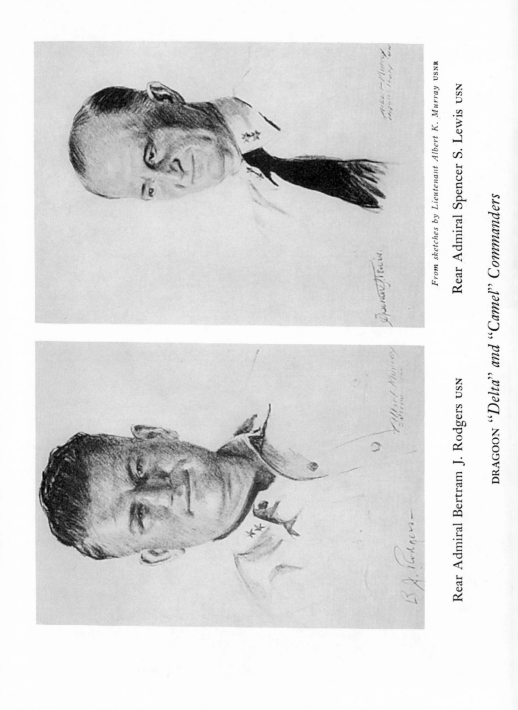

Rear Admiral Bertram J. Rodgers USN   Rear Admiral Spencer S. Lewis USN

From sketches by Lieutenant Albert K. Murray USNR

DRAGOON *"Delta" and "Camel" Commanders*

Infantry marching along Alpha Yellow beach edge to avoid mines
(Sappers removing mines at right)

General view

Pampelonne, D-day, 15 August 1944

Official Bureau of Aeronautics photo

LST–282 sunk off Cape Dramont

Dukw landing from LST
(A: Cape Dramont; B: Enemy Radar; C: Exit)

Beach Camel Green

calanques. The first of these, La Calanque d'Anthéor, was selected for an assault landing as Beach Blue.

Gunfire ships closed to the 100-fathom line at 0650 and banged away at prearranged targets until a few minutes before 0800. They succeeded in neutralizing many but not all strongpoints, and breaching or demolishing practically every villa which the air bombing had missed.

The landing on Beach Green of two battalions of the 141st RCT 36th Division, largely from LCI and LCT under command of Captain Robert Morris, went exactly on schedule. Smoke obscured landmarks until the craft were close to the beach. The assault troops landed dry-foot, met only token resistance, and suffered no losses; [16] the only casualty here was Lieutenant T. R. Evans RNVR, skipper of British *LCT-625*, killed by gunfire just as he was about to beach.

Beach Blue, only 80 yards long, lies at the head of La Calanque d'Anthéor. The Corniche road here skirts the beach, and the landmark is a high railway viaduct which the aviators had done their best to destroy. The 1st Battalion 141st RCT was landed here by a group of beaching craft under Commander L. R. Herring, composed mainly of five LST with landing craft slung on davits. More bombs had been dropped and shells fired into this small area than in any other part of the DRAGOON beaches, but several German machine guns and two antitank guns on Pointe d'Anthéor became active as soon as they got the assault craft in their sights. Two or three landing craft were sunk when retracting, and Commander Herring's LCI flagship was chased out of the cove, but there were few casualties among troops and sailors. After Beach Blue had been secured it was found to have been protected by an elaborate system of trenches, connected with underground shelters and ammunition dumps. But these defenses were manned mostly by discour-

---

[16] Report of C.O. Beach Green Assault Troops in CTG 874 (Capt. Morris) Action Report 24 Aug. However, the 36th Division has put up a monument on Beach Green which with true Texan modesty declares: "Over this defended beach the men of the 36th U.S. Infantry Division stormed ashore 15 August 1944. Together with their French Allies they began here the drive that took them across France, through Germany and into Austria, to the final destruction of the German armies and the Nazi régime."

aged Poles, some 60 of whom surrendered on D-day. That was the situation throughout the main landing zones. Enemy defenses were strong enough, but the defenders had lost all heart to fight; they knew or suspected that they were no longer on the winning side.

The battalion which landed on Beach Blue marched east along the Corniche d'Or, supported by naval gunfire; *Woolsey* destroyed two threatening German tanks. Théoule-sur-Mer on the Golfe de la Napoule was captured the following morning and survivors from the Operation "Rosie" group of French commandos were rescued. During the afternoon the obstacles that closed the Rade d'Agay were blown up by demolition teams, and a beach at the head of it was developed as an additional landing place.

During D-day Camel Beach Green, about 500 yards long, was the busiest place on the invasion coast and the noisiest, too. Enemy sniping revived every so often. Admiral Deyo's light cruisers and destroyers, at the Army's request, laid on a rapid-fire bombardment of spots around Saint-Raphaël, and just after their retirement the Luftwaffe made its only effective air raid of the entire operation, and every ship opened up on the Ju–88s. *LST–282*, fully loaded and making for the Rade d'Agay, was hit by a glider-bomb at 2225 and sank in shoal water off Cap Dramont; there were 40 casualties.

We may now turn to the Golfe de Fréjus, heavily mined and strongly defended by coast-defense batteries, some of them masquerading as Saint-Raphaël waterfront bars, kiosks and bathhouses.[17] H-hour for Beach Red at the head of this gulf, on the edge of the airdrome, was set for 1400. It was thought that this would give the bombers, gunfire ships and minesweepers enough time to destroy all defenses. But for once the enemy proved to be more tenacious than we expected.

A group of coastal minesweepers, accompanied by eight British shoal-draft minecraft, began sweeping the approach channel to

[17] The Germans had expended great ingenuity on these defenses, in some cases building an entire wooden beach cottage around a concrete casemate to conceal it. CTG 87.8 (Lt. Cdr. Maloney) and CTU 87.8.1, Action Reports 20 Aug. 1944 for events in the Gulf.

Beach Red at 1015. An hour later, as they closed to within 500 yards of the beach, they were heavily shelled by enemy batteries and forced to retire, although covered by fire from *SC–1030* and several support destroyers. While they stood out of range, 93 Army Liberators flew over the beach and dropped 187 tons of bombs. This may have minimized, but certainly did not neutralize, the opposition. Next, the "Apex" drone boats were sent in, to explode underwater obstacles. Their performance was so erratic that we credited enemy radio operators with "stealing" the radio direction of the "female" or explosive units from the "male" directing boats. Probably the trouble was organic,[18] but, in any case, the "females" went wild, running around in circles like hens with their heads cut off. Two ran aground, destroyer *Ordronaux* sank one to avoid being rammed by her, two were boarded and put out of action, and only three exploded according to plan.

Half an hour after noon, gunfire support was again called for. *Arkansas, Tuscaloosa, Émile Bertin* and four destroyers laid a heavy bombardment on all strongpoints around the Gulf. Despite these efforts, it was clear to Admirals Lewis and Deyo that, without further minesweeping, the lane to Beach Red would be bloody. H-hour was fast approaching. Landing craft carrying troops from the big transports were waiting for the word to go in. At 1405 the deputy commander of the assault group, Captain L. B. Schulten, signaled to Admiral Lewis: "Wave being held back. Request instructions." The Admiral, unable to raise the commanding general of the 36th Division, on his own responsibility ordered the landing to be shifted to Beach Green. There the entire 142nd RCT was put ashore by 1512, without loss. *Ordronaux* "did wonderful work in this whole operation. She first took station farther inshore than the boat waves off Beach Red, engaged the batteries firing into the boats, though she was narrowly missed on several occasions, then shepherded the boats around to Beach Green, displaying seamanlike skill, initiative and courage."[19]

[18] Hewitt pp. 306–8.
[19] CTG 87.7 (Adm. Deyo) Action Report, Enclosure A, p. 11.

This quick change of plan, and the landing of Beach Red assault groups on Beach Green at a time when LSTs were already discharging there, aroused the admiration of everyone but General Truscott, who was displeased at not having been consulted. General Dahlquist of the 36th Division signaled Admiral Lewis at 1740: "Appreciate your prompt action in changing plan when obstacles could not be breached. Expect to take Red Beach tonight, no matter how late. Opposition irritating but not too tough so far." [20]

Even if the defenders were not tough, Fréjus lay a good distance from Beach Green, and the van battalions of the 36th Division reached their planned assembly ground north of the town too late to attack before next day, 16 August, which opened fair and warmer. All Camel Force gunfire support ships were on station by 0645, ready to shoot on call; but their connection with shore fire control parties throughout the day was sporadic, because troops were constantly on the move. It took at least twenty minutes for an s.f.c.p. to set up its heavy equipment (which, except in unusual circumstances, it had to carry pickaback), and get word through to a ship; and the 36th Division seldom took that much time out to rest, except at night.

Attempts to sweep Golfe de Fréjus were resumed at 0700. The minecraft encountered difficulties from German anti-cutting devices, such as chain moorings with attachments which fouled the Oropesa sweep gear. A group of magnetic-sweeping YMS was committed at 0930. With *YMS-63* guiding, *YMS-200* on her starboard beam, and *YMS-24* to port, they moved in to mop up mines in waters already covered by the Oropesa sweep; but, owing to a mistake in signals, entered an area that had not been swept at all. After blowing five mines successfully, these small vessels were turning seaward at the end of their sweep, in 29 fathoms of water, when the bow of *YMS-24* hit a contact mine. It exploded, hurling the boat's anchor from the forecastle to the bridge, where it mowed down the skipper, Lieutenant (jg) Samuel R. Pruett USNR. Although the forward third of the boat was gone, she made

[20] CTF 87 Report p. 5; Truscott *Command Missions* pp. 413–14.

two complete circles out of control before her engines stopped. The wounded were taken on board *YMS–63* for treatment. British *ML–563* came up from astern to help; but she hit another mine which exploded,[21] destroying her after part and badly wounding Lieutenant Commander C. H. Pearse RNVR, flotilla commander of the British Fairmiles. She and *YMS–24* were abandoned under fire and sank or drifted ashore.

Lieutenant Commander E. R. D. Sworder RNVR now relieved the incapacitated Pearse, and, under the overall command of Lieutenant Commander J. L. Maloney USNR in *Strive*, swept a channel to Beach Red with all available small minecraft, British and American. Two motor torpedo boats, *PT–202* and *PT–218*, which ventured into the Gulf in the evening of the 16th, in an odd quest for fuel, were mined and sunk, with the loss of one man killed and six wounded. The survivors got ashore in rubber boats.[22]

Underwater obstacles, mostly mined concrete tetrahedras, were found in shoal water off Beach Red. Naval demolition teams started blowing these at 1200 August 16 and completed the job next day. The whole beach was Teller-mined and booby-trapped; and we discovered to our dismay that a German mine was not affected by the explosion of a 100-pound air bomb only four feet away.

Sweeping of the Gulf continued throughout the 17th, when British *YMS–2022* was mined and lost; and was not concluded until the evening of the 19th, when craft began to land on Red Beach.

Saint-Raphaël, with its elaborately camouflaged waterfront gazebos, was taken by the 1st Battalion 143rd RCT on the morning of 16 August. This outfit then overran Beach Red from the rear, bulldozing out of the way a row of attractive "bathhouses" that turned out to be an antitank wall. Fréjus fell in the late afternoon. At mid-

21 Chief Pharmacist's Mate D. D. Helton of *YMS–63* was on the fantail giving blood plasma to a stretcher case with a broken leg from *YMS–24* when *ML–563* blew up. The stretcher case started forward on the run, hotly pursued by the CPhM. The anchor winch from the ML, crashing down on the deck between them, ended this weird chase.

22 R. J. Bulkley "PT History" 426–7. The PTs were looking for a small gasoline tanker to refill their fuel tanks, and entered the Gulf on a rumor that one was there.

night August 16–17 General Patch, satisfied that the beachhead was firmly established, went ashore from *Catoctin*, assumed command of the Army forces of the Western Task Force,[23] and set up Seventh Army headquarters in Hôtel Latitude Quarante-trois, near Saint-Tropez. By the close of 18 August more than 30,000 troops and 5000 vehicles had been landed in Camel area; [24] over 2800 prisoners and 800 casualties had been evacuated, all objectives were attained, and the General was ready to reorganize the Seventh Army for rapid exploitation inland. Thus, a well-planned and organized attack went over with remarkably few foul-ups and a minimum of casualties.

Admiral Hewitt, for whose long career in the United States Navy Operation DRAGOON was an appropriate crown, went ashore at La Nartelle at 0900 August 16, accompanied by Secretary Forrestal, General Patch and Admiral Lemonnier. As their two jeeps rolled through the streets of Saint-Raphaël, Hewitt stood up and pointed at Lemonnier; civilians in the doorways and windows, recognizing his French naval cap, surged into the street, shouting with enthusiasm. Lemonnier made them a little speech introducing the Americans; someone started to sing the long-forbidden "Marseillaise," and everyone joined in. One can well imagine the emotion engendered by that superb national anthem on such an occasion.[25]

Thanks to the participation of their own ships, the French knew that their own Navy had had a part in their liberation. The excellent gunfire of the French cruisers and destroyers was one of the high points of the operation. And it was far from finished.

[23] Hewitt Report p. 54.

[24] On D-day alone, 17,390 troops and 2790 vehicles. (*Seventh Army Report* I p. 144.)

[25] Lemonnier *Cap sur la Provence* pp. 123–9; U.S. Naval Institute *Proceedings* LXXX (Aug. 1954) pp. 906–7; G. S. Perry in *Sat. Eve. Post* 30 Dec. 1944.

CHAPTER XVII

Objectives Won

16 August–15 September 1944

1. *Follow-up Convoys*

THE NAVY'S TASK in DRAGOON was only half accomplished by successfully landing VI Corps on 15 and 16 August. In the original plan, follow-up convoys from Italy, North Africa, Corsica, and even from the United States via Gibraltar, were scheduled for the next two and a half months; and many of these had to be speeded up, or their composition changed, owing to Seventh Army's requirements in its rapid advance. Weather continued favorable throughout this post-assault phase, gentle winds with occasional thunderstorms, and waves never high enough to impede unloading on the beaches.

Admiral Hewitt vested primary control of follow-up convoys in Comdesron Seven, Captain James P. Clay, who headed the Antisubmarine and Convoy Control Group, while Captain Sydney B. Dodds USNR acted as shore link between Army and Navy. Captain Clay in *Jouett* operated in and off the Baie de Briand, immediately east of Cavalaire. Alpha Red beach became one of the three principal landing places for follow-up convoys, the other two being Pampelonne and Beach Red at the head of the Golfe de Fréjus.[1] Initially he had 62 escort vessels at his disposal and by 21 August almost as many more. Captain Clay did a wonderful job. For instance, he managed to accelerate the arrival of two French divisions by several days, which enabled General de Lattre to maintain momentum in his assault on Toulon and Marseilles. Later, the follow-

---

[1] Alpha beaches closed down 9 Sept., Delta beaches the 16th and Camel beaches the 25th.

up convoy schedule was stepped up by as much as ten days. To avoid congestion, all convoys were scheduled to arrive off the coast in daylight and to depart at night; problems of night assembly were reduced by the use of large luminous signboards on merchant vessels. The performance of this complicated system, involving hundreds of ships and tens of thousands of different cargoes, was accomplished to the satisfaction of both Army and Navy.

By the end of 2 September, 190,565 men, 41,534 vehicles, and 219,205 tons of supplies had been landed over the DRAGOON assault beaches. On the 25th, when the last assault beach closed, the total figures for landings on beaches and in harbors were 324,069 men, 68,419 vehicles, 490,237 tons of supplies and some 325,730 barrels of fuel.[2]

2. *Eastern Flank and Escort Carriers* [3]

General Patch wished to take Cannes and Nice for "reasons more psychological than military, although harbor facilities at Nice would no doubt be useful." German batteries on Île Sainte-Marguérite off Cannes began to harass 36th Division troops near Théoule-sur-Mer on the night of 16–17 August. At the request of General Dahlquist, Admiral Deyo moved over most of his Camel gunfire support force in order to destroy the island batteries and other enemy strongpoints near Cannes. Destroyer *McLanahan*, after firing on a troop concentration at the request of her s.f.c.p., stood boldly into the Golfe de la Napoule to locate the island batteries; she drew their fire, and silenced one of them; *Tuscaloosa* was straddled by batteries located in pillboxes near the Cannes casino; *Émile Bertin* and *Brooklyn* also did some useful shooting. One of three destroyers on call during the night, *Champlin*, had the satisfaction of shooting down a Ju–88 which attempted to bomb her.

Ile Sainte-Marguérite seems to have been discouraged by the

---

[2] Hewitt pp. 94, 132.
[3] CTG 87.7 (Rear Adm. Deyo) Report 20 Aug., Enclosure A pp. 16–17; CTG 86.5 (again Deyo) Report 29 Aug., Enclosure A, and Addendum Report of 30 Aug., when he left two destroyers on the right flank and went to Propriano to fuel.

shooting on 17 August, but there were plenty more calls for supporting naval gunfire during the next three days. On the 20th the 1st Airborne Task Force (Major General Robert T. Frederick USA), which had made the parachute drop on D-day, took over this eastern flank from the 36th Division, which was about to begin its drive northward. The 1st Airborne undertook a more modest drive toward the Italian border, supported by *Brooklyn, Woolsey* and *Le Terrible.*

From 17 August on, the burden of protecting the eastern flank from surface or submarine attack, as distinct from giving gunfire support to troops, was assumed by an area screen of destroyers, commanded by Captain Harry Sanders, who had performed a similar duty in Normandy.[4] Several enemy vessels tried to penetrate this screen, but none succeeded. On the night of 17–18 August *Harding* picked up four Italian MAS boats, and with the help of *Frankford* sank three and captured the fourth, which later sank. *Carmick* and *Satterlee* got a fifth MAS boat at the same time. Two nights later a German force of three *Schnellboote* (105-foot motor torpedo boats) tried to penetrate Area Screen. *Charles F. Hughes* forced two of them to beach and sank one by gunfire; the fourth was scuttled by its crew.

On 23 August PT Squadron 15 (Lieutenant Commander Barnes), which had been doing odd jobs for the DRAGOON forces, moved up from Baie de Briande to Sainte-Maxime, in order to patrol inshore along this eastern flank. Next day it began to encounter a new German miniature nuisance, the explosive boat. This was a gasoline-driven plywood motor boat, 18 feet long, loaded with about 700 pounds of high explosive in the bow. Some were drones, operated from a control boat; others had a skipper who was supposed to jump overboard after shaping a collision course towards his target. Both kinds were completely unsuccessful. The PTs broke up three groups on three different nights, in which several of the miniature assailants exploded.

[4] Hewitt pp. 197–206; CTU 80.6.10 (Capt. Sanders) Action Report 4 Sept. 1944. See pp. 342–43 in Appendix II for the names of ships.

On 24 August, blossoming French and American flags indicated that the Germans had evacuated Cannes, and a battalion of the 1st Airborne entered the famous resort city at 1700. "The streets were lined with wildly cheering people. Some were crying openly; others threw flowers into passing American vehicles." [5] Grasse was liberated the same day.

German batteries around Nice and eastward continued to throw flowers of a different sort toward Admiral Deyo's ships, who returned them in kind — in the ten days 31 August–9 September, they answered no fewer than 80 calls for gunfire. But the Germans were pulling out to the Italian border. On 30 August, American troops occupied Nice; Monaco, as neutral, was bypassed; and the entire French coast was in Allied hands by 9 September. There the front was stabilized until April 1945.

General Frederick still needed naval support on his right flank, which rested on the sea while he was busily engaged, between 4 and 11 September, in redeploying 1st Airborne Task Force. He set up a defensive line on the heights east of Sospel, to prevent the Germans' sending reinforcements southward along the Turin–Montone highway. French destroyer *Le Malin*, on 4 September, fired 193 rounds at Germans still holding out in the heights above Monaco. Next day the Germans tried to get rid of these troublesome destroyers by means of "one-man submarines" or "human torpedoes," which had made their first appearance off Anzio in April.[6] They were then based on Mentone. Between 0800 and 0900 September 5, *Le Malin* and *Ludlow*, attacked off Monaco by three of these craft, destroyed them and captured their operators.

Destroyers *Madison* and *Hilary P. Jones* were now assigned to support troops between Mentone and Bordighera. At 0718 September 10, when *Madison* was operating in company with two PTs and with scout planes from *Philadelphia* and *Brooklyn*, a human torpedo appeared about a quarter of a mile on her

[5] *Seventh Army Report* I 232–3.
[6] See Volume IX 371–2 and Chapter XI of this volume; also O.N.I. Report "Germany . . . Navy Organization Fleets . . . Battle Units" 30 Mar. 1945.

beam. Maneuvering rapidly, the destroyer fired two depth charges at 0725, and at the same time *PT-206* (Lieutenant Edwin A. Du Bose) opened with gunfire. The torpedo disappeared, but the human pilot, recovered from the water in good condition, cheerfully disclosed the fact that his partner was working nearby. Partner, discovered twenty minutes later, was sunk; nor was he the last. By early afternoon destroyers, minesweepers, PTs and aircraft between them had destroyed ten of these gadgets.[7] Cruiser *Lorraine* and destroyers now bombarded the human torpedoes' base, which a reconnaissance plane had located near Ventimiglia.

All was quiet on this flank by 15 September, when Operation DRAGOON may be said to have officially ended. But the Germans were far from being eliminated along the Italian Riviera, and mop-up activities by the Allied Navies continued in the Gulf of Genoa until the end of the war.

Task Force 88, the escort carrier group under Rear Admiral Troubridge RN, operated in its assigned area off shore for two weeks without being subjected to a single air or submarine attack.[8] They were organized in two groups, one of five and the other of four CVEs, the larger under Rear Admiral Troubridge in antiaircraft cruiser *Royalist*, and the smaller under Rear Admiral Durgin[9] in *Tulagi*. This tactical experiment worked well, despite the fact that the American CVEs of the *Casablanca* class had a 2-knot ad-

[7] *Madison* Action Report 17 Sept. 1944; CTF 86 (Rear Adm. Davidson) Action Report 21 Oct. 1944, Enclosure C p. 34; Hewitt pp. 108–9; Bulkley "PT History" p. 439.

[8] Hewitt pp. 194–6, 269–72; Rear Admiral Escort Carriers Report of Proceedings Operation DRAGOON (enclosed in Com Eighth Fleet 9 Dec. 1944); CTG 88.2 (Rear Admiral Durgin) Action Report 6 Sept.

[9] Calvin T. Durgin, b. New Jersey 1893; Naval Academy '16; served in battleships and destroyers in World War I; naval aviator 1920 and served in aircraft tender *Aroostook* to 1922; M.S. in aëronautical engineering at M.I.T. 1924. From that time to 1930 he was constantly engaged in aviation commands or on aëronautical research afloat and ashore. In *Saratoga* 1932–4; exec. N.O.B. Norfolk to 1936, helped fit out *Yorktown* and served in her to 1938, when became successively exec. and C.O. of *Wright*. As C.O. *Ranger*, took part in Operation TORCH (See Volume II 32, 39). Com Fleet Air Quonset 1943 to June 1944, when became CTG 88.2. Comcardiv 29 Oct. 1944, and as Com CVE Group supported the Lingayen landings, Iwo Jima, and Okinawa. Various shore duties from Nov. 1945; Deputy C.N.O. for Air 1949; Com First Task Fleet 1950; retired 1951.

vantage in speed over the British of the *Tracker* class,[10] and that the British Seafires possessed only about half the endurance of the American Hellcats. Each group was screened by two British anti-aircraft cruisers and six or seven destroyers, which under the peaceful conditions in which they operated had nothing to do except to rescue pilots of planes that splashed. The observation-fighter squadron (VOF–1) on board *Tulagi* was the first United States Navy air unit to be specially trained for spotting naval gunfire and for close support of ground forces.[11]

Escort carriers had been used off Salerno, but for a different purpose, to provide combat air patrol over amphibious forces in an area where the Luftwaffe was strong. Here, their primary mission was to provide spotting planes for naval gunfire in order to prevent the waste of time and fuel involved when such planes had to be dispatched from the nearest land base. Each carrier had a group of pilots specially trained for that branch of combat aviation. They spotted for *Nevada, Texas, Philadelphia* and *Montcalm* on D-day; but for the most part the gunfire support ships preferred to be served by their own SOCs and by fast spotting aircraft furnished by XII Tactical.

The carrier groups, however, had also a second function in DRA-GOON: armed reconnaissance. While landing fields were being prepared near the beaches and the Air Force was moving up planes and equipment from its Corsican bases, these "floating fighter strips" acted as bases for fighters to cover the assault area. The Hellcats and Wildcats penetrated 120 miles up the Rhone valley and, armed with bombs, selected their own targets on retiring enemy columns, while the Seafires were used for short-range missions.

On 19 August, 110 Seafires and Hellcats flew an armed reconnaissance toward Toulouse, in the course of which they knocked

---

[10] For these classes of CVEs see Volume X 40–41. Some of the British units in TF 88 were of the *Nabob* class, with similar characteristics. See Appendix II for list of CVEs and air squadrons in DRAGOON.

[11] A. R. Buchanan *The Navy's Air War* (1946) pp. 94–8. They had been trained with Army artillery at Fort Sill.

out eight locomotives and a quantity of rolling stock that the re-
treating Germans were using. That was the first day any pilot from
the CVEs saw enemy planes – a Ju–88, three He–111s and a
Do–217 – all of which they shot down.

The CVE group in operation DRAGOON lost 16 planes to enemy
antiaircraft fire and 27 others crashed or splashed. "The U.S. aircraft, especially the Hellcats," reported Admiral Troubridge,
"proved their superiority. The Seafire is a magnificent machine,
but much too frail for operations from escort carriers. It is idle to
pretend otherwise, in spite of the splendid performance of the
squadrons equipped with these 'aristocrats of the sky.'" To the
astonishment and gratification of the naval aviators, who were unused to bouquets from the Army Air Force, Brigadier General
Saville of XII Tactical, and Général de Division Bouscat, head of
French Aviation, boarded *Tulagi* on 26 August and congratulated
all hands on their fine performance. In one day, said General Saville,
he had personally counted 202 enemy vehicles destroyed by the
Hellcats between Sainte-Maxime and Le Luc.

3. *Toulon, Port de Bouc and Marseilles* [12]

East flank activities were relatively unimportant compared with
the capture of Toulon and Marseilles, the latter being one of the
main objectives of Operation DRAGOON.

The French II Corps under Général d'Armée de Lattre de
Tassigny, initially the 1ère Division Motorisée d'Infanterie (Brosset) and the 3ème Division d'Infanterie Algérienne (de Monsabert), embarked at Taranto and departed 13 August in nine British
and one Polish transport, escorted by 15 French and three British

[12] Hewitt pp. 218–28; CTF 86 (Rear Adm. Davidson) Report; De Lattre de
Tassigny *History of the First French Army* (London 1952); Contre-Amiral Lemonnier "La marine française au debarquement de Provence" *Marine Nationale* Nov.
1944, and *Cap sur la Provence* (1954); information from French Naval Archives
in 1956.

warships, and U.S.S. *Hilary P. Jones.* They arrived off Alpha area at 1800 August 16. Admiral Jaujard's cruisers and destroyers steamed past them as in a review, a great inspiration for the French soldiers.

Debarking began at 1900 on Cavalaire and on Plage la Foux, hitherto not used, at the head of the Golfe de Saint-Tropez. There the Luftwaffe attacked, inflicting 80 casualties. Apart from that, the landing was uneventful and De Lattre was soon ashore, consulting with his friend General Patch at Hôtel Latitude Quarante-trois.

On the night of 16–17 August, U.S.S. *Endicott* and H.M.S. *Aphis* and *Scarab,* accompanied by four PT, 13 ASRC and four ML, briefly bombarded the coast near La Ciotat, hoping again to create the impression that a landing was about to take place at that unpropitious locality. On their retirement, a sharp surface battle took place. One of the air-sea rescue boats, No. 21, signaled, at 0545 August 17, to *Endicott* — then hull-down on the southern horizon — that she was being attacked by two enemy corvettes. Sensation! Lieutenant Commander Bulkeley reversed course, bent on 35 knots and at 0615 took over the fight from the two old British river gunboats which were having a running battle with vessels that looked like small destroyers. After a brisk exchange of gunfire which lasted only two minutes, the larger enemy vessel began to explode and her crew abandoned ship. The smaller in the meantime fired with 4.7-inch guns and torpedoes at *Endicott,* which, after disposing of the No. 1 enemy, closed No. 2 to 1500 yards and smothered her with gunfire. Both ships sank, leaving 210 survivors swimming or in boats. All were recovered.[13]

These vessels proved to be German corvettes *Capriolo* and *Nimet Allah.* The former, one of the new *Minerva*-class corvettes built at Genoa, had been taken over from Mussolini's Navy; the latter, originally the Egyptian Khedival yacht, had been purchased by Germany from the ex-Khedive and converted to war uses; she had

[13] This action took place 13 miles S by E of the lighthouse on Cap Croisette, the southern boundary of Marseilles roadstead. Hewitt Report p. 178; *Endicott* Action Reports 17 Aug., 23 Aug. 1944. A letter of Herr Hermann Polenz, former commander of the flotilla, gives the correct names and characteristics of the two ships.

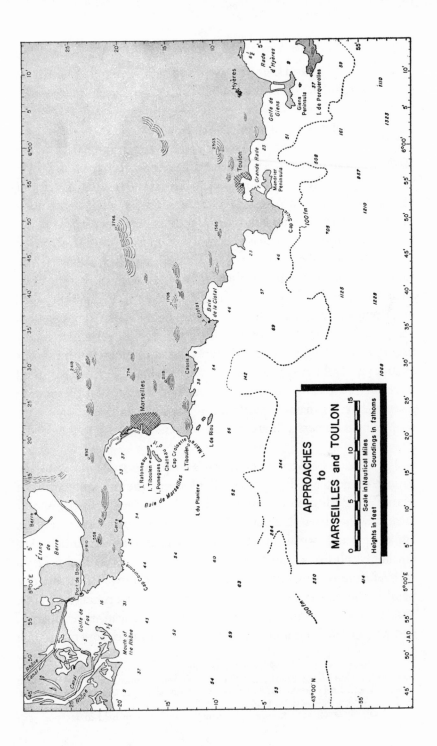

APPROACHES
to
MARSEILLES and TOULON

Scale in Nautical Miles

0   5   10   15

Heights in feet   Soundings in fathoms

two 88-mm guns and eight of 37- or 20-mm. They had been sent out of Toulon by Konteradmiral Ruhfus and were en route to Marseilles.

Another enemy sortie from Toulon, unknown and even unsuspected by us, was that of *U–230*, the last German submarine in the Mediterranean to put to sea.[14] Lieutenant Eberbach, her young C.O., with a scratch crew of sailors picked up on the beach, moved out of the harbor at 2100 August 17, hoping to get a crack at the invasion fleet. After hanging about the Mandrier Peninsula for two days he spotted *Augusta* and chased her all day on the 20th. He claims to have penetrated her destroyer screen and was just about to fire four torpedoes when the cruiser, completely unaware of his presence, was bracketed by a salvo from a shore battery and high-tailed out, completely spoiling his aim. That night *U–230* ran aground, was abandoned and blown up. Eberbach seized a French motor fishing boat in which he and the crew tried to escape to Italy; but at about 0200 August 27, when they were almost in the clear, they were intercepted by *Hambleton, Ericsson* and *Ellyson* of the area screen. The last-named sent over a boarding party and took the four U-boat officers and crew of 46 prisoners.[15]

The mission of General de Lattre's corps was to capture the historic naval port and dockyard of Toulon, and the city and harbor of Marseilles. Both places were more heavily fortified than the assault area; they had been designated "no surrender" fortresses by Hitler, and the preliminary air bombing had left many batteries intact. Accordingly, all fire support ships except those under Admiral Deyo were shifted to this flank. Admiral Davidson now had at his disposal battleships *Nevada*, H.M.S. *Ramillies* and French *Lorraine;* heavy cruisers *Augusta* and *Quincy;* two American, three British, and seven French light cruisers; [16] ten American destroyers and one

---

[14] Two were still afloat at Salamis but unable to go to sea. See Volume X 373.

[15] Oblt. z. See Heinz Eberbach "The Last German Submarine in the Western Mediterranean," a personal account trans. by Admiral Ruge; Condesron 18 (Capt. Sanders) Action Report 4 Sept. 1944.

[16] *Texas, Arkansas* and the old light cruiser division were held in reserve.

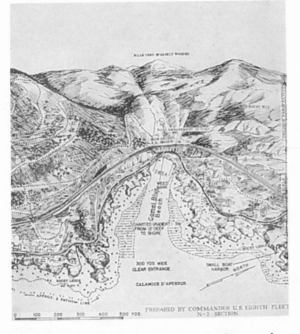

Panoramic sketch furnished to landing craft

From water color by Lieutenant Albert K. Murray USNR

Landings

Beach Camel Blue — Calanque d'Anthéor

From water color by Lieutenant Albert K. Murray USNR

Demolition Crew at Work, Golfe de Fréjus

Photo by Streicher for Bureau of Aeronautics

Rear Admiral Calvin T. Durgin (back to camera)

Conference in Ready Room, U.S.S. Tulagi

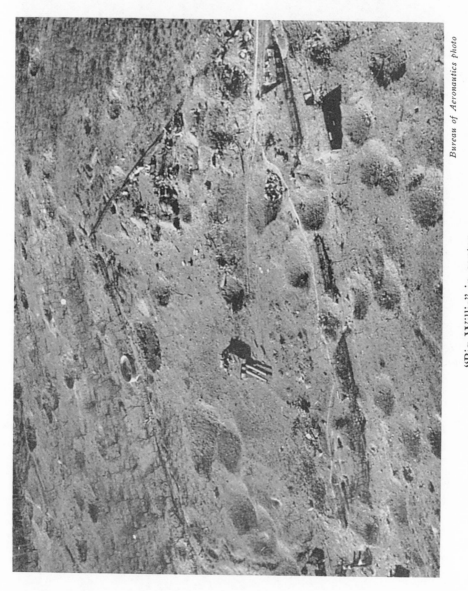

"Big Willie" in center

Mandrier Peninsula after Bombardment

British; and most of the available minecraft. These were none too many.

Admiral Davidson issued his plan to the gunfire support ships on 18 August. First phase was to sweep the Rade d'Hyères and capture Île de Porquerolles. The object here was to knock out the batteries on the Giens Peninsula and Cap de l'Esterel, which had an estimated range of eleven miles, so that the Allied ships could lie behind the peninsula and fire on the even-longer-range batteries on Cap Cépet.

The first attempt to sweep the Rade d'Hyères, on 18 August, had to be abandoned because of opposition from the enemy batteries on Porquerolles, Cap Bénat and the Giens Peninsula. Every day the gunfire support ships pounded away at these key batteries, but every day they replied, although the only effect of their shooting, as we have seen, was to spoil the aim of *U–230* on *Augusta*.

It may be assumed that, by the morning of 21 August, the face of Admiral Davidson was somewhat red. The French Army, advancing with magnificent *élan* against dug-in Germans, was breaking into the suburbs of Toulon and even approaching Marseilles, but the combined Navies had not yet attained their objectives. That afternoon, however, the results of almost continuous daylight bombardment began to be gathered. Porquerolles surrendered to contingents from *Eberle* and *Omaha* on 21 August. On the morning of the 23rd, white flags began to appear on the Giens Peninsula, which a shore party found to be evacuated by the enemy. Promptly the entire Rade d'Hyères was mineswept and secured.

In the meantime the French Corps had reached the environs of Toulon, and elements of the United States VI Corps had reached the Rhone by road up the Argens valley. Something had to be done quickly about securing a port to keep the Army supplied; logistic lines from the assault landing beaches were stretching out thin and might have to be closed if foul weather set in. Accordingly, Admiral Hewitt, after consulting with General Patch, decided to open the Golfe de Fos, 20 miles west of Marseilles, in order to provide entry for vessels into Port de Bouc, whence a canal big enough to float an LCM leads to the Rhone at Arles. If Marseilles held out longer than expected, Seventh Army could be supplied by Liberty ships and tankers unloading into landing craft at Port de Bouc, which was reported to be already under the control of the F.F.I. Actually the Germans had evacuated it on 21 August.

Minesweeping of Golfe de Fos began at first light on the 24th. The sweepers were harassed by enemy batteries on and around Cap Couronne, which were silenced by gunfire support ships after persistent efforts. After three days' work and the sweeping of 173 mines, a channel was opened to Port de Bouc; but, without waiting for the end of the sweep, Admiral Davidson on the afternoon of the 24th sent *PT–555* (Lieutenant Bayard Walker USNR), with Lieutenant Stanley Livingston and Capitaine de Frégate Bataille on board, to reconnoiter Port de Bouc.

PT–555 made the little port without incident, obtained the required information and started back. But at 0715, when she was still in the gulf, a mine exploded under her stern, killing five men, carrying away the 40-mm gun and almost everything up to the forward bulkhead of the engine room. Lieutenant Walker immediately caused his torpedoes to be jettisoned, and anchored. Life rafts were lowered to search for the missing men; the raft crews, after recovering dead and wounded, were picked up by a French rescue boat, which then towed the chopped-off PT into the little fishing port of Carro, where she moored to the dock with stern aground. Captain Ansel of *Philadelphia* sent two men ashore with a radio, by means of which Walker was able to inform Admiral Davidson about the state of Port de Bouc and enemy troop dispositions in the peninsula.

At La Couronne — nearest village to Carro — a requiem mass was celebrated on the following Sunday for the PT sailors. The church was decorated with flowers and French and American flags, the curé delivered an eloquent sermon, and four members of the F.F.I. formed an honor guard.[17] La Couronne is a poor village in

---

[17] Lt. Bayard Walker USNR Memo. 1 Sept. 1944 to Rear Adm. Davidson, Enclosure F Append. I in CTF 86 Action Report.

a barren country; but on the simple monument to its war dead was inscribed "A Nos Alliés," and the names of the petty officers killed in the mine explosion. Thus, in this remote corner of old Provence, five American sailors are kept in perpetual remembrance.[18]

On 27 August, after the channel had been properly swept, *LST– 134* and twelve salvage vessels entered Port de Bouc, carrying four causeway platoons of the 1040th Seabee Battalion and Army Engineers. The harbor and canal entrance were soon cleared, and 14 LCM from *Arcturus* and *Procyon* started up the canal to Arles on 1 September. The Army, however, made very little use of this water route, preferring to forward drummed gasoline to the front by truck. But a number of LCM worked around the clock for six days, ferrying French and American troops across the Rhone at Arles and Vallabrogues; and Port de Bouc remained the principal place for the discharge, storage and transfer inland of petroleum products.

We have left for the last the big battery on Cap Cépet, the southern cape that protects Toulon roadstead and which had to be neutralized before Toulon and Marseilles could be secured. The Saint-Mandrier battery, as the Navy called it,[19] consisted of two casemated turrets of two 340-mm (13.4 inch) each, which the Germans had removed from French battleship *La Provence* and mounted on the crest of the headland. Two had been sabotaged by French workmen, but "Big Willie," as the sailors named the other pair, could outrange any guns in the combined Mediterranean Fleet. They were surrounded by a labyrinth of tunnels and underground chambers providing living quarters for the gunners, power plant and ammunition storage; and the entire peninsula was studded with

---

[18] The monument was viewed by Mrs. Morison and Mr. Pineau in 1956. The names are not all spelled correctly, but the men commemorated can be identified as Ralph W. Bangert, Thomas F. Devaney, John J. Dunleavy, Harold R. Guest and Victor Sippin, all USNR.

[19] Saint-Mandrier is, properly, only the village and naval arsenal on the north side of Cap Cépet.

large, medium and small pieces of ordnance.[20] In addition, a partly salvaged French battleship and light cruiser were moored in the outer harbor of Toulon. Despite frequent efforts of Capitaine de Vaisseau Rosset, their commander, to assure Allied Intelligence that he was trying to save these ships for the future French Navy and that the Germans could make no use of them, the Air Forces spent a great deal of effort and bomb tonnage reducing them to junk.[21]

Twenty-year-old battleship *Lorraine*, whose 340-mm main battery was of the same caliber as "Big Willie," took a particular interest in knocking out the peninsula's guns, which had formerly been mounted in her sister battleship. Admiral Davidson gave her the privilege of firing the first shot on 19 August, after which *Nevada*, *Augusta* and *Quincy* joined in. The German gunners waited until next day, when they fired at *Émile Bertin* and *Philadelphia* off Porquerolles. On the 22nd one salvo just missed H.M.S. *Aurora*, whose C.O. sent a signal to *Nevada* just as she was moving in: "Please give Big Willie a poke in the kisser for me. Have a grudge against him since yesterday!" But Willie got in the first poke, with a 500-yard miss at a range of 30,000 yards. *Nevada* returned, with destroyers to lay smoke around her, and gave Willie the works. On the 25th, at the request of the Army, H.M.S. *Ramillies* and *Lorraine* opened fire. Admiral Davidson, then busy directing shoots by his other ships on the defenses of Marseilles, sent a signal to those off Toulon "to parade past Mandrier" to see if there was any more life in it. They complied, closing the range to 10,000 yards; and on the 26th *Lorraine*, which had fired the first shot, appropriately drew the last ever fired from the one remaining gun.

By next day the peninsula was isolated, and the German defenders were pushed into subterranean pits or dugouts. News of the liberation of Paris on 25 August gave a great fillip to the French assailants,

[20] Capt. H. L. Merillat USMCR (who was on board *Nevada*) "Big Willie Knocked Out," issued by Marine Corps Public Relations 20 Sept. 1944.

[21] It was the intention of the Germans to block the harbor entrance with these ships, but their C.O. had so moored them that they could not be moved to the channel, and they had no guns capable of firing.

and on the 28th Konteradmiral Ruhfus, the German commander at Toulon, surrendered that city and all enemy forces in the area, including 1800 sailors who had been manning the numerous batteries on Cap Cépet.

A careful study was made by French ordnance experts of Cap Cépet after this nine days' effort to destroy the big battery. The entire rocky peninsula for almost a square mile around the batteries was scarred and holed by high-caliber naval shells, whose craters could easily be distinguished from those made by air bombs. One big gun had a nick in the muzzle made by a naval shell which had knocked it out, but the second was still intact. The casemate containing the two dead guns had been completely taken apart, and all range-finding and other instruments destroyed. German prisoners who tried to escape from the fortress in a small boat on 27 August reported that most of the gunners had been killed, and a German officer told Admiral Lemonnier that during the last three days his men had refused to serve the guns.[22]

Since 24 August, the same ships that pounded Saint-Mandrier, and others in Admiral Davidson's force, had been engaged in reducing the defenses of Marseilles, especially the batteries on Cap Croisette. Actually there was more shooting by ships around Marseilles than at the defenses of Toulon, and heavy aërial bombardments were laid on at the same time. Marseilles, too, surrendered to the French Army 28 August. Isolated garrisons on Ratonneau, Pomègues and Château d'If, conveyed, through a truce mission, their desire to quit. Captain Ansel of *Philadelphia*, with Marine detachments from that ship and *Augusta*, went ashore on one of the islands and accepted the surrender of about 730 Germans.[23]

Thus the great objectives were secured within two weeks of the landings, and in less than half the time that the planners expected.[24]

---

22 Lemonnier *Cap sur la Provence* pp. 188–90, 274–85.
23 Account by Lt. Henry D. Reck USNR, who acted as interpreter for Capt. Ansel, in CTF 86 (Rear Adm. Davidson) Action Report, Enclosure F, Appendix 3.
24 De Lattre de Tassigny p. 115.

Although intensive minesweeping and salvage operations were necessary before Marseilles and Toulon could be used, unloading of supplies in the larger port began as early as 3 September, and in Toulon on the 4th; and by the 15th a greater volume of troops and matériel was being discharged in these two harbors than was sent over the assault beaches.

The liberation of Provence was in many ways a happier affair for everyone than was that of Normandy. Allied sailors and soldiers encountered jolly *gens du Midi* instead of dour, suspicious Norman peasants. The fact that French warships took a large part in the invasion, and that French troops captured Toulon and Marseilles (a part of the plan on which General Patch wisely insisted) gave the local population a feeling that this was a French campaign. Yet they were uniformly outgoing, considerate and grateful to their British and American allies. This well appeared in a liberation parade that was held in Toulon on 14 September.

Down the main streets and past a reviewing stand where the principal Allied commanders took their stations, and before the French Ministre de la Marine, a company of American sailors, with a Navy band, headed a procession. A detachment of the Royal Navy, with its own band, followed; then came 800 French bluejackets from the fighting ships, in clean blue blouses, white trousers, with the jaunty red pompon on their caps, marching along at a snappy stride, their drums and trumpets playing the traditional airs that had not been heard in France for four years. The population of that old naval port went wild with joy; for, as Admiral Lemonnier wrote, "They had recovered the France of Victory. But we did not forget that the war was still going on." [25]

The same admiral, in his book on Operation DRAGOON, writes: "I wish here to pay tribute to the high quality and the extreme courtesy of Admiral Hewitt, with whom I have kept up the closest and most confidential relations; and to note the extraordinary competence of his staff and of his task group commanders, with whom,

[25] *Marine Nationale* Nov. 1944.

for our squadron and division commanders, coöperation was at once easy, agreeable and effective." [26]

On 15 September, exactly one month from the Provençal D-day, General Patch's Seventh Army, the First French Army, and all Allied ground and service forces in Southern France were incorporated in the Sixth U. S. Army Group (Lieutenant General Jacob L. Devers), which came under the operational control of General Eisenhower.

Operation DRAGOON was over; and, when Admiral Hewitt flew to Lyons on the 17th to make his preliminary report to General Devers and inquire what more the Navy could do, all indications pointed to a speedy end of the war. It did not turn out that way; but if anyone still doubts whether DRAGOON was worth while, he should read in the military histories, especially in Kesselring's memoirs, the part that Patch's Seventh Army and De Lattre's First French Army played in the final campaign. Additional proof may be had from statistics of the enormous numbers of men and matériel handled by the port of Marseilles. By V-E Day (8 May 1945), 4,123,794 long tons of cargo and 905,512 troops had been landed at Marseilles, Toulon and Port de Bouc; the lion's share of them at Marseilles. That one port, between 1 November 1944 and 1 April 1945, received on an average half a million tons of cargo and 54,000 troops per month. These figures are in addition to those of men and matériel landed on the DRAGOON beaches. Between 15 August and 28 September, when they were closed, 380,000 troops, 306,000 tons cargo, 69,312 vehicles and 17,848 tons gasoline had passed over them. [27]

In such wise did Operation DRAGOON justify itself. In Naval history, it may stand as an example of an almost perfect amphibious operation from the point of view of training, timing, Army–Navy– Air Force coöperation, performance and results. But it must be

[26] *Cap sur la Provence* p. 86.
[27] J. Bykofsky and H. Larson *The Transportation Corps: Overseas Operations* (U.S. Army World War II Series) pp. 294, 320 of ms. Compare figures of Cherbourg at end of Chap. XII.

remembered that it met no opposition comparable to that which Operation NEPTUNE encountered in Normandy; these men were given no such challenge as the United States Navy would have to face from the Japanese air forces off Okinawa. Enemy U-boats and the Luftwaffe had been almost completely eliminated, available German surface craft were few and weak, the coastal batteries with few exceptions were poorly served, and the German ground forces, having no defense in depth, attempted no counterattack; their one idea by D-day plus 5 was to beat the Seventh Army into Germany. Moreover, DRAGOON was launched ten weeks after the Norman D-day and two weeks after the big breakthrough, on a flood tide of victory. Its great accomplishment was to swell that tide by an entire Army group, which made the Allied advance into Germany irresistible.

U.S.S. *Nevada* bombarding

Liberation parade

Toulon

General view of Toulon

The Vieux Port of Marseilles

Major Ports Secured, 28 August

PART III

The Navy's Part in the Final Campaigns[1]

August 1944–May 1945

OVERLORD and DRAGOON comprise the two main operations in the invasion of Europe in which the United States Navy played a leading part. But the Navy was far from idle during the subsequent campaign for the defeat of Germany. The last lively months of antisubmarine warfare have already been related in Volume X of this series; but there is more on the surface to be told. Small craft engaged in the tiresome routine of patrol and sweep in the English Channel, which involved occasional brushes with coastal batteries and German armed vessels. Naval landing craft, truck-borne to the Rhine, helped General Eisenhower's Expeditionary Force to cross that classic river. And Naval activity continued in the Gulf of Genoa until the German surrender.

So, if the rest of this volume seems a thing of shreds and patches, that is the way it was for the Navy. The last nine months of the European war was a soldiers' campaign in which the sailors, besides maintaining sea communications and relentlessly hunting E-boats, F-boats and U-boats, intervened only where the Army wanted help.

[1] Comnaveu Administrative History Vol. VII, Com U.S. Naval Forces France (Vice Adm. Kirk) War Diary, and Com U.S. Ports and Naval Bases France (Rear Adm. Wilkes) War Diary cover most of the naval activities included in this Part. Kenneth Edwards *Operation Neptune* (1946) and Ehrman V chap. iv are valuable for incidents and background, respectively. Jacques Mordal has an excellent summary of the final campaign in Michael Soltikow *Remagen, le Pont de la Décision* (Paris 1956).

CHAPTER XVIII

The French Out-ports

September1944–May 1945

1. *The War Continues*

ON 12 September 1944, when General Patch's Seventh Army
made contact with elements of General Patton's Third at
Châtillon on the upper Seine, and DRAGOON, as it were, merged into
OVERLORD, the war in Europe seemed to be rapidly approaching a
victorious conclusion. On the basis of strategic shortages in Germany, the liberation of Paris and Brussels, the expected breaching
of Kesselring's Gothic Line, and the Russian advance to Warsaw
and Bucharest, the British Joint Intelligence Committee on 5 September predicted that German collapse was near.[1] Field Marshals
Brooke and Montgomery were equally optimistic. For, in the last
week of August and the first ten days of September, Canadian and
British forces had overrun the flying-bomb sites in the Pas-de-
Calais, and had entered Antwerp; First United States Army had
captured a large enemy force around Mons, liberated a part of Belgium, and reached the Siegfried Line; Third Army had dashed
eastward as far as Nancy. By mid-September, the Allied armies
were on the frontiers of Germany, having cleared the enemy out
of France and most of Belgium and Luxembourg, and even penetrated the Netherlands. And several Allied Intelligence reports
gave out that the German armies were completely disorganized.
Although Generals Eisenhower and Bradley were less sanguine
than the British, possibly owing to their keener appreciation of

[1] Ehrman V 398–401.

logistical difficulties,[2] this rich harvest of victories had raised the sights of many Allied leaders to peace in 1944.

When OCTAGON Conference opened at Quebec on 12 September, the autumn colors of the Laurentian countryside were no brighter than the glow of optimism in the Citadel and the "blaze of friendship" in the Château Frontenac. "Everything we had touched," said Mr. Churchill, "had turned to gold." As evidence of the effect that success has on sometime discordant Allies: when the British again brought up their Ljubljana Gap plan General Marshall declared that he had no intention of withdrawing United States forces from Italy "at the present time," and Admiral King even promised not to remove precious LSTs from the Mediterranean as long as there was a chance of an amphibious landing in Istria, to which he now gave a qualified approval.[3]

By the end of September, the mirage of early victory had evaporated. General Alexander's Army Group, after breaking the Gothic Line in Italy, had ground to a halt on the line Viareggio–Florence–Rimini. The northern German armies were making a strong stand on their right flank, denying Antwerp sea approaches to the Allies, whose attempt to break this log jam with a paratroop attack near Arnhem met with disaster (17–25 September). This failure had strategic repercussions far and wide. General Eisenhower, anticipating a bitter winter campaign, had to recast his strategy for the invasion of Germany. Admiral Lord Mountbatten was told that his oft-postponed amphibious operation in the Indian Ocean was off again, and the Joint Chiefs of Staff prepared to continue the war against Japan without the infantry divisions which they had hoped to divert from Europe.

[2] *Crusade in Europe* pp. 304, 321; Pogue p. 245, where an estimate of 28 Aug. by Col. Oscar Koch USA, Patton's G–2, is quoted.

[3] Ehrman V 505–12. The two civilian chiefs of state were less optimistic than many soldiers. (See *Triumph and Tragedy* pp. 147–55.) Mr. Churchill had already deflated the report of his Joint Intelligence Committee; and President Roosevelt, well briefed by General Marshall, warned against forecasting the date of German collapse.

2. *Liberation of Brittany*,⁴ *August–September 1944*

Even after the liberation of Normandy, the Canadians' capture of Ostend (8 September) and the British entry into Le Havre (12 September), Hitler still held the Channel Islands, the Gironde, Lorient, Saint-Nazaire, and the harbor and city of Brest, which had been the main port of entry for the A.E.F. in World War I. In planning for OVERLORD it had been assumed that the United States Army would need some of these ports. As both Lorient and Saint-Nazaire were too small, a grand development scheme for a military port of entry in Quiberon Bay was drawn up, and in July, Rear Admiral Hall, as Com XI 'Phib, was ordered to plan a landing for part of Patton's Third Army on the Brest Peninsula.⁵ Patton's first mission, as soon as he could break the German lines in Normandy, was to liberate Brittany. German forces there were well dug in and protected by high-caliber naval batteries on off-lying islands. These garrisons had been designated "fortresses" by Hitler, which meant that they must stand and fight to the last.

Patton "busted loose" on 30 July, liberated Avranches, sent one armored spearhead south toward Rennes, a second southeast toward Le Mans and a third west toward Brest. Then Hitler tried to break up the Allied strategy. He ordered his Seventh Army to counterattack at Mortain, 25 miles east of Avranches, with the object of severing Patton from his Norman bases and rolling up American forces toward Cherbourg.

Abortive as this attempt proved to be, it created a new tactical situation from which Generals Bradley, Montgomery and Eisenhower promptly profited. It gave them an opportunity to cut off and trap the German Seventh Army between Falaise and Argentan. On 3 August, Bradley ordered Patton to clear Brittany with a mini-

⁴ Rear Adm. Wilkes War Diary; Pogue pp. 204-17; W. Bedell Smith *Eisenhower's Six Great Decisions* chap. ii.

⁵ Adm. Hall, unable to get far in planning this Operation SWORDHILT without knowing Patton's proposed scheme of maneuver, sent an officer to his HQ to find out. All he got out of "George" was the message: "Tell that s.o.b. to quit worrying – I'll be in Brest in forty-eight hours!"

mum of forces; next day, Montgomery, in a signal to Field Marshal Brooke, said, "I have turned only one American corps into Brittany, as I feel that will be enough." As soon as this was called to Eisenhower's attention he, too, agreed to hurl the major part of Third Army east, to act as the southern jaw of the trap.[6] This was taking a tremendous risk, but it worked. Most of the German Seventh Army was captured in the "Falaise bag," and Patton's spectacular rush to the Seine threw the fighting zone so far eastward that Brittany was well-nigh forgotten. The changing situation, and Bradley's decision to send Patton eastward instead of southwesterly, explains the comparative lack of naval and military activity in Brittany. Major General Troy Middleton's VIII Corps of Third Army accomplished all that was necessary in that province.

Patton crossed the ancient frontier of Normandy into Brittany on 1 August, amid scenes of wildest enthusiasm on the part of the populace. Breton granite — unlike Norman cheese — had been impervious to German propaganda. Many sailors, fishermen and other young men had long since escaped by small boats to enlist in the Fighting French Navy, or by the "underground" to form units of the F.F.I. Nowhere in liberated Europe did American soldiers and sailors have a warmer reception than in Brittany.

On 2 August, the United States Navy suffered its first casualty in this campaign. Captain Norman S. Ives, commander of the naval base at Cherbourg, headed a party of 97 naval officers and men which moved west with the Army to reconnoiter the liberated ports. They entered Granville just ahead of evacuating Germans, then proceeded along the road to Brittany, intending to reconnoiter Saint-Malo, on a false rumor that it had already fallen. At a hamlet near Pontorson, they ran into a German ambush. The Captain, Lieutenant Commander Arthur M. Hooper USNR and four sailors were killed; eight were wounded; the rest took up defensive

---

[6] *Triumph and Tragedy* p. 30; Pogue p. 209. Bedell Smith pp. 59–64 describes this as "the second of six great decisions made by the Supreme Commander which assured the annihilation of German's military power in the West." But the idea came from some 21st Army Group planner, and the decision was that of Bradley.

positions alongside the road until a column of tanks belonging to the 6th Armored Division arrived from Pontorson and rescued the survivors.[7]

Allied naval activities west and south of Cherbourg were nominally under Commander in Chief, Plymouth, but actually under the operational control of Rear Admiral Wilkes at Cherbourg. On 2 August, Wilkes ordered American PT Squadrons 30 and 34 to run night patrol between Cherbourg, the Channel Islands and Saint-Malo. In this patrol they were accompanied by a destroyer escort, whose superior radar enabled her to act as their combat information center. The O.T.C., who rode the DE, directed every attack.

On the night of 8–9 August *Maloy* and five PTs were patrolling a north-south line six miles long, west of Jersey. "The weather was good," wrote a participant, "the sea calm, with a slow easy roll coming in from the Atlantic; and, as we boomed along in the growing dusk, puffins, their crops gorged with fish, scooted out of our way. The scene was of varying tones of gray accented by the brilliant white wash from the boats as they thundered along, exhausts rumbling their steady growl into an endless carpet of foam spreading astern."[8] At 0530 August 9, after a thick fog had rolled in, *Maloy's* radar picked up six minesweepers of the German Channel Islands fleet, steaming south toward La Corbière, Jersey. Lieutenant H. J. Sherertz USNR, the squadron commander, was on board *Maloy* as O.T.C., and Lieutenant Commander Peter Scott RNVR,[9] an old hand at this game, had come along as vector controller to assist him. The two boats nearest the target were moved

[7] Rear Adm. Wilkes War Diary; Memo. of a survivor, Lt. Ewald H. Pawsat USNR (M.C.) 14 Aug.; Com Minor Naval Base 258 (Granville) Report 9 Aug. 1944; letter from another survivor, Lt. Cdr. C. U. Bishop, 2 Feb. 1957. Lt. Milby Burton USNR and other junior officers held an almost untenable position along the road until rescue arrived.

[8] J. F. Queeny USNR "The Far Shore." He was exec. of *PT–508*, whose C.O. was Lt.(jg) C. R. Whorton. The other boats were *PT–509* (Lt. H. M. Crist USNR), *PT–503* (Lt. J. A. Doherty USNR), *PT–507* (Ens. B. T. Heminway USNR) and *PT–500* (Lt. D. S. Kennedy USNR).

[9] Son of Robert Scott of Antarctic fame, and author of *The Battle of the Narrow Seas*.

up to it through the fog, fired their torpedoes by radar, and missed. *PT–508* and *PT–509* were then vectored onto the same target and approached at full speed, almost 40 knots. Each boat fired one torpedo at a range of about 400 yards, then circled to make a gunfire attack. In so doing *PT–509* emerged into a clear patch between fogbanks, in full view of the enemy, right off the port of St.-Helier. The Germans promptly opened heavy and accurate gunfire. A shell exploded in the chart house of *PT–509* and fragments spattered the deck, but Lieutenant Harry Crist, a veteran of the Pacific War, shaped a course to ram, and hit one of the minesweepers with such force that the bow of his burning and exploding boat was jammed into her side. The German crew, working frantically with crowbars, managed to clear the flaming boat, which immediately exploded and disappeared. All hands were lost except Radarman John L. Page usnr, who was taken prisoner.

PT–508, whose radar was not working, lost *PT–509* in the fog, subsequently sighted the rammed minesweeper and was about to engage her when ordered back to *Maloy* by the O.T.C. *PT–503* and *PT–507*, sent to search the coast of Jersey for the missing boat, attacked a minesweeper in St.-Helier roadstead, but were driven off by her gunfire, and two sailors were killed.

Before mid-August there were two more brushes, both inconclusive, between American PTs and German surface craft. Thereafter, for several months, the enemy kept in port, but Channel Islands coastal batteries continued to harass Allied convoys or vessels passing along the coast, despite frequent attempts by destroyers, and even by H.M.S. *Rodney*, to silence them.

Saint-Malo, the ancient "city of the Corsairs," from whose rock-studded bay Jacques Cartier had sailed for the discovery of the Saint Lawrence, was attacked by VIII Corps on 4 August and captured on the 17th. But the port, with its 40-foot rise and fall of tide, could not be used by the Allies while the Île de Cézembre, a few miles off shore, was in enemy hands. The island garrison, possessing six 194-mm guns and living in bombproof tunnels, held out two weeks longer, despite frequent bombings from the air, gunfire by 240-mm cannon mounted at Saint-Malo and Dinard, and naval bombardment by several British destroyers and battleship *Malaya*. Since it seemed impossible to batter the island into surrender, Admiral Wilkes sent 15 LCVP overland by low-bed tractors from Omaha beach to Saint-Malo, for an amphibious assault. On 2 September, just as a westerly gale was making up, and after the landing craft had embarked an infantry battalion, Cézembre showed a white flag and the garrison of 323 men surrendered. They were evacuated by the LCVP through heavy seas. This little operation, proving that it was practical to haul landing craft overland, encouraged the Army to ask for naval assistance in crossing the Rhine.[10]

On 3 August, when Bradley decided to throw the bulk of Patton's Third Army easterly, he ordered VIII Corps, which had already taken Rennes, to capture Brest after taking Saint-Malo. The Brest garrison was commanded by a fanatical and aggressive general who was considered too dangerous to leave in a position to strike against the Cherbourg-Paris supply line.[11] Naval coöperation with VIII Corps in the siege of Brest began on 11 August when three LSTs, laden with rations, ammunition and petroleum products, beached at Saint-Michel-en-Grèves, on the north side of the Brest Peninsula.[12] In six weeks' time about 60,000 tons of supplies were landed over the sand at Saint-Michel. The capacity of these beaches was insufficient; so on 21 August *PT–502* and *PT–504* were sent to reconnoiter Morlaix, a little port on the north shore of Brittany which had been bypassed by the Army. Entering at break of day, the two boats moved slowly over the mudflats and through a minefield revealed by a captured German chart, and were then startled by a spatter of small-arms fire coming from the shore. Hastily they broke out their largest ensigns, at the same time tooting their foghorns, while everyone topside waved arms vigorously and bellowed "*Américains! Amis!*" This demonstration had its effect; the firing ceased and a small boat put out from shore, almost concealed under

[10] Rear Adm. Wilkes Report 11 Sept. 1944; Dr. Paul Aubry *La Ruée sur Saint-Malo* (Rennes, 1947).
[11] Bradley pp. 362–67.
[12] Ruppenthal II chap. ii of mimeographed draft.

the folds of a French flag big enough for a battleship. As the boat came alongside, the Mayor of Morlaix, resplendent in top hat and frock coat, emerged from under the tricolor and gave a profuse and apologetic welcome. A pilot guided *PT–502* and *PT–504* up-river to the town, where officers and men were entertained around the clock by lobster, champagne and charming *bretonnes*.[13] Two days later, a British minesweeping unit cleared the approaches to the port, and on the 25th a convoy of two Liberty ships and ten LCT arrived with supplies for VIII Corps. But the pioneer PTs had all the glory — and the gravy — of liberating Morlaix.

The small nearby harbor of Roscoff was also put to use for unloading Army supplies. Both ports were operated by the Army for three months.

Convoys to Morlaix, Roscoff and Saint-Michel were covered by an outer Channel Island patrol of British and American destroyers, and by the inshore patrol of American PTs operating with a DE. *Maloy* was damaged by a near-miss from a Jersey shore battery, and *Borum* received a similar bouquet from Guernsey.

There was not much naval bombardment of Brest, because it could be reached only by long-range guns and most of the NEPTUNE fire support ships were then serving in the Mediterranean. H.M.S. *Warspite*, however, fired a few salvos which drove the Germans out of the city onto the Crozon Peninsula. On 19 September, after Brest had taken a terrible beating from VIII Corps siege artillery and German demolitions, the garrison of 20,000 men surrendered. As the harbor was full of pressure mines and scuttled ships, little rehabilitation was done in 1944. The small garrisons at Lorient and Saint-Nazaire were contained by the F.F.I., aided by a United States Infantry division, until Germany surrendered.

The British capture of Le Havre on 12 September was most opportune as the difficulty of supplying the armies was increasing and the Normandy beaches would soon have to be closed down. But Le Havre was almost as badly demolished and thickly mined

[13] Queeny "The Far Shore" pp. 39–40.

as Cherbourg. Admiral Wilkes sent in a port party on the 16th, Commodore Sullivan, salvage crew and Seabees arrived a few days later, and British minecraft began methodical sweeps. The first Liberty ships entered the inner harbor on 19 September. U.S.S. *Miantonomah*, departing Le Havre for Cherbourg 25 September, struck a mine 1500 yards from Digue Nord light, broke in two, and sank in 18 minutes, with a loss of four officers and 54 men.[14] Wilkes shifted his flag to Le Havre 11–12 October, and in early November managed to get Rouen also activated as a port of entry. In addition to these two harbors at the mouth of the Seine, Cherbourg and Morlaix continued to be operated by the United States Navy, and Granville by the United States Army, throughout the winter of 1944–1945. The Omaha beaches closed down 22 November; Utah had already been closed except to dukws. Minesweeping of the channels to the Seine and to Cherbourg, Morlaix and Brest continued all winter. Admiral Wilkes had a tremendous job overseeing dredging, sweeping, handling convoys and unloading at the several ports under his command; in January 1945, for instance, no fewer than 127 convoys arrived in and 97 departed from Le Havre.

3. *Collier Convoys and Granville Raids,*[15] *December 1944–May 1945*

Paris, liberated 25 August, was a happy city until a cold autumn set in early and the hope of an early peace had vanished. Civilian Paris was not equipped for oil heating, and her supplies of coal,

[14] Rear Adm. Wilkes War Diary; Commo. J. E. Arnold USNR in U.S. Nav. Inst. *Proceedings* LXXIII 127–35 (Feb. 1947).

[15] Comnaveu Administrative History; Comnavforfrance (Vice Adm. Kirk) to Comnaveu 21 Apr. 1945, Enclosure C "Action in Channel Islands 1 March–15 April"; Com Navbase Cherbourg (Capt. L. B. Ard USNR) "Action at Granville 8–9 March" 13 March 1945, with report of Port Commander Granville enclosed; PC–552 and PC–564 Action Reports; Hüffmeier's article in *Wehrwissenschaftliche Rundschau* Jan. 1952 pp. 24–31, trans. with notes furnished by Service Historique de la Marine; Alan and Mary Wood *Islands in Danger* (London, 1955); information from Cdr. J. W. Phillippbar, 1956. These collier convoys started in Sept. 1944 and were operated by C. in C. Plymouth. 20,135 tons of coal were discharged at Granville in Oct., 47,580 in Nov., 50,680 tons in Dec.

meager enough in wartime, were now completely cut off by German possession of the mines. Anticipating that this want of winter fuel would cause much misery to French civilians after their liberation, the Admiralty assigned a number of small coastal colliers to carry coal from Newcastle and elsewhere to Granville and Avranches, whence there were good rail connections to Paris and Tours. As both those little harbors lie deep in the Bay of Saint-Malo they can be approached only by passing the Channel Islands and Les Minquiers. Hence the colliers had to be escorted. The American PCs and SCs which had taken part in the Normandy invasion shared this new duty with the Royal Navy, which was ready to take it over entirely in December. The American craft were then prepared to return to the United States. The PCs, with reduced crews, were waiting in an English port for a break in the weather and the SCs were waiting to be loaded on Liberty ships with only skeleton crews — one officer and six men for each boat — when snorkel-equipped U-boats made their unwelcome Christmastide visits to the English Channel. Troopship *Leopoldville* was torpedoed and sunk on Christmas Eve within sight of Cherbourg, with a loss of over 800 American troops; the same U-boat sank H.M.S. *Affleck* and *Capel* off Cherbourg the day after Christmas, again with heavy loss; and on the 28th the British transport *Empire Javelin* was torpedoed and sunk in mid-channel.[16]

These events convinced Admirals Stark and Kirk that the PCs and SCs could not yet be sent home. Since there was no time to get their own men back, London and the American naval bases in England had to be combed for replacements. Yeomen, storekeepers, maintenance men and others were hustled on board with a minimum of formality, more or less in old press-gang fashion. And the SCs and PCs, remanned with green crews, resumed their winter escort and patrol duties in the rough waters of the Channel.

The Channel Islands, as we have seen, were Hitler's favorite and most valued "fortress." He refused repeated suggestions by his generals to evacuate the garrison of 36,000 soldiers and sailors, supplied

[16] For details see Volume X pp. 334-7.

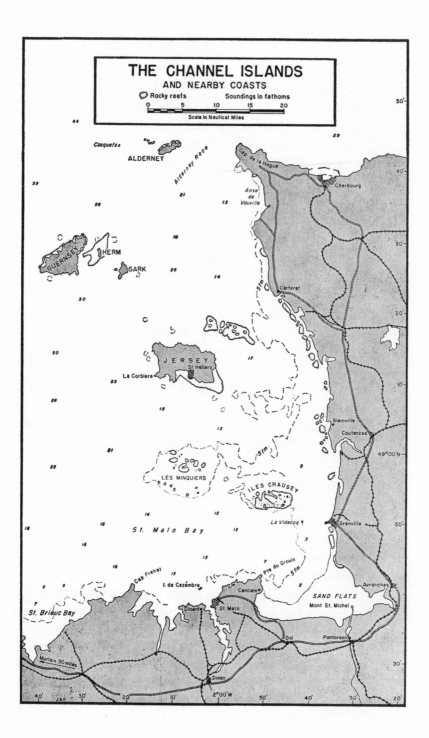

THE CHANNEL ISLANDS
AND NEARBY COASTS
Rocky reefs   Soundings in fathoms
0   5   10   15   20
Scale in Nautical Miles

50'

44

Casquets
ALDERNEY

Alderney Race

Cap de la Hague
Cherbourg

40'

29

39

81

Anse
de
Vauville

13

30'

66

19

GUERNSEY
HERM
SARK

26

14

5 fm

Carteret

20'

30

C

50

JERSEY
St Heliers

17

La Corbiere

23

18

Blainville
Coutances

10'

26

C

12

9

49°00'N

81

LES MINQUIERS

5 fm

ÎLES CHAUSEY

22

La Videcoq

Granville

50'

16

12

St. Malo Bay

12

3

18

12

7

Pte du Grouin

5 fm

2

Avranches

18

Cap Frehel

13

I. de Cezembre

Cancale

SAND FLATS
Mont St. Michel

9

9

7

St. Brieuc Bay

Dinard
St. Malo

Dol

Pontorson

30'

Morlaix 30 miles

Dinan

2°00'W

50'

40'

30'

20'

40'   30'   20'   10'

them lavishly with matériel and slave laborers from prison camps until the Islands were practically walled in concrete and bristling with high-caliber guns. On the ground that the commanding general there had become soft, Hitler placed over him Vizeadmiral Friedrich Hüffmeier, former C.O. of *Scharnhorst* and a fanatical Nazi. He had a fairly formidable fleet of small craft at his disposal, but the Islands' stock of coal was almost exhausted and his armed minesweepers burned coal. The civilian population was saved from starvation only by Red Cross supplies shipped from Lisbon.

When Hüffmeier was at his wits' end to find something to do for his Fuehrer, a suggestion came from the Continent. Five German parachutists escaped from the American P.O.W. camp at Granville, seized an LCVP, and made the German outpost at Les Minquiers, whence they were forwarded to Jersey. On the basis of their observations of collier convoys at Granville, the Admiral concocted a plan to raid that little port, and get himself a supply of coal.

The first attempt, on the night of 6–7 February 1945, failed, largely owing to the vigilance of *PC–552*. This American patrol craft, commanded by Lieutenant James S. Spielman USNR, had been posted as picket ship in Granville roadstead, to protect seven merchant vessels anchored off Cancale. Encountering an E-boat, *PC–552* opened fire and chased it for 20 miles to a point east of Cape Fréhel, thence to the westward of Les Minquiers, where the German craft turned up more speed than the PC could match and escaped to Jersey. The other raiding vessels, discouraged by bad weather and the timely action of *PC–552*, returned to Jersey without even getting a smell of the Granville colliers.

Hüffmeier decided to try again on the night of 8–9 March. This time he organized a real commando raid, built around four large minesweepers which, led by a seagoing tug, were to enter the harbor and land troops. He also employed three armed barges, three fast motor launches to land commandos on the bathing beach adjoining the town, and two small minesweepers for protection against PTs.

Search radar on the Cotentin Peninsula picked up this formation, at 2225 March 8, when it was about halfway between Jersey and Chausey. Granville was notified, the Cherbourg PT patrol, then off Cape de la Hague, was ordered south, and radar plots of the German disposition were passed to *PC–564*, then covering Granville. Her skipper, Lieutenant Percy Sandel USNR, had been on board only 12 days; she had only one gunner's mate and he was one of the first to be wounded.

PC–564 intercepted the three armed barges, set off a spread of star shell, and fired one round from her single 3-inch gun, after which the breech refused to close. Almost simultaneously the three big German vessels opened fire with 88-mm guns. Their first round hit the patrol craft's pilothouse, killing or seriously wounding all the occupants and destroying the power steering gear. The second round hit the mast, knocking out two 20-mm gun crews; the third silenced the 40-mm guns; and a fourth started a fire in officers' country. Lieutenant Sandel, considering the situation hopeless, with his ship out of control and no guns firing, ordered the engines stopped, and prepared to abandon ship. After ten men had gone over the side into a life raft, he decided to make a dash for safety; and, steering by hand and turning up flank speed, he outran the Germans to the coast, beaching southwest of Pierre de Herpin lighthouse. Two officers and 12 men had been killed and 11 wounded, and 14 were missing, out of a crew of five officers and 60 men; those who had taken to the raft were later made prisoner. But the PC was salvaged.

This engagement took place between midnight and 0030 March 9. Half an hour later the four big minesweepers were inside the artificial harbor and the three motor launches were landing commandos in rubber boats on the bathing beach.

Granville was taken completely by surprise; N.O.I.C. and the United States Army commander, although notified of the radar contacts, had treated them merely as interesting information and sounded no alert. The town was defended by 60 French soldiers and two battalions of American labor troops, there to help German prisoners handle the cargoes of the colliers, four of which were in harbor and not yet discharged. After the German minecraft had raked the quays with machine-gun fire, about 90 commandos landed, demolished portal cranes on the quay, and liberated 67 German prisoners from their quayside barracks. In the meantime the bathing-beach commandos had broken into the hotels, killed one United States Army and one Royal Navy officer and five men, and captured several American Army officers, some still clad in pajamas.[17]

Yet all did not go well with the main object of the raid. The commando unit chosen to destroy the search radar on a cliff above the harbor was effectively resisted by American troops, and the officer leading it was killed. Minesweeper *De Schelde* ran aground in the outer harbor, and had to be abandoned. That accident, as well as the fight with *PC-564* and the shore raids, retarded the timetable so that by 0300, when the German commander gave the order to retire, the ebb had run for two hours and only the smallest British collier could be towed out. Thus the net gain of this raid was a few captives and liberated prisoners, and 112 tons of coal.

The Granville raid caused security measures to be tightened along the west coast of the Cotentin Peninsula, so that when a sabotage unit of 18 Germans from Jersey landed in rubber boats on Cape de la Hague on 5 April 1945, with the mission of blowing up a railway bridge near Cherbourg, they were quickly rounded up and captured. Every so often the long-range batteries on Alderney would open a furious bombardment on the cape, apparently with the object of destroying the radar station; but these did no damage and inflicted no casualties. Admiral Hüffmeier, however, was planning a second raid on Granville for 7 May, when Doenitz notified him to call it off, as he was about to surrender to Eisenhower.

One more naval operation took place on the west coast of France. This was an attack to clear the enemy from the Île d'Oleron off the mouth of the Charente, which precluded free use of La Rochelle,

---

[17] Hüffmeier says nine, the Enclosure C in Comnavforfrance Report says six, and the Army port commander's report lists four officers, one civilian official and one private as missing.

Rochefort and Bordeaux, ports captured by the French Army in January. Organized by Vice Admiral Kirk, it consisted almost entirely of French forces. A naval task force — battleship *Lorraine*, cruiser *Duquesne*, three destroyers, a DE, three frigates, two tugs and nine minesweepers, under the command of Contre-Amiral Rue — assembled at Plymouth in early April 1945. Carrying a battalion or two of French troops and 24 American LCVP, it arrived off the Gironde estuary on the 15th. Admiral Rue, coöperating with French troops from the interior, first secured both banks of the Gironde near its mouth, and on the 30th, after a naval bombardment, landed the amphibious forces on the northern and western sides of the big island. The German garrison fought but was soon overcome, and Admiral Rue was able to announce on 2 May that all resistance had ceased.

Within a week, Germany itself had surrendered.[18]

[18] *Collection des Rapports Mensuels* at Service Historique de la Marine; Vice Adm. Kirk Report on the operation, 19 May 1945.

CHAPTER XIX

Mop-up in the Mediterranean[1]

September 1944–April 1945

ON 15 SEPTEMBER 1944, when the establishment of a continuous front through Eastern France was recognized in the
placing of all DRAGOON ground forces under General Devers' Sixth
Army Group, the enemy still held a large part of Northern Italy.
On the left (west) flank of the Allied line, General Mark Clark's
Fifth Army had overrun Leghorn and forced the Germans to evacu-
ate Florence and retreat to the hills along the north bank of the
Arno; the British Eighth Army was slugging its way over the Apen-
nines toward Rimini, which it entered on the 21st. Once more the
Allies hoped that they had the enemy on the run; once again Kessel-
ring made a stand, denying the coveted advance into the plains of
Lombardy until spring.

Seventh Army and First French Army, as they advanced north
had no worries about their left flank in France. All German forces
in that direction, except the garrisons at Bordeaux and the mouth of
the Loire, had pulled out, and De Gaulle's provisional government was in power. But they had to be on their guard against thrusts
on their right flank by mobile units of the German Army, or by
Axis light naval forces based on Genoa. Marshal Kesselring. on the
other hand, had two apprehensions: first, that American troops
might seize mountain crests north of the Alpes Maritimes and debouch into Piedmont in his rear; and, second, that the Allies

[1] There is no overall report on the operations covered in this chapter; they have
to be pieced out from the Action Reports of the U.S. ships involved, from the
Collection des Rapports Mesuels of the French Navy; R. J. Bulkley's "PT History"; records of the German naval commander at Genoa, communicated by Dr.
Jürgen Rohwer; and Kesselring *A Soldier's Record.*

might pull off an amphibious landing in the Gulf of Genoa. Coastal batteries along the Italian Riviera were strongly manned and preparations were made for counterattack at any point of landing.

Much to Kesselring's relief, neither of his fears materialized. General Eisenhower had no intention of diverting troops into Lombardy, nor did General Wilson ever seriously contemplate an amphibious landing behind Kesselring's west flank. No troops were available; and, if they had been, the landing would have been made behind the German left flank, in order to race the Russians to Vienna.

On 26 September 1944 Admiral Hewitt's Western Naval Task Force dissolved and the Admiral himself sailed for Naples in *Catoctin,* after setting up Task Force 86 to protect Seventh Army's anchor and keep the coastal batteries along the Italian Riviera stirred up. Flank Force, Mediterranean, as TF 86 was now called, stemmed from Flag Officer Northern Area Mediterranean ("Fonam," Rear Admiral John A. V. Morse RN), who was directly under Cincmed (Admiral Sir John Cunningham RN). The major part of Flank Force was French, and although its first commander was Rear Admiral Davidson, he was relieved 10 October by Contre-Amiral Jaujard. Flank Force at first comprised his *Montcalm, Georges Leygues* and *Gloire,* several French destroyers and minesweepers, PT Squadron 29 (Commander S. Stephen Daunis), and British MTBrons 421 and 378,[2] based at Golfe-Juan near Cannes. Two United States destroyers alternated with two French, returning to Toulon for replenishment when relieved. *Madison* and *Hilary P. Jones,* the first so assigned, had already broken up human torpedo attacks. On 26 September French destroyer *Forbin* sighted the last of these nuisances, then based on Genoa and San Remo,[3] sank two

[2] Jaujard alternated with Contre-Amiral Auboyneau. I have omitted frequent changes in the chain of command for, and the composition of Flank Force. In addition to ships named in the text, many others of the French Navy took part, together with a considerable number of PC, SC and YMS that had been used in DRAGOON, and which the U.S.N. turned over to the French.

[3] German Naval Staff Oper. Div. War Diary Part 8 (Naval Command Italy), which also states that 11 of the human torpedoes were then transferred to Savona to be used against an expected amphibious landing between that port and Imperia.

with the help of *Madison* and recovered their operators. Thereafter the record of Flank Force is a rather monotonous one of shooting at shore batteries on the Italian Riviera and supporting Allied troops who were thrusting at the German positions. Some of the German batteries were mounted on railroad cars, and could be moved to different locations every day. *Niblack*, by a high-speed run outside the field of fire, approached one that was located between Capes Ampeglio and Nero; she shot off 132 rounds in half an hour, and did not come under enemy fire until retiring, when two shells missed her by 200 yards.

On 27 December 1944 Rear Admiral Morse ordered *Gleaves*, *Woolsey* and *Benson* to report to him at Leghorn to support the left flank of Fifth Army, and to cover minesweeping along the Ligurian shore. They were relieved by other pairs, and six British destroyers were assigned to the Leghorn squadron in February, 1945.

On 8 March 1945, Hitler appointed Kesselring Commander in Chief West, in the vain hope that he could stem the tidal wave of Eisenhower's Expeditionary Force, and General von Vietinghoff relieved him in command of the German army group in Italy. It was now obvious that the war was nearly ended. So Admiral Jaujard gave the motor torpedo boats under his command the novel mission of launching their remaining Mark VIII torpedoes — the kind which had been unsuccessful against ships — into enemy-held harbors. Lieutenant Commander Dressling of PT Squadron 22 had the pleasure of shooting the bottom of the Mark VIII stockpile into Porto Maurizio on the night of 19–20 April 1945.

Even this late, the remains of the Axis mosquito fleet in Genoa showed that they still could sting. On the 17th an E-boat torpedoed French destroyer *Trombe* on night patrol but she managed to make Toulon safely. Two Italian motor torpedo boats which the Germans had taken over [4] were sunk by a patrol of three PTs on the night of 23–24 April. Destroyer *Kendrick* on 22 April fired five missions at

[4] *MAS-561* and *MAS-558*, according to *La Marina Italiana nella Seconda Guerra Mondiale, Navi Perdute*, I 139.

or near Ventimiglia, after which her s.f.c.p. reported "Target very well covered — Salvos together — Good firing." Two days later the Germans began pulling out and Italian partisans took over the ports.

Throughout the entire period covered by this chapter, minesweepers of the United States, British and French Navies, supported by destroyers, quietly pursued their dull, dangerous but necessary work of clearing the coasts of the Mediterranean, so that sea traffic could pursue its "lawful occasions." Twice or thrice weekly German craft sortied from Genoa to release new mines, especially "floaters" which were carried into Allied-held waters by the current; 27 of these were blown by Mindiv 32 (Lieutenant Commander H. V. Brown in *Implicit*) on one day, 11 October. A new technique was used in the operations of Mine Squadron 11 (Commander Allan M. Robinson USNR in *Improve*) and Division 18 (Commander E. A. Ruth USNR in *Sway*), in November and December. Twelve or more fleet minesweepers and nine YMS were supported by U.S. Navy Blimp *K–109*, based at Cagliari. She assisted in the search for mines, which, when the surface was calm, were visible from the air at a five-fathom depth in the pellucid Mediterranean. Eighty-six mines were disposed of in this operation without a single casualty to the sweepers, but they lost a great deal of gear on the rocky bottom. Other minecraft were substituted from time to time, and sweeping went on continuously until the end of the war.[5]

At various points in this History [6] we have followed the fortunes of motor torpedo boats in the Mediterranean. They took part in every major operation subsequent to TORCH, and continued to fight between operations. The American and British boats based at Bastia had operated so well in mixed patrols as to be known as "The Corsican Brothers." Their raids on Axis shipping in the Gulf

[5] Cdr. Robinson relieved Capt. H. G. Williams on 27 Nov. His Minron 11 Action Report of 20 Dec. 1944 describes these operations. Mindiv 21 (*Raven*, flag), Lt. Cdr. R. A. L. Ellis, USNR, also participated.

[6] Volume II, 263–6 (with illustration), 277–8; Volume IX 187 and elsewhere (see Index); and frequently in this volume. For operations that follow, R. J. Bulkley "PT History" pp. 439–53, checked by data furnished by Dr. Rohwer.

of Genoa — suspended during Operation DRAGOON — were renewed before the end of August, 1944, when Admiral Hewitt returned all boats to Senior Officer Inshore Squadron, at Bastia.[7]

The German naval commander at Genoa had at his disposal four torpedo boats originally laid down by the Italian Navy but completed by the Germans, five 700-ton Italian corvettes similarly completed, six ex-Italian MAS boats, four former French converted trawlers, a flotilla of subchasers and a considerable number of F-lighters,[8] to escort and form convoys along the Ligurian coast. It was the business of the motor torpedo boats to break these up. The German torpedo boats, in turn, prowled the coast almost nightly in search of PTs.

On the night of 24–25 August, Lieutenant A. C. Blomfield RN, riding *PT–559* with her C.O., Lieutenant R. A. Nagle USNR, led *MTB–423* in a raid on the harbor of Genoa. They sighted what they called a German destroyer (really a small harbor defense vessel) off Peglia and sank it with one torpedo. Two nights later the same team attacked a convoy of 250-foot Rhone barges, pulled out of France by the Germans and armed for escort duty, and claimed to have sunk two out of three. For nine consecutive nights, 10–20 September, the Blomfield-Nagle team engaged their natural enemies, the F-lighters, and Rhone barges as well. As a result of this novena, they claimed to have sunk eight barges, a corvette, and four F-lighters.[9] German records confirm the loss of *UJ–2216*, formerly the French corvette *L'Incomprise*.

Back in 1942, when the first PTs arrived at Bône, Commander Barnes believed that combined patrols would not work, owing to differences in tactical doctrine, training, and communications, and in the boats themselves. Now he knew better. Commenting on the

[7] Capt. N. V. Dickinson RN until 8 Sept. 1944 when relieved by Cdr. R. A. Allan RNVR, for whom see Volume IX 372.

[8] Data from German records furnished by Dr. Rohwer. The torpedo boats, classified as TA, comprised two 800-tonners, one of 1200 and one of 1880 tons. The F-lighters, more properly designated MFP, were 163-foot beaching craft similar to our LST but faster and heavily armed. See Volume IX 169.

[9] The Germans have no records of their F-lighters and Rhone barges on this coast, but all other claims of sinkings have been checked from German sources.

action off Peglia, he wrote: "Lieutenant Blomfield RN is an exceedingly capable and aggressive Coastal Force officer with three years of experience in this type of craft. The PTs working with this and other British groups have been more or less permanently assigned. · Since the normal operation group is a U.S. Elco, a British Higgins and a British Vosper, with the British Senior Officer embarked in the U.S. Elco, it is obvious that successful operations require only tactical unity and not homogeneous types." Commander Allan returned the compliment in his report to Coastal Forces: "There are innumerable memories of great occasions, both afloat and ashore. . . . To Commander S. M. Barnes USN we owe the greatest gratitude for laying the sure foundations of what has been perfect inter-Allied harmony of decision and action." [10]

At the end of September Rear Admiral Morse ordered the Bastia base to be folded up and Inshore Squadron moved into Leghorn. But their winter patrols were hampered by foul weather. On only 57 nights out of 150 between 1 November and the end of March was it possible to maintain a full patrol. The Germans were reducing their coastal convoys, as the shores controlled by them contracted, and few contacts were made. *PT–311* (Lieutenant B. W. Creelman USNR) struck a mine on the night of 17–18 November and was lost, with both officers and eight out of 13 crewmen. She was avenged two nights later by the sinking off Sestri Levante of 1034-ton *UJ–2207* (formerly French corvette *Cap Nord*) by a patrol consisting of two MTBs and *PT–308*, commanded by Lieutenant (jg) Charles H. Murphy USNR.

On the night of 16–17 December Inshore Patrol threw all it had into a sortie — five British armed trawlers, Commander Allan in *PT–302*, Lieutenant Commander Dressling in *PT–310*, five more PTs and eight MTBs. Picking up a convoy consisting of F-lighters, a coaster and a minecraft, Dressling shadowed it for 45 minutes, giving frequent position reports to Allan, until it steamed right into the jaws of the trawlers. They first threw up star shell and then let go with 4-inch shell. The F-lighters fought back savagely and were

[10] Bulkley "PT History" pp. 442, 450–1.

getting the range when the trawlers, having (as they claimed) sunk two F-lighters and minecraft, retired under cover of an MTB smoke screen.

That night battle, which took place between 0215 and 0230 December 17 off Mesco Point near Spezia, marked the height of the Christmas season for Inshore Patrol. But the most successful fight in the Ligurian Gulf was to come. On 18 March 1945, H.M.S. *Lookout* and *Meteor* engaged German torpedo boats *TA–24* and *TA–29* southeast of Genoa, sank both and recovered 108 prisoners, including the flotilla commander.[11]

On 27 April destroyer *Kendrick* proceeded to Portofino to join H.M.S. *Orion* in support of the left flank of the Fifth Army as it advanced on Genoa. But by that time, there was little left for any Allied warship to do. Word was received on board *Kendrick* at 0810 April 28 that all resistance had ceased in Columbus's birthplace; that Mussolini had been seized and killed by Italian patriots; that enemy resistance was collapsing. The Germans scuttled all their remaining small warships before evacuating Genoa.

On the night of 28–29 April Contre-Amiral Jaujard in *Gloire* led a sweep of the coast with his entire Flank Force, including Lieutenant Commander Dressling's Squadron 22. It was more in the nature of a parade than a patrol, because the Italian Riviera was already in the hands of the partisans. Von Vietinghoff signed an agreement to surrender on 29 April, and hostilities ceased on the Italian front at noon 2 May 1945, six days before the complete surrender of Germany.

[11] These were former Italian torpedo boats *Arturo* and *Eridano* (*La Marina Italiana nella Seconda Guerra Mondiale, Navi Perdute* I 161–62).

PTs at Bastia

Ile de Cézembre, seen from St. Malo

Toward the Finish

LCM Crossing the Rhine

CHAPTER XX

Plunging into Germany

October 1944–May 1945

1. Crossing the Rhine, March 1945 [1]

DURING THE LAST two months of the European War the
Navy helped the Army to cross the Rhine, whose steep banks
and strong currents have baffled military men since the days of
Julius Caesar.

By September 1944 General Bradley, assuming that the Germans
would blow all bridges, foresaw that before long his Twelfth Army
Group would be faced with crossing this formidable water barrier. Engineer Division of his staff inquired of Comnaveu what the
Navy could do to help. Admiral Stark promptly sent three staff
officers to Bradley's headquarters, where it was agreed that the
LCVP and LCM, capable of 10 and 11 knots respectively, could
best do the trick. The Army had its own assault and utility boats,
but these, it was anticipated, would be unable to cope with an
8-knot current. An operation plan, appropriately titled "Delaware,"
was drawn up, Vice Admiral Kirk assumed operational control of
the boats, and designated Commander William J. Whiteside to
command them.

[1] Third Army *After Action Report "Engineers"* II Part 12 (1945); Ninth Army
Engineer Operations in the Rhine Crossings, (a pamphlet dated 30 June 1945,
printed in Germany); Lt. W. L. Wade USNR (an eyewitness to the crossing)
"Narrative Account of Action of LCVPs on Rhine with Third Army"; Cdr. R. F.
Pryce "Memo. for Admiral Stark" 5 Apr. 1945, Enclosure in Comnavforfrance
(Vice Adm. Kirk) to Comnaveu (Adm. Stark) 21 Apr. 1945; Operation Reports
of group and unit commanders, especially of CTG 122.5 (Cdr. W. J. Whiteside):
"The U.S. Navy on the Rhine" *O.N.I. Weekly* IV 2064–77 (27 June 1945); King &
Whitehill pp. 585–86.

Four task units of 24 boats, 13 officers and 205 men each [2] were assembled in Dartmouth and Weymouth and lifted to Le Havre in British LSDs, *Oceanway* and *Northway*. Thence they were transported to training areas by Army trucks and trailers. This involved careful routing through closely built towns and villages with rubble-filled streets. The LCMs were added later for ferrying armor and heavy weapons across the Rhine. Forty-five of these 50-foot craft, weighing 26 tons each, were assigned by Comnaveu; loaded on tank-retriever trailers hooked to a truck, the unit stretched out to 77 feet and weighed 70 tons. They were transported overland without mishap, although in some towns houses had to be partly demolished to get these vehicular leviathans around tight corners.

As yet there had been no directive from the Combined Chiefs of Staff about crossing the Rhine — who should do it, when, and at what points. Field Marshal Montgomery wished to throw his army group across the lower Rhine, and head for the Ruhr from the north, while the rest of the Expeditionary Force held the enemy along the central and upper river. Eisenhower, on the contrary, wished to make several simultaneous crossings, in order to effect a double envelopment of the Ruhr. General Bedell Smith, representing Shaef, and Sir Alan Brooke threshed this out at the C.C.S. conference at Malta on 30 January 1945. In the discussion, which was vehement, General Marshall and Admiral King supported the Eisenhower plan, and to that concept the C.C.S. gave a grudging assent. Shortly after, President Roosevelt arrived at Valletta on board *Quincy*. After Marshall and King had pointed out to him the proposed crossings on a map of Germany, F. D. R., happily recalling a bicycle tour of the Frankfurt corridor which he had made as a boy, expressed his approval. And the pincer strategy worked out

[2] The LCMs were attached to the LCVP units. TG 122.5 LCVP Units, Cdr. W. J. Whiteside:
TU 122.5.1, Boat Unit 1 (Lt. Wilton Wenker usnr), for First Army
TU 122.5.2, Boat Unit 2 (Lt. Cdr. William Leide usnr), for Third Army
TU 122.5.3, Boat Unit 3 (Lt. Cdr. Willard T. Patrick usnr), for Ninth Army
TU 122.5.4, Reserve (Lt. (jg) Thomas F. Reilly usnr), at Le Havre.

brilliantly, as Brooke handsomely admitted when watching the Army cross the Rhine in American landing craft.

Lieutenant Wenker's Boat Unit 1, which had been training on the Meuse at Ardennes in Belgium, was the first to see action. It received a hurry call on the night of 7 March 1945, just after the 9th Armored Division, First Army, had captured the Ludendorff bridge over the Rhine at Remagen — the only bridge that the Germans had failed to destroy. The trip to the river, over narrow and congested roads, in competition with troops, armor and supplies, was described as "nightmarish." On 11 March the first ten boats were launched in the Rhine at Bad Neuenahr and by the 15th all 24 were operating along a 35-mile stretch of the river above Bonn. They set up a ferry service at points designated by the Army, assisted Army Engineers in building pontoon and Treadway bridges, and provided "pusher service" when the pontoon bridges sagged dangerously in the current. These bridges came into heavy use on 17 March when the Remagen span collapsed under repeated enemy air and artillery attacks. On the same day 2500 soldiers were set across the Rhine by six LCVP, while two others patrolled upstream, dropping improvised depth charges at five-minute intervals to embarrass enemy saboteurs, two of whom were blown to the surface and captured. Although Unit No. 1 did not take a leading part in an assault crossing, because of First Army's initial use of the Remagen bridge, it had ferried some 14,000 troops and 400 vehicles across the Rhine by 27 March and evacuated several hundred wounded.

At 2200 March 22 General Patton's Third Army began crossing the Rhine at Oppenheim, about ten miles above Mainz. No formal plans were drawn up for the crossing, and no artillery was laid on, because "George" wanted to beat "Monty" across the river — which he did. Lieutenant Commander Leide's LCVP Unit 2 was alerted on the 20th at Toul. It moved forward by truck, and halted about two miles short of the launching site while the initial attack wave crossed in Army assault boats. The first three craft took the water by 0300 March 23. By 0630 all 24 were engaged in ferrying troops. For the next 72 hours they operated on a round-the-clock schedule. The turnaround in this bight of the Rhine was made every six to eight minutes. One boat acted as pusher for a pontoon barge carrying tanks, and two assisted the Engineers in building bridges. All this was done under artillery fire and bombing and strafing attacks by the Luftwaffe.

By 26 March the peak of the struggle at Oppenheim was over. The Engineers had thrown two bridges across the Rhine and the boats had only to patrol the river. About 15,000 men and 1200 vehicles had been carried across at this point in LCVPs. According to Marshal Kesselring, this crossing was one of the decisive actions in the campaign for Germany. "As Remagen had been the grave of Army Group B, it seemed that the bridgehead at Oppenheim would be that of Army Group G." It was.

There were three other crossings in the Third Army sector. Unit 2 assisted the 87th Division across the Rhine Gorge at Boppard, ten miles upstream from Coblenz, on the night of 25–26 March. Every hour they made nine round trips, each ferrying 36 soldiers. This went on until 5000 men and 400 vehicles had been set across. At Oberwesel, about ten miles upstream from Boppard, the six remaining boats of Unit 2 helped the 89th Division to cross on the afternoon of 26 March. Before the landing craft arrived, assault troops were ferried across at a point downstream in Army boats and a fleet of ten dukws. "As soon as six LCVPs and six LCMs had been put into the water, the entire complexion of the picture changed, for they passed troops and equipment over the river at such a rate that within 48 hours nearly an entire division with all its vehicles and equipment had been carried over." [3]

The toughest crossing, however, was at Mainz. General Patton's staff laid this on for the 80th Division at short notice, in the early hours of 28 March. Six of the 12 LCVP employed at Oppenheim, and six of the stand-by LCM, were used here. At Mainz the Rhine was covered by enemy artillery, and the initial assault wave, which

[3] Third Army *After Action Report*, II, Part 12 p. 32.

started across at 0100 in 20 Army assault boats, was almost wiped out. At 0330 the Army officer in charge suspended the crossing, but Ensign Oscar Miller USNR, the boat officer, did not get the word and sent the first LCVP across at a point 500 or more yards below the assault line. After this boat had made an unopposed crossing the Army piled joyfully into the Navy landing craft and used Ensign Miller's route during the remaining hours of darkness. At 0630 the Germans caught on and opened up with everything they had, but did not manage to hit a single boat. Army Engineers, with the help of landing craft sailors and Seabees, at once began building a Treadway bridge at the same point.

At Mainz, states the Third Army official report, "the Navy again demonstrated its ability to be most useful and effective in a crossing operation. . . . Soon after the naval craft hit the water, they poured over such a continual stream of troops, vehicles and tank destroyers in the early crucial hours that the enemy artillery was silenced, and further ferrying and bridging was able to proceed without interference." Lieutenant Commander Leide estimated that over 10,000 troops and 1100 vehicles were ferried at this point.

In all four Third Army crossings the initial assault unit crossed without benefit of artillery preparation, and the use of Navy landing craft in the immediate follow-up enabled General Patton to build up forces on the right bank of the Rhine so rapidly that he could "plunge onward into Central Germany" without pause.

In contrast to the rapid, improvised crossings by the First and Third Armies were those by the Ninth Army (Lieutenant General William H. Simpson USA), which was under Field Marshal Montgomery's Twenty-first Army Group. "Monty," eschewing slapdash American methods, insisted on careful plans and preparations. His plan for the two American divisions of the initial Ninth Army assault was almost as detailed and elaborate as if it were an amphibious operation on the seacoast. It provided for night landings and a series of waves, at definite hours, by Army assault boats and LCVP.

The 30th Division crossed north of and the 79th south of Rhein-berg, a small town midway between Wesel and Duisburg. Lieu-tenant Commander Patrick's Unit 3 of the landing craft, including 24 LCM, was at the launching sites north of Rheinberg by 0100, when artillery preparation began and continued for two hours. The Army boats then started their outboard motors and began taking the first assault waves across. Next came the Navy landing craft. The sailors and soldiers had trouble launching them in darkness on a rough shore under German artillery fire; a dozer attempting to level the site was knocked out, and a Bay City 20-ton crane, when hit by shell fragments, dropped the first LCVP 25 feet, damaging the hull and giving the crew a bad shaking. But five more LCVP were in the water by 0930, and a bulldozer managed to shove in the LCMs, bow first, without damaging their propellers.

On D-day the two groups of Unit 3 ferried across the Rhine 3000 troops, 374 tanks and tank destroyers and antitank guns, 15 bull-dozers and 180 weasels, 80 57-mm guns, 300 loaded jeeps and 200 other vehicles; and, on the return trip, evacuated 200 casualties and 500 prisoners. Here, too, the craft assisted in bridge construction, by streaming protective nets and cables, and in patrolling. One LCM on Ninth Army front ferried across on one trip Winston Churchill, Field Marshals Montgomery and Sir Alan Brooke and General Simpson.[4]

In addition to the 72 LCVP and 45 LCM, about 4000 Navy pontoon units with their assembling "jewelry" were supplied to the Army by Comnaveu, together with a battalion of Seabees to assist in their assembly.[5] These pontoon units were used to support

[4] Churchill *Triumph and Tragedy* p. 416, who calls the boat a "small launch" (by implication British), says that his party walked about on the right bank for half an hour unmolested and that the skipper resisted pressure by "Monty" to proceed down-river and take a look at Wesel. An otherwise unrecorded incident of this historic crossing is that the Prime Minister, the Field Marshals and the General relieved themselves into the Rhine, to the delight of the bluejacket crew who had already performed this ritual.

[5] These were four detachments from C. B. Maintenance Unit 629. They also helped Army Engineers to construct the 4257-foot-long timber trestle road bridge (the Roosevelt Bridge) across the Rhine at Wesel. Information from Buyardsand-docks Historian, Miss H. R. Fairbanks.

nets protecting the Army's bridges, as lighters for piledrivers, and to ferry heavy equipment with LCMs furnishing the power.

Operating landing craft on a river hundreds of miles from the sea was one of the oddest assignments drawn by American bluejackets during World War II. They performed very well under unusual conditions, and were much appreciated by the Army, whose rapid build-up on the right bank of the Rhine was thereby rendered possible. Major General John B. Anderson USA, commanding XVI Corps, in a letter to Lieutenant Commander Patrick of Unit 3, called the crossing a "major operation" of which "your men can well be proud." [6]

General Patch's Seventh Army and General de Lattre de Tassigny's First French Army, which had landed in Provence, carried enough Army Engineer assault boats to cross the upper Rhine without help from the Navy.

Now the Allied troops that had landed in Normandy and those that had landed in Provence made a continuous line from the North Sea to Switzerland.

2. The Navy in Germany [7]

There was no stopping Eisenhower's Expeditionary Force once it had crossed the Rhine. By 1 April the First Canadian Army, on the left flank, had bridged the Rhine at Emmerich. The Second British Army, next on the right, was advancing along the Dutch-German border, and General Simpson's Ninth United States Army, which still held the right flank of Montgomery's Twenty-first Army Group, was about to join Hodges' First Army at Lippstadt in the Ruhr to surround German Army Group B, the most formidable military unit left to Hitler. On that day, 1 April, they snapped the ring around the Ruhr.

[6] CTU 122.5.3 (Lt. Cdr. Patrick) Action Report.
[7] Comnaveu Administrative History VI and VII; Pogue pp. 346–58; *Crusade in Europe* chaps. xxi, xxii; Harold Zink *American Military Government in Germany* (1947).

The two United States Armies (First and Third) in General Bradley's Twelfth Army Group, as well as General Devers' Sixth Army Group, abundantly and ably supported by the Air Forces, had made astonishing progress. Hodges' First Army reached Marburg, 70 miles east of Bonn, on 28 March; Patton's Third was then in Wiesbaden, Frankfurt and Grünberg; the Seventh occupied Mannheim on the 29th and had begun a drive on Heidelberg; and the French were about to take Karlsruhe. Germany's defenses were now overrun and her "Watch on the Rhine" overwhelmed; her entire western front had collapsed. A quarter of a million prisoners had already been taken in the Rhineland battles.

While elements of the Ninth and First Armies waited for an even bigger bag of prisoners in the Ruhr — which was secured on 18 April — the rest of Eisenhower's forces marched irresistibly to the Elbe and to the Danube. On 12 April, the day of President Roosevelt's death, an armored spearhead of the Ninth Army established a bridgehead over the Elbe at Magdeburg. First Army entered Leipzig 19 April, the same day that the Second British Army reached the lower Elbe, and First Army V Corps made contact with Russian troops at the Elbe, near Torgau, on the 25th. On 17 April, Russian troops crossed the Oder and raced to Berlin. Patton's Third Army reached the Czechoslovak border on the 17th and then swung south, crossing the Danube at Ratisbon and overrunning German defenses where

> . . . dark as winter was the flow
> Of Iser, rolling rapidly.

Seventh Army broke into the walled city of Nuremberg, the Nazi holy of holies, on the 19th, and secured it next day. The French entered Stuttgart on the 21st. Munich, revolting at last from the Nazi rule that she had spawned, surrendered to Seventh Army on 30 April, the very day that Hitler died ignobly in his Berlin bunker. At the Brenner Pass, Seventh Army on 4 May joined hands with the Fifth, which had fought all the way up Italy from Salerno. On the same day Grossadmiral Doenitz, to whom Hitler had passed his almost extinguished torch, offered a partial capitulation; and at 0341 on the 7th his representatives made a complete and unconditional surrender to the three Allied powers at Rheims.[8]

In this rout of the Germans from the Rhine to the Elbe and the Danube, the United States Navy took no part, as there were no more great rivers to cross. Coastal Command of Royal Navy patrolled the shoal, heavily mined waters off the Frisian coast, on Eisenhower's left flank.

Admiral King, anticipating that the United States Navy would take part in the administration of conquered European territory, had assigned to Comnaveu staff in July 1943 several members of the first class to be graduated from the Naval School of Military Government and Administration at Columbia University. By the end of the war, Admiral Stark had about a hundred of these specially trained officers under him. First under Cossac and then under Shaef, they served on the numerous committees and groups which were engaged in post-hostilities planning.

In London there sat the European Advisory Committee, a small body on which Ambassador John G. Winant represented the United States. This was the first interallied body officially to concern itself with the conditions of Germany's unconditional surrender, and what was to follow. After Admiral Stark had been appointed naval adviser to Mr. Winant, early in 1944, active planning started for the Navy's part in the expected occupation of Germany. In late November 1944 Rear Admiral Robert L. Ghormley[9] was designated to command U.S. Naval Forces in Germany, and in March 1945 Rear Admiral Arthur G. Robinson[10] arrived from the now tranquil Carribean to become CTF

[8] A more formal ratification of the surrender by the German High Command took place at Berlin on 9 May; but 8 May is celebrated as V-E Day because the act of the 7th became effective at 0001 on the 9th, Zone B, which in Central European Time (Zone A) was 2301 May 8th.

[9] For Admiral Ghormley's earlier career see Volume IV of this series, p. 250*n*, and Volume V Index. Since being relieved by Admiral Halsey in the South Pacific, he had been on Admiral King's staff and commanded Fourteenth Naval District and Hawaiian Sea Frontier 1943–4. Served on General Board 1946, and retired same year.

[10] For brief biography see Volume X 204*n*.

126, Commander U.S. Naval Ports and Bases, Germany. Rear Admiral Schuirmann, the former Chief of Naval Intelligence, was assigned to Comnaveu staff for post-hostilities problems.

Admiral Ramsay, after protracted staff discussions with Admiral Stark, agreed on a post-hostilities plan, issued 14 November 1944, defining the future relationship between United States and British naval forces in Europe. The essential provisions of this plan were that the Royal Navy withdraw from all French ports, which would be managed by the United States Navy in conjunction with French authorities, and that the northern coasts east of France be under British control, except for an American enclave at Bremen and Bremerhaven. The United States flag officer at Bremen and the British flag officers at Kiel and Wilhelmshaven were to be responsible to Ramsay through their respective flag officers at Berlin. Before these arrangements went into effect, Admiral Ramsay was killed in an airplane accident on 1 January 1945. His duties were assumed temporarily by Vice Admiral Kirk, who was relieved before the end of the month by Admiral Harold M. Burrough RN, who had been Flag Officer Commanding Gibraltar and Mediterranean Approaches.

In the meantime almost 500 U.S. Naval officers and over 3400 enlisted men, about half of them Seabees, were being trained at Rosneath on the Clyde for future duty in Germany. As it turned out, the Navy as such took no part in the administration of conquered Germany, exclusively an Army responsibility; but many of the Naval officers specially trained for administration were "lent" by the Navy to the Army to serve on military government teams all along the chain of command.

It was understood from the first that Russia would occupy Germany east of the Elbe, but no firm agreement was made even as to the boundaries between the British and the American zones until the Quebec Conference in September 1944 — when it was decided that the United States would occupy the southern zone, in return for Britain's relinquishing an enclave around Bremen and Bremerhaven for logistic purposes, and promising free access through the British zone. This agreement was finally ratified at Yalta on 6 February 1945, with the important modification that France obtained an hourglass-shaped occupation zone, including the Rhineland, the Palatinate, Southern Baden and a part of Württemberg, carved out of those assigned to Britain and the United States.

Thus, the one big task for Admiral Ghormley's U.S. Naval Forces Germany command was to administer the ports of Bremen and Bremerhaven. The sailors under him were drawn from the various "Drew" units which had been training in England to administer captured ports.

A Naval reconnaissance party of 48 officers and 104 enlisted men, commanded by Captain Vincent H. Godfrey, landed 4 April at Ostend, where it was shortly joined by Port Parties 1 and 2, comprising 88 officers and 703 men. A few days later they started moving toward Bremen in jeeps and trucks behind the British Second Army. They had no trouble in recognizing the German border, where the troops had erected signs, "Here ends the civilized world," and "You are now entering Germany. There will be NO fraternizing with ANY German."

That is just about what the average soldier and sailor, American or British, felt at that time, when every fresh advance revealed the incredible cruelties that had been practised in concentration camps.

On 27 April, the day after Bremen was captured by the British Second Army, Captain Godfrey's party entered. Both the waterfront and the Weser were found heavily mined and booby-trapped. A few miles down-river, at Farge, was a newly completed submarine pen with a concrete roof 25-feet thick. Eight prefabricated U-boats of the latest type were there being assembled, in addition to some 26 or more at nearby shipyards — good evidence that the war at sea had ended none too soon for the Allies.[11]

Doenitz's surrender of North Germany to Field Marshal Montgomery on 4 May cleared the way for the Navy to occupy Brem-

[11] Cdr. A. H. Cherry RNVR *Yankee R.N.* p. 501. The final chapter of this book gives a vivid account of the motorcade across Germany and conditions in Bremen, where Cdr. Cherry was the Royal Navy liaison officer.

erhaven, the harbor for ocean shipping at the mouth of the Weser. That afternoon, one of the naval port parties arrived, and by 22 May Admiral Robinson's entire command was in the northern enclave. The Weser, on which we depended for importing supplies to feed the American occupation troops and German civilians, was "the worst and most cunningly mined of any river in Germany. . . . Mines were even secured to the wharfsides." [12] Robinson's first and most important activity was to get channels swept, using minesweepers and crews of the former German Navy. These were assisted by British minecraft under Lieutenant Commander L. J. T. Pyne RNVR, and by mine disposal experts of both Navies; but over four months' sweeping was required to make the Weser safe to Bremen. The big German S.S. *Europa* was salvaged and repaired, and began a new career as a United States Army transport in September.[13] That was only one of hundreds of jobs initiated and supervised by the United States Navy in Weser shipyards, which repaired 57 German minesweepers for immediate use; and rehabilitated several hundred German fishing vessels and river barges to help reëstablish the local economy.

In the meantime Admiral Ghormley established headquarters near General Eisenhower's at Frankfurt-am-Main. He and the British eventually reached an agreement with the Russians about dividing up the few remaining ships of the German Navy.[14]

On V–E Day, there were still several German garrisons in Europe which had not been overwhelmed by the recent offensive: those in Scandinavia, Dunkirk, the Channel Islands, and the small Breton ports. Negotiations for their surrender began at the time of the conference at Rheims. Lorient, Belle Isle and Saint-Nazaire were surrendered to the U.S. 66th Division on 10 and 11 May. In the Channel Islands, as we have seen, the fanatical Admiral Hüffmeier was actually preparing another commando raid on Granville when

[12] Cherry p. 526.
[13] Later delivered to France, she is still (1957) doing service as the passenger liner *Liberté*.
[14] Of major units, the U.S.N. got *Prinz Eugen* and seven DDs, the Russians got *Nürnberg* and nine DDs, and the British, 13 DDs.

Doenitz ordered him to pipe down; and on the 9th he was still entertaining the idea of holding out when a British task group (H.M.S. *Bulldog*, flag) appeared in the roadstead and changed his mind. The German garrison at Dunkirk, after a six months' siege, surrendered on 9 May to General Lishka of a Czech armored brigade. General Eisenhower's mission to Denmark obtained the surrender of most of the Germans in that country by 5 June. But as the Germans in Norway, numbering some 400,000, had never been defeated in battle, the task of inducing them to surrender was delicate and prolonged. General Sir Andrew Thorne of the British Army, entrusted by Shaef with this mission, had to bring in some 40,000 Allied troops and a number of British destroyers as a persuasive, and did not conclude his mission until the autumn of 1945.

On 5 June 1945, the commanders of the American, British, French and Russian forces in Europe met at Berlin, formed the Allied Control Council, and assumed control of Germany in their several zones. Shaef, and dozens of combined committees and commissions, were then unscrambled into their national components, and their functions transferred to the national occupying authorities.[15] On the following day — first anniversary of the ever memorable D-day — the last of the United States Naval Forces in Europe, a division of escort craft which had brought a convoy to Le Havre, departed. Their O.T.C., Lieutenant Commander J. K. Davis USNR in destroyer escort *Borum*, had them steam back and forth in the waters off Omaha and Juno beaches, firing salutes to the memory of the men who had fallen in the great assault a year earlier.

Ten days later Admiral Stark, Commander U.S. Naval Forces Europe, announced that not a single vessel of the United States Navy was left in British waters. A convoy of LSTs, last of the 2493 U.S. ships and craft that once composed the Twelfth Fleet and XI Amphibious Force, carrying the rest of the 124,000 officers and men of the Navy who had taken part in Operation NEPTUNE,

15 When Shaef was finally wound up, Eisenhower became Commanding General U.S. Forces European Theater and American Representative on the Allied Control Council, and Admiral Ghormley became his naval adviser.

had just departed for the Pacific.[16] General Eisenhower, after returning from a brief visit to the United States, assembled all members of Shaef staff present at Frankfurt on 13 July and formally disbanded that organization, whose efforts had resulted in so outstanding a victory. He concluded his farewell speech with an aspiration that he is still endeavoring to fulfill as President of the United States, as I write these words eleven years later: —

"It is my fervent hope and prayer that the unparalleled unity which has been achieved among the Allied Nations in war will be a source of inspiration for, and point the way to, a permanent and lasting peace."

Fighting had ceased in Europe, but there was no letup for the Allied Chiefs in Germany. Problems of de-Nazifying the country, of putting liberated nations on their feet, of handling displaced persons and prisoners of war, and, above all, of Russia, were many, urgent, and almost overwhelming.

At the Quebec conference of September 1944, the C.C.S. estimated that eighteen months would be required after the defeat of Germany, to obtain the unconditional surrender of Japan. Actually, the defeat of Japan was so expedited by the Battles of Leyte Gulf and Lingayen, the occupation of Iwo Jima and Okinawa, the bombing of Japanese cities, and the submarine blockade of Japan itself, that only a little over three months elapsed between V–E Day and V–J Day.

A few days before General Eisenhower disbanded Shaef, General MacArthur announced the liberation of the Philippines. Okinawa was almost secured, and the Navy was drawing a cordon tight about Japan. Nobody — even those in the secret of the atomic bomb — could guess what the immediate future might bring.

[16] Navy Department Release 23 July 1945.

Appendices

Abbreviations in Appendices

(For abbreviations not listed here, see list before Chapter I)

AM — Minesweeper

A/S — Antisubmarine

ASRC — Air-Sea Rescue Craft

ATA — Ocean Tug, Auxiliary; ATR — Ocean Tug, Rescue

Br. — British; BYMS — British Coastal Minesweeper

CM — Minelayer

CVE — Escort Aircraft Carrier

DD — Destroyer; DE — Destroyer Escort

FT — Fleet Tug

HDML — Harbor Defense Motor Launch

LBE — Landing Barge, Emergency Repair; LBF — Flak; LBK — Kitchen; LBO — Oiler; LBV — Vehicle; LBW — Water

LCA — Landing Craft, Assault (British counterpart to LCVP)

LCC — Landing Craft, Control; LCF — Flak; LCG — Gun; LCH — Headquarters; LCM — Mechanized; LCP — Personnel; LCS — Support; LCVP — Vehicle Personnel

LCI — Landing Craft, Infantry; LCT — Landing Craft, Tank

LSB — Landing Ship, Bombardment; LSD — Dock; LSE — Emergency Repair; LSG — Gantry; LSP — Personnel; LST — Landing Ship, Tank

LSI — Landing Ship, Infantry (British; a small Transport)

ML — British Motor Launch, also called a "Fairmile"

MMS — Motor Minesweeper

MTB — Motor Torpedo Boat (British)

PC — Patrol Craft (173-foot); PT — Motor Torpedo Boat (U.S.)

RHF — Rhino Ferry

SC — Submarine Chaser (110-foot)

S.S. — Steamship, manned by merchant marine, British or American

YMS — Coastal Minesweeper

YTB — Harbor Tug, Big; YTL — Harbor Tug, Little

(A) following a lettered ship means Armored; (E) — Emergency repair (F) — Flak; (HE) — High explosive; and (R) — Rocket-equipped

APPENDIX I

The Western Naval Task Force in the Invasion of Normandy

TF 122 WESTERN NAVAL TASK FORCE
Rear Admiral Alan G. Kirk

Embarking First U.S. Army, Lt. Gen. Omar N. Bradley

Force Flagship Group: Heavy Cruiser AUGUSTA Capt. E. H. Jones; Destroyer THOMPSON Lt. Cdr. A. L. Gebelin; 3 YMS; *SC-1321; PT-71.*

TF 125 ASSAULT FORCE "U" FOR UTAH BEACH
Rear Admiral Don P. Moon

Embarking 4th Infantry Division, Maj. Gen. R. O. Barton, and units of VII Corps, Maj. Gen. J. Lawton Collins

Force Flagship Group: Attack transport BAYFIELD Capt. Lyndon Spencer USCG, FORREST Cdr. K. P. Letts; *PT-199.*

MINESWEEPER GROUP, Cdr. M. H. Brown RN

Sweep Unit 1, Cdr. Brown: H.M.S. SHIPPIGAN, TADOUSSAC, ILFRA-COMBE, BEAUMARIS, DORNOCK, PARRSBORO, QUALICUM, WEDGEPORT; 4 ML; 4 danlayers. Unit 2, Cdr. G. W. A. T. Irvine RNVR: H.M.S. ROMNEY, GUYSBOROUGH, SEAHAM, RYE, WHITEHAVEN, POOLE, VEGREVILLE, KENOVA; 4 ML; 4 danlayers. Unit 3, Cdr. Henry Plander: PHEASANT, AUK, BROAD-BILL, CHICKADEE, NUTHATCH, STAFF, SWIFT, THREAT, *TIDE, RAVEN, *OS-PREY. Unit 4, Lt. H. J. White USNR: 11 YMS. Unit 5, Lt. C. L. Rich USNR: 7 YMS. Unit 6, Lt. Cdr. J. A. Ludlow RNVR: 9 MMS. Unit 7, Lt.(jg) Irving Kramer USNR: 8 LCT; 4 LCG; 4 LCF. Marker Unit 8, Lt. A. L. Hargraves RNVR: 3 danlayers.

ASSAULT GROUPS

Beach Green Assault Group, Cdr. A. L. Warburton in *LCH-530:* Attack transport JOSEPH T. DICKMAN Capt. R. J. Mauerman USCG; LSI

* Lost in this operation.

EMPIRE GAUNTLET (Br.); 15 LST; 69 LCT; 26 LCM; 3 RHF; 1 PC; 2 LCC; 23 LCI; 1 LCH.

Beach Red Assault Group, Cdr. E. W. Wilson USNR in *LCH–10:* Attack transports BARNETT Cdr. S. S. Reynolds, BAYFIELD Capt. Spencer; 15 LST; 22 LCI; 1 LCH; 83 LCT; 25 LCM; 2 RHF; 1 PC; 2 LCC.

ESCORT GROUP, Cdr. W. W. Outerbridge

Destroyers O'BRIEN Cdr. Outerbridge, JEFFERS Lt. Cdr. H. Q. Murray (with Comdesron 17, Capt. A. C. Murdaugh), *GLENNON Cdr. C. A. Johnson, WALKE Cdr. J. C. Zahm, BARTON Cdr. J. W. Callahan (with Comdesron 60, Capt. W. L. Freseman), LAFFEY Cdr. F. J. Becton, *MEREDITH Cdr. George Kneupfer; 3 British A/S trawlers; French corvettes ACONIT Lt. de V. Le Millier, RENONCULE Lt. de V. Mithois; 7 PC; 7 SC; 7 ML.

Support Craft Group, Lt. Cdr. L. E. Hart USNR in *LCH–209:* 4 LCG; 13 LCT; 12 LCS; 20 LCP.

BOMBARDMENT GROUP, Rear Admiral Morton L. Deyo

Heavy cruisers TUSCALOOSA Capt. J. B. W. Waller, QUINCY Capt. E. M. Senn, H.M.S. HAWKINS Capt. J. W. Josselyn RN; battleship NEVADA Capt. P. M. Rhea; monitor H.M.S. EREBUS Capt. J. S. P. Colquhoun RN; light cruisers H.M.S. ENTERPRISE Capt. H. T. W. Grant RCN, BLACK PRINCE Capt. D. M. Lees RN; Dutch gunboat SOEMBA Lt. Cdr. H. H. L. Propper RNN.

Destroyers FITCH Cdr. K. C. Walpole, FORREST, Cdr. Letts, *CORRY Lt. Cdr. G. D. Hoffman, HOBSON Lt. Kenneth Loveland (with Comdesdiv 20, Cdr. L. W. Nilon), HERNDON Cdr. G. A. Moore, SHUBRICK Lt. Cdr. William Blenman, BUTLER Cdr. M. D. Matthews (with Comdesdiv 34, Cdr. W. L. Benson), GHERARDI Cdr. N. R. Curtin; DEs BATES Lt. Cdr. H. A. Wilmerding USNR, *RICH Lt. Cdr. E. A. Michel USNR.

SHORE PARTY, Brig. Gen. James E. Wharton USA

1st Engineer Special Brigade and 2nd Naval Beach Battalion, Cdr. J. F. Curtin USNR; Service and Repair Group, Lt. R. D. Cox USNR; Naval Combat Demolition Units, Lt. Cdr. H. A. Peterson USNR.

FAR SHORE SERVICE GROUP, Capt. J. E. Arnold USNR

S.S. THOMAS B. ROBERTSON, ATLAS; 2 LBK; 1 LCH; 6 RHF; 22 LCM; 36 LBV; 8 LBE; 5 fueling trawlers; 20 LBO; 3 LBW; many landing craft and dukws.

Sea Rescue Group, Lt. Cdr. A. V. Stewart USCGR: ten 83-foot U.S. Coast Guard cutters.

* Lost in this operation.

Follow-up Convoy Group, Cdr. W. S. Blair usnr: 25 LST.
Motor Torpedo Boats, Lt. R. R. Read usnr: 13 PT.
Causeway Construction Unit, Lt. Cdr. J. B. Baines usnr: 1006th
Seabee Detachment, Lt. W. C. Pietz usnr; coasters and barges.

TF 124 ASSAULT FORCE "O" FOR OMAHA BEACH
Rear Admiral John L. Hall

Embarking Landing Force, Maj. Gen. C. R. Huebner usa: 16th RCT
of 1st Division; 115th and 116th RCTs of 29th Division; 2nd and 5th
Ranger Battalions; units of V Corps, Maj. Gen. L. T. Gerow usa

Amphibious Force Flagship: ancon Cdr. M. G. Pearson.

MINESWEEPER GROUP, Cdr. J. S. Cochrane rn

Sweep Unit 1, Cdr. Cochrane: H.M.S. kellett, pangbourne, albury,
sutton, lydd, selkirk, ross, saltash, thunder; 4 ML; 3 danlayers. Unit
2, Cdr. A. H. G. Storrs rcnr: H.M.C.S. caraquet, blairmore, cowi-
chan, fort william, malpeque, vegreville, minas, wasaga, mul-
grave; 4 ML; 3 danlayers. Unit 3, Lt. Heath rnr: 10 BYM. Unit 4, Lt.
Bennett rnvr: 10 MMS.

ASSAULT GROUPS

Assault Group O–1 for Beaches Easy Red and Fox Green, Capt E. H.
Fritzsche uscg: Attack transports samuel chase Capt. Fritzsche, henrico Cdr. J. H. Willis; LSI empire anvil (Br.); 1 LCH; 6 LST; 5 LCI;
53 LCT; 18 LCM; 2 PC; 2 SC; 2 ML; 2 LCC.

Assault Group O–2 for Beaches Dog and Easy Green, Capt. W. O.
Bailey: Attack transports charles carroll Capt. Harold Biesemeier,
thomas jefferson Cdr. J. R. Barbaro; LSI empire javelin (Br.);
1 LCH; 6 LST; 17 LCI; 54 LCT; 18 LCM; 4 PC; 4 SC; 2 ML; 3 LCC.

Assault Group O–3 for Beaches Fox Green and Easy Red, Capt. L. B.
Schulten: Transports anne arundel Capt. W. S. Campbell, dorothea l.
dix Cdr. W. I. Leahy, thurston Cdr. R. B. Vanasse, 1 LCH; 12 LST;
11 LCI; 39 LCT; 1 LSB; 1 LSD; 3 PC; 2 ML.

Assault Group O–4 for Pte. du Hoc and Dog Green, Cdr. S. H.
Dennis rn: British LSI prince charles Cdr. Dennis, prince baudoin
Lt. Cdr. W. E. Gelling rnr, prince leopold Lt. Cdr. J. A. Lowe rnr,
ben-my-chree Master R. Duggan, amsterdam Master Pickering, princess maud; 1 LCT; 2 ML.

ESCORT GROUP, Capt. Harry Sanders (Comdesron 18)

Destroyers frankford Lt. Cdr. J. L. Semmes; nelson Lt. Cdr. T. D.
McGrath, murphy Cdr. R. A. Wolverton, plunkett Cdr. William

Outerson; DDs of Bombardment Group, below; H.M.S. VESPER Lt. Cdr. V. D. Ravenscroft RNR, VIDETTE Lt. Cdr. G. S. Woolley RNVR; destroyer escorts BORUM Lt. Cdr. J. K. Davis, AMESBURY Lt. Cdr. A. B. Wilbor USNR, BLESSMAN Lt. Cdr. J. A. Gillis USNR; French frigates L'AVENTURE Capt. de F. Querville, L'ESCARMOUCHE Capt. de C. Duplessis-Casso; British A/S trawlers COLL, BRESSAY, SKYE; 9 PC; 6 SC; 12 ML; 7 MTB; 2 HDML; 6 steam gunboats (Br.).

CLOSE GUNFIRE SUPPORT GROUP, Capt. L. S. Sabin
1 LCH; 7 LCR; 5 LCG; 9 LCT(R); 28 LCP; 9 LCT(A); 10 LCT(HE).

BOMBARDMENT GROUP, Rear Admiral C. F. Bryant
Battleships TEXAS Capt. C. A. Baker, ARKANSAS Capt. F. G. Richards; light cruisers H.M.S. GLASGOW Capt. C. P. Clarke RN, BELLONA Capt. C. W. F. Norris RN, MONTCALM Capt. de V. Deprez, GEORGES LEYGUES Capt. de V. Laurin (Contre-Amiral Jaujard, commanding). Destroyers FRANKFORD, MCCOOK Lt. Cdr. R. L. Ramey, CARMICK Cdr. R. O. Beer, DOYLE Cdr. J. G. Marshall, EMMONS Cdr. E. B. Billingsley, BALDWIN Lt. Cdr. E. S. Powell, HARDING Cdr. G. G. Palmer, SATTERLEE Lt. Cdr. R. W. Leach (with Comdesdiv 36, Cdr. W. J. Marshall), THOMPSON Lt. Cdr. A. L. Gebelin, H.M.S. TANATSIDE Cdr. B. de St. Croix RN, TALYBONT Lt. Cdr. E. F. Baines RNR, MELBREAK Lt. G. J. Kirkby RN.

FAR SHORE SERVICE GROUP, Capt. Chauncey Camp USNR
S.S. ELEAZAR WHEELOCK, Repair Ship ADONIS; 12 LCM. Ferry Craft: 4 LCI; 4 LCH; 72 LCT; 20 RHF; 139 LCM; 72 LBV. Service Craft: 9 fueling trawlers; 16 LBE; 20 LBO; 5 LBW; 2 LBK.

Rescue Vessels, Lt. Cdr. A. Stewart USCGR: fifteen 83-foot U.S. Coast Guard cutters.

SHORE PARTY, Brig. Gen. W. M. Hoge USA.
Units of 5th & 6th Engineer Special Brigades and units of 6th Naval Beach Battalions, Cdr. E. C. Carusi USNR, and 7th, Cdr. L. C. Leever USNR.

TF 126 FOLLOW–UP FORCE "B"

Commodore C. D. Edgar in DE MALOY, Lt. Cdr. F. D. Kellogg USNR

Embarking the rest of 1st & 29th Divisions and V Corps & Engineer Special units, Maj. Gen. C. H. Gerhardt USA

Convoy B–1, Capt. J. R. Johannesen in *LST–511:* 18 LST, 46 British LCT (Lt. Cdr. A. D. S. Dunne RN); escorted by DD RODMAN Cdr. J. F. Foley, DEs H.M.S. BRISSENDEN Lt. D. D. E. Vivian RN, WENSLEY-DALE Lt. Cdr. W. P. Goodfellow RNVR; British A/S trawlers GATESHEAD, OLIVINA, LINDISFARNE; 2 SC; two U.S. 83-foot Coast Guard cutters.

Convoy B-2, Cdr. T. F. Cameron in *LCI-414:* Attack Freighter ACHERNAR Cdr. H. R. Stevens; 1 LCH; 12 LCI; escorted by destroyer ELLYSON Cdr. E. W. Longton (with Comdesron 10, Capt. A. F. Converse), H.M. corvettes AZALEA, KITCHENER; 2 PC; 1 83-foot C.G. cutter.

Convoy B-3 (arriving 7 June), Cdr. T. W. Greene in *LST-266:* 34 LST towing 26 barges.

Convoy B-4, Cdr. B. J. Skahill in *LST-515:* 9 LST towing 9 barges, escorted by destroyer HAMBLETON Cdr. H. A. Renken; H.M. corvettes *BOADICEA, BLUEBELL; H.M. destroyers VOLUNTEER, VIMY; 3 A/S trawlers ELLESMERE, CORNELIAN, PEARL; two 83-foot U.S.C.G. cutters.

MULBERRY A, Capt. A. Dayton Clark in *SC-1329*

Numerous tugboats, net layers, bar vessels, trawlers, etc.; and Drew 3, Lt. Cdr. R. D. Moore USNR.

SALVAGE AND FIREFIGHTING GROUP, Commo. W. A. Sullivan

British wreck dispersal vessels MARIE, ADMIRAL SIR JOHN LAWFORD, TEHANA, HELP, ABIGAIL; U.S.N. salvage vessels BRANT, DIVER, SWIVEL; ATAs PINTO, ARIKARA, KIOWA, BANNOCK; various small craft.

AREA SCREEN, Capt. Harry Sanders in FRANKFORD

Destroyers and destroyer escorts of Escort and Bombardment Groups; PC and SC assigned; Lt. Cdr. John D. Bulkeley commanding 12 PT of MTBron 34 and several MTB of British 53rd and 63rd Flotillas.

Far Shore Shuttle Control: Capt. Edward C. Kline USNR in H.M.S. CAPETOWN, Capt. H. F. Nash RN.

TF 129 CHERBOURG BOMBARDMENT, *25 June 1944*
Rear Admiral Morton L. Deyo

Group 1, Rear Admiral Deyo: TUSCALOOSA, QUINCY, NEVADA, H.M.S. GLASGOW, ENTERPRISE. Screen, Capt. A. F. Converse: destroyers ELLYSON, HAMBLETON, RODMAN, EMMONS, GHERARDI, MURPHY.

Group 2, Rear Admiral C. F. Bryant: TEXAS, ARKANSAS. Screen, Capt. W. L. Freseman: destroyers BARTON, O'BRIEN, LAFFEY, HOBSON, PLUNKETT.

MINESWEEPERS, Cdr. R. W. N. Thomson RN

Unit 1, Cdr. Thomson: H.M.S. SIDMOUTH, BRIDLINGTON, EASTBOURNE, BOSTON, BANGOR, BLACKPOOL, TENBY, BRIDPORT; danlayers BRYTHER, IJUIN, DALMATIA, SIGMA; 4 ML; 8 BYMS. Unit 2, Cdr. Henry Plander: PHEASANT, THREAT, BROADBILL, CHICKADEE, AUK, STAFF, RAVEN, SWIFT; 4 ML; British danlayer THUNDER.

* Lost in this operation.

Naval Forces Engaged in Operation DRAGOON[1]

WESTERN NAVAL TASK FORCE

Vice Admiral H. Kent Hewitt

Embarking Commanding General Seventh Army, Lieutenant General Alexander McC. Patch; VI Corps, Major General Lucian K. Truscott; French II Corps, Général de l'Armée de Lattre de Tassigny

CONTROL FORCE, Vice Admiral Hewitt

Amphibious Force Flagship CATOCTIN, Cdr. C. O. Comp; destroyer PLUNKETT; Mindiv 21, Lt. Cdr. R. A. L. Ellis USNR: PHEASANT, RAVEN, AUK, BROADBILL, CHICKADEE, NUTHATCH, STAFF, SWIFT, THREAT.

SPECIAL OPERATIONS GROUP, Capt. H. C. Johnson

Western Diversionary Unit, Capt. Johnson in destroyer ENDICOTT, Cdr. J. D. Bulkeley: 4 ML; 8 PT of MTBron 29 (Cdr. S. S. Daunis); 12 ASRC.

Eastern Diversionary Unit, Lt. Cdr. Douglas E. Fairbanks Jr. USNR: H.M. gunboats APHIS, SCARAB; fighter-director ships STUART PRINCE, ANTWERP; 3 ML; 4 PT of MTBron 22 (Lt. Cdr. R. J. Dressling).

TF 86 SITKA FORCE

Rear Admiral Lyal A. Davidson in AUGUSTA

Embarking First Special Service Force, Col. E. A. Walker USA, and French Romeo Force, Lt. Col. Bouvet

GUNFIRE SUPPORT GROUP, Rear Admiral Davidson

Heavy cruiser AUGUSTA; H.M.S. DIDO Capt. T. J. Baron; French battleship LORRAINE Capt. de V. Rue; destroyers SOMERS Cdr. W. C. Hughes, GLEAVES Cdr. B. L. Gurnette; H.M.S. LOOKOUT Lt. Cdr. D. H. F.

---

[1] Commanding officers of U.S. ships not named will be found with the same ships in Appendix I.

Hetherington RN, H.H.M.S. THEMISTOCLES. Reserve: light cruisers OMAHA Capt. E. M. Tillson, CINCINNATI Capt. D. F. Worth; H.M.S. SIRIUS.

TRANSPORT GROUP, Rear Admiral Theodore E. Chandler in PRINCE HENRY
Unit A, Cdr. J. N. Hughes: destroyer transport TATTNALL Lt. Cdr. F. H. Lennox USNR; PRINCE BAUDOUIN (Br.); *PT–201*. Unit B, Capt. G. E. Maynard: H.M.C.S. PRINCE HENRY Capt. V. S. Godfrey RCN; destroyer transports BARRY Lt. Cdr. H. D. Hill, GREENE Lt. Cdr. G. O. Scarfe USNR, ROPER Lt. Cdr. U. B. Carter USNR, OSMOND INGRAM Lt. Cdr. R. F. Miller USNR; 4 PT. ROMEO Unit, Capt. S. H. Norris RN: H.M.C.S. PRINCE DAVID Cdr. T. D. Kelly RCN, PRINS ALBERT Lt. Cdr. H. B. Peate RNR, PRINCESS BEATRIX Lt. Cdr. J. D. King RNR; 4 PT.
Screen: *8 PT of MTBron 15, Lt. Cdr. Stanley M. Barnes.
Minesweeper Group: Cdr. H. L. Jenkins RN: H.M.S. LARNE, CLINTON, OCTAVIA, WELFARE, STORMCLOUD; 4 ML; danlayer KINTYRE.

TF 84 ALPHA FORCE
Rear Admiral Frank J. Lowry

Embarking 3rd Division U.S. Army, Maj. Gen. John W. O'Daniel

Force Flagship Group: U.S.C.G.C. DUANE Cdr. Harold C. Moore USCG; Fighter Director Ship ULSTER QUEEN; *LCI–953, PC–1169*.

ASSAULT GROUPS
Red Beach Assault Group, Cdr. O. F. Gregor: 46 LCI; 25 LST; 7 LCC; 43 LCT; 11 LCM; 1 LCG; 1 LCF; 7 LCS; 4 British AM; 5 PC.
Yellow Beach Assault Group, Commo. C. D. Edgar: Attack transports SAMUEL CHASE, HENRICO; transports ANNE ARUNDEL, THURSTON; attack freighters OBERON Lt. Cdr. H. T. Cameron USNR, ANDROMEDA Cdr. W. A. Fly; H.M.S. HIGHWAY; 6 SC; 4 PC; 3 LCC; 6 LST; 9 LCI; 1 LCG; 1 LCF; 17 LCT; 9 LCM; 6 LCS; 4 British AM.

GUNFIRE SUPPORT GROUP, Rear Admiral J. M. Mansfield RN
Light cruisers H.M.S. ORION, AURORA, AJAX, BLACK PRINCE; battleship H.M.S. RAMILLIES Capt. G. B. Middleton RN; QUINCY; French light cruiser GLOIRE; destroyers LIVERMORE Cdr. H. E. Seidel (with Comdesdiv 21, Cdr. G. C. Wright), EBERLE Cdr. C. B. Smiley, KEARNY Cdr. L. Williamson, ERICSSON Lt. Cdr. B. H. Meyer, H.M.S. TERPSICHORE, TERMAGANT.

* *PT–202* and *PT–218* were sunk in this operation.

MINESWEEPER GROUP, Cdr. W. L. Messmer

BARRICADE, PREVAIL, SEER, DEXTROUS, PIONEER; 6 SC; 10 YMS; 8 British and 6 French AM; 2 LCC; 2 danlayers.

SALVAGE AND FIREFIGHTING GROUP, Cdr. H. M. Andersen

Fleet tug HOPI; 1 ATA; British tugs EMPIRE SPITFIRE, EMPIRE ANN; 1 boom vessel; 1 ATR; 1 YTB; 1 YTL; 1 FT.

TF 85 DELTA FORCE

Rear Admiral Bertram J. Rodgers

Embarking 45th Division U.S. Army, Maj. Gen. William W. Eagles

Force Flagship Group: Seaplane tender BISCAYNE Cdr. E. H. Eckelmeyer; destroyer FORREST; 1 fighter-director tender.

TRANSPORT GROUP, Capt. R. A. Dierdorff

ELIZABETH C. STANTON Cdr. W. A. Wiedman USNR; LYON Cdr. T. C. Sorenson; MARINE ROBIN, SANTA ROSA, BARNETT, JOSEPH T. DICKMAN; attack freighters PROCYON Cdr. T. O. Cullins; ARCTURUS Cdr. C. R. Woodson; British LSP DILWARA, LSI ASCANIA, LSG ENNERDALE (converted tanker carrying LCM).

Escort Group, Cdr. L. W. Creighton: destroyers BALDWIN, MADISON Cdr. D. A. Stuart, CARMICK; destroyer escorts MARSH Lt. Cdr. R. A. Jordan USNR, HAINES Lt. Cdr. E. C. Powell USNR.

ASSAULT GROUPS

Red Beach Assault Group, Capt. R. E. Parker: 10 LST; 6 LCI; 7 LCT; 1 LCG; 1 LCF; 4 LCS; 2 LCM(R); 2 SC; 2 LCC; 1 LCM.

Green Beach Assault Group, Cdr. R. D. Higgins USNR: 5 LST; 5 LCI; 7 LCT; 4 LCS; 2 LCM; 2 SC; 1 LCC.

Yellow Beach Assault Group, Cdr. W. O. Floyd: 2 LST; 2 LCI; 26 LCVP; 4 LCS; 4 LCT; 3 LCM; 1 SC; 1 LCC.

Blue Beach Assault Group, Cdr. Floyd: 1 LST; 26 LCVP; 16 LCT; 1 LCG; 1 LCF; 4 LCS; 3 LCM; 1 PC; 1 LCC; 1 LCI.

Corps and Division Reserve Groups, Cdr. A. L. Warburton: 5 LST; 20 LCI; 18 LCT; 1 FT.

GUNFIRE SUPPORT GROUP, Rear Admiral C. F. Bryant

Battleships TEXAS, NEVADA; light cruisers PHILADELPHIA Capt. W. C. Ansel, MONTCALM Capt. de V. Senes and GEORGES LEYGUES Capt. de V. Laurin (Contre-Amiral Jaujard commanding); destroyers ELLYSON (with Comdesron 10, Capt. A. F. Converse); RODMAN, EMMONS, FOR-

REST, FITCH, HAMBLETON, MACOMB Lt. Cdr. George Hutchinson, HOB-
SON; French light cruisers LE FANTASQUE, LE TERRIBLE, LE MALIN.

MINESWEEPER GROUP, Cdr. E. A. Ruth
SWAY, SYMBOL; H.M.S. RINALDO, ANTARES, ARCTURUS, BRAVE, ROSARIO,
SPANKER; danlayers SATSA, CALM.

COMBAT AND FIREFIGHTING GROUP, Lt. Cdr. LePage RCNVR
Fleet tugs NARRAGANSETT, PINTO, H.M.S. ASPIRANT, ATHLETE, CHARON;
1 ATA; 2 YTL.

TF 87 CAMEL FORCE
Rear Admiral Spencer S. Lewis

Embarking 36th Division U.S. Army, Maj. Gen. John E. Dahlquist

Force Flagship Group: Attack transport BAYFIELD; British *LCH–315.*

ASSAULT GROUPS
Red Beach Assault Group, Capt. W. O. Bailey: Attack transports
CHARLES CARROLL Cdr. W. W. Chism USNR, THOMAS JEFFERSON; transports DOROTHEA L. DIX, FLORENCE NIGHTINGALE Capt. F. J. Nelson; attack
freighters CEPHEUS Cdr. R. C. Sarratt USCG, ACHERNAR, BETELGEUSE Cdr.
J. F. Grube; transport GEN. G. O. SQUIER Capt. R. D. Threshie; 5 LCI;
3 LST; 21 LCT; 20 LCVP; 9 LCS; 3 LCC; 1 LCG; 1 LCF; 2 LCM;
3 SC; 2 PC; 1 LSI (Br.); 1 LSD (Br.).
   Green Beach Assault Group, Capt. Robert Morris: 23 LCI; 1 LCH;
*14 LST; 21 LCT; 7 LCVP; 7 LCS; 3 LCC; 1 LCG; 1 LCF; 2 LCM;
2 PC; 2 SC.
   Blue Beach Assault Group, Cdr. L. R. Herring: 5 LST; 1 LCI; 3 LCS;
2 LCT; 2 SC; 1 PC.

Escort and Screening Group: Destroyers from Bombardment Group;
6 PC; 10 SC; 1 LST; 2 LCF; 1 LSF; 1 LCC; 5 LCS; 5 LCVP; 1 LCT;
2 LCM.

BOMBARDMENT GROUP, Rear Admiral Morton L. Deyo
Heavy Cruiser TUSCALOOSA; battleship ARKANSAS; light cruisers BROOK-
LYN Capt. F. R. Dodge, MARBLEHEAD Capt. G. P. Kraker; H.M.S. ARGO-
NAUT Capt. E. W. L. Longley-Cook RN; French cruisers DUGUAY-
TROUIN Capt. de V. de Quievrecourt, ÉMILE BERTIN Capt. de V. Ortoli.
Destroyers PARKER Cdr. J. F. Flynn (with Comdesron 16, Capt. C. J.
Cater), KENDRICK Cdr. A. M. Boyd, MACKENZIE Cdr. B. N. Rittenhouse,
MCLANAHAN Cdr. B. M. McKay, NIELDS Cdr. A. R. Heckey, ORDRONAUX

* *LST–282* sunk in this operation.

Lt. Cdr. J. L. W. Woodville, WOOLSEY Cdr. H. R. Wier, (with Comdesdiv 25, Cdr. R. B. Ellis), LUDLOW Lt. Cdr. W. R. Barnes, EDISON Cdr. H. A. Pearce, BOYLE Cdr. B. P. Field, CHAMPLIN Lt. Cdr. F. E. Fleck.

Minesweeper Group: Lt. Cdr. J. L. Maloney: STRIVE, STEADY, SPEED, SUSTAIN; 6 YMS; 6 BYMS; 2 danlayers; 6 British ML; 12 British AM; H.M.S. PRODUCT.

Salvage and Firefighting Group: Lt. L. R. Brown: Fleet ocean tugs MORENO, ARIKARA; 1 U.S., 2 British ATA; 1 YTB; 3 LCI; 1 LCT; 4 LCM; 1 boom vessel; 1 YTL.

TF 88 AIRCRAFT CARRIER FORCE
Rear Admiral T. H. Troubridge RN
TG 88.1, Rear Admiral Troubridge

H.M.S. KHEDIVE Capt. H. J. Haynes RN (with 24 Seafire, Lt. Cdr. R. Haworth RNVR); EMPEROR Capt. T. J. N. Hilken RN (with 24 Hellcat, Lt. Cdr. S. Hall RN); SEARCHER Capt. G. O. C. Davies RN (with 24 Wildcat, Lt. Cdr. G. R. Henderson RNVR); PURSUER Act. Capt. H. R. Graham RN (with 24 Wildcat, Lt. Cdr. L. A. Hordern RNVR); ATTACKER Capt. H. B. Farncomb of Australian Navy (with 24 Seafire, Lt. Cdr. D. G. Carlisle RNVR).

Antiaircraft light cruisers H.M.S. ROYALIST Capt. J. G. Hewitt RN, DELHI Capt. G. R. Waymouth RN; destroyers H.M.S. TROUBRIDGE, TUSCAN, TYRIAN, TEAZER, TUMULT, WHEATLAND; H.H.M.S. NAVARINON.

TG 88.2, Rear Admiral C. T. Durgin
TULAGI Capt. J. C. Cronin (with VOF-1, 24 Hellcat, Lt. Cdr. W. F. Bringle); KASAAN BAY Capt. B. E. Grow (with VF-74, 24 Hellcat *Lt. Cdr. H. B. Bass, Lt. H. H. Basore); H.M.S. HUNTER Capt. H. H. McWilliam RN (with 24 Seafire, Lt. G. Reece of New Zealand Navy); STALKER Capt. H. S. Murray-Smith RN (with 24 Seafire, Lt. Cdr. D. Eaden RNVR).

Antiaircraft light cruisers H.M.S. COLOMBO Capt. C. T. Jellicoe RN, CALEDON Capt. R. F. Nichols RN; destroyers BUTLER (with Comdesdiv 34, Cdr. W. L. Benson), GHERARDI, HERNDON, MURPHY, JEFFERS (with Comdesron 17, Capt. A. C. Murdaugh), SHUBRICK; 6 British ML.

TG 80.6 ANTISUBMARINE AND CONVOY CONTROL GROUP
Capt. J. P. Clay

Destroyers JOUETT, BENSON, NIBLACK Cdr. R. R. Conner, MADISON Cdr. D. A. Stuart, HILARY P. JONES Lt. Cdr. F. M. Stiesberg, CHARLES F. HUGHES Lt. Cdr. J. C. G. Wilson (with Comdesdiv 14, Cdr. V. Havard),

* Lost in this operation.

FRANKFORD (with Comdesron 18, Capt. Sanders), CARMICK, DOYLE, MC-COOK, BALDWIN (with Comdesdiv 36, Cdr. L. W. Creighton), HARDING, SATTERLEE, THOMPSON.

H.M. destroyers ALDENHAM, BEAUFORT, BELVOIR, WHADDON, BLACK-MORE, EGGESFORD, LAUDERDALE, PINDOS, FARNDALE, ATHERSTONE, BRECON, CALPE, CATTERICK, CLEVELAND, HAYDON, BICESTER, LIDDESDALE, OAKLEY, ZETLAND, CRETE; H.H.M.S. THEMISTOCLES.

Destroyer escorts TATUM Lt. Cdr. W. C. P. Bellinger, HAINES Lt. Cdr. E. C. Powell USNR, MARSH Lt. Cdr. R. A. Jordan USNR, CURRIER Lt. Cdr. R. McAfee USNR, FREDERICK C. DAVIS Lt. Cdr. R. C. Robbins USNR, HERBERT C. JONES Lt. Cdr. R. A. Soule USNR.

French destroyers LE FORTUNÉ, FORBIN, SIMOUN, TEMPÊTE, L'ALCYON; corvettes MAROCAIN, TUNISIEN, HOVA, ALGÉRIEN, SOMALI; sloops COM-MANDANT DOMINE, LA MOQUEUSE, COMMANDANT BORY, LA GRACIEUSE, COMMANDANT DELAGE, LA BOUDEUSE.

Minron 11, Cdr. H. G. Williams: IMPROVE, IMPLICIT, INCESSANT, IN-CREDIBLE, MAINSTAY, PINNACLE; 6 YMS; H.M. corvettes AUBRETIA, COLUMBINE.

Number of Lend-Lease Naval Vessels and Craft Built for the Royal Navy in the United States During World War II[1]

AK	Cargo Vessels	4
CGC	Coast Guard Cutters	10
AM	Minesweepers	22
AN	Net Tenders	5
APc	Small Coastal Transports	27
AR	Repair Ships, Auxiliary	2
ARB	Aircraft Rescue Boats	40
ARS	Salvage Vessels	6
AT	Ocean-going Rescue Tugs	13
ATR	Rescue Tugs	14
CVE	Escort Carriers	38
DE	Destroyer Escorts	78
LCI(L)	Landing Craft Infantry, long	220
LCM	Landing Craft Mechanized (mks. 2, 3)	671
LCP(L)	Landing Craft Personnel, large	599
LCP(R)	Landing Craft Personnel, ramped	413
LCT	Landing Craft Tank (mks. 5, 6)	171
LCVP	Landing Craft Vehicle & Personnel	321
LSD	Landing Ships Dock	4
LSI(M)	Landing Ships Infantry (merch. hulls)	13
LST	Landing Ships Tank	115
PB	Patrol Boats	5
PC	Patrol Craft, Escort	15
PF	Frigates	21
	Motor Launches, 72-foot	73

[1] Admiralty "History of the British Admiralty Delegation" in Washington, 1946, Sec. 4, Table (a), excluding vessels built under U.S. lend-lease in Canada (7 corvettes, 8 frigates, 15 "Algerine" minesweepers).

PT	Motor Torpedo Boats	113
PTC	Motor Boat Subchasers	12
SS	Submarines	9
YFD	Floating Dry Docks	4
YMS	Motor Minesweepers	150
YT	Harbor Tugs	2
PY	Yachts	4
	Pontoon Barges and Dry Docks	6
	Miscellaneous Small Craft	81

Index

Names of ships, and code names of operations, task forces and conferences, in SMALL CAPITALS
Numbers of lettered combatant ships, such as LSTs and U–boats, in *Italics*

The Appendices have not been indexed, except for main headings and flag officers.

A

ABC–1 STAFF AGREEMENT, 4
Adriatic, 227
Ægean, 224
AFFLECK, 304
Agay, rade d', 268–70
Air Force, U.S. *See* Army Air Force
Air power, and German strategy, 42
Airfields, Normandy, 108, 161–2; Provence, 244, 267
AJAX, 257
Allan, Cdr, R. A., 314*n*, 315
Allied Control Council, 329
Alpha area, landings in, 258–64; composition, Appendix II, 339–40
Amphibious Forces, U.S.N., VIII, 53; XI, 52, 58, 149
AMSTERDAM, 127
ANCON, 63, 118–9, 146, 150
Anderson, Rear Adm. Bern, ix
Anderson, Maj. Gen. J. B., 323
Ansel, Capt. W. C., 286
Anthéor, La Calanque d', 268–9
Antisubmarine patrol, 72
Antwerp, 20, 295–6
ANVIL operation, effect on OVERLORD, 28; controversy over, 221–32. *See also* DRAGOON
Anzio, effect on ANVIL, 223–4
Apex boats, 241, 256, 271
APHIS, 250, 282
APOLLO, 159
Appledore, 60
ARCADIA Conference, 4–5
ARCTURUS, 287

Area screens, Normandy, 156, 174; Provence, 277, 284
Argentia Conference, 6*n*
ARKANSAS, 56, 118, 121–3, 145, 148, 158, 160, 167–8, 197–8, 205–7, 209, 238, 268, 271
Army Air Force, opns. prior to OVERLORD, 34–8; in U.K., 67; bomb't. of Cherbourg, 198; operations, 271; 12th Tactical, 239, 280–1; 15th, 244; 1st Airborne Task Force, 277; 82nd Airborne, 89–91; 101st Airborne, 82*n*, 89–91, 105–6; IX Air Force, 100, 108, 198, 215; IX Troop Carrier Command, 89; VIII Bomber Command, 124–6; IX Tactical & Engineers Command, 108, 161
Army, U.S., Army Groups, in U.K., 50–2, 62, 64–6; statistics, 67; training & rehearsal, 64–7; arrival in Normandy, 163; First, 30, 190; Sixth, 291, 310, 324; 12th, 216; Armies, First, 29, 164, 168, 216, 324; Third, 216, 319–21, 324; Fifth, 324; Seventh, 236, 311, 324; Ninth, 321–4; Corps, V, 29, 64, 152, 158, 160, 324; VI, 236; VII, 29, 107, 156, 160, 167–8, 196–202; VIII, 298–302; XIX, 29; Divisions, 1st, 110, 130–54, 158; 3rd, 236, 262–4, 266; 4th, 105, 108, 157, 204; casualties, 103; 9th, 167, 198, 212; 29th, 110, 130–54, 158, 160; 36th, 236, 268–9, 272, 276; 45th, 236, 264–6; 79th, 198, 212; 90th, 162, 167; 1st Eng. Special Brigade, 108; 2nd Rangers, 125–9
Arnhem, 296

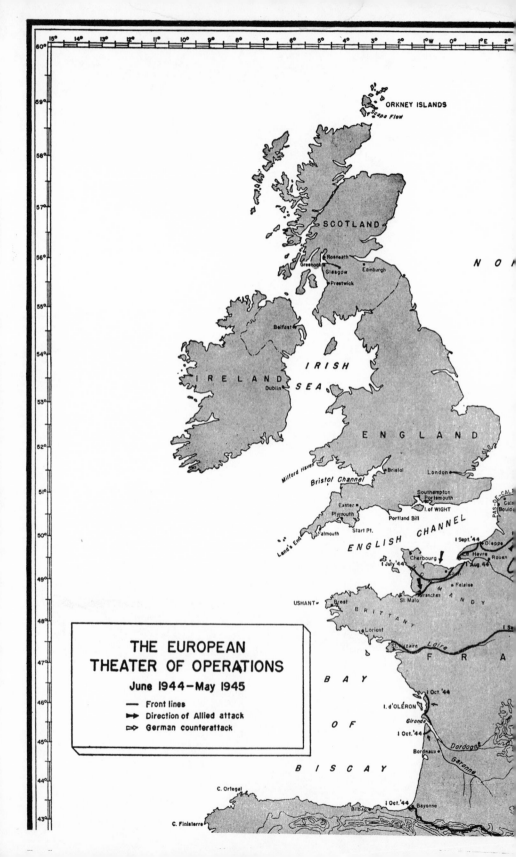

THE EUROPEAN
THEATER OF OPERATIONS
June 1944 – May 1945

— Front lines
➤➤ Direction of Allied attack
⇨ German counterattack

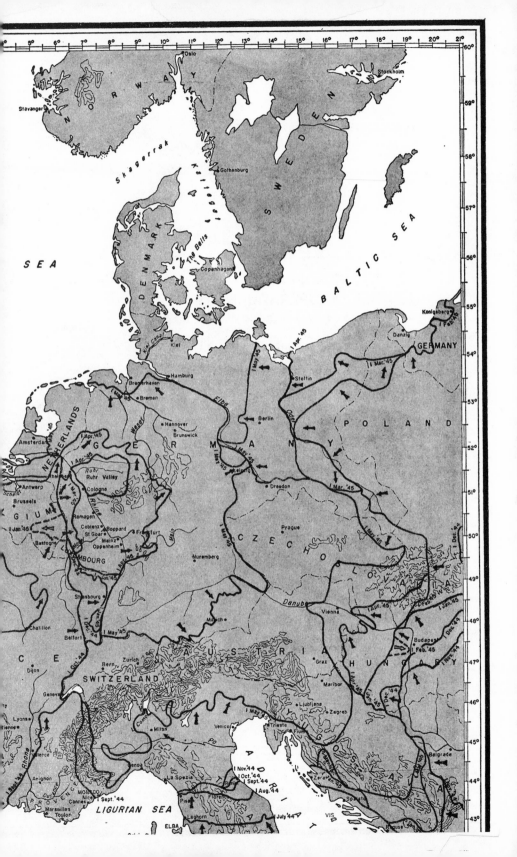

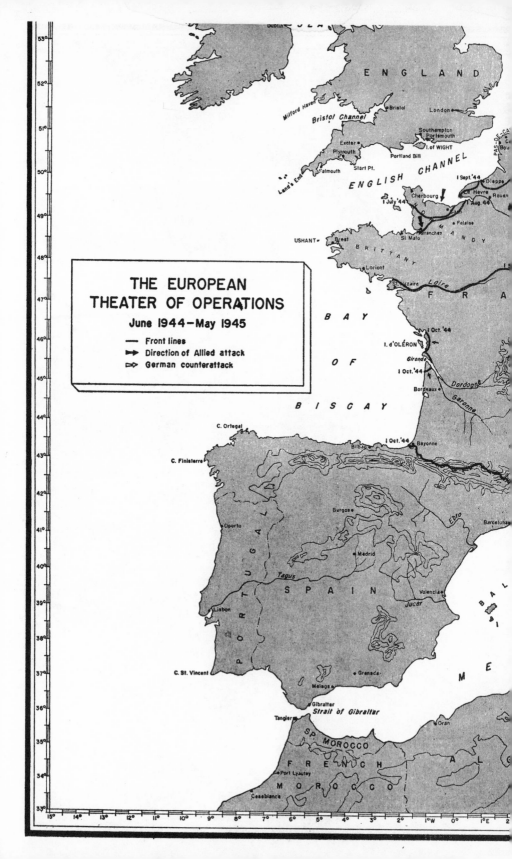

THE EUROPEAN
THEATER OF OPERATIONS
June 1944—May 1945

— Front lines
➤ Direction of Allied attack
⇒ German counterattack